A

Ronald Colman, Gentleman of the Cinema

Ronald Colman, Gentleman of the Cinema

A Biography and Filmography

by
R. Dixon Smith

with a Foreword by
BRIAN AHERNE

McFarland & Company, Inc., Publishers
Jefferson, North Carolina, and London

Also by R. Dixon Smith:

Lost in the Rentharpian Hills:
Spanning the Decades with Carl Jacobi

Jeremy Brett and David Burke:
An Adventure in Canonical Fidelity

East of Samarinda
(edited with Carl Jacobi)

Frontispiece: *Ronald Colman, who had been vacationing in England, is photographed upon his arrival in New York on July 4, 1930, en route to Hollywood to star in* The Devil to Pay.

British Library Cataloguing-in-Publication data are available

Library of Congress Cataloguing-in-Publication Data

Smith, R. Dixon, 1944–
  Ronald Colman, gentleman of the cinema : a biography and filmography / by R. Dixon Smith.
    p.   cm.
  Includes bibliographical references and index. ∞
  ISBN 0-89950-581-3 (lib. bdg. : 50# alk. paper)
  1. Colman, Ronald, 1891–1958 — Criticism and interpretation.
I. Title.
PN2287.C57S6   1991
791.43′028′092 — dc20   90-53524
                                                              CIP

Manufactured in the United States of America

McFarland & Company, Inc., Publishers
  Box 611, Jefferson, North Carolina 28640

For
Thomas R. Tietze,
Mary Ellen Gee,
and
George E. Schatz

To whom
could this chronicle
of grace and honor
more fittingly be dedicated
than to these?

Our revels now are ended.
These our actors,
As I foretold you,
Were all spirits,
And are melted into air,
Into thin air.
We are such stuff
As dreams are made on;
And our little life
Is rounded with a sleep.

—Prospero in *The Tempest*,
Act IV, Scene I, one of
Ronald Colman's favorite
quotations, engraved upon
his black marble tombstone
in the Santa Barbara Cemetery

And over the seas we were bidden
A country to take and to keep;
And far with the brave I have ridden,
And now with the brave I shall sleep.

—Laurence Housman

Contents

IV. Colman Crosses the Sound Barrier — The Goldwyn Talkies   92

V. The Image of a Star   139

VI. Years of Diversification   231

VII. Of Shadow and Substance—The Legacy of Ronald Colman   291

Acknowledgments

It is often said that making a motion picture is a complex, collaborative effort, requiring the expertise of many artists and technicians. The writing of this book has been a similarly collaborative endeavor. Thanks to the encouragement and inspiration of the following individuals and institutions, the experience has been delightful and exhilarating:

The Academy of Motion Picture Arts and Sciences (Anthony Slide); David Bradley; The British Film Institute (Tise Vahimagi); John Caruso, Jr.; Ron Colby; Basil Copper; J. Randolph Cox; Bob DeFlores; The Director's Guild of America (David Shepard); Eddie Brandt's Saturday Matinee; Douglas Fairbanks, Jr.; The George Eastman House (Marshall Deutelbaum); Lillian Gish; David D. Grothe; Ron Hall; John Hampton (The Silent Movie); Kevin B. Hancer; Michael L. Hunegs; L. Richard Landry; Ted Larson; Alford Lathrop; The Library of Congress (Barbara Humphrys, Joseph Balian); Lincoln Center for the Performing Arts; Ann McKee; Metro-Goldwyn-Mayer (Herbert S. Nusbaum, Karla Davidson); James W. Morrison; Movie Star News (Paula Klaw); The Museum of Modern Art (Charles Silver, Mary Corliss); the late Laurence Olivier; Raymond C. Olson; Stephen Rivkin; the late Raymond Rohauer; Samuel Goldwyn Studios (Tom Bodley, Thomas Seehof); Steven A. Stilwell; Kathryn A. Tietze; and the UCLA Film Archives (Charles Hopkins, Robert Rosen).

Thanks are due Juliet Colman Toland, for permission to quote from *Ronald Colman: A Very Private Person;* Kevin Brownlow, for permission to quote from *The Parade's Gone By;* Citadel Press, for permission to quote from *The Films of Ronald Colman;* and *Films and Filming,* for permission to quote from articles. I thank the following studios and institutions for reproduction of still photographs: The Academy of Motion Picture Arts and Sciences, Columbia Pictures, Metro-Goldwyn-Mayer Pictures, The Museum of Modern Art/Film Stills Archive, Paramount Pictures, RKO Radio Pictures, Samuel Goldwyn Studios, Selznick International Pictures, Twentieth Century–Fox Film Corporation, United Artists Corporation, Universal-International Pictures, and Warner Bros. Pictures.

This book owes much to Richard W. Bann and Chris Hubrig, who unearthed many rare stills in New York and Hollywood; the late Blanche Sweet, who shared her recollections of Ronald Colman; the late Brian Aherne, who contributed a lovely foreword; and Madeleine M. Henry, Carl Jacobi, Robert Milton Miller, and the late Donald Wandrei, who read the book in manuscript and made helpful suggestions.

My greatest debt is to Thomas R. Tietze, Mary Ellen Gee, and George E. Schatz, from whose critical insights I have had the good fortune to benefit. They too read the manuscript, supplying numerous suggestions for improvement in matters of detail. Their enthusiasm for the book, and especially their love and support through the years, have been indispensable.

Foreword

In the course of a long and varied life in the theatrical profession, both on stage and screen, I have been privileged to meet most of the famous names whose reminiscences now fill the shelves of our bookstores. It seems that theatrical biography has taken the place of the novel today in public favor, and this is not surprising because the twentieth century has seen the development of the motion picture, of radio and television which have carried famous names all over the world. One of the greatest of these was Ronald Colman, of whom R. Dixon Smith writes with such enthusiasm in this book.

I first met him in 1932 at the house of our mutual friend Ruth Chatterton. She was giving a party on a Sunday evening in honor of Katharine Cornell and the company of *The Barretts of Wimpole Street*, which we were then playing at the Biltmore Theater in Los Angeles. I was immediately impressed by Colman's wonderful appearance, his air of well-bred distinction and his unforgettable resonant voice, but I remember thinking that he was shorter than I had expected.

It was not until the following year, when I went to Hollywood to make a picture with Marlene Dietrich, that I met him again, and it was some time before I felt that I knew him well. He was every inch the traditional English gentleman, with perfect manners but reserved and reticent, so that I remarked to Miss Chatterton that I found it difficult to get on friendly terms with him. "Oh no, Brian!" she exclaimed. "Dine with him quietly one evening and give him a couple of drinks. You will find he has a delicious sense of humor when he feels at ease!"

He was then living a quiet bachelor life at his comfortable house in Hollywood and rarely accepted invitations, but I persevered and was finally admitted to the small coterie of friends with whom he liked to play tennis or go for a sail on his yacht. Three or four of us, all men, would go over to Catalina Island, then almost deserted, and anchor in a cove for an enchanted weekend. Slowly but surely we formed a friendship which was to last for many years and mean much to me.

Ronnie once explained to me that if he could not avoid a big party he was always careful not to stay next to any of the movie beauties for more than a few minutes for fear that one of the Hollywood columnists would headline a new romance. He knew from experience that if this happened his jealous wife, from whom he had long been separated, would raise her financial demands as the price of her agreement to divorce. Indeed it was not for several years, and then on very onerous terms, that she would consent.

The two of us used to make motor trips together sometimes and he showed me much of California, its deserts, mountains and coastline. He owned a delightful small bungalow hotel, the San Ysidro Inn, in the foothills behind Montecito. One morning when we were staying there he picked up the phone and, to my astonishment, put in a call to my old and beloved friend Benita Hume, an English actress from the London theater, asking her for dinner at his home the following week! I was delighted, for I felt that her gaiety, wit and warmth were just what he needed.

It was not long before they married and moved into a beautiful house in Beverly Hills, which became a haven for their small but select circle of friends. As I had anticipated, it was a good marriage. It brought him his beloved daughter Juliet, now married herself and living in Mallorca, and I feel sure it brought him happiness which lasted for twenty years until his untimely death. I shall always treasure his memory, for he was a great gentleman. As is said today of almost anything we need to renew, "they don't make them like that anymore!"

Brian Aherne

I

Before the Films Beckoned

Shortly before he embarked on his lengthy Hollywood career, liquor salesman David Niven attended one of Elsa Maxwell's legendary cocktail parties in New York City. The Englishman liked his hostess the minute he met her, and what she told him that night he was to remember for many years:

> Selling liquor . . . that's no good, no good at all . . . get you nowhere . . . you should go to Hollywood . . . nobody out there knows how to speak except Ronald Colman.[1]

Film historian Walter Kerr, writing 40 years later, recalled what it was like to grow up in the movie-mad twenties with but one wish: to be "as lithe as Fairbanks and as suavely persuasive as Ronald Colman."[2]

The many roles that made Ronald Colman one of the cinema's greatest stars evoked the gallantry Hemingway characterized as "grace under pressure" and that rarer virtue, serene confidence. His was an unprecedented career that successfully bridged the fields of stage, screen, radio, and television; from high adventure and delicate romance to light comedy and intense drama, Ronald Colman was the epitome of graciousness, sensitivity, and complete sincerity—always tempered and made believable by the lighthearted, unselfconscious good nature of his style, the introspective sadness of his eyes, and the indefinable fragility of that famous, exquisitely modulated voice.

He was unforgettable as the melancholy Sydney Carton in *A Tale of Two Cities*, as the idealistic Robert Conway in *Lost Horizon*, and as the dashing Rudolf Rassendyll in *The Prisoner of Zenda*. His portrayals of ill-fated Richard Heldar in *The Light that Failed* and amnesia-stricken Charles Rainier in *Random Harvest* were equally memorable.

1

In a world of apparently vanishing style and grace, Colman's uncommon charisma and distinctive urbanity made him the envy of his male audience and the idol of countless millions of female fans for some 35 years. In 1927, 1928, and 1932, he was named the top male star of the cinema. In 1935, at the height of his career, a poll of 51 actresses (including Jeanette MacDonald, Norma Shearer, Loretta Young, Bette Davis, Irene Dunne, Dolores Del Rio, Ginger Rogers, Claudette Colbert, and Barbara Stanwyck) voted him "the Handsomest Man on the Screen," with nearest contenders Clark Gable and Fredric March trailing comfortably behind. Colman's glamour was genuine, for it came from his gentility, inner strength, and irresistible charm, those qualities and characteristics which mark his finest performances.

Coursing through the Colman films are the themes of honor, duty, and self-sacrifice, concepts which were as much a part of the man himself as of the image. In Colman's self-contained world, with its own values and ethical landscapes, he played men for whom the higher demands of duty and honor always outweighed the attainment of personal fulfillment. Though his characters were dedicated, resourceful, and resilient, they were somehow vulnerable; there was always a sadness under the surface, an inherent wistfulness in the face of unfulfilled dreams. He always had that faraway look in his eyes, a slightly quizzical, averted gaze, as if he were searching for something he couldn't find.

As Colman's first biographer, Roland Wild, wrote in 1933:

> Ronald Colman is, on the whole, good for humanity. Doctors might prescribe a dose of him for depressed patients or for those with acute melancholia. He should be encouraged as a tonic for a world that is too humdrum and too respectable.[3]
>   . . . Colman is the man who makes most cinema-goers feel younger from looking at him . . . . Why did he walk straight into the hearts of men and women? Why does he appeal to men almost as strongly as he does to women?[4]

Why, indeed?

Ronald Charles Colman was born on February 9, 1891, at Richmond, Surrey, England, the second son of five children born to Marjory Fraser and Charles Colman, a silk importer of modest means. Charles was a man of considerable culture and a direct descendant of eighteenth-century dramatist George Colman, not the least of whose distinctions was the sad honor of having served as pallbearer to his friend Dr. Samuel Johnson.

Ronald attended Hadley School in Littlehampton, a boarding establishment on the Sussex coast, where he was more than moderately studious and began to take an interest in amateur theatricals. When he was 16 his father died, forever ending the boy's hopes of going up to Cambridge, wearing the old school tie, and becoming an engineer, which had been his father's fondest wish. Supporting his mother by working as a shipping clerk for the British Steamship Company at a weekly salary of 15 shillings, he added a bit of cheer whenever time permitted by acting, singing, and playing the banjo in the Bancroft Amateur Dramatic Society. Within five years, he worked his way up from shipping clerk to bookkeeper, then finally to junior accountant at 57 shillings a week. His first recorded appearance on stage came in 1908 at a Masonic smoker, long before the films, or even the theatre, had beckoned. In 1909, at the age of 18, he joined the famed London Scottish Regionals, for which he qualified because of his mother's Scots heritage, and served until 1913. During his two-week vacation in September 1912, young Colman and a friend took a troupe known as "the Mad Medicos" to the Isle of Wight and entertained by acting, singing, and playing the mandolin. In what little spare time remained in this kilted world of the British Territorials, he read voraciously.

When asked in 1928 to give a sketch of his early life, Colman offered the following summary:

> I went to school in the south of England. My people were poor and my life as a child was like the lives of millions of boys. I really didn't begin to think until the World War.[5]

On August 5, 1914, Britain found herself at war with Germany. Colman donned his kilt again and rejoined his comrades in the London Scottish, becoming one of the first 100,000 English sent over to fight on French soil. Private Colman quickly matured in war service, acquitting himself with honor and distinction on the battlefield. He took part in the first Battle of Ypres and was severely wounded at Messines. The 23-year-old volunteer, bleeding after shrapnel had ripped through his knee and ankle, had begun to crawl back toward his own lines when he realized that, should the next bullet or shell kill him on the spot, he'd be found with his back to the enemy. "Without further hesitation, he turned onto his back, and pulling with his elbows, then pushing with his good leg, he retreated from the field of battle while facing the German lines."[6]

After recuperating with his leg in a cast in a field hospital, Colman was invalided home after serving actively for only two months, and was finally discharged in May 1915. A sad bitterness and discontent, gleaned from the realities of war, had instilled in him a sense of melancholy and a longing for the privacy of a quiet life. He had always been studious and shy, but it took a war to solidify his diffidence and reserve; he rarely referred to his war experiences in later life.

Decorated, discharged, and limping, he returned to England "to get on with the business of living," he later said, "while the seventeen-year-old boys carried on the business of dying."[7]

...when ... I came back to England, my whole world had changed. I had
to have a job; so did thousands of other men just like me. Jobs were hard
to find. The only thing I knew anything about was amateur theatricals. So
I turned to the stage. I took anything I could get and that was very little.
I went along for a while. I was very unhappy in mind. London was an unhappy place to be in at that time.[8]

Significantly, he made no attempt to secure a future for himself in
business and, after toying with the idea of using family connections to
establish himself in a comfortable foreign consular career, chose to abandon
it for a turn on the stage. Whether or not he realized it at the time, a career
decision had been made, and a momentous one.

In the summer of 1916, actress Lena Ashwell, seeking a dark, handsome young man for a small walk-on part in her new play, *The Maharanee
of Arakan,* auditioned the young actor. There were not many dark, handsome young men left in London that year, and Colman landed his first professional acting position. His London stage debut was hardly auspicious; he
appeared in blackface as a herald, waved a flag, and blew a trumpet. "All
I did was toot a horn,"[9] he recalled years later.

But it was a start, and other roles included a small part in *The
Misleading Lady,* which starred Gladys Cooper and Gerald du Maurier, and
the juvenile lead in *Damaged Goods.* His older, more experienced col-
leagues found him an open, good-natured, frank-hearted fellow, with a rich,
clear voice; fine, striking looks; and a certain mature dignity which belied
his youth. The stage had the effect of loosening him up, of freeing him from
his natural barriers of shyness and restraint.

For the next few years his work on the British stage consumed most
of his time, but motion pictures were about to enter the life of Ronald
Colman.

II

The Early Silents

Our knowledge of the early years of the British film industry is at best fragmented. The dawn of film history all too often lies shrouded by the wild fancies of those who were not there and the faulty memories of those who were. Very few films exist for first-hand appraisal, and the criticisms of the trade and popular press of the time often prove worse than useless in answering the critical questions of today. Thus we not only lack much primary material, but must depend on inadequate secondary sources for what information we do possess. For most features, only bits of commentary, faded memories, and a few photographs remain.[1] The early Colman titles, therefore, are little more than a ghostly presence here.

Ronald Colman's performance as the juvenile lead in *Damaged Goods* attracted the attention of British film pioneer George Dewhurst, who went to see him in his dressing room and promptly offered him the starring role in a comedy short subject.

"I want to do the right thing by you," the producer urged. "I'll pay you a pound a day, not counting Sundays."[2]

Although hardly impressed or enthusiastic, Colman accepted the part and made the film. But *The Live Wire*, a two-reeler produced on a shoe-string budget, was never released.

For the next three years, Colman's stage activities continued to be interspersed with occasional film appearances in which he portrayed romantic juveniles in productions that circulated chiefly in the provinces. Although Colman regularly attended the cinema, being particularly devoted to Fairbanks and Chaplin, he had no great desire to star in pictures, for he felt his place was on the stage.[3] His chief work in 1919, however, was in films, during which time he made four of the eight pictures he was to make in his homeland. All were relatively undistinguished melodramas and light comedies, though he worked for such early British film pioneers as George Dewhurst, Cecil Hepworth, and Walter West.[4] His second film for Dewhurst was entitled *The Toilers*. During this time Colman met Cecil Hepworth, then considered to be the D.W. Griffith of Britain. The director asked him:

"Are you good in pictures?"

"Great!"

"How many have you done?"

"Two."

"What salary do you expect?"

"Thirty pounds a week."

"I'll give you six."

"Done!"[5]

For Hepworth he made two pictures, *Sheba* and *Anna the Adventuress*. For Walter West's Broadwest, Ltd., he made *A Daughter of Eve*, *Snow in the Desert*, and *A Son of David*, the latter his best-known and best-received British picture as well as his first leading role. Colman's last British film was *The Black Spider*, filmed on location in Monte Carlo. Oddly enough, the words "Does not screen well" appeared under his name in the lists of one London casting office. Colman's stiff leg and obvious limp continued to plague his early film career; his movements and gestures, moreover, were those he had learned on the stage, and were rather exaggerated even for accepted filmic conventions of the time.

"I persevered," Colman remembered later, "though I admit I was a very bad actor in those early films"[6]

A postwar slump hit the British film industry and Colman returned to the stage, where he appeared in *The Little Brother* with Lyn Harding and *The Great Day*, and had the lead in *The Live Wire*.[7] The theatre, it was clear, was in his blood, for he still thought of himself as a stage rather than a cinema actor, and it was the theatre which would soon take him to America.

Colman's leading lady in *The Live Wire* was the alluring musical-comedy actress Thelma Raye. While touring the play, they fell in love and decided to live together, an arrangement looked upon with some disfavor by Thelma's estranged husband, a wealthy Australian who soon divorced her. Colman, characteristically, saw it as his duty to marry her under the circumstances, and after a brief, intense courtship, the two were wed in London on September 18, 1919. Ill luck followed immediately, for Thelma, a very domineering woman, made the fatal error of mistaking her new husband's gentleness for malleability. The marriage was doomed to failure from the start, and although they were not divorced until 1934, they separated in 1923. For Colman it was an extremely lacerating emotional experience, and Thelma compounded it by plaguing him for years in Hollywood. This disastrous first marriage haunted him for much of his life and contributed to his pronounced shyness with women, turning him into the very private person he remained throughout his life.

The postwar depression in England brought with it a slump in the theatre as well as in the cinema. Two years had passed since the sounds of martial strife had died away, but Colman had yet to make his mark on either stage or screen to any appreciable extent. Unable to get work in Britain, he decided to emigrate to America to seek his proverbial fortune. Leaving Thelma behind until he could establish himself, he departed, his sole possessions consisting of three clean collars, a change of clothes, seven pounds, an abundance of confidence, and letters of introduction to D.W. Griffith and Jules Brulatour. He crossed the Atlantic in October 1920, second class on the steamship *Zeeland*.

Arriving in the United States with little to his credit but limited prior stage and screen experience, he soon discovered that work was hard to come by, even in America. Some years later, Colman recalled his last days in Britain and the tough times he faced in New York:

> And so I drifted. Then suddenly I found I was unable to buy a meal. Broke, struggling for a bare existence. Life cut deeply into one's marrow those days. America had left a strong impression on the British mind after the war. I heard of the film opportunities over here. With high hopes I shipped for New York. To be broke, hungry and out of work in one's native land is bad but to be penniless and down and out in a powerful city like New York in a strange country is one of the worst experiences in the life of man. For months I tramped the streets of New York, going from studio to studio. I was unable to get work as an extra. No one would lend a hand. Then I haunted the stage doors. I got some small parts in the theatre but always I waited for an opportunity to play in pictures. I don't know what the fascination is about Fame that makes a man struggle so to gain it. Personally I believe that the game is not worth the candle but I fought on.[8]

He took a cheap furnished room in Brooklyn, made the rounds of the agents' and producers' offices, washed dishes, ate soup and rice pudding, slept on park benches, pounded the pavement some more, and nearly starved to death in the process.

> New York—that golden gate—proved to be effectively locked. I found all the New York studios closed, as a result of a bad slump in the business. My money was soon gone; my letters of introduction could not be presented at the barred doors of the film studios and I found a return to the stage imperative.[9]

Occasionally he got a few stage parts, the first of which was in *The Dauntless Three* with Broadway star Robert Warwick. It folded after only a few days. Colman had met Warwick through the intercession of Irish-born Herbert Brenon, who was later to direct Colman's greatest silent film success, *Beau Geste*. Other small roles followed, including, finally, a walk-on as a temple priest in *The Green Goddess*, which starred George Arliss. It was the smallest part in the production, but it did buy him more than the soup and rice pudding he had become accustomed to starving on.

He also began getting small roles in films. His first was *Handcuffs or Kisses?*, an undistinguished programmer made in New York for Lewis J. Selznick (father of David O. Selznick). It didn't even rate a review in the *New York Times*. Three plays later, he went on tour with Broadway star Fay Bainter in the successful hit *East Is West*. When the coast-to-coast tour reached California in late 1921, Colman saw Hollywood for the first time, and tried, but failed, to interest the casting directors at the film studios. In the film capital, he was on the outside looking in, for he had but one American picture to his credit, and an inconsequential one at that. Despite an enthusiastic mention by famed drama critic Alexander Woollcott in the *New York Times* on August 16, 1921, for his work on the stage as a butler in a mystery-comedy ("Ronald Colman makes a little part tell"), the frustrations continued to mount. In November 1921, for instance, the young man walked into a Hollywood agent's office and inquired:

"Do you think there might be a chance for me in Hollywood?"

"I wonder," the agent replied.

Colman made a fast exit, deeply chagrined, and returned to New York a badly disappointed man.[10]

Finally an earlier Broadway role in *The Nightcap* led to a significant part as "the other man" in *La Tendresse* with Ruth Chatterton and Henry Miller. As Alain Sergyll, the plum juvenile lead, Colman made an immediate impact in this widely touted love-triangle drama. The critics singled him out in their reviews, with Alexander Woollcott again praising his work in the *New York Times* on September 26, 1922: "One fine, direct and authentic performance is given by an actor named Ronald Colman." Such appraisal failed to produce any film offers at first, but the monetary horizon was about to brighten, for agents and producers were at last beginning to sit up and show some interest in the young Britisher. By now, Thelma had joined him in New York, and together they managed to keep poverty from their door. And then the big break came.

Director Henry King had been looking for a handsome, Italian-looking young man to play opposite Lillian Gish in *The White Sister*, her first picture since leaving Griffith after *Orphans of the Storm* (1922). By a stroke of luck, James Abbé, Miss Gish's stills photographer, had spotted Colman in *La Tendresse;* he thought the Englishman would be just right for the part, and persuaded King and Miss Gish to go see him. Sitting in the audience that evening, the two knew at once that they'd found their leading man. They went to see him backstage, and King asked the youthful-looking 31-year-old to come to his office the next morning.

Colman arrived and greeted King: "I do appreciate more than anything in the world someone calling me for an interview, but I'm no good in pictures. I have been told both in London and New York that I don't photograph well, and I've decided that I'm through with them. I'm going to stay in the theater where I know my way, and apparently I don't know my way in pictures."[11]

He agreed to make a screen test, but insisted that King was wasting his time: "I know you won't like it when you see it."[12]

King asked Colman if he'd mind having some liberties taken with his appearance. The director slicked down Colman's dark hair and, with a makeup pencil, added a thin moustache. The actor had appeared sans moustache in all his roles to date.

After completing the test late that afternoon, Colman told King, "You know, I've enjoyed this work very much. I'm just sorry I know you won't like it!"[13]

As Lillian Gish remembers, "Once we had run the test we knew our search was over. Ronald Colman was perfect for the part."[14]

And so the silent medium, unable to take advantage of Colman's voice, hired him for his looks. This was the first great turning point. Overnight he had vaulted from his first substantial Broadway role into an incredibly meaty part in a major American motion picture.

Miss Gish sent a note to *La Tendresse* producer-star Henry Miller, explaining that Colman was in a predicament. Since *The White Sister* was to be shot on location in Italy, the actor would have to leave the cast of *La Tendresse* immediately; but he felt a large debt of gratitude to Miller for giving him his opportunity in the play, and was reluctant to back out on such short notice. Miller fully understood the situation and gave him his blessing. Forty-eight hours later Colman and the rest of the cast and crew sailed for Italy.

During the long sea voyage he was coached in screen-acting techniques by King and Miss Gish, and also grew a moustache to replace the one Henry King had pencilled in. Thus came into being the famous Colman moustache, which would remain a part of the image for the next 35 years.

The company of *The White Sister* took the reserved Englishman to their hearts immediately. The crew filmed for six months in and around Rome, and when the picture, stunningly photographed by Roy Overbaugh, went into general release early in 1924, it made millions for both Inspiration and Metro. As the dashing, tragic Captain Giovanni Severi, Colman projected polish and humor; his whole aspect suggested power, acute intelligence, and quiet strength of character. Guided for the first time by a really top-notch director, Colman photographed well, in a creditable role, and was surrounded by a superb cast.[15] Although he initially considered it a mere pleasant interlude, still thinking of himself as a stage actor, Colman changed his opinion once he saw the edited print, and realized that he was indeed a film actor.

"They toned down my theatrical mannerisms and refined my style," he remembered later; "they saw that I was photographed to maximum advantage."[16]

Thirty-two years of age was rather late to make it big in the movie capital by Hollywood standards, where Lillian Gish, Mary Pickford, and others became superstars in their early teens, but Colman had made an auspicious beginning. *The White Sister* made him an immediate star.

On the personal front, things weren't as bright. Thelma had joined her husband in Rome and they were having difficulties during the filming. They soon separated for good.

While awaiting a good script offer, Colman bided his time by making an uncredited appearance in *The Eternal City*, a Samuel Goldwyn production shot on location in Rome and New York. Boasting a cast of 20,000, it starred Barbara La Marr, Bert Lytell, Lionel Barrymore, Richard Bennett, and Montagu Love. Colman next appeared as George Arliss' son in an insignificant programmer entitled *$20 a Week*. It was to be his last undistinguished effort.

Colman joined director Henry King in Italy to make George Eliot's *Romola*, a big-budgeted historical spectacle produced by Inspiration and scheduled for release by Metro-Goldwyn. Starring Lillian and Dorothy Gish, William Powell, Colman, and Charles Lane, this late-medieval saga of political intrigue in Florence made a big splash when it opened in December 1924, but Colman was lost in the production, "in a role which proved to be no more than a decorative lovesick cipher."[17] While shooting the picture in Florence, Colman struck up a friendship with stage actor and co-star William Powell. Refined, lean, and similarly moustached, Powell shared Colman's sense of humor, shyness, and reticence. Their friendship was to last a lifetime.

Although Colman didn't know it, fortune was about to smile: Sam Goldwyn was about to enter the picture.

The Live Wire

1917. *Producer, director, screenplay, and cinematographer:* George Dewhurst. 2 reels. Never released. No print known to have survived.
Cast: Ronald Colman, Phyllis Titmuss.

The time—1917; the place—a primitive studio on the outskirts of London. Ronald Colman was making his very first motion picture.

A vacant room in an old house served as the tiny studio. Besides acting, Colman doubled as scene shifter and helped set up lights. George Dewhurst wrote the script, directed, and personally photographed the production.

The film was completed in one day. For his efforts, Colman was paid the munificent sum of one pound. The results, according to Colman, were "lamentable and uneven."[18] To his relief, the two-reeler was never released.

"If it had been," he later recalled, "and I had been able to see myself as others would have seen me, I'm sure I would have dashed back to my three-legged stool at the British Steamship Company in a jiffy."[19]

The Live Wire, together with all seven of Colman's later British releases, was presumed destroyed in the London Blitz of 1941. Even the basic plot of his film debut is unknown today.

Such was the inauspicious start of a forty-year film career.

The Toilers

1919. *Production:* Diamond Super, Ltd. *Distribution:* Neville Bruce, Ltd. *Producer:* George Dewhurst. *Director:* Tom W. Watts. *Screenplay:* Eliot Stannard, R.C. Sheriff (from the novel *The Toilers of the Sea* by Victor Hugo). *Cinematographer:* Egrot. 5 reels (5,000 feet). Released in England in March 1919. No print known to have survived.

Cast: Manora Thew (Rose), George Dewhurst (Jack), Gwynne Herbert (Mother), Ronald Colman (Bob), Eric Barker (Jack as a child), John Corrie (Lighthouse Keeper), Mollie Terraine (Merchant's Daughter).

Colman's second production for George Dewhurst was *The Toilers,* shot on location in a Cornish fishing village and released in 1919. In a substantial supporting role, Colman played the selfish adopted son of a fisherman's widow who deserts his foster mother (Gwynne Herbert) for a flighty London socialite (Mollie Terraine). But the romance fails and, after a series of disheartening adventures in London, the rejected and chastened suitor returns to the fisherfolk and the forgiving arms of his foster mother. In addition to producing the picture, Dewhurst starred as Colman's brother.

Colman's acting style at this time was awkwardly theatrical.

"My hands and arms went round and round like windmills," he later remembered, "and I was all over the place like a jumping jack, giving highly 'nervous' accounts of myself."[20]

Moreover, his limp, a result of the war injury, was more apparent on the screen than it had been on stage. The actor was appalled to notice how pronounced it seemed in films.

Despite beautiful location photography, this simple romantic tale had little to recommend it. *The Bioscope* called the picture "poor and unconvincing material," deeming it a "thin, commonplace and rather weak drama which possesses . . . very little human interest."[21]

A Daughter of Eve

1919. *Production:* Broadwest, Ltd. *Distribution:* Walter Daw & Sons, Ltd. *Producer and director:* Walter West. 5 reels (5,000 feet). Released in England in 1919. No print known to have survived.

Cast: Violet Hopson (Jessica Bond), Stewart Rome (Sidney Strangeways), Cameron Carr (Charles Strangeways), Ralph Forster (John Bond), Edward Banfield (Sir Hugh Strangeways), Vesta Sylva (Jessica as a child), Ronald Colman.

Later in 1919, producer-director Walter West offered Colman a small role in his latest production, *A Daughter of Eve*. As stage assignments were difficult to come by and he needed the money, Colman accepted the part. Apparently, no record of his appearance in this crime drama exists, for it was insignificant and uncredited.

Violet Hopson played the lovely young wife of a British Lord. Hopelessly enamored of her former lover, an impoverished cad portrayed by Stewart Rome, she advances him 500 pounds of her husband's money. When the husband is murdered and the money is discovered missing, the lover is convicted of murder and sentenced to death.[22] He is in fact innocent, for on the night the murder took place he and Miss Hopson had met for a tryst, but he steadfastly refuses to invoke his only alibi to spare her the ignominy of a scandal. A desperate, D.W. Griffith–inspired, last-minute rescue attempt fails to save him, and the young man is executed. Miss Hopson then awakens to realize that the entire story has been a dream.

The Bioscope was highly critical of this undistinguished, overmelodramatic concoction, calling attention to its "rather conventional and obvious construction . . . [in which] there is mechanical artifice rather than justifiable coincidence. And the 'surprise' at the end is unconvincing and rather irritating, making one feel that a great deal of fuss has been made about nothing."[23]

Sheba

1919. *Production:* Sutherland, Ltd. *Distribution:* Butcher's Kimemagraphic Distributors, Ltd. *Producer and director:* Cecil M. Hepworth. *Screenplay:* Blanche McIntosh (from the novel *Rita*). 5 reels (5,475 feet). Released in England in 1919. No print known to have survived.

Cast: Alma Taylor (Sheba Ormatroyd), Gerald Ames (Paul Meredith), James Carew (Levison), Lionelle Howard (Count Pharamond), Eileen Dennes (Bessie

Saxton), Mary Dibley (Rhoda Meredith), Diana Carey (Mrs. Ormatroyd), Eric Barker (Rex Ormatroyd), Ronald Colman.

The one name that mattered in the British cinema during this period was that of Cecil Hepworth. The director had entered the industry in 1896 at the age of 21, and made his first motion picture in his own studio at Walton-on-Thames in 1898. A meticulous craftsman distinguished for his artistic and technical excellence, Hepworth scored notable successes with several early Dickens adaptations, among them *Oliver Twist* (1912), *David Copperfield* (1913), and *The Old Curiosity Shop* (1914).

In 1919, he cast Ronald Colman in another small, unbilled role in *Sheba,* which featured the director's best-known star, Alma Taylor. She portrayed a rich Jew's stepdaughter who weds a famous opera singer's son (Gerald Ames), only to learn that he is already married. The picture was well received, and one London paper commented: "Rather outlandish in its plot convolutions but effectively acted by Miss Taylor and Gerald Ames, and the talented hand of Cecil Hepworth is everywhere apparent."[24]

Although Colman's part was trivial, it gave evidence that he was at last beginning to tone down his theatrical mannerisms; and although he had not yet mastered the technique of cinematic underplaying, he was noticeably more relaxed in front of the camera.

In his 1951 autobiography, *Came the Dawn,* Cecil Hepworth wrote:

> His was an unknown name, and I, knowing nothing of his ability, cast him for a part of no great importance. There was, consequently, nothing very distinguished in his acting, for the part did not give him much opportunity. I also noted that he appeared to have some slight awkwardness which prevented him from walking really naturally in the film. It may have been merely temporary or he must have overcome it, for I have not noticed it in any of his films since.[25]

Snow in the Desert

1919. *Production:* Broadwest, Ltd. *Distribution:* Walter Daw & Sons, Ltd. *Producer and director:* Walter West. *Screenplay:* Benedict James (from the novel by Andrew Soutar). 6 reels (7,000 feet). Released in England in 1919. No print known to have survived.

Cast: Violet Hopson (Felice Beste), Stewart Rome (William B. Jackson), Sir Simeon Stuart (Sir Michael Beste), Ronald Colman (Rupert Sylvester), Poppy Wyndham, Mary Masters, A.B. Caldwell.

Colman's final picture of 1919 was Walter West's *Snow in the Desert,* a romantic drama which reunited him with Violet Hopson and Stewart Rome. The plot concerned the extra-marital entanglement of a wealthy business magnate's wife (Violet Hopson), who deserts her neglectful husband (Sir Simeon Stuart) to elope with a dashing poet (Stewart Rome). When the husband falls dangerously ill, she regrets her indiscretion, rejoins her husband, and saves his business from ruin.

As the well-bred Rupert Sylvester, Colman had a small but attractive part which earned critical praise, but the film itself was harshly condemned for its trivial plot contrivances and predictability. Despite handsome location shooting in Cornwall, one reviewer called it "a foolish romance of the kind that has become the essence of triteness."[26]

A Son of David

1920. *Production:* Broadwest, Ltd. *Distribution:* Walter Daw & Sons, Ltd. *Producer:* Walter West. *Director:* E. Hay Plumb. *Screenplay:* Benedict James (from the short story by Charles Barnett). 5 reels (4,700 feet). Released in England in February 1920. No print known to have survived.

Cast: Poppy Wyndham (Esther Raphael), Ronald Colman (Maurice Phillips), Arthur Walcott (Louis Raphael), Constance Blackner (Miriam Myers), Robert Vallis (Sam Myers), Joseph Pacey (Maurice as a child), Vesta Sylva (Esther as a child).

Ronald Colman's first important screen role was that of a Jewish prizefighter in Walter West's 1920 production, *A Son of David.* Set in London's squalid Whitechapel district, this drama starred Colman as a young man, Maurice Phillips, who grows up believing that his father had been murdered in a boxing match. To avenge the death, he becomes a skilled boxer and finally meets his father's alleged killer in the ring. Although his hulking opponent is almost twice his weight, the Son of David manages to defeat him, only to discover that his father had not been murdered after all: a heart attack had struck him down after the bout. His honor satisfied, Phillips weds his true love, a rabbi's daughter (Poppy Wyndham).

A Son of David was directed by kindly, jovial ex-vaudevillian E. Hay Plumb, who patiently urged Colman to tone down his theatrical movements and gestures. The advice apparently worked, for reviewers were beginning to notice the young actor and praised his performance highly. They were equally enthusiastic about the picture, and *A Song of David* went on to become the most popular of Colman's British films. As *The Bioscope* observed, "It strikes an original note and should prove very attractive to a majority of audiences."[27]

Colman, however, felt that he had overacted badly, and found the final fight sequence rather silly.

"My screen shadow seemed to me terrible, unspeakably dreadful," he later said. "In the big moment I had to knock out a man, an ex-professional who could have killed me and eaten me."[28]

Anna the Adventuress

1920. *Production:* Sutherland, Ltd. *Distribution:* National Photoplay Distributors, Ltd. *Producer and director:* Cecil M. Hepworth. *Screenplay:* Blanche McIntosh (from the novel by E. Phillips Oppenheim). 6 reels (6,280 feet). Released in England in 1920. No print known to have survived.

Cast: Alma Taylor (Anna and Annabel Pellissier), James Carew (Montague Hill), Gerald Ames (Nigel Ennison), Gwynne Herbert (Aunt), Christine Rayner (Mrs. Ellicote), Ronald Colman (Walter Brendan), James Annand (Sir John Ferringhall), Jean Cadell (Mrs. White).

Colman's second picture for renowned director Cecil Hepworth, *Anna the Adventuress*, reunited him with one of Britain's top film stars, Alma Taylor. During this period, Colman and Miss Taylor were among the few British performers working under fixed contracts, which guaranteed them a steady income whether or not they were making pictures.

In this 1920 murder melodrama, based on the novel by E. Phillips Oppenheim, Alma Taylor starred in a dual role, portraying identical twin sisters. After some extremely involved plot twists, the film rushes headlong through an exchange of identities, bigamy, and murder to its hopelessly muddled conclusion.

Anna the Adventuress failed to impress either the public or the critics, who found its complexities overwhelmingly confusing. Despite Miss Taylor's versatility and some ingenious special effects in the dual-role sequences, reviewers grumbled that the sisters were all too often indistinguishable; as one critic complained, "Audiences go to a movie to be entertained, not to be mind-teased and twisted."[29]

Colman, in a minor role, did a commendable job of underplaying, which earned him some fine notices that praised his "pleasant manner and acting authority."[30] However, when he attended a theatre screening to observe the audience's reaction to his new style, he was startled to overhear a woman remark that he didn't know how to walk: the effect of his war wound was still evident.

Although Colman would soon emigrate to America and aspire to stardom in Hollywood, misfortune was about to strike Cecil Hepworth. Engulfed by bankruptcy a few years later, he eked out a living for the next 30 years by making promotional trailers. Largely forgotten, he died in 1953.

The Black Spider

1920. *Production:* B & C Shows, Ltd. *Distribution:* Butcher's Kinemagraphic Distributors, Ltd. *Producer:* Edward Godal. *Director and screenplay:* William J. Humphrey (from the novel by Carlton Dawe). 5 reels (5,800 feet). Released in England in May 1920. No print known to have survived.

A moustacheless Colman, in an early British film, Anna the Adventuress, *already displays the kind of intensity he would later make his trademark.* Left–right: *Jean Cadell, unidentified actor, Colman, and Alma Taylor.*

Cast: Lydia Kyasht (Angela Carfour), Bertram Burleigh (Archie Lowndes), Sam Livesey (Reginald Conway), Ronald Colman (Vicomte de Beauvais), C. Hayden Coffin (Lord Carfour), Adeline Hayden Coffin (Lady Carfour), Mary Clare (Coralie Mount), Dorothy Cecil (Marjorie West).

In *The Black Spider,* his third 1920 release as well as his last British picture, Colman was cast as the gallant Vicomte de Beauvais, "a French nobleman who broke hearts and safe deposits throughout Europe."[31] Beautiful Riviera scenery shot on location in Monte Carlo provided the glitter, and exotic Russian dancer Lydia Kyasht, starring as Colman's fiancée, furnished the glamour.

An infamous international crook known only as "the Black Spider" terrorizes the wealthy resort crowd up and down the Riviera coast. The intricate plot is sown with false trails and red herrings—including an imposter who copies the Spider's methods—but the mysterious jewel thief is finally unmasked and brought to justice.

This sophisticated thriller was a delightful change of pace for Colman, and clearly anticipated his later early-talkie success, *Raffles,* in which he also impersonated a dashing gentleman thief. The critics praised his portrayal of "the Black Spider," and the picture caused a sensation among cinema audiences in Britain due to its authentic location photography. As *The Bioscope* noted, "Ronald Colman makes the bold, bad Vicomte a romantic figure in the short glimpses we have of him. The drama itself offers no great opportunities to its players. Delightful Monte Carlo exteriors and well-staged studio scenes are the pleasantest features of this complex mystery story, the plot of which is told in so involved a style as to be difficult to follow."[32]

Thus Colman's early British period came to a close. His next pictures would be produced in America.

Handcuffs or Kisses?

1921. *Production:* Lewis J. Selznick Pictures Company. *Distribution:* Select Motion Pictures Corporation. *Producer:* Lewis J. Selznick. *Director:* George Archainbaud. *Screenplay:* Lewis Allen Browne (from the short story "Handcuffs and Kisses" by Thomas Edgelow). *Cinematographer:* Jules Cronjager. 6 reels. *Release Date:* September 5, 1921. No print known to have survived.

Cast: Elaine Hammerstein (Lois Walton), Julia Swayne Gordon (Mrs. Walton), Dorothy Chappell (Violet), Robert Ellis (Peter Madison), Alison Skipworth (Miss Strodd), Florence Billings (Miss Dell), Ronald Schabel (Leo Carstairs), George Lessey (Elias Pratt), Ronald Colman (Lodyard).

"I was offered a very insignificant part in a very insignificant picture," Colman later remembered of this film, "and all they wanted was a sharp-looking dress suit and someone to fill it."[33]

Shot in New York on a shoestring budget, *Handcuffs or Kisses?* starred Elaine Hammerstein as a young orphan, Lois Walton. Swindled out of her father's fortune by an avaricious aunt, she is shuttled off to a reformatory, where she and other inmates are cruelly abused. Fearful of the consequences if she were to complain, Lois refuses to testify against the vicious matron (Alison Skipworth) when an investigation is conducted. However, she arouses the compassion of investigative attorney Peter Madison (Robert Ellis) and is soon paroled. After further misadventures, including the lecherous advances of a physician and unsuitable employment as social secretary to a gambling-house operator (Florence Billings), she accepts Madison's proposal of matrimony, and all ends happily.

Colman's first appearance in an American film was limited indeed, and was hardly guaranteed to open the doors of stardom. As a rich playboy angling for the heroine's affections, he had a brief scene of no consequence whatsoever with Miss Hammerstein, and then dropped out of the picture. The Selznick people seem to have sealed the fate of *Handcuffs or Kisses?*

even before they released it. It opened early in September of 1921, but distribution was haphazard, and the popular press ignored it. Trade papers dismissed the picture as an embarrassment, and gave it only perfunctory notices. *Exhibitor's Herald,* for instance, tossed it aside by commenting: "Too much like anti-reformatory propaganda. . . . It is steeped in gloom without a bit of comedy relief."[34]

The White Sister

1923. *Production:* Inspiration Pictures, Inc. *Distribution:* Metro Pictures Corporation. *Director:* Henry King. *Screenplay:* George V. Hobart, Charles E. Whittaker (from the novel by Francis Marion Crawford). *Cinematographer:* Roy Overbaugh. *Assistant Cinematographers:* William Schurr, Ferdinand Risi. *Art Director:* Robert M. Haas. *Production Manager:* Joseph C. Boyle. *Stills Photographer:* James Abbé. *Titles:* Will M. Ritchey, Don Bartlett. *Film Editor:* Duncan Mansfield. *Musical Score:* Joseph Carl Breil. 13 reels (13,147 feet). Cut to 10 reels (10,055 feet) for national release in February 1924, and again to 9 reels (9,361 feet) for general release in April 1924. *New York Premiere:* September 5, 1923.

Cast: Lillian Gish (Angela Chiaromonte), Ronald Colman (Captain Giovanni Severi), Gail Kane (Marchesa di Mola), J. Barney Sherry (Monsignor Saracinesca), Charles Lane (Prince Chiaromonte), Juliette La Violette (Madame Bernard), Signor Serena (Professor Ugo Severi), Alfredo Bertone (Filmore Durand), Ramon Ibanez (Count del Ferice), Alfredo Martinelli (Alfredo del Ferice), Carloni Talli (Mother Superior), Giovanni Viccola (General Mazzini), Antonio Barda (Alfredo's Tutor), Giacomo D'Attino (Solicitor to the Prince), Michele Gualdi (Solicitor to the Count), Giuseppe Pavoni (The Archbishop), Francesco Socinus (Professor Torricelli), Sheik Mahomet (The Bedouin Chief), James Abbé (Lieutenant Rossini), Duncan Mansfield (Commander Donato).

The first American picture to be shot on location in Italy, this "Romance of a Love that Outlived Passion" was set on the Italian slopes beneath the ever-threatening Vesuvius. It is the story of Donna Angela Chiaromonte (Miss Gish)—principal heiress to the vast estate of her father, Prince Chiaromonte (Charles Lane)—and her devotion to the dashing Captain Giovanni Severi (Colman). Before Severi can ask Chiaromonte for his daughter's hand in marriage, the prince is thrown from his horse while riding to the hounds and dies. Angela's scheming half-sister, the Marchesa di Mola (Gail Kane), steals her father's will. Since she knows that it divides the inheritance between the two daughters, she burns it and calls for a quick settlement of the prince's estate. In the absence of a will, everything goes to the older daughter, the Marchesa. A crushing sense of utter loss overwhelms Angela as she realizes that she has been tricked out of her fortune, and when she turns to her sister for comfort and support, she is callously rebuffed, for the Marchesa is insanely jealous of Giovanni Severi's affection for Angela.

Colman's first big break came with the opportunity to work with silent-screen legend Lillian Gish. Here, in The White Sister, *Colman as Captain Giovanni Severi prepares to leave his sweetheart for active duty.*

Homeless and penniless, Angela flees to the residence of her old friend Madame Bernard (Juliette La Violette). Captain Severi visits her there and informs her that he has received orders form the Italian War Department assigning him to command an expedition to Africa. As they sit before the fireplace with hands entwined, he tells her that the troops sail at dawn. He doesn't want to leave her, but he must serve his country.

Angela sees him off at the dock at daybreak.

"The day I return will be our wedding day," Giovanni promises.

"I'll wait for you, Giovanni," she vows; "I'll wait for you forever."

Months later, as an unsuspecting Angela dreams of her lover's return, Severi's encampment in North Africa is savagely attacked by marauding Arab bandits. Word of the massacre quickly reaches Italy, where Monsignor Saracinesca (J. Barney Sherry), an old friend of the Chiaromonte family, gently breaks the news to Angela. Clutching Giovanni's last letter, she faints as she hears a newsboy shout outside, "Captain Severi killed!"

Angela lies for weeks in a trance-like, emotionless state of dry-eyed despair in a convent hospital. Finally she recovers and, believing her lover dead, informs the Monsignor of her decision to become a nun and devote her life to Giovanni's memory by serving God.

But miraculously, Giovanni Severi lives. Bronzed, bearded, and ragged in a crude Arab cell, he is one of the lucky few who were taken prisoner rather than slaughtered on that fatal day in the desert. While Angela serves her novitiate and prepares to take her final vows, Severi manages to escape and finally reaches an outpost of civilization. He returns to his homeland on the first warship bound for Italy.

Content to forsake the outside world forever, Angela garbs herself in bridal array and becomes a "bride of Christ." In the house of the Lord, she is divested of her worldly garments and her long, golden tresses are symbolically shorn.

When Severi's ship arrives, he is taken ashore and ordered to report to the War Department immediately, where he is informed that his brother, Professor Ugo Severi (Signor Serena), a noted scientist, has collapsed and been hospitalized. Giovanni is granted permission to visit his brother at the same hospital where Angela is now a nun and a nurse. Inevitably he comes face to face with her. Unwilling to believe that his beloved has become a nun, Severi embraces her as recognition dawns on her face. When he tries to kiss her, Angela swoons, reaches up to touch his cheek, and start to kiss him. Then, remembering her new role, she recoils in horror and flees. Observing the proceedings is the Archbishop (Giuseppe Pavoni), who tells Giovanni that marriage to the Holy Church is as sacred as that to a man.

"Had Angela married another man," asks the priest, "would you ask her to break her marriage vows?"

An anguished Severi swears he'll make Angela renounce her contract. Angry and brooding, he lures the white sister to his brother's laboratory, where he insists that she sign an appeal to the Pope for a dispensation. The emotional complexity of this scene is visually reinforced by Henry King's deft juxtaposition of shots of the distraught captain with shots of nearby Vesuvius and bubbling lava, similarly seething ferments of unrest.

"I have pledged my word to God," Angela maintains, "and He alone can release me!"

"You promised to wait for me forever. Forget your vows," insists Giovanni.

Meanwhile the spiteful Marchesa, aware that Severi has returned, informs the Monsignor that Ugo Severi's observatory is the secret meeting place of Sister Angela and her lover. Severely shocked, the priest sets out for the laboratory.

Severi, dominated by his unquenchable passion, threatens to keep Angela his prisoner. She'll be an outcast nun, he warns, for everyone will believe that she's been living with him. But finally Angela's protestations prevail, and Giovanni comes to realize that she belongs to God alone. Angela quietly leaves.

The air outside is stifling; a sense of foreboding fills the atmosphere: Vesuvius is about to explode. As smoke begins to bellow forth from the top of the volcano, Severi determines to warn the villagers below. Skillful cross-cutting dominates the film's final scenes and creates tension as Vesuvius erupts and pours mountains of liquid fire onto the village. While Severi races to warn the townspeople, the Marchesa's carriage plunges off a narrow road and is demolished. A bloodied, mortally wounded Marchesa drags herself from the wreckage and manages to stagger back to town and into a small chapel, where Angela listens to her dying confession. In her delirium, the Marchesa assumes that her sister is a priest, and she confesses that she burned her father's will and turned Angela out of her house.

"Will she forgive me, Father?" whispers the Marchesa.

"God is love. She forgives you," Angela replies softly, cradling her sister in her arms.

Villagers flee through the night and the smoke as Severi shouts his warning. Then water from a burst reservoir floods the streets of the town. Catastrophic flood scenes deluge the screen; buildings collapse and Severi valiantly rescues a drowning child. Finally, however, he succumbs to the raging torrent and drowns.

At dawn, the sun begins to shine down upon a steaming slope of desolation. Vesuvius is at rest again. The people of the village pray for the unknown soldier who saved many lives while sacrificing his own. Sister Angela prays for the soul of Giovanni Severi, and the church bells toll.

Religious stories, often based rather loosely on the Bible, were legion in the silent era—*Intolerance, The Ten Commandments, The King of Kings*—but *The White Sister* was, according to Lillian Gish, the first *modern* religious story to be filmed. The inspiration for the picture came when Miss Gish read F. Marion Crawford's popular 1909 tear-jerking novel. Recognizing its cinematic potential, she immediately signed with Inspiration Pictures for $1,000 a week plus a percentage of the profits after double the cost of the negative had been returned to Inspiration. Once Ronald Colman had been cast as Miss Gish's leading man (at $450 a week, which was what Henry Miller had been paying him on Broadway), Henry King shepherded cast and crew onto the S.S. *Providence* and departed for Rome, where interiors were constructed in a studio on the outskirts of the city. Various location shots were filmed throughout Italy—in Sorrento, Capri, Rome, Lago Montagna, and Tivoli. "We didn't go over there to make a picture of interiors," King later remembered.[35]

For the scenes of Vesuvius, King went to Naples:

The only way you can get up to the top of the mountain is on horseback. So I took the cameraman, Roy Overbaugh, his assistant, a guide, and one other person. We rode up to the top, then we started down inside the volcano.

Using ropes, we somehow got down to the bottom. There were little craters which would burst into life every few minutes, discharging gases. Then the wind would change and all you could do was lie on your stomach and put your handkerchief over your face. You'd be asphyxiated if you didn't. Fortunately, we were all young and full of enthusiasm. When the gas cleared, we set off again and came to a crack in the lava. . . . The camera assistant began to have fainting spells and had to go back. The craters kept bursting and firing little stones that looked about the size of pebbles. One of them fell near Roy Overbaugh and me, and it was at least a foot in diameter.

Well, the heat was so intense I couldn't stand it. It singed my eyebrows and my hair. . . . That little expedition took twelve hours — but we got our film. It so happened that Vesuvius was in a kind of semi-eruption. When we intercut this with the scenes we had made in the studio, and with what we had shot on the side of Vesuvius, it looked rather convincing.[36]

On the way over . . . I met an archbishop, the papal delegate to Washington.

"You have a vivid imagination," he said, "and that is what worries me. The scene in The White Sister — where she becomes a nun — is sacred to the Catholic Church. I wish you'd eliminate it."

"I'll make a deal with you," I said. "Would you prefer me to do this sequence with my imagination or with your help?"

"By all means, with my help," he said. "If you must do it, I will give you someone who will guide you so that you will not go wrong."

We arrived in Rome, and on the morning we were to shoot the sequence a short, fat little priest came on the set. He had his script with him, and it was very thick. . . . It took him from eight in the morning until seven at night to get through it. . . .

Now, I have worked with a lot of New York stage directors, but I never saw a man with such quiet authority. . . . When I saw the archbishop, I thanked him for sending the priest over.

"You know," I said, "he is the greatest stage director I ever saw."

"Well," said the archbishop, "he's had a lot of experience. The last show he put on had sixteen thousand people in the cast."

The priest was the head ceremonial director from the Vatican![37]

Other problems were overcome without the help of such high authorities. When Lillian Gish encountered difficulties in getting Colman to overcome his natural reserve and play his love scenes with appropriate passion and abandon, Henry King solved the problem by taking the actor out to dinner, giving him a few drinks, and then bringing him back to face the cameras. Miss Gish describes what happened next:

It worked! Ronnie was so relaxed he could just walk straight. We did the scene over several times, and finally he was yelling and gesticulating as the

Italians always do—however well born—when they are in a temper. We got the scene that is in the picture around two in the morning. The next day, he was so contrite! He kept asking people what he had said. He'd only gone so far as to say "Damn," but I think he was teased for some time by the men in the company. Even if he had been unconscious, though, he couldn't have ceased being a gentleman.[38]

After six months of filming in Italy, plus a side trip to Algeria, where the desert sequences were shot, the company returned to New York, but was unable to find a distributor willing to release the picture, despite the fact that religious films had always served as commercial trump cards for the major distributors. "People get religion free on Sundays," they were told; "you can't make them pay for it during the week."[39]

But Miss Gish was determined. "I'll tour it in a tent if I have to," she insisted.[40] Unable to open the picture in movie theatres, Inspiration staged its premiere at New York's prestigious Forty-fourth Street Theatre, and it caused an immediate sensation. God proved big at the box office, and Nicholas Schenck, head of the eastern office of Metro Pictures, quickly agreed to distribute it. Contributing to the film's smashing success were Roy Overbaugh's glowing cinematography and magnificent night shots of Vesuvius in eruption. Overbaugh had used panchromatic film, a newly developed, highly sensitive stock which accentuated his shadowed, atmospheric lighting. Henry King masterfully manipulated editing techniques to generate suspense (including frequent shots of bubbling lava—visual metaphors for seething passion and frustrated sexuality). And, of course, Lillian Gish and Ronald Colman both contributed fine performances. Although *The White Sister* had cost only $300,000 to produce, it soon earned fortunes for both Inspiration and Metro.

For once, Hollywood's chronic insistence upon happy endings was reversed, but only because the film was an independent production, made without the film capital's influence. The novel had ended happily once Angela had renounced her vows, but Lillian Gish felt that the only plausible conclusion for the picture was a tragic one. "We couldn't expect to hold the sympathy of audiences," she recalls, "if a half-hour after our heroine had taken solemn vows she repudidated them."[41]

Lillian Gish's ethereal beauty, that physical frailness and delicacy best described as a Dresden-china quality, was exhibited here to the best advantage yet. Shrouded in holiness, dreamlike and subdued, she embodied an unattainable ideal.

Ronald Colman's earlier performances in London and New York had been the work of a very young, inexperienced actor. With *The White Sister*, the right man had met the right moment, for his portrayal of the reckless Captain Severi was an automatic stepping-stone to stardom.

Critics turned in rave reviews of Miss Gish's restrained performance, and proclaimed Colman a new screen star. As *Motion Picture Classic* reported, "A newcomer is Ronald Colman who plays the broken-hearted lover, and he gives a performance of quiet force and dignity. He never seems to be acting, which makes his expression all the more natural and genuine."[42] Movie-goers everywhere began asking the same question: Who was that dark, attractive, young Italian whom Lillian Gish had selected as her new leading man? Ronald Colman had begun his rapid climb to the top of the ladder.

Essanay had produced a version of *The White Sister* in 1915, with Richard Travers and Viola Allen playing the leads. When M-G-M remade it in 1932, Clark Gable and Helen Hayes failed to recapture the poignancy of the Gish-Colman teaming.

The Eternal City

1923. *Production:* Samuel Goldwyn, Inc. *Distribution:* Associated First National Pictures. *Producer:* Samuel Goldwyn. *Director:* George Fitzmaurice. *Screenplay:* Ouida Bergere (from the novel and play by Hall Caine). *Cinematographer:* Arthur Miller. 8 reels (7,929 feet; cut to 7,800 feet for general release). *Premiere:* December 17, 1923. *Release Date:* January 20, 1924. No print known to have survived.

Cast: Barbara La Marr (Donna Roma Valonna), Bert Lytell (David Rossi), Lionel Barrymore (Baron Bonelli), Richard Bennett (Bruno Rocco), Montagu Love (Charles Minghelli, Leader of the Reds), Betty Bronson, Joan Bennett (Pages), Ronald Colman.

After completing *The White Sister,* Colman signed on for an uncredited stint in this World War I historical epic produced by Samuel Goldwyn. Based on the 1901 novel by Hall Caine, which was originally staged on Broadway in 1903, it was a remake of the 1915 Famous Players–Lasky picture which had featured Pauline Frederick. George Fitzmaurice, who was to guide Ronald Colman through eight later productions, directed this version, which starred Barbara La Marr, Bert Lytell, Lionel Barrymore, Richard Bennett, and Montagu Love. *The Eternal City* is a tale of romance and political intrigue amid the splendor and majesty of Rome. With Sir Hall Caine's permission, scenarist Ouida Bergere (the future Mrs. Basil Rathbone) updated the story by making its hero an Italian war veteran who joins Mussolini's black-shirted Fascisti in a patriotic effort to defeat scheming Bolsheviks.

Enamored since childhood, Donna Roma Valonna (Barbara La Marr) and David Rossi (Bert Lytell) are separated when David goes off to war. Believing him killed in action, Roma studies art and becomes a celebrated sculptor, helped by the patronage of an unscrupulous politician, Baron Bonelli (Lionel Barrymore), secret leader of the Bolsheviks. In the stormy aftermath of the war, David joins Mussolini's Fascist movement and leads the Blackshirts against the Reds. When their paths cross again, David denounces Roma for her liaison with Bonelli. After killing the Baron in a pistol struggle, David learns that Roma had not been Bonelli's mistress, and the lovers are happily reunited.

Filmed on location in Rome and New York, *The Eternal City* boasted handsome, authentic Italian settings and rich pictorial design. Although reviewers found the plot contrivance of Fascisti versus Reds generally turgid and heavy-handed, they praised the beauty and realism of the Roman exteriors; the romance was gripping, and the stars' performances were widely acclaimed. Lionel Barrymore played the merciless villain to the hilt; Bert Lytell convincingly portrayed the romantic hero; Montagu Love was appropriately malevolent as the Red leader; and Barbara La Marr, famous as "the girl who was too beautiful," made a lovely heroine.

The inclusion of newsreel footage of King Victor Emmanuel, and of the Duce reviewing his victorious troops, added to the film's timely appeal, and *The Eternal City* was an unqualified success at the box office. Rounding out the picture's epic proportions was an impressive cast of 20,000 extras, one of whom was the unbilled Ronald Colman. This appearance kept him busy and paid his bills, but was an odd assignment indeed for Lillian Gish's new leading man.

$20 a Week

1924. *Production:* Distinctive Pictures Corp. *Distribution:* Selznick Distributing Corp. *Director:* Harmon F. Weight. *Screenplay:* Forrest Halsey (from the short story "The Adopted Father" by Edgar Franklin). *Cinematographer:* Harry Fischbeck. 6 reels (5,990 feet). *Release Date:* April 12, 1924. *New York Premiere:* June 8, 1924. No print known to have survived.

Cast: George Arliss (John Reeves), Taylor Holmes (William Hart), Edith Roberts (Muriel Hart), Walter Howe (Henry Sloane), Redfield Clarke (George Blair), Ronald Colman (Chester Reeves), Ivan Simpson (James Pettison), Joseph Donohue (Little Arthur), William Sellery (Clancy, Restaurant Keeper), George Henry (Hart's Butler).

After returning to New York and shooting *The Eternal City*, Colman visited Henry King to inquire whether he and Lillian Gish might have any work for him in the coming months. The director assured Colman that they had a part for him in their forthcoming production, *Romola*, to be shot on location in Italy later that year. In the meantime, King sent the young actor over to the old Biograph studio with a recommendation that George Arliss use him in his new comedy *$20 a Week*, set for release by Lewis J. Selznick. Having worked with Lillian Gish was enough to get anyone through the door in those days, and Colman got the part.

Arliss played millionaire John Reeves, who is challenged by his son Chester (Colman) to live on $20 a week and whatever else he can earn without divulging his true identity. Reeves accepts the wager and goes to work in a mill owned by steel tycoon William Hart (Taylor Holmes). Hart's sister Muriel (Edith Roberts) adopts a son (Joseph Donohue), a thoroughly nasty little fellow, whereupon Hart retaliates by adopting a father—John Reeves. He manages to save Hart's corporation from financial ruin and accepts a partnership in the business. Chester marries Muriel and thereby inherits both a fortune and misfortune—mischievous little stepson Arthur.

As with most George Arliss pictures, everyone and everything in *$20 a Week* was subordinate to its star. But despite the distinguished presence of Mr. Arliss, the film was an insignificant programmer which most critics dismissed as a trivial and only mildly humorous misfire. The *Morning Telegraph* called Arliss' performance "a bright spot in an otherwise dull picture,"[43] while the *New York Tribune* found Colman merely "quiet and attractive."[44] The *New York Times*, however, praised it as "splendid light entertainment."[45]

Colman, who had already worked with Arliss on Broadway, knew that appearing in an Arliss film could only help his career. The role was certainly more substantial than the one that had preceded it; and, as Colman later recalled, Arliss had been extremely helpful to him on the set, urging director Harmon Weight to make the most of Colman's scenes and prompting cameraman Harry Fischbeck to be sure to photograph Colman to best advantage. Besides, he had Italy and a new picture with Henry King and Lillian Gish to look forward to.

Romola

1924. *Production:* Inspiration Pictures, Inc. *Distribution:* Metro-Goldwyn Pictures Corporation. *Director:* Henry King. *Screenplay:* Will M. Ritchey (from the novel by George Eliot). *Cinematographers:* Roy Overbaugh, William Schurr (assisted by Ferdinand Risi). *Art Director:* Robert M. Haas. *Assistant Director:* Joseph C. Boyle. *Technical Advisor:* Dr. Guido Biagi. *Shipbuilder:* Tito Neri. *Titles:* Jules Furthman, Don Bartlett. *Film Editor:* Duncan Mansfield. *Laboratory Work:* Gustav Dietz. *Musical Score and "Romola" Theme:* Louis H. Gottschalk. 12 reels (12,974 feet). *New York Premiere:* December 1, 1924. *Los Angeles Premiere:* December 6, 1924.

Cast: Lillian Gish (Romola), Dorothy Gish (Tessa), William H. Powell (Tito Melema), Ronald Colman (Carlo Bucellini), Charles Lane (Baldassarre Calvo), Herbert Grimwood (Girolamo Savonarola), Bonaventura Ibanez (Bardo Bardi), Frank Puglia (Adolfo Spini), Amelia Summerville (Brigida), Tina Ceccacci Renaldi (Monna Ghita), Eduilio Mucci (Nello), Angelo Scatigna (Bratti), Alfredo Bertone (Piero de Medici), Ugo Uccellini (Bishop of Nemours), Afredo Martinelli (Tornabuoni), Gino Borsi (Captain of the Barque), Pietro Nistri (Pirate Captain), Alfredo

Fossi (Pirate Galley Master), Attilio Deodati (Tomaso), Pietro Betti (Fra Sylvestro), Ferdinando Chianese (Archbishop), Toto Lo Bue (Fra Benaducci), Carlo Duse (Bargello), Giuseppe Zocchi (Executioner), Eugenio Mattioli, Giuseppe Becattini (Papal Legates), Rinaldo Rinaldi, Enrico Monti, Baron Giuseppe Winspere, Francesco Ciancamerla, Baron Alfredo Del Judici, Baron Serge Kopfe, Gastone Barnardi, Giovanni Salvini (Members of the Council of Eight), Countess Tolombi, Marchese Imperiale, Princess Isabella Romanoff, Countess Tamburini, Princess Bianca Raffaello, Marchese Fabrizio Gonzaga, Prince Alexander Talone, Baron Alfredo Del Judici, Baron Giuseppe Winspere (Banquet Members).

With considerable profits flowing in from *The White Sister,* Inspiration advanced nearly $2,000,000 and sent Henry King and Lillian Gish to Italy to film *Romola,* George Eliot's 1862 novel of romance and political intrigue in Renaissance Florence. Director Henry King had intended to shoot the picture in Florence itself, but streetcar tracks, telephone poles, and other constant reminders of modernity necessitated the construction of a "new" fifteenth-century Florence on a set just outside the city. Under the guidance of art director Robert Haas, whose work in *The White Sister* had been so highly praised, a huge Florentine set was erected with painstaking accuracy, covering 17 acres and rendering an exact replica of the architecture which had marked the Golden Age of the Florentine Renaissance. Scrupulously researched and pictorially exquisite, the production starred Lillian and Dorothy Gish, William Powell, Ronald Colman, and Charles Lane.

Arriving in Florence, which is at the mercy of mob rule following the departure of Piero de Medici, Greek adventurer Tito Melema (William Powell) meets and courts Romola (Lillian Gish), the devoted daughter of blind scholar Bardo Bardi (Bonaventura Ibanez). Another suitor and frequent visitor to her book-cloistered world is patient, gentle Carlo Bucellini (Ronald Colman), who is quick to discern a formidable rival. But he cannot prevent Romola from marrying the fortune-hunting Tito shortly after the death of her beloved father.

A stranger, clad in filthy rags, arrives in Florence in time to behold Tito and Romola leaving the church following the wedding ceremony. It's Baldassarre Calvo (Charles Lane), Tito's foster father, whom Tito had betrayed many months before. Calvo rushes up to his son on the church steps.

"My son! My son!" he cries. "I thought you were dead!"

"Take this madman away," Tito orders disdainfully. "I know him not!"

His suspicions aroused, Carlo Bucellini approaches the crestfallen old man, who proceeds to relate a dastardly tale of filial betrayal. While sailing to Italy, Calvo and his foster son were beset by pirates. Promising to rescue Calvo, Tito fled and finally made his way to Florence, where he conveniently forgot the old man's plight. Calvo was sold into Turkish slavery, but escaped and has been searching for his son ever since.

Tea-time on the set of Romola. *Dorothy Gish, Ronald Colman, director Henry King, unidentified woman, and Lillian Gish.*

Through ill-gotten gains and reprehensible political machinations, Tito rises to eminence in the new Florentine government, and is quickly elevated to the position of Gonfalonier, chief magistrate of the city and leading member of the vindictive Council of Eight. Terror, tyranny, and intimidation stalk the streets of Florence with drawn sword.

Night after night Calvo lurks in the shadows outside the Bardi palace with a gleaming knife, ready to avenge his betrayal. At a banquet held in honor of Tito's rise to power, Calvo manages to gain entrance and denounces him by disclosing details of the shipwreck: he had adopted and educated him, and is repaid thus. Tito insists that this ragged old clown was once a servant in his father's household, and has become obsessed by the notion that he was robbed of his fortune and name.

After deceiving both his wife and Tessa (Dorothy Gish), a simple peasant girl whom he seduces and leaves the child, Tito incurs the wrath of the Florentine populace when he condemns Savonarola, beloved priest and champion of the people, to execution at the stake, and imprisons anyone (including Carlo Bucellini) who dares to speak out against the new government. Pursued to Tessa's dwelling by an enraged mob, he barely escapes through an open window into the canal below. The faithful Tessa, although unable to swim, follows him and leaps into the water, but Tito pushes her away and she drowns. Reaching the banks of the Arno, Tito collapses and is drowned by his vengeful foster father. This scene, startling in its terrifying realism, shows Tito's head under water, with his tongue bulging out, as Calvo grasps his throat until death comes.

The picture ends with Romola caring for Tessa's baby and finding happiness with Carlo Bucellini, her faithful suitor.

Romola was one of Hollywood's most lavish projects; the vibrancy and authenticity of its sets and costumes made it one of the most awe-inspiring of all silent films — from the standpoint of art direction, at least, a genuine masterpiece. Metro-Goldwyn premiered the picture in New York at the George M. Cohan Theatre on December 1, 1924, and in Hollywood at Sid Grauman's Chinese Theatre five nights later.

"This is a film to be remembered," rhapsodized Mordaunt Hall in the *New York Times.*[46] Douglas Fairbanks called it "the most stunningly beautiful picture in every last detail."[47] And from Santiago Alba, Minister of Arts in Spain, came another accolade: "It is a page of the most delicate art and appeals like few other films."[48]

Lillian Gish gave an exquisite portrayal of the quiet, gently incisive lily maid of Florence.[49] Dorothy Gish radiated a lively warmth as Tessa. Newcomer William Powell, then little known, was superbly chilling as Tito Melema, and dominated the picture. Ronald Colman, looking quite the dandy in a shoulder-length wig and tights, gave a sympathetic performance in the thankless part of Carlo Bucellini. Though nominally the hero, he served a purely ornamental function and was quite overshadowed by the suave villainy of William Powell and the dramatic presence of the Gish sisters.

Although enormously popular with the critics, *Romola* was not nearly as successful at the box office as *The White Sister* had been, and it made very little money for Inspiration and Metro-Goldwyn. Despite Henry King's superb sense of romanticism and cameraman Roy Overbaugh's lustrous cinematography, the film displayed only a plodding intensity, and audiences found it dull and lacking in melodramatics.[50]

By the time *Romola* was released, Ronald Colman was busy filming in Hollywood and had already completed *Tarnish*, his first picture for his new producer, Sam Goldwyn.

III

The Early Goldwyn Years—
The Image Is Shaped

The Sam Goldwyn story is the story of American opportunity, the rags-to-riches tale of a Jewish-immigrant glove salesman from Warsaw who became one of Hollywood's greatest showmen. Samuel Goldfish (his original American name from an immigration authority's translation of his Polish name) was, above all, a fiercely determined businessman. Totally independent of any studio, board of directors, or any authority but the box office, he was a solidly professional independent producer and star-maker who insisted on quality rather than quantity, interpreting rather than creating, influencing rather than controlling, developing rather than inventing. Ronald Colman was just another leading man until Sam Goldwyn made him a star; no one was knocking down any doors to sign him for pictures until Goldwyn put him under contract.

In 1924 the producer saw *The White Sister* and at once decided to bring "Gish's new leading man" to Hollywood. While in Florence filming *Romola*, Colman received an urgent wire from Goldwyn, imploring him to drop everything and head straight for California. Before he had even received the actor's reply, Goldwyn announced Colman for the lead opposite May McAvoy in *Tarnish*.

Colman's second trip to Hollywood was to be very different from his first. When he arrived this time in the movie capital, it was the province of Chaplin, Keaton, and Lloyd; of Fairbanks, Valentino, and Novarro; of Pickford, Chaney, and the Barrymores; of Tom Mix, William S. Hart, Jackie Coogan, Clara Bow, Colleen Moore, and Rin-Tin-Tin. Under Sam Goldwyn's shrewd guidance, Colman would soon command a top position in the Hollywood pantheon. Within a few short years, he became one of the most popular young men in the film colony, despite his reserve and the fact that he eschewed the more glittering aspects of lavish parties and opening-night celebrations. Combining a fraternal spirit with a quiet disposition, he was likeable but not part of the scene, attractive but somewhat remote.

Tarnish, his first effort for his new producer, was directed by Goldwyn favorite George Fitzmaurice. Trained in Paris as a painter, this genial Irishman had a strong pictorial sense of light and shadow and was always at his best with glowing romantic themes. "Fitz" was to direct no fewer than eight Colman pictures in the coming years, including two of the finest Colman-Banky extravaganzas, *The Dark Angel* and the first of the Valentino-inspired costume swashbucklers, *The Night of Love.*

Satisfied with Colman's performance in *Tarnish,* Goldwyn signed his new discovery to a long-term contract at $2,000 a week in May 1924. So began the long association that was to span a decade and include 18 pictures.

At first, however, Goldwyn used Colman only infrequently, lending him out to other companies instead. And although Colman turned in some consistently good performances, he was generally relegated to supporting top leading ladies: he made polished comedies with Constance Talmadge (*Her Night of Romance* and *Her Sister from Paris,* both for First National); romantic dramas with Blanche Sweet (*The Sporting Venus* for Metro-Goldwyn, *His Supreme Moment* for Goldwyn); and a light comedy with Norma Talmadge (*Kiki* for First National). In 1925 he hit his stride, turning out eight pictures, the most notable of which were *The Dark Angel* (his first with Vilma Banky) and *Lady Windermere's Fan* for Ernst Lubitsch at Warner Bros. *A Thief in Paradise,* made for Goldwyn and co-starring the lovely Doris Kenyon and Aileen Pringle, was the first film in which he played the leading role as distinguished from the female star's mere romantic interest. And though many of these pictures were of no particular distinction and were vehicles designed to showcase the talents of their female stars rather than Colman, the choice of Ronald Colman as their leading man was a fortuitous one, for Colman's name on a bill was quickly coming to signal box-office success. In 1925 *Photoplay* started comparing him to John Gilbert; Colman was already becoming a big star personality, and audiences were beginning to request Colman pictures.

Then came the first of five films he was to make with the 22-year-old Hungarian beauty Vilma Banky, another Goldwyn discovery, who came to Hollywood via the Austrian cinema. According to Goldwyn legend, the producer had spotted Miss Banky in the train station in Budapest while he was waiting to catch a train. Before he left, he had signed her to a handsome five-year contract. Banky arrived in Hollywood early in 1925, passed her screen test with flying colors, and Goldwyn quickly announced her first picture: *The Dark Angel* with Ronald Colman. The film was directed by the durable George Fitzmaurice, who in 1926 was to guide Miss Banky through

Rudolph Valentino's last picture, *Son of the Sheik*. Banky spoke only limited English, and in fact delivered her lines in Hungarian, but her flaxen-haired beauty photographed like magic.

When the film was released, it became an immediate sensation and was an important landmark in Colman's career. In this, the first picture in which he was billed above the female lead, Colman was no longer merely the leading man; he was the indisputable star. *The Dark Angel* was the second great turning point in Colman's career, for it shaped the image to come. As the British soldier who is blinded in the war and schemes to keep this fact from his sweetheart for fear that she might marry him out of pity, Colman for the first time played a gallant gentleman who places honor and self-sacrifice above all. It was clear that this kind of characterization was well received by the public, in addition to being congenial to Colman's own personality.

The actor later stated that, of all the roles he had done to date, he far preferred this one as the tragic, blind soldier: "It was a sympathetic part of course, but it demanded a repression, a subdued tone that I try so hard to get into my work."[1]

One role succeeded another very quickly until, by graceful and easy stages, Colman found himself at the pinnacle of Hollywood stardom. In Henry King's moving melodrama *Stella Dallas*, Goldwyn's first production under his new distribution arrangement with United Artists, Belle Bennett's outrageous, pitiable Stella dominated the film, but Colman lent solid support as her aggrieved husband. Then came an adaptation of Oscar Wilde's *Lady Windermere's Fan* for Ernst Lubitsch at Warner Bros., in which Colman exhibited his flair for comedy and shared the limelight with May McAvoy, Bert Lytell, and the superb Irene Rich. The picture demonstrated that Lubitsch had not lost his vaunted "touch." Light comedy, a genre for which Colman always felt the warmest affection, was fast becoming one of his real fortes. Ample proof of this came in his next romp for First National, *Kiki*, in which that endearing little spitfire Norma Talmadge chased him through nine reels to the delectation of audiences everywhere.

The most magnificent of his silent films was *Beau Geste*, made on loan-out to Paramount and shot on location in the scorching Arizona desert. Expertly directed by Herbert Brenon, it offered romance and adventure in the Foreign Legion, became one of the most financially successful silents of all time, and was "the film which really established Colman in his own right as a major star, as well as one of the best actors around."[2] Colman won top honors with his romantic portrayal of the gentleman who died to save a woman's honor. Dashing, reckless, clever, and brave, Beau possessed all the virtues with which Colman was coming to be identified; the image had arrived to stay, indelibly stamped with all the characteristic traits of honor, duty, and self-sacrifice which were to be forever associated with Ronald Colman. Colman himself said that he could never watch this mighty picture without getting a lump in his throat. His fan mail after *Beau Geste* was second only to that of John Gilbert.

Colman was never a part of the fabulous Hollywood society. For most, the movie capital was a bewitching, enchanting place; for Ronald Colman, it was simply where he worked. Privacy was always important to the star who, next to Garbo, was least often seen, talked with, or talked about. As May McAvoy, Colman's co-star in *Lady Windermere's Fan*, remembers:

> I never knew anybody to have more beautiful manners than he had and who always did the right thing at the right time. . . . It would never have occurred to me to ask him anything personal. . . . Although he was kind and gentle, very friendly and sweet, there was a little wall built around him, and you never got beyond that. Not that he ever put it in words, but he wanted his private life to be his own, and he had a right to it.[3]

Warm and convivial if one took the trouble to get through that first layer of defense and reticence, Colman was never aloof, but there were deep elements of reserve that made it quite impossible for him to confide his most intimate thoughts to any except his closest companions. Very few people, for instance, knew that Colman was married. Thus he could discuss only with a handful of trusted friends the problems being caused by his wife Thelma, who had recently descended upon Hollywood and was doing her best to make his life — and pocketbook — miserable.

As fellow English actor Percy Marmont recalls:

> Insofar as women were concerned . . . he was scared of them. When friends started to match-make during the course of a conversation, he would just clam up.[4]
> I soon discovered he would never talk about himself to people unless it was somebody he liked very much and with whom he was intimate. . . . But you took Ronnie into a room with a lot of people he didn't know, and he'd be perfectly genial and perfectly friendly with everybody, but there'd be no question of getting him into a corner and pumping him because he'd get out of that corner very quickly.[5]

Nonetheless, it was possible to be a popular figure without being a public one, especially when one's popularity was the result of an image flashed across a cinema screen. And there were jolly times too, most frequently among the inhabitants of Hollywood's English colony. Colman had purchased a large, Spanish-style home with ample acreage, nestled among the nearby hills on Mound Street. Tennis, golf, and poker were among the chief avocations he shared with close friends Clive Brook, William Powell, Richard Barthelmess, Warner Baxter, Tim McCoy, Charles Lane, and Percy Marmont.

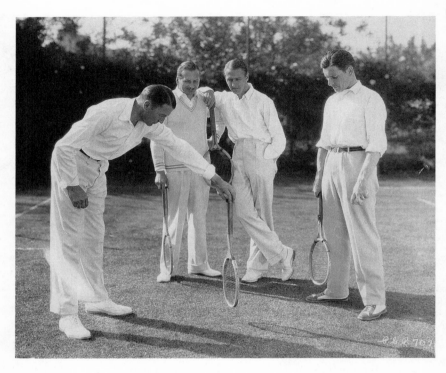

A few fast sets of tennis in Clive Brook's back yard on a Sunday morning. This interesting group of Englishmen includes Brook, Philip Strange, Percy Marmont, and Ronald Colman.

The phenomenal success of *Beau Geste* determined Goldwyn not to lend his star out thereafter, and his chief preoccupation in 1926 was devising a series of vehicles in which to star his new Colman-Banky team. He reunited them in *The Winning of Barbara Worth*, a contemporary western directed by Henry King and featuring Montana cowboy Gary Cooper in his first major screen appearance. Since the public was in love with the new team, Goldwyn gave audiences what they wanted and soon produced a series of immensely popular costume swashbucklers which established Colman and Banky as one of the screen's foremost love duos, rivalling the John Gilbert-Greta Garbo and Charles Farrell-Janet Gaynor teams in their appeal, and further linking Colman with the Italianate image of Rudolph Valentino.

In *The Night of Love,* set in seventeenth-century Spain, an enormous castle created by masterful set designer Carl Oscar Borg provided the setting around and in which Colman romped, wooed Miss Banky, and battled evil Montagu Love. *The Magic Flame,* another adventurous concoction, had Colman playing his first dual role, which anticipated such later successes as

The Masquerader and *The Prisoner of Zenda.* In the following year, he was cast as "Leatherface," the Flemish righter of Spanish wrongs, in the sumptuous sixteenth-century period piece *Two Lovers.* These three pictures, full of love and hatred, loyalty and treachery, and battles of both wit and swordplay, were classic romantic make-believe. Colman's strong, witty, and dashing characterizations made him an irresistible hero. But he was aware that his producer had teamed him with Miss Banky chiefly to capitalize on his physical appearance; "as a flamboyant lover *à la* Ramon Novarro, a characterization completely at odds with his real life type,"[6] Colman felt himself decidedly miscast.

On January 27, 1927, Vilma Banky and actor Rod La Rocque were married against a backdrop of Goldwynesque splendor. Goldwyn spent $25,000 and masterminded the entire affair. Cecil B. De Mille was best man; ushers included Ronald Colman, Harold Lloyd, Donald Crisp, and George Fitzmaurice; and Goldwyn himself gave the bride away. With thousands of curious spectators milling about, Tom Mix drew up to the church in a coach and four. Other invited guests included Charlie Chaplin, Doug Fairbanks and Mary Pickford, William Randolph Hearst and Marion Davies, and Will Rogers.

When asked after the formalities what her first child would be named, Banky replied, "I don't know, you'll have to ask Sam Goldwyn."[7]

Fearing that this spectacular affair would hurt the popular image of Ronald Colman and Vilma Banky as contented lovers, Goldwyn decided to split the duo, teaming Miss Banky for one picture with Britisher Walter Byron and Colman with tempestuous French import Lily Damita. Neither experiment found favor with the public.

So Ronald Colman and Vilma Banky went their separate ways, Colman going on to greater triumphs, Banky to swift obscurity.[8] After completing *Two Lovers,* Colman sailed for his homeland with friend and fellow English actor Philip Strange to renew his acquaintance with friends and relatives he had not seen since 1920. Grateful as he was to the country which had sheltered him and taken him to its heart as one of its own, he retained to the last an abiding loyalty for England.

Waiting to greet him on the dock at Southampton was a surging crowd of eager fans, a cluster of old companions, and a young British director named Alfred Hitchcock. Not expecting such a demonstration from his native land, Colman was flattered but rather astonished. His mother, now in her seventies, awaited his arrival in London. A few days later, Colman took her to the London premiere of *Two Lovers;* as their car slowed to a crawl in front of the theatre, a rush of autograph-seekers surrounded the vehicle.

"My dear Ronnie," she queried fearfully, "what in the world are all these people doing here? Has there been an accident?"

"And that," Colman said later, "is about how seriously my family took me!"[9]

Revitalized, Colman returned to Hollywood to make what was to be his last silent film, Herbert Brenon's ambitious adaptation of Joseph Conrad's *The Rescue*. Filmed off an island not far from Santa Cruz, the picture was the first for which Colman received exclusive star billing above the title. Lily Damita's good looks, intelligence, and obvious wit matched well with those of her co-star, but she failed to catch on with the public, who regarded her as Vilma Banky's usurper. And with the sudden demand for all-talking pictures, *The Rescue*, too, failed to catch hold of popular esteem.

Nevertheless, by 1929, Colman was one of Hollywood's most charismatic romantic idols. He had enjoyed one of the most rapid ascents to stardom that the movie capital had ever know, but with talking pictures on the horizon, a big question in filmland was how Ronald Colman would fare before the microphones.

Tarnish

1924. *Production:* Samuel Goldwyn, Inc. *Distribution:* Associated First National Pictures. *Producer:* Samuel Goldwyn. *Director:* George Fitzmaurice. *Screenplay:* Frances Marion (from the play by Gilbert Emery). *Cinematographers:* William Tuers, Arthur Miller. *Art Director:* Ben Carré. *Film Editor:* Stuart Heisler. 7 reels (6,831 feet). *Release Date:* October 12, 1924. No print known to have survived.

Cast: May McAvoy (Letitia Tevis), Ronald Colman (Emmet Carr), Marie Prevost (Nettie Dark), Albert Gran (Adolf Tevis), Mrs. Russ Whytall (Josephine Tevis), Priscilla Bonner (Aggie), Harry Myers (Barber), Kay Deslys (Mrs. Stutts), Lydia Yeamans Titus (Mrs. Healy), William Boyd (Bill), Snitz Edwards (Mr. Stutts), Norman Kerry (John Graves).

While making *Romola* in Florence, Colman was signed by Sam Goldwyn to star opposite May McAvoy and Marie Prevost in *Tarnish*. Adapted from a recent Broadway hit by leading scenarist Frances Marion, the film was to be directed by the always-active George Fitzmaurice. Colman would have preferred to remain under the protective aegis of Henry King, but he took King's advice, accepted Goldwyn's offer, and headed for Hollywood to make his first picture in the film capital.

Colman played Emmet Carr, a man whose past has been "tarnished" by an escapade with the far-from-virtuous manicurist Nettie Dark (Marie Prevost). When he falls in love with Letitia Tevis (May McAvoy), daughter of once-prosperous womanizer Adolf Tevis (Albert Gran), things quickly get out of control as Adolf falls victim to the same honeyed charms of Nettie Dark. After wheedling the old man out of most of his money, she steals the rest. On New Year's Eve, Nettie lures Emmet to her apartment on the pretext that she is seriously ill. Letitia, in the meantime, suspects Nettie of having picked her father's pocket and rushes off to demand that she return the money. Astonished to discover Emmet in Nettie's chambers and crushed by his apparent infidelity, she leaves. Grim and determined, Emmet forces Nettie to accompany him to the Tevis home, where she confesses that she had not seen Emmet for a year. Letitia snuggles happily into Emmet's arms, realizing that he is her true love after all.

Released seven weeks before *Romola, Tarnish* opened to favorable reviews, though some critics found it tame when compared with the original stage version. Still, it was rather racy in its treatment of sexual affairs and barely escaped the censorial cutting shears of the Hays office.[10] That it reached the screen with any fidelity was due in large part to Frances Marion's suspenseful screenplay, George Fitzmaurice's delicacy and energetic direction, and, to be sure, Marie Prevost's patent and perpetual naughtiness. Singled out for critical praise were May McAvoy's wholesome, soul-searching heroine; Marie Prevost's seductive little temptress; Albert Gran's self-indulgent old sinner (the same part he had played on Broadway); and Ronald Colman's strong, restrained hero.[11]

Exhibiting all the assurance and poise which his tutelage under Henry King had brought him, Colman did full justice to the role and displayed troubled dignity to good advantage. As Mordaunt Hall commented: "He is a convincing screen actor with a pleasing personality."[12] *Variety* added, "Ronald Colman . . . is the best thing in the film."[13] On the strength of this performance, Goldwyn put him under a long-term contract; Colman's output in the coming year would total eight pictures.

Her Night of Romance

1925. *Production:* Constance Talmadge Productions. *Distribution:* First National Pictures. *Producer:* Joseph M. Schenck. *Director:* Sidney A. Franklin. *Screenplay:* Hans Kräly. *Cinematographers:* Ray Binger, Victor Milner. *Film Editor:* Hal Kern. 8 reels (7,211 feet). *Release Date:* January 11, 1925.

Cast: Constance Talmadge (Dorothy Adams), Ronald Colman (Paul Menford), Jean Hersholt (Joe Diamond), Albert Gran (Samuel C. Adams, Dorothy's father), Robert Rendel (Prince George), Sidney Bracey (Butler), Joseph Dowling (Professor Gregg), Templar Saxe (Dr. Wellington), Eric Mayne (Dr. Scott), Emily Fitzroy (Nurse), Clara Bracey (Housekeeper), James Barrows (Old Butler), Claire De Lorez (Paul's Artist Friend).

Colman's next picture after *Tarnish* was *Her Night of Romance,* made on loan-out to Joseph M. Schenck at First National. Schenck, who was married to the enormously popular Norma Talmadge, had been eager to obtain Colman's services as leading man to sister-in-law Constance Talmadge, that delightful comedienne whose box-office following had mushroomed since her early days with D.W. Griffith.[14] Witty scenarist Hans Kräly whipped up a lively confection and the fun began.[15]

This jolly farce had Miss Talmadge as wealthy American heiress Dorothy Adams, who, to discourage fortune hunters, poses as a penniless and thoroughly unprepossessing spinster while traveling in England with her father (Albert Gran). Enter Lord Menford (Colman), a supremely giddy and impoverished Britisher who spends most of his time getting spiffed and the rest of it squandering borrowed money. Urged by money-lender Joe Diamond (Jean Hersholt) to court the recently arrived heiress, Menford impersonates a wealthy physician and meets the millionaire's daughter, after agreeing to share whatever wealth he stumbles upon with Diamond.

Forced to sell his ancestral estate for lack of funds, Menford returns home in the wee hours after a round or three at his club, inebriated as usual and forgetful that the house has been sold. Unknown to him, the new owners have already moved in — the undisguised Dorothy and Mr. Adams. Menford runs full tilt into Dorothy, who has chosen to occupy the tipsy aristocrat's own bedchamber. One thing leads to another, as it so often does, and they agree to avoid an embarrassing situation by posing as newlyweds. When Menford eventually proposes legitimate marriage, Dorothy accepts, until she learns of his financial arrangement with Joe Diamond. Fur starts to fly, but Dorothy's father, realizing that Menford is a solid chap after all and has never guessed his daughter's true identity, reunites the pair.

This comedy of deception was as light as light comedy could be, but its good, wholesome merriment proved more than enough to satisfy both audiences and critics alike. The lovely Constance Talmadge made an immediate hit, while Ronald Colman's "skillful blend of outraged dignity, lordly disdain and wry spoofing"[16] made him "a handsome foil for Connie's scintillating talents."[17] As one reviewer commented: "Connie is grand and Colman makes a dashing leading man with that irresistible brand of charm only Englishmen born and bred can muster."[18] Colman's lighthearted mischief showed that he had a natural flair for light comedy, a talent soon to be demonstrated to even better advantage.

A Thief in Paradise

1925. *Production:* Samuel Goldwyn, Inc. *Distribution:* First National Pictures. *Producer:* Samuel Goldwyn. *Director:* George Fitzmaurice. *Screenplay:* Frances Marion (from the novel *The Worldings* by Leonard Merrick). *Cinematographer:* Arthur Miller. *Art Director:* Ben Carré. *Film Editor:* Stuart Heisler. 8 reels (7,355 feet). *Release Date:* January 25, 1925. No print known to have survived.

Cast: Doris Kenyon (Helen Saville), Ronald Colman (Maurice Blake), Aileen Pringle (Rosa Carmino), Claude Gillingwater (Noel Jardine), Alec B. Francis

(Bishop Saville), John Patrick (Ned Whalen), Charles Youree (Philip Jardine), Etta Lee (Rosa's Maid), Lon Poff (Jardine's Secretary).

After *Her Night of Romance* Colman returned to Goldwyn to star opposite luscious Doris Kenyon (wife of actor Milton Sills) and exotic Aileen Pringle (on loan from Metro-Goldwyn) in *A Thief in Paradise,* a George Fitzmaurice-Frances Marion production shot partially on location in San Francisco.

After years of misfortune and failure, derelict Maurice Blake (Colman) earns a precarious living as a pearl diver in the Samoas with Philip Jardine (Charles Youree), the disowned son of a San Francisco millionaire. Quarreling over a pearl on their small raft, the two engage in underwater combat, and during the struggle Philip is killed by a shark. Maurice manages to swim ashore, where he is informed by Rosa Carmino (Aileen Pringle), Jardine's half-caste common-law wife, that Philip has been forgiven and asked to return home by his estranged father. Since Maurice bears a striking resemblance to Jardine, Rosa persuades him to assume the dead man's identity and claim the inheritance. Maurice successfully impersonates Philip, as the elder Jardine (Claude Gillingwater) has not seen his son for many years. Against his will, the imposter falls in love with, and soon marries, Helen Saville (Doris Kenyon), Philip's childhood sweetheart. But before he can confess his deception, Rosa interferes. She appears as a dancer at an elaborate Jardine soirée, and after her performance as an ersatz Venus, arrayed in strings of pearls and rising from a huge oyster shell, she jealously informs Helen that her husband is a fraud. But his wife forgives him, Jardine decides to adopt his newfound "son," and all ends on a predictably joyous note.

Released just two weeks after *Her Night of Romance, A Thief in Paradise* met with mixed reviews. One critic, praising the film's shark-infested underwater struggle and its striking San Francisco locales, called it "indisputably . . . brilliant entertainment,"[19] while another commented: "Lavish, charmingly set and costumed, and rather empty, but Ronald Colman and the lovely Misses Pringle and Kenyon make the viewing . . . worthwhile."[20] Pictorially beautiful and high on fast-paced thrills, including a remarkably dizzy polo match between teams of females in bathing suits, this was Hollywood's conception of how the rich customarily disported themselves, and audiences ate it up; the picture's more implausible plot contrivances were soon forgotten once the box-office receipts began pouring in.

In his most strenuous dramatic achievement since *The White Sister,* Ronald Colman turned in an outstanding performance and reaped fine critical reviews; and when *Photoplay* launched its campaign to establish Colman and John Gilbert as "Rival Nordic Lovers," it quickly proved that

the public's frenzied idolatry of stars now included the shy Britisher who
was fast becoming a major figure in the film capital.

The Sporting Venus

1925. *Production and distribution:* Metro-Goldwyn Pictures Corporation.
Director: Marshall Neilan. *Screenplay:* Thomas J. Geraghty (from the short story by
Gerald Beaumont). *Cinematographer:* David Kesson. *Art Director:* Cedric Gibbons.
Assistant Director: Thomas Held. *Wardrobe:* Ethel P. Chaffin. *Film Editor:* Blanche
Sewell. 7 reels (5,938 feet). *New York Premiere:* May 10, 1925.

Cast: Blanche Sweet (Lady Gwendolyn Grayle), Ronald Colman (Donald
MacAllan), Lew Cody (Prince Marno), Josephine Crowell (Countess Van Alstyne),
Edward Martindel (Lord Alfred Grayle), Kate Price (Housekeeper), Hank Mann
(Marno's Valet), Arthur Hoyt (Detective), George Fawcett (Sandy MacAllan).

Blanche Sweet was another mainstay from the old Griffith stock company. In one of Hollywood's earliest package deals, Sam Goldwyn agreed
to send Colman over to Metro-Goldwyn to make a film with Miss Sweet,
if she in turn would do a subsequent picture with Colman at the Goldwyn
Studios. Their first effort together was *The Sporting Venus*, directed by Miss
Sweet's husband, the talented but mercurial Marshall Neilan. Principal
location shooting was in Scotland, with further exteriors shot in England,
France, and Spain. It was the last time Colman would journey abroad to
make a film.

When the author interviewed Blanche Sweet in New York late in 1979,
she reminisced about Ronald Colman and *The Sporting Venus:*

> We were making films for M-G-M as a unit. We were under contract to
> deliver to M-G-M any picture that we might want to make. They had nothing
> to do with the story; we were the only ones who had anything to say about
> cutting, about producing, about who was to be cast in it. It was our doing,
> not M-G-M's. They had nothing to do with our unit at all, except that we
> turned the film over to them and they exhibited it.
>
> I don't know whether I said it, or whether it was Marshall who said it, or
> whether we both did, but we wanted him for the role in *Sporting Venus*. He
> was very handsome in his kilt and he had marvelous knees. I didn't know
> at the time that Ronald had Scottish blood. He was very pleasant to work
> with. When we did the bit of comedy walking in the country, he had a very
> good sense of humor, in a typically British style—light and gay and
> amusing.[21]

This romantic drama of misunderstanding opens at Grayloch Hall, the
Scottish estate of Lord Grayle (Edward Martindel), proud patriarch of a
stiff-necked clan. Lady Grayle dies after giving birth to a baby girl, and for
18 years Lord Grayle follows the round of fashionable resorts, leaving his
daughter in the hands of servants.

Deprived of a mother and neglected by her father, Lady Gwendolyn

(Miss Sweet) grows up with the sporting blood of the Grayles, and falls in love with Donald MacAllan (Colman), a young medical student far below her station.

Lord Grayle returns home from Biarritz to celebrate his daughter's eighteenth birthday. He has invited the dubious Prince Marno of Portugonia (Lew Cody), an impoverished continental cad, to join them for the hunt. Marno's creditors have already refused to extend him further credit and have decided that they must marry him off to a rich dowager so that he may satisfy his outstanding debts. Naturally, he readily agrees to come to Scotland, for Lady Gwendolyn is the richest lass in all the British Isles. He'll take part in the hunt, all right, but for entirely different game.

Lord Grayle arranges a coming-out party to present his daughter to society. The persistent prince can't take his eyes off her, but Lady Gwendolyn has eyes only for Donald, who meets her outside the castle to inform her that he must return to medical school in London on the morrow.

"I'll be here—when you come back," she promises, despite her father's opposition to the match.

Months later, careers are swept away when the First World War erupts. Donald enlists, and a certain noble lady motors to London to bid him good-bye. A smile masks Gwen's tears as Donald, garbed in a kilt and tam-o'-shanter, salutes her and departs for France.

Two years pass, and Donald returns from the front on his first leave. While hurrying through London on his way to Scotland and Gwen, he meets Prince Marno, who manages to convince him that he and Gwen are engaged and planning to be wed soon. Donald believes Marno's lie, makes no attempt to see Gwen, and spends his leave alone in London, bitterly disappointed. On his last night, he unexpectedly encounters Gwen and the prince at a military ball.

"How long have you been in London, Donald?" she inquires, obviously hurt.

"About two weeks," he replies uncomfortably, looking very grave.

Gwen mistakes his studied indifference for scorn. When Donald returns to active service, she tries to forget him by seeking excitement on the Riviera and elsewhere. She transforms herself from the lass of Grayloch into the Sporting Venus, creating a ravishing spectacle indeed.

Two more years of the war pass, and Donald returns home a successful surgeon. When he learns that Gwen has gambled away millions of francs following her father's death and that she has announced her engagement to Prince Marno, he determines to save her from her reckless pace. At the Quadrant Club, a wild London jazz emporium, Donald confronts Gwen and protests that she's ruining herself through riotous living.

"Why this sudden interest," she asks, "after your long silence?" Provoked, she informs him that she and the prince are soon to be married.

Marno, meanwhile, has received a cable informing him that he must marry immediately or his creditors will take action. Gwen's gambling losses lead her attorneys to investigte the scheming prince, and once they discover that he's never owned any estates in Portugonia, Gwen refuses to receive him. When he arrives unannounced at Grayloch Hall and attempts to kiss her, she slaps him and hurls a perfume bottle at him for good measure.

Eventually, with her fortune exhausted and her health ruined, the Sporting Venus pays with shattered nerves for her heedless ways. In a secluded spot on the coast of France, she learns that the Grayle estate has been sold. A commoner has become the new master of Grayloch Hall: the now-wealthy Donald MacAllan. Gwen returns to Scotland and the same little cottage where Donald used to study. When she becomes ill, and in her delirium cries out for Donald, her housekeeper (Kate Price) quickly summons the surgeon. Donald hurries to the cottage, but discovers that Gwen has wandered off into the night in a raging storm. He sets out after her, and watches in horror as she plunges off a cliff into the icy water below. Ripping off his coat and hat, he dives in and manages to pull her to safety.

Donald slowly nurses Gwen back to health, and finally they are wed. Another wedding takes place the very same day, as the bogus "Prince" Marno receives his comeuppance, for his creditors have taken a cruel revenge and found him a bride—an ugly, fat, old hag who happens to be disgustingly rich. The camera cuts from the wedding of Donald and Gwen to that of Marno. As the "prince" stares in shocked disbelief at the ancient monstrosity waddling down the aisle, director Neilan deftly dissolves to a shot of an armored tank bearing down in the same direction. While Marno and his bride are joined in matrimony, a hearse winds its way past the church to the accompaniment of a doubly appropriate funereal dirge. Nice comic touches. Our story ends with Donald and Gwen happy in each other's arms in a lovely cameo, silhouetted against the sunlight.

One of Hollywood's top directors in the twenties was Marshall Neilan, whose sharp tongue and abrasive Irish wit failed on more than one occasion to ingratiate him with the studio executives for whom he worked. He once antagonized M-G-M's Louis B. Mayer by quipping, "An empty taxicab drove up to the M-G-M gates yesterday and Louis B. Mayer got out."[22] According to Blanche Sweet, Neilan was in a most accommodating mood when she accompanied her husband and Ronald Colman to Scotland to shoot *The Sporting Venus*. Exteriors were filmed at Cortachy Castle, the ancestral estate of the Airlie family in Kerriemuir, with further location photography shot in the surrounding Scottish hills. Although it has long been rumored that an acerbic Neilan clashed with the more reserved Colman on the set, Miss Sweet finds such claims the result of entirely uninformed guesswork. "Marshall wanted Ronnie for the part," she said. "He respected him, and they got along just fine."[23]

Mordaunt Hall found *The Sporting Venus* lacking in suspense,[24] but most observers found it witty and stylish, and the film did well for Metro-Goldwyn. As the last of the sporting Grayles, Blanche Sweet was endearing as the capricious, headstrong Scots heiress; Ronald Colman, appearing for much of the picture's footage in his kilt, turned in an effective performance as the gallant medical student, in a role highly reminiscent of his own experiences at the outbreak of the First World War; Lew Cody was delightfully nonchalant as the fortune-hunting debtor.

By the time *The Sporting Venus* was released, the second film which teamed Blanche Sweet and Ronald Colman, *His Supreme Moment*, had already been playing in theatres for a month.

His Supreme Moment

1925. *Production:* Samuel Goldwyn, Inc. *Distribution:* First National Pictures. *Producer:* Samuel Goldwyn. *Director:* George Fitzmaurice. *Screenplay:* Frances Marion (from the novel *World Without End* by May Edginton). *Cinematographer:* Arthur Miller (with Technicolor sequences). *Art Director:* Ben Carré. *Film Editor:* Stuart Heisler. 8 reels (6,565 feet). *New York Premiere:* April 12, 1925. No print known to have survived.

Cast: Blanche Sweet (Carla King), Ronald Colman (John Douglas), Kathleen Myers (Sara Deeping), Belle Bennett (Carla Light), Cyril Chadwick (Harry Avon), Ned Sparks (Adrian), Nick de Ruiz (Mueva), Anna May Wong (Harem Girl in play), Kalla Pasha (Pasha in play), Jane Winton.

After making *The Sporting Venus*, Blanche Sweet came over to the Goldwyn Studios to film *His Supreme Moment* with Ronald Colman. In this picture, written and directed by Frances Marion and George Fitzmaurice respectively, Colman played mining engineer John Douglas, who falls in love with celebrated Broadway star Carla King (Miss Sweet). An old flame, Sara Deeping (Kathleen Myers), agrees to back Douglas in a new mining venture; then he and Carla depart, agreeing to live together platonically in South America before committing themselves to matrimony. But after a year of hardship and primitive conditions, Carla longs for the comfort and luxury of New York, and John becomes despondent over the apparent failure of his gold-mining operation.

About this time, Sara arrives, still hopelessly in love with John, and schemes to rekindle his affection. Compounding Douglas' troubles, the miners strike, and a fire rages out of control, almost claiming his life. Carla saves him and they leave South America, and Sara follows. Upon their return to New York, John resumes his affair with Sara, while Carla decides to sacrifice her own happiness by marrying an elderly millionaire (Cyril Chadwick) in return for his financial support of the mine. When John learns

Something of the stereotypes of romantic passion depicted in the films of the twenties can be gleaned from this shot of Ronald Colman and Blanche Sweet in His Supreme Moment.

of her plan, however, he leaves Sara and manages to acquire independent financing, whereupon the two lovers return to South America to find a future together.

Goldwyn's publicity department, with its flair for inspired advertising, touted *His Supreme Moment* as "Supreme in All That You Could Ask!" Reviewers for the most part agreed, and its commercial success was immediate and impressive. Widely acclaimed was Arthur Miller's use, in two remarkable scenes, of Technicolor photography, a novelty fast becoming common practice in the mid-twenties. The first of these was the opening sequence, an elaborate Turkish harem setting which turns out to be the Broadway musical in which Colman first spots, and becomes smitten by, the comely Miss Sweet. The second comes toward the end of the film, when Carla courageously rescues John during a fiery uprising in the South American jungle.

Blanche Sweet gave an excellent account of herself as the sincere, restrained Carla King. As one reviewer remarked, "Miss Sweet never falters in her work, giving a really remarkable performance."[25] Critics considered Ronald Colman's portrayal of idealistic dreamer John Douglas his finest to date, and Mordaunt Hall commented that Colman was "better in this picture than in any other in which he has appeared since *The White Sister*. He . . . looks every inch a man, rugged and good-looking and thoroughly at his ease, whether he is in dress clothes or in his rough mining suit."[26] Oddly, though, Hall added, "It would, however, improve his appearance if he wore a more decided mustache instead of a thin line which is only faintly visible."[27] Indeed.

In conversation with the author, Blanche Sweet recalled that Colman

was a very restrained man. He never exaggerated anything; he rather underplayed everything. He was never too demonstrative. As Lillian Gish wrote in her book, she and Henry King had a little difficulty with Ronald in *The White Sister*, because he didn't have the relaxed, demonstrative manner that they wanted him to have in the scene where he was making love to her and trying to get her to give up her vows. When I played with him in *His Supreme Moment*, I had the same trouble. Fitzmaurice, who was directing, said to Ronald, "Come on, loosen up. I need some *fire* here! You know this girl. You love her. You want to make love to her. *Loosen up!*" We had to make I don't know how many takes, and I don't think we ever did get really the desired effect we wanted. It took me a while to figure it out. It rather intrigued me. Then I thought, well, it's the man himself; it's his disposition. It's his *natural* way, in his personal life, of acting; and he carries it over into whatever part he is playing. "Reticent" is the word to be used about Ronald. It's no comment on his acting ability—he just didn't want to act *that* way.[28]

Her Sister from Paris

1925. *Production:* Joseph M. Schenck Productions. *Distribution:* First National Pictures. *Producer:* Joseph M. Schenck. *Director:* Sidney Franklin. *Screenplay:* Hans Kräly (from the play by Ludwig Fulda). *Cinematographer:* Arthur Edeson. *Art Director:* William Cameron Menzies. *Assistant Director:* Scot R. Beal. *Wardrobe:* Adrian. 7 reels (7,255 feet). *Release Date:* August 23, 1925.

Cast: Constance Talmadge (Helen Weyringer/Lola), Ronald Colman (Joseph Weyringer), George K. Arthur (Robert Well), Margaret Mann (Bertha), Gertrude Claire.

So successful was the first pairing of Constance Talmadge and Ronald Colman that Sam Goldwyn agreed to First National's request for a rematch, and *Her Night of Romance* was followed soon thereafter by another wacky farce, *Her Sister from Paris.* Miss Talmadge had a field day in a diverting dual role, portraying both a neglected housewife and her devastatingly sexy sister from Paris.

Celebrated Viennese author Joseph Weyringer (Colman) is, quite frankly, bored. It's his wife, Helen. In fact, she's in imminent danger of driving him to distraction, madness, or worse. Hoping to salvage her ailing marriage, Helen decides to pose as her saucy twin sister, Lola. Joseph may have lost interest in his drab spouse, but he is eagerly attentive to the lively charms of this vivacious Parisian vamp. Both he and his friend Robert Well (George K. Arthur) fall all over themselves in their quest for her favors. Joseph, first in line, professes his love for the seductive dancer, whereupon she reveals herself to be his own wife. The drastic measure pays off, for Helen wins her husband back, after he sees her in an entirely new and more sparkling light.

This second teaming of Talmadge and Colman was as magical as the first, and *Her Sister from Paris* opened to enthusiastic reviews which proclaimed it an unalloyed delight. Audiences loved it and lined up at the box office, making this chic comedy of errors one of Colman's biggest hits of 1925. Despite some feeling that Sidney Franklin's direction lacked the merry sparkle of his earlier *Her Night of Romance,* Hans Kräly's mischievous screenplay kept things bouncing along, and the film just barely squeaked by the Hays office, which cast an admonitory glance or two at its deliciously risqué sexual scuffles.

Constance Talmadge's elfin charm and hilarious scene stealing effectively complemented Colman's unruffled nonchalance, and Miss Talmadge found him an ideal leading man. As she remarked in an interview given the following year, "He forced me to give my very best, not by any overt or direct means but because working opposite him proved so galvanic that one was shamed into doing a little more with one's character than usual."[29]

Two loosely adapted remakes later appeared. In 1934, Franchot Tone took the Colman part in *Moulin Rouge,* and Greta Garbo and Melvyn Douglas reworked the theme in *Two-Faced Woman* (1941), Garbo's last picture.

The Dark Angel

1925. *Production;* Samuel Goldwyn, Inc. *Distribution:* First National Pictures. *Producer:* Samuel Goldwyn. *Director:* George Fitzmaurice. *Screenplay:* Frances Marion (from the play by H.B. Trevelyan). *Cinematographer:* George S. Barnes. *Art Director:* Ben Carré. *Film Editor:* Stuart Heisler. 8 reels (7,311 feet). *Release Date:* October 11, 1925. No print known to have survived.

Cast: Ronald Colman (Captain Alan Trent), Vilma Banky (Kitty Vane), Wyndham Standing (Captain Gerald Shannon), Frank Elliott (Lord Beaumont), Charles Lane (Sir Hubert Vane), Helen Jerome Eddy (Miss Bottles), Florence Turner (Roma), Billy Butts (Boy).

There had been a number of war pictures since D.W. Griffith's *Hearts of the World* (1918), but the only really striking ones were Rex Ingram's *The Four Horsemen of the Apocalypse* (1921), King Vidor's *The Big Parade* (1925), and George Fitzmaurice's *The Dark Angel.* Teamed for the first time in *The Dark Angel* were Ronald Colman and lovely Hungarian actress Vilma Banky, Sam Goldwyn's newest discovery, in the poignant romantic drama of a gallant officer who returns blinded from the First World War.

In his most important role since *The White Sister,* Colman portrayed British officer Alan Trent, who is unexpectedly ordered back into action before he and his fiancée, Kitty Vane (Miss Banky), can be married. Blinded in battle and held prisoner by the Germans, Trent is presumed dead. After the war, his friend, Captain Gerald Shannon (British actor Wyndham Standing), gently soothes Kitty's sorrow with a discreet proposal of marriage. At first she resists, ever hopeful that her lover will return. Finally, however, she pledges herself to Shannon, unaware that Captain Trent is very much alive.

Trying to forget Kitty forever, lest he burden her with his blindness, Trent reappears from the trenches and settles down to a successful career as an author of children's books. On the very day of his wedding, Shannon learns that Alan is living nearby and, loyal to his former comrade in arms, informs Kitty that Trent still lives. Forewarned of Kitty's imminent arrival, Trent devises a clever plot to convince her that he has perfect eyesight. Arranging his room so that everything is at his fingertips — furniture, drinks, pipe, tobacco, matches, even the newspaper from which he has memorized an extract read to him by his housekeeper — he receives his former fiancée with studied grace, never missing a step. Coolly and with deliberation, Trent terminates their relationship. The war has left him a changed man, he tells her; preferring to forget the past, he simply wishes to be left alone.

Director George Fitzmaurice (second from left) *sets up a shot with Ronald Colman, who plays blinded veteran Alan Trent, and little Billy Butts in* The Dark Angel. *George S. Barnes is seen at the camera. The easel carries a sun reflector, while the man at the right is holding gauze between the performers and the bright sun.*

Brokenhearted, Kitty rises to leave, but turns to offer him a final handshake. When he fails to notice her outstretched hand, she departs, assuming that he has purposely rebuffed her gesture of friendship. But when she returns moments later, standing silently in the room while Trent addresses her as if she were his housekeeper, Kitty sees through his deception and her unfailing devotion is rewarded. The star-crossed lovers are reunited, free to find happiness together at last.

    The Dark Angel brought Ronald Colman further acclaim and recognition, and replaced *The White Sister* as the critical yardstick by which his performances were to be measured. The first of five films he was to make with Vilma Banky, it contributed significantly to the image with which Colman would forever be associated: the wistful, melancholy gentleman who willingly sacrifices his own happiness for that of the woman he loves.

    To effect his convincing performance of a man who has been plunged into darkness, Colman undertook the uncomfortable task of periodically staring into a full battery of klieg lights and sun arcs. "It called for little effort," he later recalled. "After a few moments of the lights, I felt as blind as could be desired!"[30]

Frances Marion, by now coming to be known as Colman's scenarist, fashioned her screenplay from the London stage hit by Guy Bolton (whose nom de plume was H.B. Trevelyan). With sincerity and subtlety, she transformed the play's unhappy ending into the rapturous romantic finale without which few Hollywood productions were made in the twenties.

Nearly five decades later, Marion praised Colman's assured sense of dramatic restraint and underplaying:

> Ronnie always made excellent suggestions, but he refused to take any credit for them, although often these suggestions became highlights of the finished picture. He had a tremendous influence on the style of acting then. His controlled performances, his lack of posturing and his economy of gesture conveyed more power to a scene than the thrashing mode a lot of actors still indulged in. Even in the most melodramatic scenes, with others in the cast whirling around like windmills in a storm, he appeared convincingly calm on the surface, yet one sensed his deep-rooted emotions.[31]

Director George Fitzmaurice, similarly identified as part of the same Colman team, made this classic tear-jerker a sympathetically felt and tastefully executed romance, as well as one of the most stirring war pictures of the decade.

The Dark Angel established Vilma Banky—with her radiant blonde hair, blue eyes, and perfectly chiseled features—as an important new star, and made Colman and Banky one of the screen's leading romantic teams. In one of the studio's less inspired moments, publicity releases touted the picture as "a story of blind love," but it electrified audiences everywhere and became an immediate smash hit. Goldwyn sent Colman to New York for the much-heralded premiere, and the following morning columnist Louella Parsons shrewdly observed: "Singly, Vilma Banky would have been charming, but with Ronald Colman, she is part of a team that Mr. Goldwyn should copyright for his future pictures."[32] And that, in effect, is exactly what the producer did.

Goldwyn remade *The Dark Angel* a decade later, less successfully, with Fredric March, Merle Oberon, and Herbert Marshall heading the cast.

Stella Dallas

1925. *Production:* Samuel Goldwyn, Inc. *Distribution:* United Artists Corporation. *Producer:* Samuel Goldwyn. *Director:* Henry King. *Screenplay:* Frances Marion (from the novel by Olive Higgins Prouty). *Cinematographer:* Arthur Edeson. *Art Director:* Arthur Stibolt. *Costumes:* Sophie Wachner. *Film Editor:* Stuart Heisler. 11 reels (10,157 feet). *Release Date:* November 16, 1925.

Cast: Ronald Colman (Stephen Dallas), Belle Bennett (Stella Dallas), Alice

Joyce (Helen Dane), Lois Moran (Laurel Dallas), Jean Hersholt (Ed Munn), Douglas Fairbanks, Jr. (Richard Grosvenor), Charles Lane (Stephen Dallas, Sr.), Vera Lewis (Miss Matilda Philiburn), Beatrix Prior (Mrs. Grosvenor), Maurice Murphy, Newton Hall, Jack Murphy (Morrison Children), Robert Gillette, Winston Miller, Charles Hatten (Morrison Children, some years later).

This phenomenally successful sob story of mother love stars Ronald Colman as a young man of refinement and sensitivity who impulsively marries a socially unacceptable woman and lives to regret it. Told with simplicity, conviction, and sincerity, it proved to be one of Samuel Goldwyn's most prestigious pictures of the twenties.

Wealthy young socialites Stephen Dallas (Colman) and Helen Dane (Alice Joyce) are soon to be married, but disaster and disgrace intervene when Stephen's father, exposed as an embezzler, commits suicide. Shame turns Stephen from all that is dear to him, and takes him to a small mill town, where he achieves distinction in the legal department of the town's biggest mill.

Shortly after reading of Helen Dane's marriage, the lonely bachelor meets and weds Stella Martin (Belle Bennett), the attractive but limited daughter of a mill worker. Although aware of his new bride's little crudities of taste and grammar, Stephen at first has great hopes for Stella, and a daughter is born.

Wishing to help her husband because of his social position, Stella becomes a noticeable ornament at the smart country club to which she and Stephen belong. Bedecked in gaudy dresses and plumed hats, Stella cuts a ridiculous and pitiful figure, the object of mockery among the idle rich. Her coarse behavior, lacking the most ordinary of social graces, and her conspicuous flirtation with the club's crude and loud-mouthed riding master, Ed Munn (Jean Hersholt in a brash performance), only hasten her husband's growing dissatisfaction.

The breaking point occurs the day Stephen is appointed chief of the mill's legal department in New York City. Enchanted, he dashes home to share the good news with his wife, only to discover her in the company of Ed Munn. They have argued about this offensive individual before. After their final quarrel, Stella refuses to resettle with her husband, and Stephen leaves for New York alone. The marriage, condemned to failure from the start, is over.

The years pass swiftly, and Stephen prospers while Stella sinks into a self-indulgent quagmire of personal neglect. Their daughter, Laurel (Lois Moran), now almost ten and lovelier every day, has inherited her father's dark, contemplative eyes and refined tastes. Stella's apartment is a shabby affair, but only by living in such lodgings can she afford to take Laurel to exclusive resorts where she can meet "nice young people." And the summer hotels they patronize are indeed impressive. For Stella, such excursions require tight-fitting corsets, absurd regalia, and lavish expenditures of powder, rouge, and lipstick. At home she is a flabby, shapeless mess, with a double chin and ratty hair.

Except for the pain which his separation from Laurel causes him, Stephen has never regretted his decision. His visits with his daughter are frequent, and although there is much to criticize, he has never influenced the child against her mother. In recent years, Stephen has renewed his relationship with Helen Dane, now the widowed Mrs. Morrison, whom Laurel regards with wide-eyed admiration. Stella steadfastly refuses to grant Stephen a divorce, and as each new year succeeds the last, Stephen's sufferings lie heavily upon his heart.

Laurel, now in her late teens and part of the young country club crowd, is quite taken with Richard Grosvenor, a devastatingly good-looking college lad (played with considerable charm by 15-year-old Douglas Fairbanks, Jr.). One day, as she strolls with Richard, Laurel spots her mother bustling across the lawn from the hotel, looking like an over-the-hill tart with a parasol. Unaware that the creature approaching them is Laurel's mother, her friends scream with laughter and call the woman a freak. Unable to face the confrontation, a panic-stricken Laurel slips off her wristwatch, pretends she's lost it, and rushes off to find it. When she later insists they return home at once, Stella uncomprehendingly complies. As the train hurtles them through the night, Stella is drifting off to sleep in her berth when the mention of Laurel's name in an adjoining compartment prods her wide awake.

"To think that dreadful creature we saw today is Laurel's mother!"

"Of course Richard Grosvenor would never marry her with *that* mother."

So that's the story, Stella realizes with a start, as she hears herself described for the first time in cruel detail. Maternal instinct now triumphs over self-interest, and the theme of self-sacrifice dominates the latter portion of the film.

Stella secretly visits Helen Morrison and agrees to divorce Stephen if he and Helen will provide Laurel with a proper upbringing. But Laurel loyally refuses to leave her mother. With no other way to ensure her daughter's future, Stella steps out of Laurel's life by marrying the drunken nitwit Ed Munn.

Stephen and Helen are quietly wed, followed not long thereafter by Laurel and Richard Grosvenor. In the famous, tear-stained climax, Stella is part of the crowd which gathers outside the front gate of the Morrison mansion to watch the fashionable wedding. Standing in the cold rain, she peers through a lighted window and observes her daughter's happiness from afar. Stella's face glows faintly as she watches Laurel join her destiny to Richard's, and slow tears course down Stella's cheeks as they kiss. Then a policeman in a rain-drenched slicker abruptly tells her to move along.

"Yes, sir, I'm going," she murmurs. "I was only seeing how pretty the young lady was."

Stella walks off into the dreary night and is consumed by the darkness.

Although faithfully adapted from the 1923 heart-throb novel by Olive Higgins Prouty, this movie rose above its trite source and emerged an authentically tragic, deeply felt human drama. Melodrama and sentimentality gave way to sensitivity, warmth, and humanity—qualities altogether lacking in the original.[33]

Demonstrating the same sincerity and conviction which characterized his work in *The White Sister,* director Henry King refrains from using his camera as a battering ram with which to bludgeon his audience's sensibilities. He instead allows it to observe potentially over-indulgent scenes just long enough to establish the appropriate mood, and then moves on. A fitting example is the heart-wrenching closing scene in which Stella stands unnoticed in the rain and watches her daughter's wedding through a window. The ending as it appears in the novel is both interminable and hackneyed, but the sequence in the film is relatively brief, the camera rarely lingering on Stella's face. Such control obliterates the histrionics of the original and endows the scene with genuine dramatic power and emotion.[34] Another scene which effectively illustrates King's deft treatment of melodramatic source material is the suicide of Stephen Dallas, Sr. The elder Dallas reads the newspaper which discloses his financial misdoings, then drops it to the floor. The camera cuts to a close-up of the discarded newspaper, and a smoking revolver falls across the headline which screams "STEPHEN DALLAS EMBEZZLER!" A nice touch, handled with sureness, economy, and dispatch.

Ronald Colman's ingratiating performance not only advanced his growing reputation as a major box-office star, but further enhanced his developing image as the distinguished gentleman willing to suffer sacrifice for his loved ones. Despite his top billing, Colman did not by any means dominate *Stella Dallas,* for his was merely a supporting role; it was Belle Bennett who garnered most of the critical praise. So although *Stella Dallas* is often considered one of his most memorable pictures of the twenties, it pales when compared with the earlier *Dark Angel,* in which the Colman image was for the first time fully articulated, or the forthcoming *Beau Geste,* which firmly established the bittersweet image for the next 30 years. *Stella Dallas* was designed to showcase Belle Bennett's talents, and it did. She stole the show.

Miss Bennett gives an overwhelmingly convincing performance as a crude and uncultivated woman who makes an arch attempt to be genteel, fails miserably, and then sacrifices everything for her daughter. The characterization is vulgar, but the interpretation is one of great depth and beauty. Especially moving is the scene in which Stella, realizing that Laurel is unwilling to forsake her mother, stands alone in the dimly lit apartment and comtemplates suicide. In a lingering medium shot—the left side of her face shadowed, the right side lit—Stella thinks of herself, her coarseness, her failures. The lighting of veteran cinematographer Arthur Edeson, the perceptive direction by Henry King, and Miss Bennett's remarkably controlled performance capture perfectly an anguished moment of self-confrontation. As is so often true of the best silent films, no words are spoken because no words are needed. The utter, simple tragedy is all there visually.

Lovely Lois Moran, a young American actress whom Samuel Goldwyn had discovered working in pictures in France, made her Hollywood screen debut as Stella's daughter. As Laurel grows up, Miss Moran ages convincingly, from a little girl of 10, through adolescence, to some years later when, no longer a child and yet not quite a woman, she falls in love and marries. These transitions, and Miss Moran's capable handling of their intricacies, add a further dimension of delicacy to the film's charm.

With its first-rate cast and direction, *Stella Dallas* was an enormous box-office hit and received high praise from the critics.[35] The picture worked, for the emotions were real. When Samuel Goldwyn remade the film in 1937, Barbara Stanwyck starred and John Boles took the Colman part. Handkerchiefs were damp once again in theatres throughout the country. A 1990 remake, *Stella,* starred Bette Midler, with Stephen Collins as Stephen Dallas.

Lady Windermere's Fan

1925. *Production and distribution:* Warner Bros. Pictures, Inc. *Director:* Ernst Lubitsch. *Screenplay:* Julien Josephson (from the play by Oscar Wilde). *Cinematographer:* Charles Van Enger. *Assistant Cinematographer:* Willard Van Enger. *Assistant Directors:* George Hippard, Ernst Laemmle. *Art Director:* Harold Grieve. *Costumes:* Sophie Wachner. *Electrical Effects:* H.W. Murphy. *Art Titles:* Victor Vance. *Titles:* Maude Fulton, Eric Locke. 8 reels (7,815 feet). *Release Date:* December 27, 1925.

Cast: Ronald Colman (Lord Darlington), May McAvoy (Lady Windermere), Bert Lytell (Lord Windermere), Irene Rich (Mrs. Erlynne), Edward Martindel (Lord Augustus Lorton), Carrie Daumery (The Duchess of Berwick), Helen Dunbar, Billie Bennett (Gossipy Duchesses), Larry Steers (Party Guest), Wilson Benge (Butler).

That fatal fan! It first surfaced in London in 1892, courtesy of Oscar Wilde, to stain the honor of lots of respectable vulgar people. It takes thoroughly good people, Wilde was fond of reminding his audiences, to do thoroughly stupid things, like complicating their trivial lives with gossip and slander. And it took Lady Windermere's fan to bring temptation, sin, and folly to the doorsteps of the honorable.

When Warner Bros. decided to film *Lady Windermere's Fan,* Oscar Wilde's delicious satire of scandal and smugness in high society, the studio fortunately had Ernst Lubitsch, master of the sophisticated sex farce, under contract. Already specializing in films which brought a new and frivolous attitude toward sex to the comedy of manners, Lubitsch was ideally suited to transform the abrasive Wildean cleverness to the screen. The director set out to adapt the play with his customary light malice and sardonic wit. Ronald Colman was borrowed from Samuel Goldwyn to play Lord Darlington, the amorous *bon vivant* in whose lodgings the fan was found. A splendid Lubitschean cast was assembled to portray the dull dowagers and backbiting nobility of a bygone generation. Tongues were placed in cheek thus and so, the screechingly clever British drawing rooms were invaded, and the social shams which pass for polite society began to tremble.

Edith Erlynne (Irene Rich) is a lady with a past. Beautiful, shameless, and indiscreet, she has drifted back to London after a life of adventure on the continent. Although she was once loved and respected, her social standing has long run its course. She has just sent a note to Lord Windermere (Bert Lytell), whom she must see at once if he would avoid "certain unpleasant disclosures."

"I am the mother of your wife," she informs him quite matter-of-factly.

"You know very well that your daughter was brought up to believe her mother is dead," Windermere replies indignantly. "You also know why!"

Accepting his offer of payment for her secrecy, Mrs. Erlynne soon lives in extravagant style, unaccepted by society but the subject of its chilly gossip.

Lord Darlington (Colman) pays Lady Windermere (May McAvoy) a visit on her birthday and, having failed earlier to convince her that his protestations of love and undying affection are genuine, reveals that her husband is deceiving her for another woman. A disbelieving wife is persuaded only when Darlington indicates that her husband's checkbook contains the name of Mrs. Erlynne.

At this very moment Mrs. Erlynne is pleading with Lord Windermere for an invitation to his wife's birthday party.

"To be seen at your house tonight means my social recognition, possibly my marriage to Lord Augustus. I am desperate; if you refuse to invite me, I will go to my daughter and tell her who I am!"

A preoccupied Windermere returns home and is confronted by a wife who now believes that her husband has turned "from the love that is given to the love that is bought." Uncompromised, Windermere explains that his benevolence was not at all improper and that he has in fact invited the lady in question to the forthcoming birthday gala.

"If she dares to come here," Lady Windermere threatens, brandishing her husband's all-important birthday gift, "I will strike her across the face with this fan!"

Lady Windermere (May McAvoy) displays her famous fan as Lord Darlington (Ronald Colman) and Lord Windermere (Bert Lytell) look on, in Ernst Lubitsch's sparkling adaptation of the Oscar Wilde play.

Windermere hastily dispatches a prudent letter of refusal to Mrs. Erlynne who, without opening the envelope, mistakes it for the expected invitation and departs for the Windermere estate. Discovering that she is not on the guest list, she produces her note from Windermere, but its message signals defeat until Lord Augustus Lorton (Edward Martindel) appears and escorts his intended through the portals as his guest. Looking like "a deluxe edition of a wicked French novel," the notorious Edith Erlynne sails into the crowded room and explodes a bombshell. While the conceited aristos and gossipy biddies go bananas, an outraged Lady Windermere clutches at her fan and an astonished Lord Windermere regards both women — and the fan — with grave discomfort. As Lady Windermere approaches her uninvited guest, the camera cuts to a tight close-up of that deadly fan in clenched fist. But alas, the scandalmongers are denied their sensation when the honorable lady drops her fan, bows coldly, and addresses Mrs. Erlynne with quiet reserve.

"How kind of you to honor us! I have heard so much about you — from every side."

Mrs. Erlynne blanches, forces a smile, and quickly circulates among the

rest of the guests, as Lady Windermere, in her pain and anguish, slips out
to the terrace. While the virtuous dowagers chatter like so many cackling
hens, the "swells" outdo themselves in their attempts to gain the approval
of the exquisite Edith Erlynne. Cornering the worst-whispering matron,
Mrs. Erlynne purchases her social acceptance as she gushes, "I have
yearned—positively yearned—to meet the best-dressed woman in London!"

That's all it takes. Crude flattery converts the snobs, brazen infamy has
its hour, and Mrs. Erylnne has arrived.

Moments later Lord Darlington departs, having first informed Lady
Windermere that he is leaving London and that she will never see him
again. The good lady, believing that her husband has broken the bond of
matrimony and dishonored her in her own house, hurries to her disappointed suitor's apartment.

Mrs. Erlynne, having spied Lady Windermere leaving the estate, reads
the note the jealous wife has left her husband: "You may have your Mrs.
Erlynne. I am going to Darlington who loves me." Snatching up the incriminating note, she rushes off to save her daughter—and the day.

Reaching the apartment shortly after Lady Windermere but only
moments before Darlington, Mrs. Erlynne confronts her daughter with the
compromising note and makes her plea.

"I swear to you there is nothing between Lord Windermere and
myself! Please go home! Trust me, child; trust me as you would your own
mother. I did just what you are doing tonight, and ruined my life. If they
find you here you will be dishonored—an outcast!"

Footsteps approach. It is Lord Darlington, and Lord Windermere and
the rest of the good old boys are with him! The two women retreat to the
study just in time, but Lady Windermere has left her fatal fan in the drawing
room. All is lost. Lord Lorton discovers it, realizes that Lady Windermere
is in the apartment, and, with customary tact and discretion, immediately
informs all and sundry. Darlington, in shock, denies all charges as Mrs.
Erlynne, thinking quickly, glides into the room, retrieves the fan, and
rescues her daughter from a hideous precipice of shame.

"I am afraid I took your wife's fan by mistake," she announces coolly.
"So sorry!"

Lord Lorton glowers reproachfully, the haughty snobs exit in embarrassment, Lady Windermere slips away unnoticed, Mrs. Erlynne begs a
bewildered Darlington's forgiveness for her intrusion, and all is delivered
from harm. All except a twice-stained but stainless heroine.

The following morning Lord and Lady Windermere embrace.

"You were right about Mrs. Erlynne," he tells her. "She is thoroughly
bad."

The butler announces Mrs. Erlynne, whose departure for France is imminent. After Windermere withdraws without acknowledging her presence, she makes a final plea to her daughter.

"Don't tell him! You would kill his love, and spoil the only decent thing I ever did."

Taking leave of Lady Windermere, Mrs. Erlynne meets Lord Lorton on the front step and minces no words.

"Your conduct last night was outrageous!" she snaps. "I have decided not to marry you."

Won over by her audacity, an astonished Lorton begs her to reconsider. With little reluctance, she does, and they drive off together. And well they should, for this has been, after all, the story of "a good woman."

It seems incredible that an Oscar Wilde play was produced as a silent picture, without the benefit of all the sparkling Wildean dialogue. But it was — successfully. And the reason for its success was Ernst Lubitsch. The earliest German director to come to Hollywood, Lubitsch specialized in light bedroom farces, becoming famous for the so-called "Lubitsch Touch," the subtle visual innuendo or nuance. "Art," Debussy once said, "is the art of leaving out." Lubitsch knew what to reveal and what to conceal. His art was the art of omission, of saying little but implying much. Without the use of a single Wildean epigram, Lubitsch conveyed the unconscionable smugness of Victorian society in purely visual terms, through the attitudes, facial expressions, and reactions of his actors and the sardonic wit of his images. From the opening scene, in which Lord Darlington (Colman) enters Lady Windermere's chambers, the Wildean tone is immediately set. Darlington bows courteously, shakes her hand, and then holds it just a trifle longer than is polite. The inference is discreet but unmistakable: Darlington is in love with a married woman. In a later sequence, an intertitle informs us that a "gentleman's relation to a lady is indicated by the manner in which he rings her doorbell." Lord Lorton hesitates before ringing Mrs. Erlynne's bell, removes a pocket mirror from his vest pocket to check his moustache, buttons his coat, then presses the buzzer. The maid relieves him of his hat and coat, but, unsure of which drawing room his intended awaits him in, he enters hesitantly. "But when the relation becomes more friendly," he rings the bell impatiently, not once but thrice, hangs up his hat without assistance and, thoroughly familiar with his surroundings, marches briskly into Mrs. Erlynne's chambers. Although Wildean in spirit, such psychological portraiture is Lubitschean, a specifically cinematic form of wit which amplifies emotions through the use of visual, rather than spoken, epigrams. "Truth," as Stendhal remarked, "is to be found only in details."

It is, of course, these intellectual glints that matter, but an invariably superb comedic cast increased the sparkle. May McAvoy is pleasingly proper and over-virtuous as Lady Windermere, Bert Lytell contributes an earnest and restrained Lord Windermere, Edward Martindel adds a commendable touch of blasé snobbery as the stuffy Lord Lorton, and Ronald Colman is amply witty and amusing as the clever, dapper Lord Darlington. The film's most memorable performance is easily that of Irene Rich as Mrs. Erlynne, for it is through her balanced portrayal of a devoted mother-in-disguise that the Wildean attack on Victorian priggishness is realized. Willingly accepting public disgrace to save her daughter's reputation, Mrs. Erlynne, by her spontaneity and nobility, gives complacency its comeuppance.

Throughout the film, supporting characters are gorgeously orchestrated and consistently add merriment as excessively trivial aristos. In a particularly amusing sequence, the socially unacceptable Mrs. Erlynne is spotted at the racetrack, and the high-society dowagers prepare to pounce. They know who she is. Better still, they know *what* she is. As they regard their prey disapprovingly through binoculars, the following exchange takes place among the Duchess of Berwick, Lady Plymdale, and Mrs. Cowper-Cowper:

"She is getting gray—"
"She is quite gray—"
"She is perfectly gray—"

Of course they never talk scandal; they merely remark on it.

As for Ronald Colman, if his Darlington was a bit less roguish and more reserved than Wilde might have imagined, his performance was comfortable and polished, and showcased his flair for light comedy. In light of Colman's earlier comedic successes (most notably *Her Night of Romance* and *Her Sister from Paris*), it is curiously revealing that at this time he considered himself better suited to star in romantic adventures than in light comedies.[36] His first major comedy, *Lady Windermere's Fan*, clearly anticipates such later comedic romps as *The Devil to Pay* and *The Talk of the Town*, in which Colman turned in some of his most delightful performances.

Although only a medium-sized success at the box office, *Lady Windermere's Fan* was generally well received by the critics, although some reviewers complained that the omission of the Wildean epigrams deprived the picture of "the sparkle of the author's words."[37] Recent evaluations, far from dismissing the film as inferior to the play, rate it more highly: Andrew Sarris calls it "an improvement on Wilde's original,"[38] and Herman G. Weinberg observes that the "effect . . . is that of having seen a witty play, though not a word of dialogue has been spoken."[39] A more fitting tribute to Lubitsch's abilities to tell a story through pictures can hardly be imagined. Unfortunately it sometimes takes decades for a classic to be recognized as such.

Consider the 1949 remake, *The Fan*, which starred George Sanders in the Colman part, along with Jeanne Crain and Madeleine Carroll. Despite the benefit of Wilde's dialogue and direction by Otto Preminger, it managed to misplace most of the wit and satire of the original, and the result was "a disaster."[40] The Lubitsch version, on the other hand, was voted one of the ten best films of 1925.[41] Its glowing narrative, pictorial wit, graceful performances, and Lubitsch's finely honed satirical gifts allow one to suspect that Oscar Wilde had no cause to turn over in his grave.

An amusing sidelight: By 1925 Ronald Colman had become Samuel Goldwyn's most valuable property, and when the producer agreed to lend his star to Warner Bros. for *Lady Windermere's Fan* he insisted that Colman receive top billing. Unfortunately Irene Rich's contract assured *her* of top billing in all of her pictures. Finally Miss Rich, delighted to work with Colman, accepted Goldwyn's stipulation (inexplicably, she received fourth billing) and all appeared resolved until an infuriated Goldwyn telephoned Lubitsch after having read the script. Under no circumstances would he allow Ronald Colman to portray a villain.

"Villain? I don't know what is villain," the director replied reassuringly, a bit uncertain of his English. "He love a beautiful girl if that is villain."

Would Colman make a sacrifice?

"Ya, he lose the girl!"[42]

That was all Goldwyn wanted to hear. Colman would be available, but only on the further condition that his credit line read "Courtesy of Samuel Goldwyn." Agreed. But Lubitsch was to have his revenge.

The director's prankishness was as consummate as his English was imperfect, and during the filming he never let his star forget the anxious moments Goldwyn had caused him.

"Mr. Colman," he would say, "you walk across the room, you stop by the table, you pick up the book, then you look into the eyes of Miss McAvoy by courtesy of Sam Goldwyn!"[43]

Colman accepted the good-natured needling with characteristic aplomb. His admiration for Oscar Wilde was boundless (according to his daughter, Colman knew most of the playwright's works by heart), and he was doubly pleased to be working with a director of Lubitsch's stature.[44]

Kiki

1926. *Production and distribution:* First National Pictures. *Producer:* Joseph M. Schenck. *Director:* Clarence Brown. *Screenplay:* Hans Kräly (from the play by David Belasco as adapted from the French play by André Picard). *Cinematographer:* Oliver T. Marsh. 9 reels (8,279 feet). *Release Date:* April 4, 1926.

Cast: Norma Talmadge (Kiki), Ronald Colman (Victor Renal), Gertrude Astor (Paulette), Marc MacDermott (Baron Rapp), George K. Arthur (Adolphe), William Orlamond (Brule), Erwin Connelly (Joly), Frankie Darro (Pierre), Mack Swain (Pastryman).

This clever and breezy slapstick farce stars Norma Talmadge as Parisian gamine Kiki, an energetic waif whose theatrical and matrimonial ambitions complicate the life of stage producer Victor Renal (nattily portrayed by Ronald Colman). Miss Talmadge's ingratiating comedic talents are in evidence from the opening scene, in which she brashly obtains an audition, to the final fade-out, which leaves her happily snuggled in Renal's arms.

Kiki, a lowly newspaper vender, secretly adores Renal and longs to join the chorus line. When an aspiring actress is fired from chorus rehearsals, Kiki sees her opportunity, profits by it, and lands a position as a chorus girl. But her unpredictable habit of interfering and committing perfectly dreadful blunders arouses the wrath of Paulette, the patronizing star of the show and Renal's sweetheart (played with appropriate disdain by Gertrude Astor), and Kiki is fired. Renal takes pity on the perky trouper and invites her to dinner and then to his home. Becoming as intrigued by his companion's charms as she is by his, Renal embraces and kisses her, and the fun starts. Kiki resists, wrestles her disbelieving suitor to the ground, and locks herself in his bedroom. Renal decides that retreat is the better part of valor and withdraws to sleep elsewhere.

When Kiki awakes the next morning, she is confronted by Renal's antagonistic valet, Adolphe (George K. Arthur). In a wildly cascading series of clownish catastrophes, Kiki, clad in a baggy pair of her host's pajamas, precipitates a hair-pulling free-for-all with the valet and then, with grim determination, intrudes upon Renal's telephone conversation with Paulette by rattling the fireplace grill. Renal concedes defeat, hangs up in dismay, and drags the diminutive terror by the ear to the bedroom and locks her in.

Paulette, now aware that she has a rival, soon arrives, accompanied by the scheming backer of the show and Paulette's secret lover, Baron Rapp (Marc MacDermott). Kiki realizes that Paulette has conspired with the baron to lure Renal away from her and, for some good reason probably unknown to her at the time, sets about spraying the living room with perfume and ripping off her clothes. Paulette's haughty condescension provokes Kiki, by now scantily clad in her undergarments and clutching a knife between her teeth, to chase her jealous antagonist through the house. Renal intervenes and snatches up the infuriated buccaneer just as she "passes out" in his arms, as rigid and flat as a board. A hastily summoned doctor diagnoses a cataleptic fit. After failing at several attempts to revive the supposedly stricken Kiki, Renal places her on his bed and props a pillow under her head. Finding herself alone with Renal at last, Kiki reaches up suddenly and, without warning, grabs him passionately and kisses him. Renal reacts in innocent comic panic, his eyes wide with shock and stupefied amazement. Then she calmly pretends to pass out again. Paulette, who in the meantime has returned to the theatre, calls Renal and urges him to join her there. The time for pretense is over, and Kiki once more "recovers." Renal

Director Clarence Brown on the set of Kiki *with star Norma Talmadge, Ronald Colman, and—of all things—a baby goat.*

embraces her, drops the phone, kisses her, and proposes marriage. The clever little actress has received her most ecstatic review: Renal's sympathy has turned to love.

Having scored major triumphs in *The Dark Angel, Stella Dallas*, and *Lady Windermere's Fan*, Ronald Colman was by now a big-name star much in demand at the box office. He had, moreover, been so successful in his two pictures with Constance Talmadge (*Her Night of Romance* and *Her Sister from Paris*) that sister Norma Talmadge specifically requested Colman as her leading man in this screen version of the popular David Belasco stage hit.[45] Clarence Brown, soon to become Greta Garbo's favorite director (he directed no fewer than seven of her pictures), regarded the casting of Colman opposite Miss Talmadge as a decided coup.[46]

The combination of a lively screen play by Ernst Lubitsch's witty collaborator Hans Kräly, gay and snappy direction by Clarence Brown, Miss Talmadge's comic versatility, and Colman's "restrained and charming performance"[47] made for more than enough merriment to please both public and critics. The gags come at such a rapid and well-timed pace that one laugh frequently dissolves into another, with the momentum building toward the film's most hilarious highlight — Kiki's feigned cataleptic fit. Like so many fine comedy scenes, this set piece is built around a very few simple and physical gags, and then milked for all it's worth — which, in the case of as clever a comedienne as Talmadge and as lighthearted a leading man as Colman, is plenty.[48] Kiki's catalepsy is but an act, designed to keep her in the house with Renal, and she carries it off perfectly. Renal lifts her arm and lets it go, but it doesn't drop; it remains outstretched, suspended in mid-air. He raises her leg and releases it; it too stays there, hanging stiffly in mid-air. An exasperated Renal resolves to get her coat on and get her out of the house, but it simply can't be done. He balances her precariously in an upright position, gingerly lets her go, darts away to grab a coat, and dashes back to catch her just as she topples toward the floor. After a second attempt proves equally futile, Renal realizes, once Kiki "recovers" and plants a firm kiss on his lips, that the only thing a gentleman can do with a resourcefully rigid lady is to marry her. Love among the sight gags.

Beau Geste

1926. *Production and distribution:* Famous Players-Lasky Corporation and Paramount Pictures Corporation. *Producers:* Adolph Zukor, Jesse L. Lasky. *Director:* Herbert Brenon. *Screenplay:* Paul Schofield. *Adaptation:* John Russell (from the novel by Percival Christopher Wren). *Associate Producer, Eastern Studio:* William Le Baron. *Cinematographer:* J. Roy Hunt (with Technicolor sequences). *Assistant Director:* Ray Lissner. *Art Director:* Julian Boone Fleming. *Production Superintendent:* Frank Blount. *Supervising Film Editor:* Julian Johnson. *Musical Score:* Dr. Hugo Riesenfeld. 11 reels (10,600 feet). *Release Date:* August 1, 1926. *New York Premiere:* August 25, 1926.

Cast: Ronald Colman (Michael "Beau" Geste), Neil Hamilton (Digby Geste), Ralph Forbes (John Geste), Norman Trevor (Major Henri de Beaujolais), Noah Beery (Sergeant-Major Lejaune), Alice Joyce (Lady Patricia Brandon), Mary Brian (Isobel Rivers), William Powell (Boldini), Victor McLaglen (Hank), Donald Stuart (Buddy), George Regas (Maris), Bernard Siegel (Schwartz), Paul McAllister (St. André), Redmond Finlay (Cordere), Ram Singh (Prince Ram Singh), Maurice Murphy (Young "Beau"), Philippe De Lacey (Young Digby), Mickey McBan (Young John).

> *The love of a man for a woman waxes and wanes like the moon — but the love of brother for brother is steadfast as the stars, and endures like the Word of the Prophet.*

Pulsating with a vitality which still thrills more than half a century after its release, *Beau Geste* is an exotic tale of three brothers who join the French Foreign Legion and go to war. It is full of mystery, intrigue, suspense, romance, adventure — the stuff of which "big" pictures are made. Big, but not necessarily enduring. *Beau Geste* is something more, as big thematically as its panoramic Sahara setting. Its elemental themes — courage, honor, duty,

The impressive Fort Zinderneuf set, shot on location near the Mexican border in Arizona, from Beau Geste. *This is the picture that made Ronald Colman a major star.*

renunciation, self-sacrifice, and, above all, brotherly love, all caught in the swell of war and brutality—are developed with a strength and dignity as inspirational as the Arabian proverb from which its central theme is taken. This is escapism ennobled.

A caravan of legionnaires snakes across the windswept sands of the Sahara. Through sweltering sun and desert waste, it advances to the relief of Fort Zinderneuf, isolated from life on the edge of the unknown. A strange, sinister sight awaits them at the lonely outpost: no lookout in the watchtower. Neither sound nor movement from those men in the ramparts high above. Major Henri de Beaujolais (Norman Trevor), commander of the relief detachment, fires his revolver to alert the garrison, but the sharp report goes unnoticed and the silent vigil is maintained.

Suddenly, from one of the embrasures, a rifle protrudes from behind a sentry and fires at the approaching battalion. A greeting? A warning? Or an Arab trap? The camera cuts to the deathly still ghosts poised in the parapets and to a chilling close-up of one bearded legionnaire—pipe clenched firmly between his teeth, rifle ready at his shoulder, face frozen and staring lifelessly out across the desert whiteness. This poor wretched warrior will never step smartly, nor will his comrades. Corpses cannot march.

When the scout he has sent over the wall fails to return, Major de Beaujolais enters and finds every soldier within slain. Sprawled next to a dead legionnaire is the commandant, a crushed letter clutched in his hand, a French bayonet protruding from his chest. Murdered by one of his own men! After a hasty search of the barracks fails to produce signs of life, Beaujolais returns to the spot where, moments ago, he had discovered the murdered commandant and the dead soldier near him, but the bodies are no longer there. *Someone* must be alive, the major realizes. Someone fired that shot, someone propped those bodies up in the ramparts and placed their rifles in position, and someone has snatched two corpses. But why?

No sooner does Beaujolais return to his troops than billowing clouds of black smoke begin to pour forth from the fort. In minutes, Fort Zinderneuf is swallowed by flames.

The mystery of Fort Zinderneuf is but a part of the tale of three brothers — Beau, Digby, and John Geste — whose code of honor and loyalty begins in childhood and ends in the desert sands. The story flashes back 15 years to boyhood days in England, where the three youths engage in thrilling exploits of soldierly valor by launching stately model ships from the edge of their aunt's lily pond at Brandon Abbas. When young John is accidentally wounded in the leg, oldest brother Beau performs minor surgery with his jacknife, congratulates the "Stout Fella" for "bravery under fire," and pronounces him worthy of the highest honor — a full-dress Viking's funeral. They lay a toy soldier on the deck of one of the boats, drape a miniature flag over the "body," build a pyre of matches round him, and place a tiny dog at his feet. The vessel is then set ablaze and solemnly shoved forth.

"Digby," Beau requests presently, "you must promise that if I die first, you'll give me a Viking's funeral." And thus the pact is made.

Lady Patricia Brandon (patrician beauty Alice Joyce, who played Ronald Colman's second wife in *Stella Dallas*) entertains the Rajah Ram Singh, who is visiting the country estate to view its priceless Indian sapphire, the "Blue Water." They are joined by Aunt Patricia's old friend Captain Henri de Beaujolais of the French Foreign Legion, who is aware that since she and her husband have lived apart, her financial difficulties have been considerable. Later that evening, Beau, hiding behind a suit of armor, overhears his aunt tell the Rajah:

"— but, Your Highness, I consent, only because I see no other way out of my difficulties."

The story now flashes forward to a time when the boys have all grown into splendid manhood. Aunt Patricia's husband is returning from Shanghai and must sell the Blue Water immediately. But the fabulous stone has disappeared, and with it the brothers Geste. Beau (Ronald Colman) confesses that he stole the jewel, and flees to avoid the consequences. Digby (Neil Hamilton) is the next to shoulder the blame, claiming that Beau's act of gallantry was meant to shield him, the true culprit. John (Ralph Forbes), admitting his own guilt, follows worthily in his brothers' footsteps and decides to join them in disgrace and shame. Hence it comes to pass that the mysterious theft of a precious family heirloom sets these three out on as eventful and fateful a journey as ever a man took.

The fugitives join the exile of the self-condemned — the French Foreign Legion — and embark for the unquestioning solitude of the Sahara. Trouble brews at Sidi-bel-Abbès when a cowardly sneak thief, Boldini (William Powell), overhears the trio joking about a stolen sapphire and a flight from justice, and reports the conversation to his crooked commanding officer, Sergeant-Major Lejaune (Noah Beery). Digby is soon assigned to Major de Beaujolais' battalion at Tokotu, while the treacherous Lejaune, vowing to get the gem for himself, takes Beau and John with him to the last outpost under the burning African sky — Fort Zinderneuf.

Things begin badly and rapidly grow worse at the fort, until finally Lejaune's brutal tyranny so enrages his subordinates that a mad scheme of murder and mutiny is planned. Beau and John remain faithful to the tricolor and refuse to join the rebels, but Lejaune is to die, and they must either join or be slaughtered with the commandant. Lejaune hatches a little plot of his own, and plans to leave no living witnesses to his robbery of Beau's jewel. His scheme is to use the loyal ones to murder the mutineers and then see to it that the survivors perish. When the relieving force arrives from Tokotu, he will be proclaimed a hero for suppressing the revolt single-handedly.

But out of the night, from beyond the desert crests, sweeps a shrieking swarm of massed Arab invaders. A wild rush, a fierce orgy of slaughter, and the garrison is reduced to a small score of weary defenders. From atop the crimson-stained ramparts, Lejaune mounts a daring and resourceful defense. Even the dead cannot be spared. As each man falls, the commandant props him up in place and forces rifles into dead hands, so that every wall appears to be fully manned. Springing furiously from embrasure to embrasure and exposing himself fearlessly, Lejaune fires each weapon from behind its lifeless sentinel.

The desperate counter-stroke works, but not before a merciless bullet claims another victim: Beau. Lejaune and John are now the sole survivors. Still determined to get the jewel, Lejaune pounces on Beau and finds a note of confession addressed to Scotland Yard. Enraged, the younger Geste leaps forward and attacks him for daring to touch his fallen brother. A fierce struggle ends when John drives his bayonet through the commandant's chest, and then kneels to cradle a dying brother in his arms.

"Get away quickly," Beau whispers, managing a smile, "before the relief comes. They'll shoot you for killing Lejaune. Take — letter — to Aunt Pat."

A brief silence.

"Where are you — Stout Fella?" he asks, groping for his brother's face. "Isn't that silly, Johnny," he smiles. "I'm — going — blind —"

John Geste (Ralph Forbes) comforts his dying brother Beau (Ronald Colman) in Beau Geste, *a tribute to love between brothers based on the best-selling novel by P.C. Wren.*

And then he quietly dies.

Hours later, the relief patrol arrives. After firing a warning shot to gain the few precious seconds he needs to effect his escape, John scrambles over the back wall. Major de Beaujolais' scout scales the front wall only to find slain soldiers sprawled everywhere. Two of them—Beau and Lejaune—he recognizes, for the newcomer is Digby. And Digby knows what must be done.

He hides in the guardhouse while Beaujolais enters and discovers the bodies of the commandant and the legionnaire lying next to him, and then quickly carries his brother to his bed in the barracks while the major searches the garrison for survivors. A vow is remembered, a promise made 15 years earlier is kept. Digby covers the body with blankets and sheets and then, remembering that Beau must have a dog at his feet, fetches Lejaune's body and drags it to the foot of the bed. Setting the funeral pyre ablaze, he snaps to attention, and then disappears over the back wall. Moments later, in the desert, he and John are reunited.

"I kept my promise, Stout Fella," Digby stammers. "I gave him—a Viking's funeral—"

The brothers salute as they watch the fort go up in smoke, and then set off over the rise.

Digby perishes in the desert, but John survives to bring the Zinderneuf story home to England and Brandon Abbas. There he fulfills Beau's dying request and hands Aunt Patricia the letter, which clears up the mystery of the Blue Water and brings the tale of the Geste brothers to a close:

"What a name you gave me as a little boy — 'Beau' Geste! But I fear the 'beautiful gesture' I've tried to make has turned out a sorry prank. I was behind the armor the day you sold Ram Singh the real Blue Water, and when Uncle Hector's cable came I realized how desperate things would soon be for you, so I took the glass imitation. You contrived that, I know, in love and fear — in fear and love I took it, and if that has helped you at all, perhaps you will still call me 'Beau' Geste."

Immediately after reading P.C. Wren's tremendously popular 1925 novel of the French Foreign Legion, director Herbert Brenon enthusiastically set about persuading Paramount producers Adolph Zukor and Jesse Lasky to purchase the film rights.[49] Its action, heroics, and archetypal romantic-idealist central figure, he assured them, were tailor-made for the silent screen. Brenon's zeal was contagious, and Paramount dispatched an advance man to Algeria to select suitable desert locations, but the outbreak of hostilities involving the real Foreign Legion made filming in North Africa impossible.

Fine substitutes for the Sahara were soon found at two locations: a stretch of desert waste east of Burlingame, California, and an equally barren area near the Mexican border southwest of Yuma, Arizona. The environment was as uncompromising as Herbert Brenon's insistence on realism, fidelity of detail, and authentic locales.

With cast's and crew's adrenaline coursing, Brenon assembled his own Foreign Legion on this American Sahara, amid 150-foot-high dunes, scorching sun, and howling wind. Among the nearly 2,000 extras hired to play legionnaires and Arabs were representatives of 18 different countries, many of whom were bona fide ex-legionnaires. Seventeen freight trains hauled camels, horses, mules, equipment, and supplies from Los Angeles to Yuma, from there transported by truck across plank roads out into the desert. Location shooting commenced in March 1926 and ended three months later. By then it was apparent that *Beau Geste* would be Paramount's most prestigious project of the year, costing an almost unprecedented $900,000 to produce.[50]

The production values, cinematography, and direction are near-perfect. Julian Fleming's towering recreation of Fort Zinderneuf, isolated like a tiny island in the midst of an immense sea of sand, is an impressive centerpiece. J. Roy Hunt's location photography offers much in the way of pictorial beauty; especially remarkable are his panoramic compositions of mounted legionnaires winding their way across baked sands in long shot, and of Digby wandering off over billowing dunes in silhouette against an awakening sky. The spectacular battle scenes, with hordes of Arab marauders closing in on the fort, and the legionnaires' desperate stand in the desert are well mounted and forcefully underscored by an oppressive motif of stifling, sweltering heat.[51]

Not that those scenes were easily obtained. Neil Hamilton remembers:

> One of my favorite moments in the film was when the fort was attacked by the foe. There was Ronnie and I and twenty men inside, defending it. Attacking were one thousand five hundred horses and riders. The day started and finally, when the sun was exactly right and the clouds were exactly in the right position, you could see in the entire one-hundred-eighty-degrees view of the horizon little specks way in the distance. As they converged on the fort, they were recognizable as riders. It was an absolutely magnificent sight. The desert was black with them, and finally they got to within an eighth of a mile of the fort, and Brenon was seized by a stroke of genius. He picked up his megaphone and shouted, "For every man that makes a good fall during the firing of the rifles, an extra ten-dollar check!" So they came closer and closer and when they were within one thousand feet of the fort, the signal was given for us to fire. And the twenty-two men including Ronnie and me inside the fort fired, and one thousand five hundred men fell *dead* in the desert. They couldn't use one *inch* of film.
>
> And then Ronnie started to laugh, and he laughed so hard I thought he was going to lose his eyeballs. The whole day's work was ruined, and there was nothing else we could do except some little shots around the inside of the fort, but even then, each time we would start, Ronnie would break up into screams of laughter to the intense disgust of Herbert Brenon.
>
> The next day, once only twelve men had been told to fall when we shot, the entire thing was set up again, and went off perfectly until we had fired and they had fallen off and Ronnie just exploded into hopeless laughter again and ruined the whole thing. It took us about three days to get that shot. Brenon finally said something dreadful to him like, "If you laugh tomorrow I'm going to drag you out and have all those one thousand five hundred horses run over you!"[52]

What finally rises above the clamor of the action sequences is the simplicity and strength of Herbert Brenon's direction, which skillfully weaves the great themes of brotherly love, unswerving loyalty, and self-sacrifice against a backdrop of grim, elemental forces — sand, sun, wind, and heat. This elevates a simple mystery-adventure to epic proportions.

Beau Geste boasts one of the most impressive supporting casts ever assembled for a silent picture. As the sadistic Lejaune, Noah Beery gives one of the most chilling "dirty-dog" performances of his career. His finest moment comes when he whips his exhausted troops to battle pitch just before the Arabs mount their final whirlwind assault on the fort. He forces them to sing the Legion's Marching Song and then orders them to "laugh —

you jolly carefree swine! Let the Arabs know we're awake and merry and still all here!" Smiles are forced through gritted teeth, then succeeded by a roar of infectious laughter, while the commandant bellows fiercely with the anger and laughter of a madman. Fine, virile, vicious stuff. William Powell (off-screen one of Ronald Colman's closest friends) offers a bravura character study of the slimy stool-pigeon Boldini. Caught in the barracks trying to steal the elusive jewel from Beau's sash, he is held over a table by the enraged recruits with his arms outstretched, while swords are pierced through his hands. Pop-eyed, screaming, and sweating in a tight close-up, Powell is unforgettable. Victor McLaglen and Donald Stuart score a hit in comic-relief roles as American recruits Hank and Buddy. Neil Hamilton (veteran of many earlier D.W. Griffith pictures) and Ralph Forbes (an English actor making his American screen debut) are capable and determined as the younger Gestes, but their heroics are so overshadowed by Colman's presence that their performances appear to lack the inspiration the parts call for. Simply stated, Colman stole the works.

Beau Geste was in every way Ronald Colman's greatest personal triumph of the twenties, and the most magnificent of his silent films. It brought recognition of his artistry and versatility as an actor, and firmly established his position as one of the top male stars in Hollywood. The casting of Colman as Beau Geste was both perfect and natural, almost an inherent necessity. Described in the novel as an enigmatic, incurable romantic possessing "remarkable physical beauty, mental brilliance, irresistible charm, stubborn determination, and the reckless courage of a youthful d'Artagnan,"[53] the character not only fit the star's on-screen image but was also the embodiment of many of Colman's own personal values and moral precepts. Colman here for the first time presents a fully realized portrait of "the man who lives by 'the code,'"[54] whose principles of duty and unswerving loyalty prompt him to sacrifice his very honor to preserve untarnished a lady's reputation. Colman's bittersweet performance moves audiences and tugs at the heart strings because his sacrifices are so "quiet, personal, and unsung,"[55] and because of the restrained intensity and inherent nobility the actor brought to the role. The aura of wistfulness, loneliness, and melancholy, first developed to a finely honed edge in *The Dark Angel*, became a staple in *Beau Geste* as Colman forged the image with which audiences would forever associate him, and from which he would rarely depart for the next 20 years. Never again would his legions of fans expect of a Colman picture the happy ending almost obligatory in other Hollywood productions. Colman *was* Beau Geste; he made the character live with such subtlety and sensitivity that Beau remains one of the most vividly remembered and best-loved heroes of all silent cinema.

An immediate smash hit with the public, *Beau Geste* was hailed by many critics as one of the finest action pictures of all time as well as one

of the best silent films ever made. As the forerunner of scores of similar pictures, it is arguably the greatest Foreign Legion film ever produced; the
passage of time has done nothing to dim its electrifying, timeless appeal.
One of the top ten money-makers of the silent era, it was awarded a
prestigious *Photoplay* Gold Medal in 1927, and one can only imagine how
Colman and the picture would have fared had the industry's Academy
Awards become an institution just one year sooner.

Colman made the film on loan-out to Paramount, and once again his
shrewd producer had demanded, and obtained, a special credit line for his
star which read "By Arrangement with Samuel Goldwyn." When the critics
praised Colman as highly as the picture, Goldwyn realized that the actor
was now a *very* major box-office attraction in his own right, and quickly
made the decision never again to lend his most valuable property to other
studios. *Beau Geste* was *the* turning point in Colman's career: the star had
suddenly become a meteor.

When William Wellman filmed a superb talkie version for Paramount
in 1939, with Gary Cooper, Ray Milland, Robert Preston, and Brian
Donlevy heading the cast, he paid tribute to the power of the original by
shooting an almost scene-for-scene remake. Cooper made a charming Beau,
but his otherwise excellent performance lacked Colman's innate strength.[56]
The 1966 rendition, which starred an inept Guy Stockwell, was a monumen-
tally inferior travesty, while *The Last Remake of Beau Geste*, released in 1977
with Marty Feldman and Ann-Margret, was played strictly for laughs.

The Winning of Barbara Worth

1926. *Production:* Samuel Goldwyn, Inc. *Distribution:* United Artists Corpora-
tion. *Producer:* Samuel Goldwyn. *Director:* Henry King. *Screenplay:* Frances Marion
(from the novel by Harold Bell Wright). *Cinematographers:* George S. Barnes, Gregg
Toland. *Special Effects:* Ned Mann. *Art Director:* Carl Oscar Borg. *Location
Manager:* Ray Moore. *Titles:* Rupert Hughes. *Film Editor:* Viola Lawrence. *Musical
Score:* Ted Henkel. 9 reels (8,757 feet). *Los Angeles Premiere:* October 14, 1926. *New
York Premiere:* November 28, 1926.
Cast: Ronald Colman (Willard Holmes), Vilma Banky (Pioneer Woman and
Barbara Worth), Charles Lane (Jefferson Worth), Paul McAllister (The Seer), E.J.
Ratcliffe (James Greenfield), Gary Cooper (Abe Lee), Clyde Cook (Tex), Erwin
Connelly (Pat Mooney), Sam Blum (Horace Blanton), Edwin Brady (Cowboy),
William Patton (Little Rosebud), Fred Esmelton (George Cartwright).

The Winning of Barbara Worth was shot in Nevada's barren Black Rock
Desert. Reuniting Ronald Colman with Vilma Banky and director Henry
King, it depicts the settling of California's Imperial Valley and the vast irrigation project which harnessed the Colorado River and diverted its waters
into the arid California desert.

Against a grim and desolate landscape, a young pioneer woman (Vilma Banky) buries her husband beside their Conestoga wagon in the unconquered California desert. She and her little daughter struggle ahead on foot, into the teeth of a blinding sandstorm. A merciless scourging by the screaming wind, and then a lull. The mother, too, has perished in the sand, but rancher Jefferson Worth (Charles Lane) and his hired hands find the little girl and take her with them.

Years later, in Rubio City, Jefferson Worth initiates a land reclamation project to make the desert bloom into a fertile paradise — the dream of his lovely adopted daughter, Barbara Worth (Miss Banky in her principal role). New York financier James Greenfield (E.J. Ratcliffe) arrives to build a new empire with his foster son, Willard Holmes (Colman), the engineer who is to head the enterprise. At a banquet thrown in honor of the Easterners, Abe Lee, one of Worth's chief surveyors (Gary Cooper in his starring debut), casts a disapproving glance at Holmes when the newcomer begins to court Miss Worth, whom Lee is determined to marry.

The engineering expedition begins the following morning. Food, water, supplies, and equipment are dragged across the desert by 20-mule teams. Their goal: the untamed Colorado River, and the construction of a gateway through which the waters of the Colorado can reach thirsty soil. The town of Kingston is built and still more homesteaders move westward, carrying with them life and hope and energy. Finally, Barbara and Jefferson Worth watch their dream come true as water begins to pour through the irrigation canal at dawn. The project is a success, and Barbara rewards Holmes with a kiss as Abe Lee watches with increasing jealousy.

Now the unscrupulous Greenfield, a man with an insatiable thirst for gold, plots to take the territory for himself and takes control of the King's Basin Land and Irrigation Company. Disregarding the probability that the river might eventually rise and flood Kingston, he refuses to reinforce the gateway, causing panic among the townspeople. Holmes returns from the desert, finds the entire settlement moving toward new land, and discovers that his foster father has fired all of Worth's men for spreading word of a flood. When Holmes insists that the gateway must be strengthened, Greenfield promptly fires him too.

At Jefferson Worth's month-old town of Barba, high up on a mesa, Worth's followers continue to regard him as the savior of the desert, but Greenfield has him right where he wants him, for he knows that Worth has fallen short of cash and cannot meet his next payroll. Holmes, snubbed by Miss Worth when Abe Lee tells her that the engineer is in league with Greenfield, intercedes on Worth's behalf and contacts George Cartwright, an influential New York banker (Fred Esmelton). Insisting that Cartwright can make millions and found a new empire, Holmes pleads with him to extend credit to Jefferson Worth. Meanwhile, in Barba, Greenfield's agents

The Winning of Barbara Worth: *Young Gary Cooper*, at top *(as Abe Lee), in one of his earliest film appearances, shows the naturalism that would make him a star. With Barbara Worth (Vilma Banky) and Willard Holmes (Ronald Colman);* bottom, *Vilma Banky entertains Ronald Colman at afternoon tea on location in the Nevada desert.*

incite the workers to riot for their pay, burn the town, and return to Kingston. Cartwright quickly pays Worth a visit and explains that Willard Holmes is his friend, not his enemy. It was Holmes who persuaded Cartwright to invest in the project and advance the necessary funds. When Worth learns that the men are threatening to torch Barba, he orders Abe Lee to race there with the payroll. Holmes insists on accompanying his rival, and they set out on a desperate ride across the mountains.

As the sun sinks behind the mountains, Greenfield's gang ambushes them in Devil's Canyon, in an attempt to steal the payroll. Lee is shot, but Holmes pulls him to safety, receiving a flesh wound in his left shoulder. They escape to Coyote Wells, where the wounded Lee hands the payroll over to Holmes, shakes his hand, and urges him to make the rest of the journey alone.

Nightfall at Barba, and no sign of Abe Lee. An angry, sullen mob rages out of control as Willard Holmes storms into town, hands the payroll over to Barbara Worth, and collapses from his wound after telling her that Abe Lee lies wounded at Coyote Wells. After Barbara dresses Holmes' wound, Lee is brought in on a stretcher. He tells her that he recognizes her love for him as that of a sister for a brother. Moments later, Barbara overhears Holmes telling Greenfield that he'll never ask her to marry him; she returns in despair to Lee's bedside before Holmes finishes his sentence: ". . . because she loves another man."

In the film's spectacular finale, a sudden cloudburst threatens the already weakened dam. Sandbagging efforts fail, the Colorado bursts its banks, and the gateway collapses. Sufficiently recovered from his wound, Holmes leads the men to Kingston in a heroic attempt to warn the ranchers and townspeople of the impending flood. The entire town slides and collapses into chaos; a mass exodus is reminiscent of the land-rush sequence in William S. Hart's *Tumbleweeds* (1925). The tornado of panic is in full fury, and many of the townspeople are whirled away like leaves before its breath.

Most of the flood victims reach Barba, where, the following morning, Willard Holmes exhorts them to further effort. "Our battle with the River has just begun," he shouts. "We've got to drive it back and keep it there!" After Barbara assures him of her love, Holmes rides off into the desert to redirect the Colorado into the valley, vowing to return for her once the fight is won.

Several years later, the glorious dream has become a glorious reality and a new empire blooms in the wilderness. Amid scenes of orange groves, vineyards, and thriving little cities, Willard and Barbara Holmes find happiness together.

"While companies like Biograph and American re-created the struggles of the early pioneers in the pitiless desert," film historian Kevin Brownlow points out, "the California desert was being settled all around them."[57] Sam Goldwyn, long eager to bring Harold Bell Wright's epic 1911 novel of desert reclamation, intrigue, and romance to the screen, purchased the film rights and dispatched director Henry King and location manager Ray Moore to northern Nevada, where they found the perfect site for location shooting: the Black Rock Desert, at an elevation of 6,000 feet, near the Idaho border. There, at a cost of almost $800,000, they constructed a camp which accommodated nearly 1,200 extras and technicians; drinking water had to be hauled in from 200 miles away.

> Art director Carl Oscar Borg drew up plans for the three towns that had to be built in the desert, and the Western Pacific Railroad built a spur line to the new city of Barbara Worth, Nevada (Barba, in the film)—based on El Centro, California. A vast tent city housed the extras, and a mess hall, bakery, and recreation center were built. . . . The fierce temperature changes—from 120 degrees during the day to freezing at night—were accompanied by baby tornadoes. One of these destroyed most of the motion picture town of Kingston, doing $10,000 worth of damage.[58]

After a three-month ordeal of desert filming, during which the company endeavored, with no particular success, to teach Vilma Banky how to speak proper English, the picture was completed; and audiences, welcoming this second teaming of Colman and Banky, made it an immediate box-office smash. Colman, however, became disgruntled when Goldwyn's publicity department began creating rumors of an off-screen romance between himself and Miss Banky, and both stars were said to have had misgivings about making a western. "You're wasting yourself here, Miss Worth," Holmes tells Barbara early on, "like an orchid in a bucket of sand." Many reviewers agreed, finding Miss Banky "essentially a hothouse flower,"[59] and Colman's polish and sophistication at odds with his rugged characterization. Recent screenings indicate that both judgments were unduly harsh. Gary Cooper scored an unexpected success as the gangling ranch hand who loves and loses Barbara Worth. Tall, lanky, and overpoweringly shy, the young cowpoke from Helena, Montana, had been working as an extra for some time before Henry King cast him as Abe Lee, a role in which he literally played himself. While rehearsing the scene in which he lies wounded in the desert, Cooper began to overplay until Colman gave him some advice based on experience: "Easy does it, old boy. Good scenes make good actors. Actors don't make a scene. My own feeling is that all you have to do is take a nap, and every woman who sees the picture is going to cry her eyes out!"[60] Cooper took Colman's suggestion to heart, became a star overnight, and launched a career which was to last for more than three decades. He often told interviewers in later years that the actor he most admired was Ronald Colman.

Romance and the box-office appeal of Colman and Banky made *Barbara Worth* one of the biggest hits of 1926, but its true place in film history lies in the fidelity of its documentary-like scenes of desert reclamation and the settling of the Imperial Valley. As Kevin Brownlow observes,

> The documentary reconstruction . . . is of such a high standard that it places the film on a level with the other Western epics, *The Covered Wagon* and *The Iron Horse*. But whereas those films were set in the nineteenth century, this is an epic of twentieth-century pioneering. The difficult transition between the Old West and the New is captured with fascinating fidelity, even though the exact date is smudged somewhat. How startling to see buckboards and prairie schooners sweeping through the desert, leaving in their wake an immobilized Model T Ford![61]

With superb and surprisingly mobile camerawork, George Barnes and Gregg Toland captured the construction of the dam, the building of new cities, the sowing of grain in newly fertile soil, and, of course, the catastrophic flood scene: carefully constructed in its montage and horrifyingly realistic in its impact, it at least rivaled, if it didn't surpass, the parting of the Red Sea in Cecil B. De Mille's *The Ten Commandments* (1923), and made *Barbara Worth* even more visually stunning.

The Night of Love

1927. *Production:* Samuel Goldwyn, Inc. *Distribution:* United Artists Corporation. *Producer:* Samuel Goldwyn. *Director:* George Fitzmaurice. *Screenplay:* Lenore J. Coffee (from "the famous old Spanish Dramatic Poem" by Pedro Calderón de la Barca, 1600–1681). *Cinematographers:* George S. Barnes, Thomas E. Brannigan. *Art Director:* Carl Oscar Borg. *Technical Director:* John K. Holden. *Titles:* Edwin Justus Mayer. *Film Editor:* Grant Whytock. 8 reels (7,440 feet). *Release Date:* January 24, 1927.

Cast: Ronald Colman (Montero), Vilma Banky (Princess Marie), Montagu Love (Bernardo, Duke de la Garda), Natalie Kingston (Dame Beatriz), Laska Winter (Gypsy Bride), Sally Rand (Gypsy Dancer), John George (Jester), Bynunsky Hyman, Gibson Gowland (Gypsy Bandits), William Tooker (Spanish Ambassador), Charles Holt (Grandee).

The Night of Love! The very title was enough to send countless millions of Ronald Colman's female fans flocking to theatres to see their handsome idol teamed for the third time with that vision of loveliness, Vilma Banky, in one of the most lavishly mounted costume romances of the twenties. This rousing melodrama of feudal passions, blood, and tears was given added box-office clout by an exotically costumed Ronald Colman portraying a Robin Hood–like avenger who swashbuckles his way into the heart of the fairest princess in the land.

Hollywood stills photographers were often skilled artists in their own right. Here, in a shot from The Night of Love, *the photographer captures not only the glamour of Ronald Colman and Vilma Banky, but also the classic romanticism of pre–Raphaelite painters.*

The setting is early seventeenth-century Spain, an age when the lord of the manor possessed unlimited powers over his vassals. Most notorious of these privileges was the dread *droit du Seigneur*—the cruel right of the nobleman to his subject's betrothed for the "first night."

Montero (Colman), an adventurous gypsy soldier of fortune, is about to wed his gypsy bride (Laska Winter) according to ancient custom, when Bernardo, Duke de la Garda (Montagu Love), raids the wooded encampment and claims his feudal prerogative—Montero's virgin bride.

"I'll send her back—tomorrow!" he thunders contemptuously as his mounted troopers disperse the enraged but powerless gypsies and disappear in a cloud of dust through the forest.

At the duke's castle, the panic-stricken bride seizes the nobleman's knife and chooses an honorable death by her own hand rather than accede to her host's lustful advances.

The duke keeps his word and returns Montero's bride to her own people the following morning. That night, the funeral over, a heartbroken

Montero thrusts his arm into the roaring flame of a campfire and promises a swift retaliation.

"I swear in this flame," he hisses grimly, dark eyes ablaze, "she shall be avenged—in blood and fire."

The hour of retribution approaches on the night the duke arrives at the castle with his own bride, the beautiful Princess Marie of France (Vilma Banky). Having planned an entirely different wedding night, Montero abducts the princess from the duke's very bedchambers and hauls her off in his arms, while his confederates—bloodthirsty ruffians all—hold the duke at bay and engage the castle forces in a massed battle on the grand stairway.

"I'll send her back—tomorrow!" cries Montero before he gallops off, with the duke's soldiers in hot pursuit.

At the remote castle stronghold of Montero and his robber band, perched high atop a barren aerie overlooking the sea, the swaggering bandit chieftain regards his new prize with mingled rage and laughter, and then sends for another prisoner—the disheveled duke.

"A toast, my Lord, to your bridal night—and mine!" he gloats. "And as the Duke claimed my bride," he explains, turning to the princess, "so I—the Lord of these mountains—claim you!"

"Take her—revenge yourself on *her*—" pleads the duke, begging on his knees that his own life be spared.

Montero has the simpering coward removed, then approaches his terrified princess with a studied air of hot-blooded triumph. The hour of vengeance is at hand.

"Tonight you are a Gypsy girl," he says, forcing her to kiss him, "and *I* am lord of the castle!"

Her protestations unheeded, Marie races to a large open window and, pausing but a moment, plunges to the sandy beach below. To her death? No, for this is a fairytale; at the moment, she is merely an unconscious and somewhat battered princess.

The next day, the duke is delivered to the steps of his own castle, his face branded with an eternal mark of shame, while Montero removes Princess Marie to a wooded refuge. Pity follows intitial resentment, until finally she learns to love her dashing bandit hero. Passionately.

". . .the night is sweet—and my heart is yielding," she tells him.

Unwillingly at first, she succumbs. They embrace. "Now I can never escape you!" she whispers.

"Now I can never let you go!" Montero replies.

And so it goes, in the misty dreamworld of romance. But like all love stories, this one is beset by obstacles, and the lovers must part, for the princess is not free to love Montero. Though her desires and her heart tell her otherwise, she knows she must return—to the duke.

"And we who have found each other—must lose each other!" she sobs, still clinging to his embrace. "But my heart remains with you forever."

Even bandits are prompted to do the gentlemanly thing—especially when they are impersonated by Ronald Colman. Honor-bound, he takes her back.

"No—no—I cannot let you go—" he pleads, kissing her cheek as they stand on the castle steps.

"I shall always need you—in my heart," she sighs, composing herself; "give me strength not to falter—not to turn back." Honor binds a woman too.

Morning comes, but the heart of the beautiful lady is dark with despair. Consigned to a dank dungeon cell, she awaits her love, whom the duke has lured to the castle. And awaiting Montero's effort to rescue his beloved is a fiendish death-trap.

Under cover of darkness, Montero stealthily makes his way to the dungeon and frees the princess. But the trap is sprung, and, after a fierce struggle with the castle guards, he is captured and handed over to a gloating villain, who has prepared his hated rival's fate with grandiose viciousness— torture followed by death at the stake.

News of their chieftain's capture brings gypsies and peasants swarming to the castle. But they are powerless to help Montero; he struggles help- lessly while the fagots are lit and smoke envelops his body.

Just when all seems lost, Princess Marie effects a plan of her own. High atop the castle ramparts is a statue of the Blessed Virgin. Changing places with it and placing its crown on her own head, the princess raises her arm as a sign to stop the vengeful atrocity below.

"A miracle!" gypsies and soldiers alike cry out, falling to their knees. "Let the Blessed Virgin speak—let her say who is guilty in the eyes of Heaven!"

The duke is denounced, of course, and in the pitched battle which follows, Montero's massed followers free him from the funeral pyre just in time, storm the castle, and slaughter the duke, clearing the way for the two lovers to be reunited—in a luminous close-up—for the final embrace.

Need we doubt that they lived happily ever after?

With sizable box-office returns pouring in from *The Dark Angel* and *The Winning of Barbara Worth*, Ronald Colman and Vilma Banky were both riding a crest of popularity, so Samuel Goldwyn shrewdly rushed *The Night of Love,* the first of their three costumers, into production. Colman and Banky were never more appealing together, and the added bonus of stun- ning visuals and lustrous production values automatically assured their pro- ducer another smash hit.[62]

Deeply bronzed by the Hollywood sun and the very picture of muscular health as the dark gypsy lover, Colman was as strong and virile as the story itself. With long, dark sideburns and longer, curly hair, and sporting a tight black outfit with studded vest, bandana, and wide-brimmed hat, he made a dashing bandit indeed, rather reminiscent of the sartorial splendor showcased the same year by Douglas Fairbanks in *The Gaucho*. Cavorting through sun-drenched woods and dimly lit castles with a decidedly Fairbanksian flair, Colman performed some agile swashbuckling and displayed a towering range of emotions—from rage and fury to gentle love-play.

Typically Hollywood, of course, was the casting of reserved Englishman Ronald Colman as a swashbuckling gypsy, and his Hungarian leading lady as a matchless French beauty. Colman had been widely touted after *The White Sister* as "the new Valentino," and now that Valentino was dead Goldwyn decided to continue teaming Colman and Banky in a series of costume romances. The fact that Miss Banky had co-starred with Valentino in *The Eagle* and *Son of the Sheik* did little to lessen Colman's surprise when he suddenly found himself and John Gilbert hailed as the Great Lover's successors. His diffidence and essentially private nature convinced him that he was miscast as a passionate, extroverted Latin lover, solely on the strength of his dark physical appearance. But, as Joe Franklin perceptively observes:

> Even when he was playing a gypsy outlaw or a fiery lover, he always somehow contrived to remain suave, debonair—and above all, polite and well-mannered. And if this sometimes lessened the conviction of the performance he was giving . . . well, that was amply compensated for by the charm and grace he exuded.[63]

But even if Colman thought himself miscast in hot-tempered Latin-lover roles, audiences didn't, and the costume spectacle became his forte for the next few years.

With a cataract of golden hair streaming down over her shoulders, Vilma Banky once again proved herself Ronald Colman's perfect match. She was called upon to personify a glamorous romantic ideal, and if this was a somewhat limited dramatic task, it cannot be denied that she made the most of her luxurious gowns, cameo features, and radiant beauty.

One is hard put to recall a more blackguardly villain than the superb Montagu Love, who rounds out the cast with a sinister presence as enjoyable as it is menacing.

The film was directed with considerable energy by George Fitzmaurice, veteran of no fewer than five earlier Colman pictures, and little expense was spared to make the production as visually exciting as possible. The pictorial highlights of the film are the lavish wedding feast held by the duke in honor of his young bride and the brilliantly mounted burning-at-the-stake finale, courtesy of art director Carl Oscar Borg and cinematographer

George S. Barnes. The thousands of extras gaping at looming shadows and soaring flames as Montero is strapped to the stake, and the excellent long shots of massed rebels storming the castle gates, are equally impressive and produce a smooth, strong narrative that never lacks in dash and speed.

An appropriate blend of humor persistently enlivens the heroics and derring-do, giving the picture a lighthearted quality akin to that of Douglas Fairbanks' delightful *Robin Hood* (1922). The results are at once neat, symmetrical, and pleasing. When Princess Marie returns to the castle after her night of love with Montero, for instance, she runs full tilt into one of the duke's full-fledged orgies, complete with assorted scantily clad mistresses, much groping, and an erotic slave dance. When the duke announces that he will bestow a prize upon the best dancer, he is asked what the prize will be.

"I am the prize!" he booms lecherously.

If the parallels with *Robin Hood* are striking, the suggestion of a later and finer swashbuckler is even more pronounced, for the themes of honor, sacrifice, and renunciation weave their way through *The Night of Love* just as they do ten years later in *The Prisoner of Zenda*. In both films, Colman renounces the princess he loves for a clearly defined mandate of honor; in both pictures, the princess belongs to another man, and the sacrifice must be made. Acting upon the code by which he has been reared, his choice of action is clear. All this is etched in his face as he bids Princess Marie farewell on the steps of the duke's castle—he could keep her, but he won't.[64]

Not surprisingly, the theme of *droit du Seigneur*—rather racy for 1927—was immediately attacked by the censors, who took the issue to court, alleging that it was "salacious and entirely too intimate for presentation to young people as entertainment."[65] Fortunately, however, the judge decided that the theme was treated appropriately, and ruled in favor of Goldwyn.

The critics, while praising the film's visual merits and the charm of Mr. Colman and Miss Banky, carped that a certain predictability in the plot structure weakened the overall dramatic impact, and that the *droit du Seigneur,* while a medieval reality, was a mere plot contrivance designed to unite the lovers, separate them for a while, and then reunite them for the final romantic clinch. What they failed to perceive was that the dauntless heroes, virtuous heroines, and cloak-and-dagger villains who inhabit the realm of dreams are never unreal, but merely enhanced versions of an elemental reality. *The Night of Love* served up ample portions of unadulterated escapism, and it was never for a moment to be doubted that the delicate princess and her tempestuous gypsy lover were destined to be united forever.

By teaming Colman and Banky, Sam Goldwyn had hit a box-office jackpot. It was by now a certainty that more of their on-screen magic would follow, for as *Photoplay* magazine rejoiced, "What a combination, those two."[66] Colman was determined that the combination remain on screen only, and he objected to his producer's persistence in publicizing the star's supposed off-screen romance with Vilma Banky. Good press or not, Colman found the matter the height of bad taste, but, as he told director Fitzmaurice, "It's no use making Sam see reason when he has a publicity gimmick all flared up inside of him."[67] Six years later, similar tactics led to an irreparable break and finally drove Colman from the Goldwyn studio.

When asked by an interviewer whether his lovemaking in *The Night of Love* would be as tempestuous as in his previous two pictures with Miss Banky, the shy Britisher gave a response as curiously reticent as it was quick and ready: "We have learned that there is always something new about love making and that no two people in love ever behaved precisely the same."[68]

The Magic Flame

1927. *Production:* Samuel Goldwyn, Inc. *Distribution:* United Artists Corporation. *Producer:* Samuel Goldwyn. *Director:* Henry King. *Screenplay:* Bess Meredyth (from the play *König Harlekin* by Rudolf Lothar). *Cinematographer:* George S. Barnes. *Art Director:* Carl Oscar Borg. *Continuity:* June Mathis. *Titles:* George Marion, Jr., Nellie Revell. *Assistant Director:* Robert Florey. *Technical Advisor:* Captain Marco Elter. *Film Editor:* Viola Lawrence. *Theme Song:* Sigmund Spaeth. 9 reels (8,308 feet). *Premiere:* August 26, 1927. *Release Date:* September 18, 1927. No print known to have survived.

Cast: Ronald Colman (Tito, the Clown and Cassati, the Count), Vilma Banky (Bianca, the Aerial Artist), Augustino Borgato (The Ringmaster), Gustav von Seyffertitz (Duke Umberto, the Chancellor), Harvey Clarke (de Bono, the Aide), Shirley Palmer (The Wife), Cosmo Kyrle Bellew (The Husband), George Davis (The Utility Man), André Cheron (The Manager), Vadim Uraneff (The Visitor), Meunier-Surcouf (The Sword Swallower), Paoli (The Weight Thrower), David Mir (The Manicurist).

Designed, like *The Night of Love*, to further exploit the exotic charm of Ronald Colman and Vilma Banky, *The Magic Flame* was an artfully contrived costume romance which featured its stars as circus performers caught in a web of intrigue and mistaken identity while touring one of those mythical kingdoms so popular with audiences in the twenties. This plot provided generous doses of suspense, thrills, masterful photography, and gorgeous sets and costumes, but what brought the fans flocking to the box office was the added attraction of Ronald Colman in his first dual role.

The circus has arrived in the land of Illyria, where a new king is soon to be crowned. With the wagons and the tents comes beautiful trapezist Bianca (Miss Banky), who soon attracts the lustful, monocled eye of the wicked Count Cassati (Colman). The "count," it seems, is none other than the crown prince himself, heir apparent to the Illyrian throne. In love with faithful, humble Tito the Clown (Colman again), Bianca spurns the count's lecherous advances. Maddened by her disdain and determined to make her his own, Cassati entices Bianca to his hotel under false pretenses. But before he can ravish her, Bianca saves the night and preserves her virtue by demonstrating just how handy acrobatic skills can be. In a flash she's out the window and into a conveniently located tree. An impressive lady. Tito, meanwhile, rushes to the rescue and kills the count by tossing him out the aforementioned window into the sea below. Finding himself in a serious predicament, Tito capitalizes on his striking resemblance to the late villain and accompanies the Illyrian noblemen to the royal palace, posing as the heir presumptive. For the moment, masquerading as a crown prince appears less disagreeable than being executed for the murder of one. Bianca learns that the count/prince is safe and about to be crowned. Drawing the obvious conclusion that the evil one has slain her beloved Tito, she conceals a revolver in a bouquet of flowers and proceeds to the palace to assassinate the new king. At the last moment Tito reveals his identity to her, but their troubles have just begun, for the power-hungry chancellor (icily sinister Gustav von Seyffertitz) has seen through the deception and plans to arrest the imposter on a charge of murder. Tito takes up the call to action, and plays it with a brave tongue and a swift, unmatched sword. Coolly he informs the chancellor that it would be indeed difficult to prove that the real king was never crowned. The two lovers finally make good their escape and return forthwith to the circus, joyful that they are reunited at last.

Sporting sumptuous Goldwyn production values as well as stunning performances by Ronald Colman and Vilma Banky, *The Magic Flame* demonstrated its audience appeal immediately and quickly became the most successful of the team's pictures to date. The critics accorded it smashing reviews which lavished praise on the glittering costumes, Carl Oscar Borg's looming sets, and George Barnes' heavily shadowed German Expressionist visuals (which won an Academy Award nomination). Director Henry King, working with Colman for the last time, deftly juggled alternating moods of romance, melodrama, pathos, and comedy against both circus and palace settings; his style and skill made *The Magic Flame* arguably the finest of the five films Colman and Banky made together.

In the role of Bianca, Vilma Banky was delightfully energetic, creating a character markedly different from her earlier, more reserved portrayals. Once again she soared straight into the hearts of movie-goers everywhere. As *Photoplay* exulted, she "surpasses all her previous work as Bianca. She is extraordinarily lovely."[69]

A full decade before his most famous dual role in *The Prisoner of Zenda*, Ronald Colman acquitted himself with distinction, dash, and verve in this one. Early on, Henry King decided he wanted to emphasize subtle facial dissimilarities between the two characters. The director recalls:

We couldn't put wool in his cheeks because that would have made him look ridiculous, but I suggested we have some teeth made to put over his own, just to give him a different expression. He thought it was a good idea, so I sent him down to a dentist and they took a cast and made him some that gave him a tough kind of look. Then Frances Marion saw him with these on, and she and Sam couldn't believe we had done this to one of the handsomest men in pictures. I got into an awful hassle with them. Ronnie liked the teeth, he felt they gave him a character to work with. Anyway, they went on hassling for so long that we did away with the teeth and changed his moustache a bit instead.[70]

Thus the count sported a longer and somewhat curled moustache and cut a far more swaggering figure than his adversary Tito, whose face, with a minimum of contrasting makeup, appeared sad, sympathetic, and less well nourished. It was in the part of the prince's double that Colman really took off; gone was Tito's reticence, replaced by the virile dash and swashbuckling heroics with which audiences had come to associate the actor during this phase of his career.

Oddly enough, reviewers for the most part failed to discuss the handling of what must have been a crucial scene, in which the clown vanquishes the count. A regrettable oversight in any case, but all the more unfortunate here, since the picture is lost, unavailable for reappraisal. We shall perhaps never know whether superimpositions and split-screen techniques were employed, or if the use of a double, careful camera angles, and skillful editing conveyed the illusion. Mordaunt Hall, at least, called attention to Colman's use of heavy makeup in one of the film's early scenes: "At first the features of Ronald Colman are hidden under putty and grease-paint, but this Clown sits at a mirror and gradually wipes off the disguise until the well-known physiognomy of the popular player is revealed."[71]

Of the two roles, Colman far preferred that of the wicked, monocled count to that of the sensitive lover Tito, but indicated in interviews that he didn't particularly relish playing either part. It was evident that he was losing interest in the costume melodrama. While he recognized that he owed much of his position at the box office to the popularity of such undemanding assignments, he was already beginning to dream of more challenging roles.

Two Lovers

1928. *Production:* Samuel Goldwyn, Inc. *Distribution:* United Artists Corporation. *Producer:* Samuel Goldwyn. *Director:* Fred Niblo. *Screenplay:* Alice D.G. Miller (from the novel *Leatherface: A Tale of Old Flanders* by the Baroness Emmuska Orczy). *Cinematographer:* George S. Barnes. *Art Director:* Carl Oscar Borg. *Assistant Director:* H. Bruce Humberstone. *Titles:* John Colton. *Film Editor:* Viola Lawrence.

Musical Score: Dr. Hugo Riesenfeld. *Songs:* Wayland Axtell ("Grieving"), Abner Silver ("Lenora"). 9 reels (8,706 feet silent; 8,817 feet with musical score and synchronized sound effects). *Release Date:* March 22, 1928.

Cast: Ronald Colman (Mark Van Rycke), Vilma Banky (Lenora De Vargas), Noah Beery (The Duke of Azar), Nigel de Brulier (William, Prince of Orange), Virginia Bradford (Gretel, the Tavern Girl), Helen Jerome Eddy (Donna Inez, the Duenna), Paul Lukas (Don Ramon De Linea, the Spanish Captain), Fred Esmelton (Meinherr Charles Van Rycke, the High Bailiff of Ghent), Eugenie Besserer (Madame Clémence Van Rycke, His Wife), Harry Allen (Jean), Marcella Daly (Marda), Scotty Mattraw (Innkeeper), Lydia Yeamans Titus (Innkeeper's Wife). .

The land of mist and dreams revisited.

In the days when dauntless heroes beleaguered enchanted castles and did battle with giants, the byways of a luckless country lie silent as a tomb, save for the unending tramp and rattle of the hosts of an alien conqueror. The year is 1572, and the once-free land of Flanders suffers under the yoke of Spain. Blood dogs and butchers roam the countryside in search of William, Prince of Orange, leader of the Flemish. But suddenly, across the conquerors' path sweeps the shadow of a dark and mysterious figure— "Leatherface," protector of the Prince of Orange, in whose heart beats the spirit of Flanders, defying the Spanish presence.

His Magnificence, the Governor of Flanders and Duke of Azar (Noah Beery), hatches a plot to capture William and the elusive Leatherface and complete the Spanish triumph by crushing the Flemish resistance. The cruel "Spanish Butcher" has summoned his niece to Ghent. Fresh from a convent in Seville comes the "Flower of Spain," Lenora De Vargas (Vilma Banky), little suspecting her scheming uncle's ruthless plan. For he has arranged her marriage to the son of the High Bailiff of Ghent—ostensibly to cement relations between the victors and the vanquished, but in reality to ferret out the secret whereabouts of William and Leatherface and arrange their downfall. Her protestations ignored, affairs of state conspire to turn the lovely, tearful noblewoman into a spy.

Enter Mark Van Rycke (Ronald Colman), son of the High Bailiff, stoically unperturbed at the prospect of wedding and bedding a beautiful Spaniard, for, after all, the union will bring the blessing of peace and safety to his people—or so he has been led to believe.

"Some men die for their country!" he shrugs with demurest innocence, a mischievous twinkle in his eye. "I'll marry for mine!"

The Bailiff's son and the Flower of Spain meet for the first time at a formal betrothal reception in the great hall of the Kasteel—he regarding his intended's matchless form and elegance with undisguised approval, she responding with a frosty reserve.

The nuptial knot is soon tied, but trouble besets the wedding night.

"Be just a little patient with me tonight," a sorrowful bride beseeches

Ronald Colman and Vilma Banky became enormously popular in a series of costume romances. This still from Two Lovers *suggests why: they were both actors of unquestioned attractiveness.*

her new husband. "Everything is so strange. Can there be happiness without love? I don't love you—you don't love me—"

"You're wrong! As it happens—I do love you—"

"Please—please don't speak to me of love," she pleads, backing away. "Yes, I am your wife. You have rights. Take them!"

"I don't want rights," he replies gently; "I want your love!"

But Lenora tells him that she loves another—Don Ramon De Linea, captain of the Spanish forces which occupy Ghent, the dread "Blood Dog" charged with the destruction of the Prince of Orange and Leatherface.

Moved deeply by this news, Van Rycke turns to leave the bedchamber, pausing but a moment to say with tender understanding, "Poor Flower of Spain! It wasn't fair of them—to force you into this."

With this sensitive gesture, he has earned her respect; touched, the lady weeps for the gentleman she cannot love.

Later that night, in a dimly lit garret above the Three Weavers' Tavern, the mysterious hooded avenger known as Leatherface kills the vicious Don Ramon (Paul Lukas) in a bloody skirmish, escaping through a window just seconds before the captain's troops arrive on the scene. Before he dies,

Blood Dog gasps that Leatherface has been wounded. The identification and apprehension of this Renaissance Zorro is thus assured.

In safety afterwards, his hand and arm bloodied, Leatherface removes his sinister leather hood and reveals himself to be—Mark Van Rycke!

Still later, in a secret cellar deep below the Van Rycke estate, Leatherface meets with a throng of adherents and produces a secret list of 2,000 loyal men of Flanders, armed and ready to mount an attack on the Spanish. But Lenora has discovered the sliding panel which leads through a black, meandering passageway to the concealed basement and, hidden in the ghostly darkness, overhears all that is said. After the rebels disperse, she removes the incriminating document from its hiding place behind a loose stone in the masonry and hurriedly returns to her second-floor bedroom. There she is startled to find her husband already awaiting her.

"Why do you fear me so?" he asks. "If you would only believe—I love you."

"If it's true that you love me," she replies, her face ashen, "allow me to go to Brussels and get permission to return to Spain."

A saddened Van Rycke kisses the hand of the wife he has never known and smiles gravely.

"A coach will be waiting for you an hour after sunrise."

Torn between two loyalties and weeping softly as she makes her decision, Lenora attempts to smuggle a note to her uncle. But the ever-watchful Leatherface waylays the messenger and retrieves the letter.

That morning, Van Rycke, now fully aware of his wife's duplicity, insists on accompanying her to Brussels. But in a beautifully lit sequence flooded by rain and lightning, the pair meet with a road accident when their elegantly appointed carriage loses a wheel. Mounting one of the horses and spurring it into action, they race off into the night.

Seeking refuge at a nearby inn, Van Rycke is captured by the cunning duke and his henchmen. Exposed as Leatherface, he is beaten savagely, yet despite the mobbing and the mauling to which he is subjected, he stalwartly refuses to reveal the prince's whereabouts.

In the early hours of dawn, Van Rycke—dusty, dirty, and bedraggled—is paraded through the streets of Ghent by Spanish troops and hauled off to a monster of a medieval fortress, where a torture chamber awaits him. But Lenora, having witnessed her husband's brutal treatment and by now realizing the justice of the Flemish cause, acts with a quick and ready resolve and spreads the alarm. There is but one hope: the Kasteel drawbridge leading from the swamp is always unguarded. If only she can get there to lower it before the rebels attack at dawn!

Meanwhile, back in the torture chamber, the Spanish Butcher hisses through tightly compressed lips: "Put him to death! First make him speak!"

As Van Rycke is strapped and whipped and thrashed, thousands of armed rebels — brandishing knives, cutlasses, sledgehammers, swords, and clubs — come storming through the swamps.

Lenora, having slipped into the castle, tries to lower the drawbridge, but the chains won't budge. As expected in the best suspense sequences, however, of course they finally give at the last possible moment, just when we are almost obliged to abandon our hero to his fate. Her hands bleeding from the powerful chains, Lenora lowers the bridge. The rebels pour into the castle, and the wild melee begins.

Van Rycke, his back lacerated, is freed to confront the seething, defeated governor. Hastily issuing a proclamation which orders the permanent removal of all Spaniards from Flanders, a determined Van Rycke hands the document defiantly to the duke for his signature. The insurgents — to a man — hoist their swords in jubilation.

And now, in a quiet corner by himself, the sad and lonely patriot who has saved a kingdom gazes wistfully out a window at the carriage which is preparing to convey his wife safely to the sea, and thence to her Spanish homeland.

At this point, William of Orange (Nigel de Brulier) enters with the news that their long-sought victory has been made possible by a Spaniard. "That Spaniard is now in our hands and begs permission to remain in Ghent," he tells his savior. "The decision rests with you!"

Relief and joy mingle as Van Rycke beholds "the Spaniard" and recognizes his wife. That Lenora loves her husband at last is reflected in her eyes. Drawing her cut and bleeding hands to his lips, he embraces her in his strong, yet gentle, arms, as her upraised face meets his in the final lustrous close-up.

For the screen team of Colman and Banky, 1927 had been a banner year and *Two Lovers* followed quickly on the heels of their two enormous box-office successes, *The Night of Love* and *The Magic Flame*. By 1928, both Colman and Banky were drawing top salaries, and as neither was satisfied sharing top billing, Goldwyn announced that *Two Lovers* would be the last picture in which the team would appear together.

As Colman told an interviewer that year:

> There's always the possibility, you know, that our work may become mechanical. Perhaps it is now. We are so thoroughly familiar with each other's reaction to any situation a script may call for that quite unconsciously we may anticipate such reactions. We can't be certain that we're not playing scenes today quite in the manner we played certain scenes in *The Dark Angel*.[72]

In addition, Vilma Banky had recently married actor Rod La Rocque, forever ending the fantasy that the two great screen lovers were as inseparable off-screen as they were in front of the cameras. Goldwyn accordingly decided thereafter to feature Colman and Banky separately in only one picture a year, each teamed with a different partner.

And so an unusually extravagant budget—nearly a million dollars—was allocated for what would become the most elaborately costumed and possibly the best remembered of the romantic team's efforts together. In a shrewd publicity gimmick, Goldwyn had offered a prize of $2,500 to the public for a suitable story suggestion, and of the 40,000 entries which swamped the studio, the scenarists finally chose the Baroness Orczy's popular 1916 novel, *Leatherface*. And an ideal selection it was, for the leading roles were perfectly suited to the Colman-Banky mystique; the film's authentic sets, costumes, uniforms, and weapons, glittering cinematography by George S. Barnes, striking period atmosphere by art director Carl Oscar Borg, and vigorous direction by Fred Niblo made *Two Lovers* the perfect swashbuckling swan song for the greatest Hollywood love team of the twenties.[73]

Ronald Colman again proved himself a most accomplished and diverting swashbuckler, once more rivaling the great Fairbanks and demonstrating an athletic agility which bore no little resemblance to the earlier Niblo-directed costumer, *The Mark of Zorro* (1920).[74] Enlivening the gallantry and dashing heroics was the star's Fairbanksian sense of good-natured humor, shown to best effect when he is betrothed to the Flower of Spain in her villainous uncle's castle. Lenora is standing hidden behind the duke, in bridal raiment and white veil. Not seeing her, Van Rycke assumes that the lady who is to be his future bride is Lenora's duenna, the none-too-attractive Donna Inez (Helen Jerome Eddy). The duenna has seen him, too, and beams with undisguised pleasure.

"Calamity!" Van Rycke grimaces, whispering to his father. "Is *that* the Flower of Spain?"

Obviously bored, Van Rycke persists with several such remarks whispered out of the corner of his mouth, much to his parents' dismay, until, accepting Lenora's hand and seeing her finally for the first time, he beams broadly.

In the portrayal of tender solicitude for a radiant bride, Colman was very much in his element, bringing debonair charm and an obvious enjoyment to his fiery impersonation of the noblest of Flemish freedom fighters. But, as he modestly remarked to an interviewer, "The role was, let's be honest, superficial, but it *was* colorful and gave me, I suppose, a chance to demonstrate a shallow but highly theatrical virtuosity."[75]

Colman may not have believed his own publicity, but audiences did, and the critics accorded him high praise for his swashbuckling. Reviewers, however, were quick to point out that the story itself was on occasion a bit unbelievable. Mordaunt Hall commented that

> You might expect Leatherface to be slightly worn out after being beaten, tormented and then flogged, but it is to be presumed that this fellow is a glutton for punishment, and where other men might crumple up and faint, he struts into a room looking as fresh as if he had just had a cold plunge.[76]

Hall further observed that Miss Banky "appears to have been told to look as lovely as she possibly can. And she does."[77] For example, when Lenora arrives at the inn after galloping through a storm, she is drenched but unruffled, her hair remaining immaculate.

> Lenora is a girl of mettle, who only gives in when she hears the voice of Mr. Niblo via his megaphone. She works and works on the drawbridge, while the Flemish are swimming through the stagnant and none-too-inviting waters, and finally it gives a little, then a little more. What suspense! Will she be able to hold out until she has pulled the wheel around a couple more times? She does and then falls, white and beautiful, her dress torn but, thank heaven, her hair is not disarranged! It could not look more charming if she had walked out of a hairdresser's but an instant before.[78]

So although in spots the tale is none too credible, that is a fault only if we demand that a picture be an approximation of "reality." In the silent cinema of romance, the surface tensions and sinister goings on — bursting with masked avengers, sliding panels, and secret papers — are menacing and suspenseful because the viewer has entered the world of an enchanted fairytale, where the derring-do is always lighthearted, vile intriguers are always as despicable as Noah Beery, and both heroes and heroines always bounce back triumphant with a jaunty, determined spring to their step.

As a concession to the growing demand for talking pictures, *Two Lovers* was released with a synchronized musical soundtrack, sound effects, and two songs. The expense of such lavish accoutrements contributed heavily to the film's cost. But the results were worth it, for the Colman-Banky star quality and Goldwyn's sumptuous production values made "this latest hymn to romantic love"[79] one of the finest and best-received of all silent swashbucklers.

There were several successful Hollywood love teams in the twenties — including Charles Farrell and Janet Gaynor, John Gilbert and Greta Garbo — but none matched the popularity that Ronald Colman and Vilma Banky commanded in their five pictures together. In the thirties, only Errol Flynn and Olivia de Havilland would match their flair for sheer swashbuckling escapism.

The Rescue

1929. *Production:* Samuel Goldwyn, Inc. *Distribution:* United Artists Corporation. *Producer:* Samuel Goldwyn. *Director:* Herbert Brenon. *Screenplay:* Elizabeth

Meehan (from the novel by Joseph Conrad). *Cinematographer:* George S. Barnes. *Art Director:* William Cameron Menzies. *Assistant Director:* Ray Lissner. *Titles:* Katherine Hilliker, H.H. Caldwell. *Film Editors:* Marie Halvey, Katherine Hilliker, H.H. Caldwell. *Musical Score:* Dr. Hugo Riesenfeld. 9 reels (7,910 feet silent; 7,980 feet with musical score and synchronized sound effects). *Release Date:* January 13, 1929. No print known to have survived.

   Cast: Ronald Colman (Tom Lingard), Lily Damita (Lady Edith Travers), Alfred Hickman (Mr. Travers), Theodore von Eltz (Carter), John Davidson (Rajah Pata Hassim), Philip Strange (d'Alcacer), Bernard Siegel (Jorgensen), Sojin (Daman), Harry Cording (Belarab), Laska Winter (Immada), Duke Kahanamoku (Jaffir), Louis Morrison (Shaw), George Regas (Wasub), Christopher Martin (Tenga).

Colman's first post–Banky picture, as well as his last silent film, was *The Rescue,* Herbert Brenon's exotic adaptation of the 1920 novel by Joseph Conrad, which introduced to American audiences Sam Goldwyn's new discovery, French actress Lily Damita.

The tropic moon shines brightly on the waters of the Java coast, where English adventurer Tom Lingard (Colman) combs the shores of a thousand islands in his trading brig, the *Lightning.* When Pata Hassim, the Rajah of Wajo (John Davidson), is exiled after saving Lingard from hostile natives, the trader feels duty-bound to restore the rajah to his throne. But before they can mount their assault, a British yacht blunders onto the scene and runs aground. Fatefully stranded in the midst of what will soon be a dark theatre of war are Mr. Travers, a wealthy member of Parliament (Alfred Hickman), and his young wife, Edith (Miss Damita). When Lingard helps them to safety, Edith is attracted to the adventurer, while Travers takes an immediate dislike to him. Travers and one of his party are later seized and held captive in a native stockade. Upon Lingard falls the choice of saving them and destroying his own trading operation or allowing the natives their kill and fulfilling his promise to Hassim — the duty of a white man to his fellow countrymen or the unbreakable word of "King" Tom to a native chieftain. Lingard chooses to save Travers, and the film plunges headlong through a native uprising and a passionate affair between Lingard and Mrs. Travers, until finally the derelict tramp steamer carrying the rajah's loyal supporters is blown up, killing all aboard. A remorseful Lingard sends Edith back to her husband. The affair is over. Grim-faced, from the *Lightning* he watches Travers' yacht heading south into the blackness of the night.

   "Steer north," he commands.

The Rescue was filmed on and around Santa Cruz, off the Santa Barbara coast, where for three months the company coped with unenviable living conditions (primitive shacks shared with goats), persistently uncooperative weather, mounting production costs, and Herbert Brenon's broken ankle. Once the shooting was completed, Goldwyn quickly inserted a sequence of synchronized sound effects to meet the challenge of talking pictures and unleashed a publicity campaign designed to capitalize on the fact that no

Conrad novel had ever previously been transferred to the screen with any notable success. To the producer's surprise, critical response to this tale of the Java seas was lukewarm. Reviewers tended to complain that the story limped and was excessively ponderous, and that the predictable Hollywood triangle eventually smothered Conrad's original intentions. George Barnes' inspired cinematography, however, offered much in the way of pictorial beauty; dark, brooding, and doom-laden, it captured admirably the mystic grandeur so prevalent in Conrad's works. Though the author's deep philosophical concerns might be expected to impose almost insuperable limitations on a film director, Mordaunt Hall concluded that Herbert Brenon had "skillfully preserved the essence of the narrative . . . by more than a mere suggestion of the masterful writer."[80] But he noted that Lily Damita's elaborate attire and immaculate makeup were regrettable box-office concessions, considering the rough surroundings in which the drama was enacted.

Once again, Ronald Colman played a hero for whom the demands of love and duty are in perpetual conflict. In the balance hangs Captain Tom Lingard's affair of honor involving the throne of a Malayan prince. When he is forced to choose between love and duty, duty wins, as it always does in a Colman picture, and the lovers must go their separate ways. As *Photoplay* observed,

> Ronald Colman . . . is right out of the Conrad pattern, one that suffers deeply without any flamboyant emotion . . . The repressed acting of Colman makes the figure very real. . . . It isn't another *Beau Geste*, but director Herbert Brenon has brought out in Colman the same quality that characterized him in that earlier work.[81]

Mordaunt Hall added:

> Even though Ronald Colman may not answer Conrad's description of Tom Lingard, his performance is so earnest and sensitive that in spite of his coal-black hair, his clean-shaven chin and small mustache he is not only far from disappointing but he reflects the spirit of "King" Tom.[82]

The Rescue was a commercial failure, and made only a small profit. It had aspired to be both art and escapist entertainment, and wound up not completely fitting either category. Audiences ignored it, and the film quickly vanished into undeserved oblivion as a result of the advent of all-talking pictures. The public simply wouldn't attend a silent picture in 1929, when it could see something — anything — that squawked. Discriminating devotees who remember *The Rescue* consider it one of the most visually exciting of all late silents, containing one of Colman's most finely shaded performances, but, alas, it too has long since joined the swollen ranks of lost films.[83]

IV

Colman Crosses
the Sound Barrier —
The Goldwyn Talkies

"And just at that moment there came a whisper in Hollywood, no more than a whisper. It was a croaking voice from behind the silver screen, uttered by one Al Jolson."[1]

Since the days of Thomas Alva Edison, who had tried to couple a moving image with his new phonograph in 1887, early film pioneers had worked on sound synchronization. The marriage of visual image and accompanying sound could have been achieved many years sooner than it in fact was, but motion picture companies were making huge profits with silent films and were reluctant to risk those profits by experimenting with an unknown commodity; also, there was the problem of exhibitors having to wire their theatres for sound pictures, a costly undertaking at the very least. By 1908, the steady torrent of nickels and dimes was increasing daily in nickelodeon parlors throughout America, and every two months the number of people patronizing cinemas throughout the world was greater than the entire population of the globe. Within two decades, a crude novelty had become the dominant cultural force of the mechanized world. The cinema galloped into the 'teens, never to be the same after the arrival of D.W. Griffith's monumental *The Birth of a Nation*. That film's New York debut on March 3, 1915, was heralded as "The Dawn of a new Epoch in the Theatres of the World"—one memorable occasion when advertisements did not lie.

Novelty has always enticed the public and played a major role in the history of the cinema. Once the fascination with motion's sake had waned, producers turned in the 'teens to longer "feature" pictures. But by the mid-twenties, that novelty had begun to wear off, box-office receipts weren't what they had once been, and the scene was set for the arrival of the "talkies."

In 1926, Warner Bros. began working in earnest on sound synchronization. It all began in August of that year with *Don Juan*, which starred the swashbuckling John Barrymore. The film was silent, but its Warner Vitaphone accompaniment, a sound-on-disc system perfected by Western Electric, offered an orchestral score plus synchronized sound effects. In October 1927, Warner Bros. released *The Jazz Singer* starring Al Jolson. It was basically a silent film with a few synchronized dialogue and musical sequences, but these few "talking" sequences were the novelty the industry needed. When theatres installed sound equipment, attendance nearly doubled. As the earliest silent films had afforded the thrill of movement for movement's sake, so the first talkies were popular merely because they "talked." William Fox soon brought out the Fox Movietone system, a sound-on-film process, and by the spring of 1928 all the major studios had begun converting to sound. Theatres immediately began to apply artificial respiration to their sagging box offices, and the slick gimmicks and advertising campaigns — which boasted "This theatre wired for sound" and "100% all-talking" — lured in the customers. The first entirely talking picture, *Lights of New York,* only proved that the movies had suddenly forgotten everything they had learned in 30 years. Overnight, the cinema had lost its sophistication and became primitive again; a novelty revived an industry, but destroyed a highly perfected art.

The stars and directors whose careers weren't ruined by the advent of sound found themselves still working at the same studios, but in a completely different medium. "Nobody in the movie business knew much about sound. Nobody in the sound business knew much about movies. Everybody in both businesses resented everybody in the other."[2]

Mechanical limitations were the worst liabilities. The camera now had to be placed in a soundproof booth to prevent the whirring noise from reaching the microphones, thereby rendering it crudely immobile. Microphones were hidden in stage props, from which actors could not stray, thereby restricting their action. And as films began to depend more on dialogue than on the artistic manipulation of visual images, increasing numbers of stage plays were photographed, throwing the cinema back to the stationary conventions of its turn-of-the-century infancy.

The most noticeable casualties, of course, were the actors and actresses whose glittering careers were tragically cut short because their voices clashed with their screen personalities. Norma Talmadge's heavy Brooklyn accent, for instance, wasn't altogether convincing in talking pictures, and her career quickly ended. But stars with stage training, such as John and Lionel Barrymore, William Powell, George Bancroft, Marie Dressler, and

Clive Brook, had nothing to fear. Many character actors, including Boris Karloff, Jean Hersholt, and Nigel Bruce, had also learned to speak in the theatre. And a few actors with no stage background, like Janet Gaynor, Charles Farrell, Norma Shearer, and Gary Cooper, made the transition through the sheer magnetism of their dramatic presence.

Hollywood moguls watched—and listened—with trepidation as their silent idols faced the microphones and uttered their first recorded words. Hedging their bets, the studios began to hire scores of Broadway stars— George Arliss, Fredric March, Leslie Howard, Clark Gable, Sylvia Sidney, Fred Astaire, Helen Hayes, Paul Muni, Spencer Tracy, Katharine Hepburn, James Cagney, and Edward G. Robinson—just in case.

The silent screen had been unable to exploit Ronald Colman's voice, which was to prove his greatest asset. Sam Goldwyn, apprehensive that the public might not accept Colman's English accent, hurriedly scheduled a screen test to measure his protégé's voice quality. The producer's fears were unfounded. It was perfect.

> Undoubtedly Colman possessed one of the finest voices of all the major stars—it was soft, it was cultured, it was friendly, it was well modulated; above all, it fitted in with his physical appearance to an incredible degree. Colman, who had, indeed, played Latin lovers, was fortunately just as familiar to the public playing an Englishman. . . . His impact, when it was discovered that his voice was exactly as audiences had imagined it, was in every way tremendous.
>
> One thing Goldwyn noticed more than any other was that the Great Lovers of the Silent Screen, spouting dialogue which was an almost word for word adaptation of the florid and flowery titles which had traditionally accompanied the stars' wordless miming, were now greeted by hoots of derision. If only other producers had given careful thought to a new form of dialogue and a more restrained approach to the mummer's art, many of the silent casualties could have been avoided. It was this lack of foresight more than any weaknesses of voice which rang the death knell of the giants.[3]

The unhappy fate of John Gilbert provides an ideal illustration.

> Legend has it that his voice, in his first talking film, proved too high-pitched and reedy to survive the demands of sound. Not so: his voice was neither better nor worse than the voices of a dozen other stars whose careers continued. . . . What happened to Gilbert was that his studio obtusely decided to introduce him to sound in a film *exactly like* the films in which he had sinned glamorously with Garbo . . . the ardent wooing that had been so seductive was translated into speech. Instantly, the audience laughed. What the audience had been so willing to fantasize for itself by way of lovemaking under silence could not be believed for a moment in a world made more dimensional by words.[4]

Thus the choice of Colman's first talking role was crucial. Goldwyn made no attempt to carry over the tradition of the costume romance into talkies; with tastes changing and swashbucklers out of fashion, the craze was to be up-to-date. The producer recognized instantly the direction Colman's career must take: that of the *modern* lover, in genteel, gentlemanly roles which would complement the Colman voice. Goldwyn quickly recast the Colman screen personality and set the pattern for his future screen roles, giving him a new look, a new style, and witty, entirely plausible dialogue.

Colman's experience on the boards, first in London and later on Broadway, paid off handsomely once the movies learned to talk.

> For Colman, the voice, the good looks, the moustache, the quizzical expression—all these were a help, but the main reason for Colman's sudden rise as the first really great male star of the early talkies is that even in silent films, his acting had been restrained, whereas many other stars who had not been so restrained were unaware of the sudden need to be so—until after the damage had been done.[5]

And so Ronald Colman, armed with superb poise and a convincing but restrained ardor, crossed the sound barrier. Sam Goldwyn assigned playwright Sidney Howard the task of adapting H.C. ("Sapper") McNeile's action thriller, *Bull-Dog Drummond,* to the screen. Filmed rapidly and with few retakes, it gave audiences drama, high speed, laughter, and thrills. The lighthearted approach, carefully chosen to accent comedy rather than romance, worked; critics cheered and crowds queued up for the film in New York, London, and other cities for months. As Colman later told an interviewer for *Film Weekly,*

> I believe in comedy. I believe that properly handled, it may contain all the essentials of drama. This is on the surface a light-hearted and courageous generation. People do not go about beating their breasts and being tragic in public when they suffer. At least I am certain that Anglo-Saxons do not! Why not, then, let us show characters on the screen who are like the people we know—who meet their difficulties with poise and perhaps the tongue in the cheek a little? For some reason, it seems easier to do this in talking pictures than it did in silent ones, and I am glad.[6]

Colman's performance in *Bulldog Drummond,* along with his lighthearted heroics in *Condemned!,* a prison-escape picture released six months later, earned him his first Academy Award nomination for Best Actor. His third talkie, *Raffles,* had him cast as a gentleman crook in a reprise of the role Gerald du Maurier had made famous on the stage and John Barrymore had portrayed in the silents.[7] Filled with humor, wit, and the glamour of leading lady Kay Francis, it provided evidence of Colman's undiminished popularity as a star and box-office attraction.

Soon after the coming of sound, Colman and close friends Bill Powell,

Dick Barthelmess, Warner Baxter, Ernest Torrence, Neil Hamilton, and Ruth Chatterton all leased beach frontage in Malibu, where they spent weekends swimming, sailing, water-skiing, and deep-sea fishing; it was at this time that the film colony dubbed the inseparable trio of Colman, Powell, and Barthelmess "The Three Musketeers." Through actress Bessie Love, Colman met William Hawks, brother of director Howard Hawks; Bill soon graduated from the role of tennis partner to that of permanent business manager.

"Go in and do what you can for me," Colman told him. "Before God, I'm probably worth thirty-five dollars a week. Before the motion picture industry, I'm worth anything you can get!"[8]

After their marriage, Bill and Bessie Hawks introduced Colman to lovely actress Mary Astor, recently widowed by the death of a third Hawks brother, Kenneth. A brief love affair ensued. More than 40 years later, Mary Astor recalled:

> Ronnie asked me to marry him. Unfortunately, I was all entangled with a man who didn't want to marry me, and whom, also unfortunately, I later married. I was certainly attracted to Ronnie. He had wit and charm in abundance. But I wasn't using my intelligence about relationships in those days. It was a brief encounter—and a lovely one![9]

Shortly after completing *Raffles*, Colman went on holiday with Percy Marmont and sailed for England, where he visited his sisters Edith and Gladys, and stopped by old haunts (even popping into Bramlin's, one of his old theatrical booking agencies, to inquire mischievously whether they had any work for him). He later joined Bill Powell and the Ernest Torrences in Paris, returning with Powell to Hollywood in time to deny Goldwyn-inspired gossip of a romance with leading lady Kay Francis.

Meanwhile, Wall Street and the economy had already toppled the country into the throes of the Great Depression, which Americans weathered with a succession of light, frothy comedies; undemanding trifles they may have been, but such heartwarming morsels were needed. Goldwyn rushed his star into production on *The Devil to Pay*, a distinctive and irresistible side-splitter written specifically for Colman by playwright Frederick Lonsdale. As a "slightly disreputable, wholly likeable young ne'er-do-well,"[10] Colman went into full swing, wooed leading ladies Loretta Young and Myrna Loy simultaneously, and carried it off with perfect aplomb.

The Unholy Garden, which he made against his better judgment, was a barnloft abomination and a great flop. Colman played a dashing thief who tangles with a den of outlaws in a North African oasis. Although scripted by Ben Hecht and Charles MacArthur, the picture had precious little to recommend it. But later in 1931, Colman turned in one of his most sensitive performances to date as a quietly heroic research scientist in John Ford's

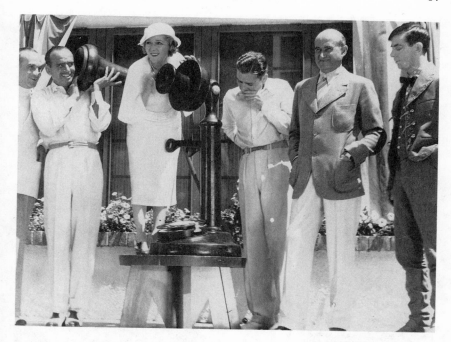

Ronald Colman apparently stifles a laugh as Douglas Fairbanks and Mary Pickford clown with a giant telephone at the Goldwyn studio. Looking on are Al Jolson, Sam Goldwyn, and an unusually somber Eddie Cantor.

Arrowsmith. Adapted by Sidney Howard from the best-selling novel by Sinclair Lewis, it was enlivened by Colman's and Helen Hayes' charm, winning humor, and magnificent portrayals.

Arrowsmith completed, Colman set out once more for Europe with his friend Al Weingand. After revisiting Colman's First World War battlefields en route to Berlin, they stopped off in Vienna, Budapest, Venice, Rome, Naples, and Genoa before returning to France. From Marseilles, they sailed to Egypt to see the Nile and the Sahara, stopped in French Somaliland, made their way to Ceylon, and finally pushed on to the Far East. In Shanghai, Colman called on his uncle, the same gentleman who had enticed him with the possibility of a diplomatic post in 1915. A brief jaunt to Kyoto, Japan, where he joined Richard Barthelmess and toured the Nikitsu movie studio, rounded out the expedition.

By the time he returned to Hollywood in the spring of 1932, Colman was a bona fide superstar, and Goldwyn had decided to feature him in only one picture per year. This seldom-seen-but-always-welcomed approach almost backfired later that year when Colman starred with Kay Francis in King Vidor's *Cynara,* an astute but somewhat dated psychological melodrama

Ronald Colman, with Bessie Love and her husband, William Hawks (brother of director Howard Hawks), having fun at an October 1932 costume party celebrating Ernest Torrence's thirtieth wedding anniversary.

of marital infidelity. Although his performance was one of subtlety and depth, and critics hailed it as Colman at his very best, the public was simply unwilling to accept Ronald Colman as an adulterer, and the film was only moderately successful. It miscarried because its star had taken the liberty of stepping out of his own image, and audiences firmly refused to countenance him in roles which departed from that image.

Colman's final picture for Goldwyn was *The Masquerader,* chiefly remembered today as the film responsible for the celebrated Colman-Goldwyn feud which led to the actor's severing all connection with the Goldwyn studio. Colman again played a dual role, one of which was that of a dipsomaniac. Goldwyn, never remiss when it came to publicity-grabbing gimmicks, ordered press releases to the effect that Colman played his love scenes better after fortifying himself with a considerable amount of alcohol and that, as a result, he looked better when mildly dissipated than when completely fit.

> The accusations had been given slight credence by the fact that as long ago as 1923, when Colman was making *The White Sister*, Henry King had plied the actor with whisky in an effort to break down his very English middle class reserve duing his love scenes with Lillian Gish. The results had been highly successful, and Miss Gish recalls that Colman went so far as to utter a thoroughly ungentlemanly "Damn!" on one occasion.[11]

Although such tactics might have worked in 1923, they hardly justified Goldwyn's blatantly false pronouncements. To Colman these statements, no matter what the intention, reflected not only upon his ability as an actor but also upon his character. Calmly, but with an air of determination and assurance, he sued his producer for libel and $2,000,000 in damages. Goldwyn retaliated by refusing to cancel Colman's contract and threatened to keep him off the screen for the remaining two years. The case was eventually settled out of court, but Colman insisted he would never work for Goldwyn again. And he never did.

His career at stake, Colman walked out on his studio and defiantly set off on an extended round-the-world tour. Like the screen characters he so often portrayed, he was risking everything on a point of honor.

So ended the decade during which the Colman image was firmly established under Sam Goldwyn's tutelage. Colman had been Goldwyn's biggest prestige star; the producer's concern for his protégé's career was so obsessive that he had neglected to groom any other male stars to follow in Colman's footsteps, an oversight which became apparent after 1933. Colman would remain a top favorite for two more decades, and much of that success he owed to to a brassy former glove salesman named Samuel Goldfish.

Bulldog Drummond

1929. *Production:* Samuel Goldwyn, Inc. *Distribution:* United Artists Corporation. *Producer:* Samuel Goldwyn. *Director:* F. Richard Jones. *Screenplay:* Sidney Howard (from the novel *Bull-Dog Drummond* by Herman Cyril McNeile ["Sapper"] and the play by "Sapper" and Gerald du Maurier). *Continuity:* Wallace Smith. *Cinematographers:* George S. Barnes, Gregg Toland. *Art Director:* William Cameron Menzies. *Assistant Director:* Paul Jones. *Associate Director:* A. Leslie Pearce. *Film Editors:* Frank Lawrence, Viola Lawrence. *Song:* Jack Yellen, Harry Akst ("[I Says to Myself Says I] There's the One for Me"). *Running Time:* 92 minutes. *New York Premiere:* May 2, 1929.

Cast: Ronald Colman (Captain Hugh Drummond), Claude Allister (Algy Longworth), Lawrence Grant (Dr. Henry Lakington), Montagu Love (Carl Peterson), Wilson Benge (Danny), Joan Bennett (Phyllis Benton), Lilyan Tashman (Irma Peterson), Charles Sellon (John Travers), Adolph Milar (Marcovitch), Tetsu Komai (Chong), Gertrude Short (Barmaid), Donald Novis (Country Boy), Tom Ricketts (Senior Conservative Club Member).

Within the portals of London's Senior Conservative Club, a stately old butler glides noiselessly past a dozen or so ancient members, bearing countless rounds of whiskies and sodas to those comfortably ensconced with their evening papers in somber armchairs. Suddenly a hallowed tradition is broken. The butler drops a spoon, shattering the silence. Horror-struck, a cluster of ill-tempered, crusty octogenarians protest this infernal invasion. To make matters worse, Captain Hugh Drummond (Ronald Colman), known more familiarly to his intimates as "Bulldog," enters like a breath of fresh air and adds to the relative din by whistling, just to wake the place up. Perhaps unintentionally, this opening scene subtly announces Samuel Goldwyn's *Bulldog Drummond* as Ronald Colman's first all-talking picture.

Captain Drummond is bored. Since the armistice, he has found life impossibly dull. In fact, he tells his friend Algy Longworth (a singularly horse-faced individual played by the deliciously absurd Claude Allister), he believes he is going positively mad. Looking for a piece of just about any action he can find, Drummond advertises in the *Times:* "Demobilized officer, finding peace unbearably tedious, would welcome any excitement."

From the deluge of letters he receives, Drummond responds to the most promising one, a communication from one Phyllis Benton, imploring him to meet her at the Green Bay Inn on the London road at midnight; she's in hideous danger. Back into the thick of adventure again, Drummond packs a toothbrush and a revolver, and he's off.

Moments after he's shown to his room at the inn, there comes a knock on the door. It's midnight, and a vision of loveliness appears (18-year-old Joan Bennett in her starring debut). She's given them the slip. Them? Why, Lakington, Peterson, and Irma, of course. It seems they're treating her uncle, wealthy American John Travers, for a nervous breakdown. Only their hospital isn't a hospital. They're torturing him. Although it sounds awfully like a penny thriller, Drummond assures Miss Benton that he believes her fantastic tale, and she leaves with his promise of assistance.

Another knock. The face of the villain who enters is surely one of nature's danger signals, for this blackguardly countenance belongs to Dr. Lakington, an authentic, dyed-in-the-wool lunatic if ever there was one (sinister Lawrence Grant). Outside, the ruthless Carl Peterson (Montagu Love, no slouch himself in the villainy department) forces Phyllis into a waiting auto and whisks her back to the asylum.

Dashing Bulldog Drummond (Ronald Colman) shows Algy Longworth (Claude Allister) the essential equipment required by any self-respecting adventurer—toothbrush and revolver.

It is at Dr. Lakington's "nursing home"—a grim, brooding affair—that Drummond comes face to face with all these worthies for the first time. Set upon by as vicious a gang of cutthroats as ever wielded a blade, he succeeds in spiriting Miss Benton off to the inn with Algy, then returns to settle the account. From his perch on the skylight overlooking Lakington's ominous central chamber, where the heavily drugged Travers (Charles Sellon) is being forced to sign over his securities and jewels, the Bulldog pounces, shoots out the light, and makes a clean getaway with Travers in the ensuing confusion.

Back at the inn, Phyllis and Algy await the return of Bulldog Drummond.

"I say, you're not getting Drummonditis too, are you?" asks Algy with anticipation.

"What's Drummonditis?"

"A complaint most women get soon after they meet Bulldog Drummond!"

The adventurer arrives with Travers in tow, but the next round is played by Lakington and the dressy wench, Irma (slinky Lilyan Tashman). Hired thugs abduct Miss Benton and "Travers" (Drummond in disguise), and transport them back to their lair, where they soon discover their mistake.

"Can't you stay away from here?" Peterson flashes angrily.

"I find it very difficult," Drummond admits lightheartedly.

Strapped to a chair, with the gloating Lakington bending over him, Drummond makes a rather odd request: "Would you mind deflecting that blast in the other direction?"

"What blast?" Lakington inquires.

"Even your best friends won't tell you!"

"Where's Travers?" Peterson demands.

"I wonder," Drummond muses.

Peterson and Irma depart, leaving their captives in Lakington's loving hands.

"And now we are — we are going to *amuse* ourselves," the doctor drools with a suggestive, twisted leer as he hovers over Phyllis' unconscious body.

While Lakington retreats into his laboratory to prepare a deadly poison, Phyllis recovers and frees Drummond. A vengeful Bulldog springs into action and throttles the life out of this archfiend, moments before Peterson and Irma return.

"If you move a muscle," Peterson threatens, "I'll shoot!"

"Then I certainly shall *not* move a muscle!"

But Drummond plays his ace, presses a hidden switch, and an electronic door slams shut, trapping Peterson inside the central chamber. Downstairs, Irma works "the old circus game," aware that Algy's on his way with reinforcements from Scotland Yard. A score of hirelings, disguised in full police regalia, arrive to "arrest" the Petersons, and march off with them in "custody." When Drummond learns that he's been had, he gallantly allows Pete and Irma to escape their thoroughly well-deserved fate, for Phyllis has confided that she has, indeed, caught Drummonditis.

When distinguished playwright Sidney Howard was summoned from New York to provide Ronald Colman with witty dialogue for his talkie debut, Sam Goldwyn encouraged him to fashion his screenplay as a vehicle for the actor and, above all, to underscore the element of comedy. Howard, a longtime Colman admirer, deftly tailored the Drummond character to fit the specific characteristics of the Colman image. F. Richard Jones, whose lighthearted blend of farce and adventure had contributed to make *The*

Gaucho, one of Douglas Fairbanks' finest swashbuckling romps two years earlier, was brought in to direct. Meticulously rehearsed until every scene was letter perfect, and then swiftly shot, *Bulldog Drummond* emerged as a frothy, exuberant thriller clearly played as much for laughs as for action. With its first-rate script and snappy dialogue; superb, German-influenced sets by William Cameron Menzies; heavy-laden, Expressionist cinematography by George Barnes and Gregg Toland; surprising mobility, flexible cross-cutting, and breathless pace; impressive supporting cast; and — most important — Ronald Colman's effortlessly debonair characterization, it was clear that Sam Goldwyn had another smash hit on his hands.

Joan Bennett's wearisome, expressionless portrayal of a damsel in distress was the sole weak spot in an otherwise admirable roster of supporting players, and while this might be excused by the fact that she was only 18 at the time, it should be noted that she never got any better. As Drummond's dubiously qualified assistant Algy, Claude Allister turned in a glorious piece of eccentric excess. In an amusing scramble, the sheer balminess of this meddlesome jackass is shown to good advantage: Algy, disguised as Drummond, hops off a balustrade to elude the Bulldog's pursuers, but in so doing loses his raincoat, hat, and scarf when a covetous tree limb gets in the way. Standing in the pouring rain in his familiar tux, he is approached by one of Peterson's thugs. Adjusting his ever-present monocle, the nonplussed Algy remarks, "Jolly night for the ducks, what?"

Montagu Love and Lilyan Tashman were quick-witted and sympathetic in their roguery, but Lawrence Grant stole their thunder as the impossibly malevolent Dr. Lakington, whose malignant brain continued to hatch new atrocities to perpetrate upon those unfortunate enough to cross his path. These hilariously melodramatic scoundrels concocted a clever scheme that was as cunning in its conception as it was merciless in its execution. But they made a cardinal error — they tangled with Bulldog Drummond.

Colman's genteel English adventurer bore less than a family resemblance to H.C. McNeile's original hero, whose exploits were first novelized in 1920 and then, with the assistance of Gerald du Maurier, brought to the stage in 1925. As envisioned by "Sapper," Drummond was a huge, square-jawed, phenomenally unprepossessing crime fighter with fists like jackhammers. Colman's Drummond, shorn of all the rough edges, was more cultivated, chivalrous, and verbally playful. What made the *real* difference, of course, was Colman's striking good looks.

> . . . it was a debonair and sophisticated interpretation, a Drummond who was really a twentieth-century D'Artagnan. In fact, there was a good deal of Fairbanksian flair in Colman's performance, and the character shared a great many of the qualities that had made up the Fairbanks "image" in his

modern silent comedies—good society connections, an educated background, and an unstressed but apparently unlimited private income.[12]

Colman's winning, sunny manner carried the show. Soon after his arrival at the asylum, for instance, after being assured that nothing is amiss, he hears the tortured Travers cry out for help.

"Somebody step on the cat's tail?" Drummond inquires brightly.

In a diverting exchange, Irma informs Drummond that Phyllis cannot be allowed to leave the premises. "At the moment," she adds, "I'm not sure whether you're leaving yourself."

"Are you planning to prevent me, Miss Peterson?"

"I *shall* prevent you, Captain Drummond!"

"I don't wish to seem curious," he asks cheerfully, "but would you tell me how?"

And finally, even when he gets down to business, he maintains an unruffled, jaunty exterior. In a scene using only shadow images, Phyllis screams in horror as Drummond chokes the evil Lakington to death.

"I'm being as *gentle* as I can!" he assures her with determined nonchalance.

> Colman's flawless diction, his beautiful timing, and the sense of fun he brought to the role not only dominated the film, but influenced the tongue-in-cheek playing of the rest of the cast. . . . [T]he whole mood [was] dictated by the frequent shots of Drummond roaring through the night in his open roadster, grinning at the sheer joy of it all, his white scarf flapping in the wind, streaming out behind him like the white scarves of cavalier airmen in World War I movies.[13]

Such effortless nonsense was never for a moment intended to be taken seriously. Most talkies so far had been little more than leaden-paced, photographed stage plays, with all talk and no action, but *Bulldog Drummond* was something new—a rattling good satire that moved. Audiences went wild, and critics called it the finest talking picture yet produced. Colman's voice was heralded as the find of the year, and he received his first Academy Award nomination for Best Actor.[14] And although George Arliss won the Oscar for *Disraeli*, it was apparent that Colman's talkie career had been spectacularly launched.

"What Chaplin is to the silent film," Goldwyn predicted, "Colman will be to sound!"[15]

When *Bulldog Drummond* premiered on May 2, 1929, at New York's opulent Apollo Theatre, Ronald Colman donned his tight smile for the crowd and made a rare personal appearance to help launch this all-important talkie, accompanied by both Mr. and Mrs. Samuel Goldwyn. Percy Marmont recalls the aftermath:

We had arranged for the car to be at the stage door, as there was a vast crowd out front, since everyone knew Ronnie was there. We were going to burst through the back door into the car, and the chauffeur had instructions to start the engine the minute he saw us. We dashed out of the door and there was no car but a vast crowd waiting. We couldn't go back because the stage door wouldn't open inward. Ronnie just said, "Jesus!" and we rushed along the side of the cinema until we found a side door we could open, pushed in and slammed it to. It was a dreadful ordeal getting through that mob of people. Ronnie was shaking like a leaf. Eventually we got a message through to Sam, and the car came around to the front of the house. It was an awful experience for him, and it might have been one of his reasons for not attending opening nights later in his career when there was no pressure.[16]

Several earlier silent treatments of the "Sapper" stories had been filmed in England, starring Carlyle Blackwell and Jack Buchanan, and, later, many others took over the role in less ambitious films, among them Ray Milland, John Howard, and Ralph Richardson. Colman himself returned as Drummond in 1934, but the 1929 version was to remain *the* definitive Drummond picture, "the yardstick by which all others were measured—and from which they copied."[17]

Condemned!

1929. *Production:* Samuel Goldwyn, Inc. *Distribution:* United Artists Corporation. *Producer:* Samuel Goldwyn. *Director:* Wesley Ruggles. *Screenplay:* Sidney Howard (from the book *Condemned to Devil's Island* by Blair Niles). *Dialogue Director:* Dudley Digges. *Cinematographers:* George S. Barnes, Gregg Toland. *Art Director:* William Cameron Menzies. *Film Editor:* Stuart Heisler. *Song:* Jack Meskill, Pete Wendling ("Song of the Condemned"). *Running Time:* 86 minutes (also released in a silent version: 10 reels, 9,000 feet). *New York Premiere:* November 3, 1929. Reissued in 1944 as *Condemned to Devil's Island.*
   Cast: Ronald Colman (Michel Auban), Ann Harding (Mme. Vidal), Louis Wolheim (Jacques Duval), Dudley Digges (Jean Vidal), William Elmer (Pierre), Albert Kingsley (Felix), William Vaughn (Vidal's Orderly), Constantine Romanoff, Stephen Selznick, Harry Ginsberg, Baldy Biddle, John George, Arturo Kobe, Emile Schwartz, John Schwartz, Bud Somers (Convicts).

Death hovers over a pitiable cargo of human flesh as a convict ship crosses the storm-swept Atlantic. Its destination: Devil's Island, the dread penal colony in French Guiana, where fever-ridden jungle and shark-infested sea permit no hope of escape. The prisoners are quickly landed, stripped to the waist, and issued uniforms. Among these emaciated wrecks of men is Michel Auban (Ronald Colman), a handsome, athletic Parisian thief who's been stealing from the moment he learned to walk. His refined speech and aristocratic bearing seem oddly out of place as he fairly bounces up to the inspection desk when his name is called.

Jacques Duval (Louis Wolheim) and Michel Auban (Ronald Colman) make a desperate escape from Devil's Island in Condemned! *Though Wolheim's excellent performance was overshadowed by even more memorable work the following year in* All Quiet on the Western Front, *Colman was nominated for the Academy Award.*

"You're an unusual type for a criminal," the warden growls.

"That's been the secret of my success!" he beams, further attracting the attention of Warden Jean Vidal (Dudley Digges), a nasty, dictatorial martinet hardened by years of service on the island. Auban will make an excellent houseboy for his young wife (Ann Harding).

The results are inevitable: Mme. Vidal—lonely, unhappy, and terrorized by her detestable husband—soon develops a strong attraction for Michel. When Vidal confronts Auban with his suspicions, the prisoner retaliates with a well-aimed punch to the warden's chin, for which offense he's given six months' solitary confinement. In a frenzy, Mme. Vidal insists that Michel is not her lover, but confesses that she does love him.

Marking the endless days and nights in solitary, the convict finally receives a smuggled message from the woman he has come to love: her husband is sending her home on the next day's ship. Auban effects an escape, eludes his pursuers, and conspires to meet Mme. Vidal on a steamer bound for France. Tension mounts as Michel and fellow escapee Jacques Duval (Louis Wolheim) are forced to abandon their stolen boat and seek the concealment of the jungle swamps; finally Vidal, combing the backwaters with a vengeance, spots them and opens fire. Silently, stealthily, the two comrades creep, always keeping just out of reach of the heavily armed guards.

Desperation drives Michel on, until finally, without further mishap, he joins Mme. Vidal as planned when her ship docks. But Vidal stages a sudden raid on his wife's stateroom, and Auban is apprehended. Faithful Jacques slips aboard, grabs the warden in a stranglehold, and pulls him overboard. Vidal is drowned, and Jacques, mortally wounded by a guard, sinks with a sickening gulp, having done his best to save Michel. The law takes its course, and Auban is returned to Devil's Island to serve his time, while Mme. Vidal waits for him in Paris.

Time passes. A train hurtles through the night, and finally, in a railway station in Paris, Michel Auban is reunited with the woman he loves.

Directed in fine, bravura style by Wesley Ruggles, *Condemned!* was adapted from Blair Niles' semi-fictionalized account of life, anguish, and death on Devil's Island. As with *Bulldog Drummond*, Sam Goldwyn insisted upon hours of thorough rehearsal before the cameras rolled. Beautifully lit and photographed by George Barnes and Gregg Toland, the production offered stage veteran Ann Harding in a restrained portrayal of the warden's abused wife, Louis Wolheim in a capital piece of work as Colman's sidekick, and Dudley Digges, playing his part to the hilt as the vindictive Vidal (he also served as the film's dialogue coach).

Despite the picture's authentically grim prison settings, playwright Sidney Howard's script was not without its lighter moments. In an especially delightful sequence, Vidal delivers a lecture to his wife over breakfast, while Michel sits in the kitchen and mimics the warden's every gesture and word in pantomime. Later, Vidal summons Auban to his office and accuses him of having made love to his wife:

> *Vidal:* Can you guess why you've been brought here?
> *Auban:* Come on, now you tell me and save us the trouble of guessing.
> *Vidal:* Are you or are you not my wife's —
> *Auban:* Ah, ah, oh, oh, I wouldn't ask that if I were you.
> *Vidal:* Why not?
> *Auban:* 'Cause your mother wouldn't be proud of her little boy speaking such *nasty* thoughts about a lady!

It has been alleged that Colman's elegant insouciance was more enchanting than convincing, and lacked the grit demanded by the narrative. When the basic plot of *Condemned!* was used again in Franklin Schaffner's *Papillon* (1973), Steve McQueen turned in a more effective performance than Colman did in the earlier film. The main reason is that Hollywood was simply not ready in 1929 to depict the torment of life on Devil's Island in all its horrifying reality. Forty-four years later, however, times had changed, and *Papillon* gave us an uncensored account of the filth, malnutrition, and despair that *Condemned!* had carefully avoided. Within the earlier picture's limitations, and despite his agreeable impudence, Colman adapted his style to the role and gave a suitably serious, dramatic performance.

Colman's daughter recounts her father's serious brush with danger on the set of *Condemned!*:

> During a scene following his prison escape, he hides beneath a floating bridge while the guards walk over it. The exact amount of space was measured to fit his head between the water level and the bridge, so that he could surface when he had run out of breath. Action: The guards approach. He takes a deep breath and submerges, holding it as long as possible, then finds that their weight upon the bridge has lowered it, leaving no space for his head to come up. Some astute man on the set sensed something was wrong, climbed into the water, and dragged out the choking star. . . . The bridge was heightened several inches, and the sequence reshot successfully.[18]

Colman, Miss Harding, Dudley Digges, and Wesley Ruggles were all present when this stirring drama of escape, flight, and capture opened at Grauman's Chinese Theatre in Hollywood. *Condemned!*, along with *Bulldog Drummond*, later earned Colman an Academy Award nomination for Best Actor.

Raffles

1930. *Production:* Samuel Goldwyn, Inc. *Distribution:* United Artists Corporation. *Producer:* Samuel Goldwyn. *Directors (uncredited):* Harry d'Abbadie d'Arrast, George Fitzmaurice. *Screenplay:* Sidney Howard (from the short story "Gentlemen and Players" by Ernest William Hornung and the play *Raffles, the Amateur Cracksman* by Hornung and Eugene Wiley Presbrey). *Cinematographers:* George S. Barnes, Gregg Toland. *Art Directors:* William Cameron Menzies, Park French. *Assistant Director:* H. Bruce Humberstone. *Technical Directors:* John Howell, Gerald Grove. *Film Editor:* Stuart Heisler. *Sound:* Oscar Lagerstrom. *Running Time:* 70 minutes (also released in a silent version: 7 reels, 6,509 feet). *New York Premiere:* July 24, 1930.

Cast: Ronald Colman (A.J. Raffles), Kay Francis (Lady Gwen), David Torrence (Inspector Mackenzie), Frederick Kerr (Lord Harry Melrose), Bramwell Fletcher (Bunny Manders), John Rogers (Crawshay), Wilson Benge (Barraclough), Alison Skipworth (Lady Kitty Melrose), Frances Dade (Ethel Crowley), Virginia Bruce (Blonde).

It is a moot point, H.G. Wells once observed, whether burglary be considered sport, trade, or art. The technique is scarcely rigid enough for a

Goldwyn prop man hands Ronald Colman a grip as the actor prepares to make an entrance in a scene from Raffles.

trade, and its mercenary concerns disqualify its claim to be an art. On the whole, he decided, it would seem rather most justly deemed a sport, one for which no rules exist. It is precisely this informality that led to the successful career of A.J. Raffles (Ronald Colman)—debonair cricketer by day, devil-may-care safecracker by night.

We meet the Amateur Cracksman under cover of darkness, plying his sport in a Bond Street jewelry establishment. Immaculately attired in formal wear, he is seen—entirely in silhouette—removing a diamond bracelet from its case and replacing it with a calling card which announces that this has been his farewell appearance. For Raffles is to be married to the beautiful Lady Gwen (Kay Francis) and has resolved to begin a new life. He has relished the use of his wits to procure illegal gain and elude the law, but that is now behind him. He later gives Lady Gwen the diamond bracelet as a token of his affection, and that's that.

Or so he thinks. For Bunny Manders (Bramwell Fletcher), one of Raffles' closest chums, is in a deuce of a jam. He's lost heavily at cards and has written a bad check, the discovery of which will disgrace him as a common cheat. To save Bunny's honor, Raffles decides to sacrifice his own; he'll accompany his friend to Melrose House for an afternoon of cricket, and later burgle Lady Melrose's priceless necklace.

A gang of third-rate crooks, however, determine to steal the same necklace on the same night. After the cricket match, Scotland Yard's Inspector Mackenzie (David Torrence) interrupts a dinner party to warn Lord Melrose (veteran character actor Frederick Kerr) that burglars plan to rob his home — perhaps a *particular* burglar.

Late that night, the thief Crawshay (John Rogers) removes the necklace from the neck of the slumbering Lady Melrose (Alison Skipworth), but is collared by Raffles, who pockets the necklace before the crook is apprehended. Mackenzie suspects Raffles of being his real quarry when he discovers that Lady Melrose failed to place her necklace in her safe upon the advice of Mr. A.J. Raffles. The inspector has Raffles followed the next morning, when the cracksman returns to his London flat to cover Bunny's bad check. Deciding to use a thief to catch a thief, Mackenzie allows Crawshay to escape, hoping that he'll lead him directly to Raffles. When Crawshay does exactly that, the cat-and-mouse game begins in earnest.

After Bunny leaves the flat to buy Raffles an airline ticket to Amsterdam, Gwen arrives. She also suspects her affianced of being the infamous cracksman. Yet she loves him, and wants to flee with him and share his fate. Mackenzie enters unexpectedly, and Raffles quickly hides the necklace in his tobacco humidor. A suspenseful moment occurs, as the inspector reaches into the container to help himself to some pipe tobacco and nearly discovers the prize. Bunny returns, Mackenzie spots the ticket, demands to know what business Raffles has in Amsterdam, the diamond capital of Europe, and accuses him of being the Amateur Cracksman. Raffles confesses and turns over the necklace, assuring Bunny that he will receive the handsome reward Lord Melrose has offered for the return of the sparklers. But the warrant Mackenzie holds for Raffles' arrest is not for the theft of the Melrose necklace, but for the robbery of the Bond Street jewelry shop on the previous Friday. Gwen quickly surrenders the bracelet. Once more Raffles uses his wits; locking the inspector and his men into another room, he makes his escape into the London fog, nonchalantly sauntering past the

Opposite: *Thirty-nine and willing to admit it. Ronald Colman cuts his birthday cake on the set of* Raffles, *while the crew gathers around for a share. Director Harry d'Arrast, soon to be fired by producer Sam Goldwyn, is seated at Colman's left, with Wilson Benge at d'Arrast's left. John Rogers, Kay Francis, and David Torrence are standing across the table from Colman.*

bobby guarding the entrance to the flat, bundled up in a perfect disguise — Mackenzie's wide-brimmed hat and cloak. When the inspector reaches the street, he spies what he takes to be Raffles, only to discover that that clever gentleman has draped hat and cloak over a police callbox and has made a clean getaway.

"Well," Mackenzie grins, "one can't help likin' him."

Based on a short story in the best-selling 1899 collection, *The Amateur Cracksman,* written by Arthur Conan Doyle's brother-in-law E.W. Hornung, and on the drama that Hornung soon co-authored, *Raffles* had proved itself a hugely successful star vehicle for nearly three decades. Kyrle Bellew and Gerald du Maurier had distinguished themselves in the title role on the stage shortly after the turn of the century; John Barrymore had made the part famous on the silent screen in 1917, which was followed by an unsatisfactory remake starring House Peters in 1925.

Overjoyed by Colman's triumph in *Bulldog Drummond,* Sam Goldwyn saw the similar *Raffles* as an ideal follow-up, quickly obtained the property for his star, and retained the services of scenarist Sidney Howard, who had already scripted *Drummond. Raffles* was rushed into production upon completion of *Condemned!* The director originally assigned to direct the film was Harry d'Abbadie d'Arrast, one of Hollywood's most colorful directors of the late twenties and early thirties. Of French parentage but born in the Argentine, d'Arrast had come to Hollywood in 1922, where he began working as Charlie Chaplin's assistant on *A Woman of Paris* and *The Gold Rush.* He then made his mark with a series of deftly sophisticated comedies which starred Adolphe Menjou. D'Arrast's style was witty, ironic, and Lubitschean. Such elegance unfortunately failed to suit Sam Goldwyn's needs, and he fired the director after viewing early rushes. George Fitzmaurice, veteran of five earlier Colman pictures, was brought in to complete the film. But d'Arrast had worked on the script with Sidney Howard, and much of its sparkling wit is directly attributable to the departed d'Arrast. Curiously, neither director received screen credit.

Colman played the lead role in the same engaging, playful vein that had marked his portrayal of Hugh Drummond. The result was another light-comedy thriller in the *Bulldog Drummond* mold, with its star at his polished best as the gentleman thief. The picture does have several lovely moments. The verbal sparring matches between Raffles and Inspector Mackenzie have great charm, for each man knows exactly what the other is up to, and each is equally determined to outwit his opponent. Similarly humorous is the following exchange between the cracksman and his valet (Wilson Benge), as the former announces his decision to abandon his life of crime:

"Have a watch," Raffles insists, proffering the object.

"A watch, sir?" asks the dumbfounded valet.

"You're a stout fellow, Barraclough. You've been a good servant, and I want you to have my watch — well, uh, *a* watch, anyway."

But although this tasteful, urbane romp received wide acclaim at the time of its release, its stage origins — especially the finale in Raffles' flat — creaked, and the picture was soon forgotten. Goldwyn remade it almost scene for scene in 1939, with Colman replacement David Niven following in his predecessor's footsteps as the debonair thief. It is this version that is most often shown on television; until comparatively recently, the Colman rendition had been out of circulation for years.

As Julian Fox put it: ". . . Colman had become, through these undemanding trifles, the most popular star of the early talkies."[19]

The Devil to Pay

1930. *Production:* Samuel Goldwyn, Inc. *Distribution:* United Artists Corporation. *Producer:* Samuel Goldwyn. *Director:* George Fitzmaurice. *Screenplay:* Frederick Lonsdale, Benjamin Glazer. *Dialogue Director:* Ivan Simpson. *Cinematographers:* George S. Barnes, Gregg Toland. *Musical Score:* Alfred Newman. *Art Director:* Richard Day. *Assistant Director:* H. Bruce Humberstone. *Technical Advisors:* Lady Maureen Stanley, Lt. Col. G.L. McDonell. *Film Editor:* Grant Whytock. *Running Time:* 74 minutes. *New York Premiere:* December 18, 1930.

Cast: Ronald Colman (Willie Hale), Loretta Young (Dorothy Hope), Florence Britton (Susan Hale), Frederick Kerr (Lord Leland Hale), David Torrence (Mr. Hope), Mary Forbes (Mrs. Hope), Paul Cavanagh (Grand Duke Paul), Crawford Kent (Arthur Hale), Myrna Loy (Mary Crayle), Ivan Simpson (Owner of Pet Shop), Forrester Harvey.

Ronald Colman's on the loose again, and the fun is unrivaled as *The Devil To Pay* chronicles the hilarious doings of dashing ne'er-do-well Willie Hale, scion of one of London's noblest families. In and out of trouble — mostly in — since his departure for East Africa two years ago, this altogether unredeemed rascal returns to England, blaming his misfortunes on horses with short noses and good cards — but not good enough. Awaiting his arrival is that venerable peer of the realm, Lord Leland (crotchety Frederick Kerr), who has decided that his worthless dum-dum of a son has failed him for the last time: "If he ever sets his foot in this house again," the old man harrumphs, "I'll — I'll kick him out. That's what I'll do; I'll — I'll personally kick him out, the villain!"

No sooner does Willie set foot in London than he chances to spot George. Although intending to squander his few remaining pounds at tomorrow's Derby, Hale engages in animated conversation through a window with George, enters the pet shop, and buys him on the spot. George is a wire-haired fox terrier. From there, it's off to take up with old girlfriend and celebrated stage actress Mary Crayle (sexy Myrna Loy).

The camera cuts discreetly to the palatial Hale residence the following morning, where, after a hearty breakfast, wicked Willie bows his head penitently and ventures forth to his father's study. For the tenth time, the old boy blusters in a positively tearing rage, his son has disgraced him — this time by selling the house and furniture he had given him in Africa.

"Now — now let me — let me tell you, young man, you've been nothing but trouble since the day you were born."

"Well, now, as an intelligent man, I wonder if you didn't anticipate that possibility."

"Now," laughs Lord Leland, "now you're blaming me for bringing you into the world."

"I should be extremely mortified for your sake if I had to blame anyone else!" Hale chuckles, grinning in deep travail of soul.

Willie's insouciance carries the day, for he emerges from the confrontation with the old codger's blessings — and a hundred pounds. With that, he's off to the Derby with sister Susan (Florence Britton) and her friend, London socialite Dorothy Hope (17-year-old Loretta Young), destined that very evening to become engaged to an attack of indigestion more commonly known as the Grand Duke Paul (Paul Cavanagh). But when this worthy beholds Miss Hope at the racetrack in company with W. Hale, Esq., and insists she never see that disreputable cad again, Dorothy breaks off her engagement. Later, Willie is summoned to the Hope mansion; Dorothy's father, the linoleum king (David Torrence), wishes to see him.

"It may be coincidence," Mr. Hope begins, "but since knowing you, my daughter has broken off her engagement to a young man for whom I have the highest regard."

"Ah, how tragic it is that children so seldom do what their parents want them to," sympathizes Willie with carefree aplomb. "My father has the most awful trouble with me."

"So I accuse you of being the cause of that engagement being broken. She was in love with him until you arrived."

"I? What business is it of mine?"

"Because she's a rich girl and you want to marry her yourself!"

"Mr. Hope, I trust your linoleum is better than your manners!" asserts Willie in a tone of amused protest.

"How *dare* you speak to me like that!"

"Why?" he chuckles. "Are you ashamed of your linoleum?"

If his daughter dares to marry Willie Hale or anyone like him, Hope swears, he'll cut her off completely. "This information alters your point of view on marriage considerably, doesn't it, Mr. Hale!"

"Yes. I can't quite tell you how considerably!"

His mind made up, Willie bounds onto the terrace and at once asks Dorothy if she has any objections to his becoming her father's son-in-law.

Loretta Young would make three pictures with Ronald Colman. In the first of these,
The Devil to Pay, *she is already a star who, like Colman, would sustain her popularity
in various media through several decades.*

Miss Hope, of course, has adored him from the start and accepts on the spot,
but extracts a promise that he will never see Mary Crayle again.

Homeward bound, our hero halts an elderly passerby on the street and
heartily shakes his hand. "Of all the men in the world I don't know," he cries,
"I should like you to be the first to congratulate me!"

Seeking advice on how best to terminate his relationship with Mary
Crayle, Willie thoughtfully consults George, who, in his inimitable panting
fashion, suggests that a letter will do the trick. It doesn't. When a telephone
call also fails, Willie catches Miss Crayle after her performance, but before
he can tell her he's betrothed to another, the actress whisks him off to her
apartment.

Misunderstandings abound in every romance, and this one is no exception. Unbeknown to our principals, a private detective has trailed Hale to
Mary Crayle's residence, and relays this juicy morsel of news to Dorothy's
father. Wishing to spare his daughter the embarrassment of an unfortunate
alliance, Hope encourages her to dial Miss Crayle's number. Willie's just

broken the bad news to Mary, all right, but makes the fatal mistake of answering Dorothy's phone call himself.

Later at the Hope residence, Willie's explanations miss the mark. Huffily contending that one should pay for one's experiences, Dorothy hands him a check for 5,000 pounds. When her check is cashed and Mary Crayle departs for the south of France, it appears that Dorothy has paid all the expenses for still another Willie Hale fling. But a message arrives from the formerly destitute Grand Duke Paul, thanking her for the generous gift of 5,000 pounds, with which he'd paid off all his creditors; they'd held off, it seems, only because they believed he was going to marry the linoleum heiress. That does it; by sending Paul the money with a note indicating that it had come from Dorothy, Willie wins the day and proves that it was her titled suitor, and not he, who was the fortune-hunter.

Meanwhile, Willie's booked two tickets for New Zealand—the second, of course, for George. A contrite Dorothy rushes to him, only to discover her beloved packing his suitcase. She's now ready to become a poor man's wife, and all is forgiven. But Dorothy's father arrives, insisting that they needn't go to New Zealand; he wants to buy them a farm here in England, as a wedding present.

"Next time you go broke," Lord Leland bellows with laughter, "it will be *his* furniture you're sellin', and not mine!"

One of Sam Goldwyn's highest priorities was the careful selection of properties for his brightest star, Ronald Colman. Since audiences were clearly enchanted by Colman's lighthearted performances in *Bulldog Drummond* and *Raffles*—both comedy thrillers—the producer quickly engaged the services of playwright Frederick Lonsdale, master of the sophisticated light comedy, whose first screen assignment was to fashion a screenplay specifically suited to the Colman persona. After a bit of shuffling, George Fitzmaurice replaced director Irving Cummings; and Loretta Young, whose soft, purring voice and lovely, large eyes made her a perfect match for Colman, won the part originally intended for stage actress Constance Cummings.

Young recalls how her lifelong crush on Ronald Colman caused difficulties on the set:

> . . . my crush on him grew with the years, as he grew in his stature and attractiveness and ability. I watched his career, what he was doing and who he was doing it with and wishing it could be me. . . . Then I got a call from Goldwyn's studio saying, "Come over, we want you to make a test for the lead with Colman." Goldwyn had decided to change Constance Cummings.
>
> So there I am doing my test and all of a sudden I see him and my mouth went dry and I couldn't swallow and it was sad! I was too embarrassed to tell anyone how I felt about him. Anyhow, I got the part.
>
> I would be fine in rehearsals, then I'd get with Ronnie and I'd forget

everything except him — my dreamboat! Finally, Fitz . . . said to the coach, "What's the matter with her? She's OK until we turn the camera and then nothing comes out." So the coach called me into the dressing room and I burst into tears and said, "Well, I'm just so crazy about him. I think I'm bad in the part and he knows I'm bad."

Well, he must have said something to Ronnie, and he explained it to Fitz. Ronnie was almost a psychiatrist in the way he handled the situation because he wooed me enough to fulfill all my romantic dreams about him . . . and still not enough to encourage me beyond our eight hours on the set. He was so darling, such a mature man and always so tender with women. I really fell head over heels in love with him on that picture.[20]

Elderly English actor Frederick Kerr, who had been so delightful as Lord Melrose in *Raffles*, was awarded the role of Colman's father, and with Myrna Loy on hand, as well as a winsome terrier named George, shooting began.

Lonsdale's sparkling script gave its star a sunny landscape through which he bounced with grace and infectious good humor. Clearly in his element, Colman made the most of his bright lines. Numerous happy touches include the opening sale in Africa, where Willie auctions off his bed to raise money for passage back to England.

"With or without the owner?" a sprightly lass inquires.

"Without."

"Ten."

"It's yours," he replies without hestiation. "I've always wanted you to sleep in it!"

And later, in one of his finest vignettes, he tips his hat to an elderly lady as he alights from a cab in London: "Have no fear for the day," he beams irrepressibly; "you look divine!"

Here and throughout the picture, Colman put everything the public had learned to expect of him into his performance. The film's superabundance of charm flowed consistently and smoothly under George Fitzmaurice's deft direction, and audiences and critics alike caught the spirit. As the *New York Herald Tribune* put it,

Six reels of Mr. Colman being charming, but since it happens that Mr. Colman can be charming without offense, ostentation or self-consciousness, and that Frederick Lonsdale is an expert at making something out of nothing, the result is a polished, tasteful and entirely likable screen comedy.[21]

The Devil to Pay was judged Colman's best work to date, and the actor always considered it one of his favorites. "It may not be great acting," observes William K. Everson, "but it's a great *performance* — debonair, attractive, the fine lines flawlessly delivered with tremendous flair."[22]

The Unholy Garden

1931. *Production:* Samuel Goldwyn, Inc. *Distribution:* United Artists Corporation. *Producer:* Samuel Goldwyn. *Director:* George Fitzmaurice. *Screenplay:* Ben Hecht, Charles MacArthur. *Cinematographer:* George S. Barnes. *Musical Score:* Alfred Newman. *Art Directors:* Richard Day, Willy Pogany. *Film Editor:* Grant Whytock. *Sound:* Frank Grenzback. *Running Time:* 74 minutes. *New York Premiere:* October 28, 1931.

Cast: Ronald Colman (Barrington Hunt), Fay Wray (Camille de Jonghe), Estelle Taylor (Hon. Mrs. Elize Mowbry), Warren Hymer (Smiley Corbin), Tully Marshall (Baron Louis de Jonghe), Lawrence Grant (Dr. Shayne), Ullrich Haupt (Colonel von Axt), Kit Guard (Kid Twist), Henry Armetta (Nick-the-Goose), Lucille LaVerne (Mme. Lucie Villars), Mischa Auer (Prince Nicolai Poliakoff), Henry Kolker (Police Inspector), Charles H. Mailes (Alfred de Jonghe), Morgan Wallace (Captain Kruger), Arnold Korff (Louis Lautrac), Nadja (Native Dancer), William von Brincken, A.E. Anson.

Much ado about almost nothing. Ronald Colman falls in with a band of deteriorated, demoralized ruffians, woos leading lady Fay Wray, and makes a gallant sacrifice in *The Unholy Garden*, one of his least memorable pictures.

British bank robber Barrington Hunt (Colman) flees from Marseilles to Algeria, where he seeks refuge in hostile Arab territory. Local military authorities, eager to apprehend him, hire Elize Mowbry (Estelle Taylor) to lure him into a trap, but Hunt kidnaps her, steals her auto, and drives off into the Sahara. There he finds sanctuary at a desert oasis, in a broken-down hotel which caters to the needs of murderers, thieves, and fugitives on the run. In this raffish milieu, Hunt joins forces with a host of hardened cases. Among them are Dr. Shayne (Lawrence Grant in a role which recalls his performance in *Bulldog Drummond*), who murdered his three wives and now stores his tobacco in the skull of one of them, and Colonel von Axt (Ullrich Haupt), who sold out his division in the war. Hunt conspires to help them rob an elderly hotel resident. Their target is the Baron de Jonghe (Tully Marshall), a blind Parisian banker and embezzler who's stashed some ten million ill-gotten francs somewhere on the premises. In an effort to discover the whereabouts of the old man's loot, Hunt romances the baron's granddaughter, Camille (Fay Wray). He unearths the spoils, but falls in love with the girl and decides to double-cross his partners.

The baron's brother, Alfred de Jonghe (Charles Mailes), arrives and pleads unsuccessfully with his brother to return the money and live out his remaining days in peace and freedom in Paris. Meanwhile, the resourceful Hunt climbs stealthily through the baron's window, removes the money box from its hiding place in the fireplace chimney, and makes off with the cache. The villains murder the baron, find the money box empty, and realize that Hunt has swindled them. The chase is on. Hunt, Camille, and Alfred de

Fay Wray, best known for her performance as a blonde opposite an even taller, darker leading "man" the following year, is seen here as a brunette succumbing to the charms of adventurer Barrington Hunt (Ronald Colman) in The Unholy Garden.

Jonghe steal through the garden to Alfred's car, where Hunt, refusing to burden Camille's life with constant peril and flight, gives her the money and insists that she leave without him. He bids her adieu with a kiss, and then watches wistfully as their auto lurches off into the desert. Hunt and a loyal companion elude their pursuers and head out into the Sahara.

The script came from nowhere, and it went nowhere. Ben Hecht and Charles MacArthur, commissioned by Sam Goldwyn to furnish the screenplay for *The Unholy Garden*, were working under great pressure from Howard Hughes to complete their script for *Scarface*; and, although Hecht later boasted that he had dictated the Goldwyn script in one night, some believe that he and MacArthur delegated the assignment to subordinate writers.[23] Either way, it was knocked out in record time, and it shows. A skewed moral environment in which nothing and no one can be trusted is a fair enough start, but the story soon slides into a morass of hopelessly clichéd situations and improbable melodramatics entirely devoid of originality. When a fugitive thief hides out in a Sahara oasis, which just happens to sport a conveniently placed haven for criminals, and just happens to hook up with a merry gaggle of predictable villains, the whole affair becomes an unconvincing *Grand Hotel* in the sand. It simply doesn't work.

It was intended to be taken as a jocular spoof, and on this level it plays well in spots, for the sprightly, tongue-in-cheek, and surprisingly risqué dialogue does provide some witty moments. In his eighth and final collaboration with Ronald Colman, George Fitzmaurice supplied an unflagging directorial pace, but was unable to disguise the essential thinness of the plot, the obvious studio backdrops, or the fact that his leading players had little to do. Fay Wray, whose screen presence is staggeringly forgettable, proved, two years before her date with King Kong, that she couldn't act, but she was lovely to behold as the distraught beauty who reaches out for love in the midst of thieves. Ronald Colman had portrayed gentleman crooks before, of course, and turned in an effortlessly lighthearted, debonair performance as the knight of rueful countenance whom chance had blown into the Sahara. Dissatisfied with the film's obvious shortcomings, he walked through it with jaunty determination rather than genuine belief, substituting polished, wisecracking humor, nonchalance, and savoir faire for whatever the part lacked in dramatic opportunity. This didn't save the picture, but it made its failure somewhat less obvious. And, in one of the film's most effective moments, he got to play a heart-tugging renunciation scene, by now an almost obligatory part of the Colman image. When Hunt decides that he cannot share his life of ceaseless flight with Camille, he tells her that

> ". . . it's the one thing I've done that's any good. Don't spoil it. I love you more than I said. That's why you must go on — alone. Oh, it would be nice, my dear, but it's nicer this way. It would only mean a little while together, and then the police. You wouldn't find Paris very nice as a convict's bride. I would keep you with me, but — but, don't you see, I planned it this way. A better job than I've ever done before. Go back to life. And someday, when your eyes are shining, and you go to meet an honest man, look at Paris once for me, and think of it as my wedding present."

When *The Unholy Garden* was released, some reviewers found it a thoroughly enjoyable "packet of fun and excitement,"[24] but most gave it poor notices. Why Sam Goldwyn ever decided to film it in the first place remains a well-kept secret. It is known that he was displeased with the screenplay, but by then the picture had already gone into production. Colman remained solidly professional on the set, but resented the fact that, after all their triumphs together, Goldwyn had handed him such a role. He considered it his weakest film to date, but his next production, *Arrowsmith*, released just six weeks later, would soon make up the lost ground.

Arrowsmith

1931. *Production:* Samuel Goldwyn, Inc. *Distribution:* United Artists Corporation. *Producer:* Samuel Goldwyn. *Director:* John Ford. *Screenplay:* Sidney Howard (from the novel by Sinclair Lewis). *Cinematographer:* Ray June. *Musical Score:* Alfred Newman. *Art Director:* Richard Day. *Assistant Director:* H. Bruce Humberstone. *Film Editor:* Hugh Bennett. *Sound:* Jack Noyes. *Running Time:* 110 minutes; 95 minutes (subsequent rereleases). *Release Date:* December 7, 1931.

Cast: Ronald Colman (Martin Arrowsmith), Helen Hayes (Leora Tozer), Richard Bennett (Dr. Gustav Sondelius), A.E. Anson (Professor Max Gottlieb), Clarence Brooks (Dr. Oliver Marchand), Alec Francis (Cecil Twyford), Claude King (Dr. A. DeWitt Tubbs), Bert Roach (Bert Tozer), Myrna Loy (Joyce Lanyon), Russell Hopton (Terry Wickett), David Landau (State Veterinarian), Lumsden Hare (Sir Robert Fairland), Charlotte Henry (Pioneer Girl), James Marcus (Doc Vickerson), DeWitt Jennings (Mr. Tozer), Beulah Bondi (Mrs. Tozer), John Qualen (Henry Novak), Adele Watson (Mrs. Novak), Sidney DeGrey (Dr. Hesselink), Florence Britton (Miss Twyford), Ward Bond (Policeman), Pat Somerset, Eric Wilton (Ship's Officers), Erville Alderson (Pioneer), George Humbert (Italian Uncle), Raymond Hatton (Drunk), Theresa Harris (Native Mother), Kendall McComas (Johnny), Walter Downing (City Clerk), Bobby Watson.

Unforgettable glimpses: a rural South Dakota village in midsummer, ravaged by "blackleg" cattle disease . . . a horde of menacing, plague-ridden rats scurrying aboard a steamer . . . a devastated lane of thatched huts in the West Indies, infested by the dread bubonic plague . . . New York cloaked in a blinding snowstorm, as a tall, haggard research scientist hunches over a tier of beakers, impelled by a zealous sense of duty to mankind. The doctor is Ronald Colman; the picture, Samuel Goldwyn's legendary *Arrowsmith*.

From the moment Arthur Hornblow first pressed Sam Goldwyn to purchase the rights to Sinclair Lewis' Nobel Prize–winning 1925 novel, Ronald Colman urged his producer to bring it to the screen. Goldwyn was enthusiastic but wary. Its episodic nature would make adaptation difficult, the death of its heroine spelled potential box-office poison, and a story about experimental research for the good of humanity wasn't exactly surefire either. Lewis himself was anxious to see it filmed, but Goldwyn wavered until playwright Sidney Howard, who had already scripted *Bulldog Drummond* and *Condemned!*, seconded Colman's promptings and offered to undertake the scriptwriting chores. Goldwyn gave the go-ahead, determined at last to spare no expense in transferring this powerful saga of dedication and sacrifice to the cinema. Colman was granted his request to portray Martin Arrowsmith, and Helen Hayes, the scintillating stage actress recently imported to Hollywood by M-G-M, was awarded the role of his loyal, loving wife. A superior supporting cast was assembled, John Ford was brought in to direct, and shooting commenced. The imagination,

The first lady of the American stage, Helen Hayes, made few forays into the cinema. Her intelligent portrayal of Leora in John Ford's Arrowsmith *showcased her expertise in what was for her a new medium.*

resourcefulness, and intensity of the next months were to make *Arrowsmith* one of Sam Goldwyn's most prestigious pictures of the thirties.

Born of stubborn pioneer stock, young Martin Arrowsmith (Colman) studies medicine at Winnemac College and dreams of a successful career as a research scientist. But when he meets lovely Leora Tozer (Helen Hayes), a petite, outspoken nurse at the local hospital, he forsakes his goal and settles for the less risky ambition of becoming a general practitioner. The two are soon wed, and as a man cannot marry on what a laboratory assistant makes, he has to practice medicine after all. To hell with bacteriology and other advanced *materia medica;* he'll command glory as a great healer in the land of opportunity, Leora's home town of Wheatsylvania, South Dakota—366 inhabitants, and not a doctor in the lot.

Though he is never free form the burning desire to become a great researcher, Arrowsmith accepts his altered circumstances, hangs out his shingle, and practices his trade. Eventually his yearnings for experimentation are fed anew when he journeys to Minneapolis to attend a lecture on yellow fever and bubonic plague delivered by Dr. Gustav Sondelius (Richard Bennett[25]), famed researcher and member of the Royal Swedish Medical Academy.

Returning home with a new lease on life, Arrowsmith renews his passion in the war against disease and vows not to stagnate any longer in his country practice. Converting his humble kitchen into an improvised research laboratory, he launches his experiments in earnest. But his successful efforts at effecting a cure for the mysterious "blackleg" cattle disease are resented by a jealous state veterinarian (David Landau), Leora loses the child she is carrying, and the young doctor reaches the limits of his frustrated endurance. What is he, he asks himself, but an inconspicuous, discouraged country practitioner? With Leora he is contented enough, but the routine of prescriptions and bandages he cannot—and will not— tolerate any longer. He'll make himself succeed—in New York, where his old Winnemac mentor, the renowned immunology specialist Max Gottlieb (A.E. Anson[26]), now heads an experimental research team. Infinities ago, the professor had promised Martin he'd make a place for him.

And so the young couple from the midwest plains arrive at the McGurk Institute, an awesome edifice which grows story upon story until it scrapes the sky. Embarking upon a lively existence in his own research laboratory, Arrowsmith stands alone in his new sanctuary, surrounded by clean rows of test tubes, and prays:

> "God give me clear eyes and freedom from haste. God give me anger against all pretense. God keep me looking for my own mistakes. God keep me at it till my results are proven. God give me strength not to trust to God!"

Two years of diligent and fruitless work find a despondent Arrowsmith impatient at not accomplishing anything of substance and almost ready to give up the fight. But then the unexpected occurs. He has been experimenting with three beakers thick with deadly microbes. He notices that one of them has become clear overnight. Something in that flask has killed those bugs. But what? Perhaps—just perhaps—this could be the breakthrough he's sought during long months without food or sleep.

Research wipes out everything else—makes him forget Leora, Gottlieb, everything except the bugs. Weeks later, he surfaces, bedraggled, unshaven, wilted sick from the madness of overwork, to inform Professor Gottlieb and associate Terry Wickett (Russell Hopton) of his startling new discovery:

"All I know is it's hell on the bugs!" he cries out in a voice which fights to render itself steady. "Dissolves 'em, eats 'em up, slaughters 'em, wipes 'em off the—" he breaks off, slumping exhausted onto the nearest chair.

But disappointment soon dulls the edge of his discovery: Martin's cure has been anticipated by an eminent French scientist, who has already published his results. There follows a year of frustration and more disappointment. Then, finally, comes the opportunity of a lifetime. The great Sondelius enlists Arrowsmith's assistance in his struggle against killer rats and a raging outburst of bubonic plague in the West Indies. The crusading soldier of science teaches Martin everything he's learned about the dread disease in China and India, but Arrowsmith is deeply troubled. He learns he is to administer his new serum to only *half* his patients, as he had once done with the cattle in South Dakota. Yet a physician is duty-bound to save *all* his patients. Those wretched, half-mad natives will come to him for help, begging for their lives. Has any man the right to sacrifice human lives just to prove the effectiveness of a new drug?

Finally, still torn between conflicting duties but heeding Professor Gottlieb's advice that he spare his pity for generations yet unborn, he departs for the Indies, determined to be the man who ends all plague. Leora, now as in years past, vows she'll not leave her husband's side and insists upon accompanying him on his desperate mission.

When the Arrowsmiths and Sondelius arrive on the darkly infested island of Blackwater, British governor Sir Robert Fairland (Lumsden Hare) accuses Martin of wanting to use his quarantined inhabitants as one would guinea pigs in a lab and refuses to allow the experiment to proceed. Arrowsmith in turn warns him that if he prevents the proposed measures, his instructions permit him to withhold the serum entirely until the governor comes to his senses.

Unable to persuade them to endure a test which might well lead to the eradication of plague forever, Arrowsmith and Sondelius set out for the worst infected island in the entire colony, a tropical hell where the epidemic is swallowing village upon village.

The great experiment dominates the latter portion of the film, as image after haunting image dramatically evokes a fevered atmosphere of tension, menace, and lurking horror — Arrowsmith in his emergency clinic, inoculating every second inhabitant as outstretched black arms reach out to him for help; huts and villages exploding in flame as the frenzied Sondelius, already infected and soon to die, lumbers through the night, preaching the gospel of rat extermination; death-dealing rodents, swiftly darting and turning as the contagion spreads; the dead, borne on stretchers through the oozing black mud; and always the beating of tom-toms, chants, and the soft, mournful sounds of Negro spirituals.

From time to time the camera takes us back to the little Blackwater bungalow where Leora, in great distress over her husband's safety, awaits his return. So magnificent are these scenes in their restrained dramatic intensity that they are worth recalling in detail. Earlier we had seen Martin lay his half-smoked cigarette on the edge of the research table, close to the ominous rows of test tubes containing enough plague virus to wipe out half an army. We watched as the camera cut to a tight close-up when a drop of the deadly virus spilled onto the cigarette, and we knew that, sooner or later, Leora would smoke it. Now she does. These next brief scenes, alternating with those of her husband's rescue operation, as she lies dying and alone, feeling weaker by the minute and crying out to Martin for help, remain the visual as well as the dramatic high points of the film. Shot almost entirely in silhouette and highlighted by rippling light and latticed shadow, they were exactly what director John Ford and cinematographer Ray June intended them to be: poignant reminders that although the early talkies might indeed talk, a picture was still worth a thousand words.

Arrowsmith finally learns that Blackwater has been dangerously contaminated, but he arrives too late and discovers Leora lying on the floor, very thin, very frail, and quite still, as if asleep.

He cradles his wife in his arms.

"I loved you, Lee. You knew that, didn't you?" he pleads. "Didn't you know I *couldn't* love anyone else? Didn't you *know* that, Lee?"

Robbed of Leora's silent, assuring presence, Arrowsmith grimly resolves that his experiment shall not be continued, and begins inoculating every frightened native he can find, hour after hour, injection after injection. Then, finally, wild-eyed, tousled, and drunk, living on whiskey and hate, he goes to pieces:

"Give 'em *all* the serum! Shoot 'em *full* of it! C'mon, open the doors, let 'em *all* in!" he cackles a little insanely, choked by his own tears. "Kill *all* the rats! Burn *all* the villages! To *hell* with experiments! To *hell* with science! To *hell* with Gottlieb!"

Tears mingle with sobs. "Lee, oh Lee—"

Days pass, some of them sober. Then the drinking stops altogether, and he gets on with his work. The heroic attempt is a success, the plague is wiped out, and Arrowsmith returns to New York a hero. But Lee is gone, Gottlieb has suffered a stroke and can't even recognize him, and if he stays at McGurk, he'll be a faithful mechanic in a competent, visionless medical factory for the rest of his life. His close associate Terry Wickett has the right idea; he's leaving the institute to build an experimental research cabin in the Vermont woods, and wants Martin to join him. Unwilling to serve two masters at once, Arrowsmith follows the dictates of his own conscience and chooses the isolation of Vermont, peace within himself, and a focus for his life's work. Even the arrival at McGurk of beautiful Joyce Lanyon can't hold him. Cool, trim, and sure (and portrayed seductively by Myrna Loy), she'd met him in the tropics, and has stopped off at the institute to console him by offering—well, herself. He'd resisted her advances then, while Lee was alive, and he politely rejects them now, for what she represents to him is everything he's always been willing to sacrifice for his work.

Dr. Tubbs (Claude King), publicity-seeking director of the institute, enters Arrowsmith's laboratory and informs him that the reception committee is ready to proclaim him an official hero.

"Ready, are you? Well, *so* am I!" he snaps, rushing out of the building with a smile to hail his new partner.

"Terry, wait! I'm coming with you; Lee and I—we're *both* coming with you!"

Following a vigorous advance publicity campaign, *Arrowsmith* opened on December 7, 1931, to exciting reviews and became an immediate hit with the public, attracting huge crowds for months. Nominated for four Academy Awards—Best Picture (M-G-M's *Grand Hotel* won), Best Adapted Screenplay, Best Cinematography, and Best Art Direction—it also made both *Photoplay's* and the *New York Times'* lists of the year's best. Author Sinclair Lewis acclaimed it as the only film he'd ever seen produced with such a delicate sense of respect for an author's original intentions. He was so pleased that he presented Ronald Colman with a copy of his book inscribed, "To Ronald Colman, who to me *is* Martin Arrowsmith,"[27] and sent an appreciative letter to Sam Goldwyn: "I want to thank you and Sidney Howard and Ronald Colman and Helen Hayes and Richard Bennett for a film which has completely carried out everything I tried to do in *Arrowsmith.*"[28] Goldwyn used the novelist's recommendation to promote the film, and it proved to be good publicity.

Today *Arrowsmith* lives up to its reputation on at least five levels: extraordinary direction, superb cinematography, superior production values, ambitious treatment of themes, and—most important—masterful performances from Ronald Colman and Helen Hayes.

The verve and snap of director John Ford's visual storytelling enabled him to achieve some forceful effects. The almost hallucinatory tension of the inoculation and rat-killing scenes and the shadowy stylization of Leora's death are handled with assurance and a firm, knowing hand. Intelligent, powerful, and mesmerizing, the film moves and is moving.

Some reviewers pointed out that Sidney Howard's screen treatment dispensed with scenes that were necessary to the advancement of the narrative and oversimplified the novel's interwoven themes. But this was to be expected, for to have brought every single page of such a complex and episodic novel to the screen would have resulted in a four-hour picture. Instead Howard drastically revised the story and eliminated whole sections of the book. By substituting a uniquely cinematic means of propelling the narrative forward, he condensed the themes into a series of succinct visual images which reveal the entire substance of the original.

In one memorable scene, for instance, the Arrowsmiths arrive for the first time at New York's McGurk Institute. Cameraman Ray June first films the soaring skyscraper directly from below in a subjective, low-angle shot, showing us exactly what they see. Then the camera cuts to an extreme high-angle shot from above, as the couple look up, overpowered by the building's proportions. In one brief, telling sequence, these deliberate false perspectives emphasize the alienation, both physical and psychological, that these rural strangers feel in their new urban surroundings. This effectively incorporates one of the major themes of the novel: mammoth Science dwarfing the insignificant practitioners who make possible its gigantic strides.[29]

And in a significant departure from the novel, *Arrowsmith* verifies the effectiveness of his experimental serum by vaccinating only half of the cattle threatened in a South Dakota epidemic. In the book, this episode had been mentioned only in passing, but by restructuring and emphasizing it as a parallel sequence to the later experiment on human lives in the Indies, Howard rendered more forceful the scenes in which Arrowsmith wrestles with the ethics of using human beings for the benefit of science as one does animals.[30]

Yet it must be acknowledged that some of *Arrowsmith's* scripting difficulties remain unsolved. Because of its severe condensing, the picture is too cramped to do full justice to the novel. Professor Gottlieb's eccentricities and inspiring brilliance, of such consequence throughout Arrowsmith's career, are inadequately etched and only hinted at, while the Terry Wickett character, so important in the novel for providing Arrowsmith with the impetus to strike out on his own, is never developed and remains a cardboard figure.[31] Omitted entirely is Martin's youthful rebelliousness and iconoclasm as a medical student, which in part explained his obsession with research in general and his repeated frustrations both as a country doctor and as the scientist he had so much wanted to become. But most significantly, the picture obliterates the immediate reasons behind Arrowsmith's decision to sever his ties with McGurk. In the novel, he did marry Joyce Lanyon and toiled at the institute for some time thereafter, only gradually — and hence more understandably — learning that he could not combine outside pursuits with the consuming round-the-clock vigil of a dedicated researcher. Thus when, in the film, he rejects Miss Lanyon and strikes out for Vermont on the very day he returns from the West Indies, most of his motivations for doing so are lost.

Yet if such dilutions flaw the picture, this is a small price to pay for what it does contain — marvelous, riveting, dramatic stuff, especially Ronald Colman's idealistic doctor and Helen Hayes' devoted wife. From their very first encounter at the hospital — she scrubbing the floor because she's been caught smoking a cigarette, he scolding her for not showing him proper respect and then promptly asking her to dinner — the stage is set for a perfect complementing of personalities: Colman with his wry and winning manner, self-deprecatory charm, and cheery disposition; Miss Hayes with her ingratiating, nervous little stutter, tender warmth, and unswerving loyalty.

"Well, we're married," he says as they leave the little courthouse after a brief, impersonal civil ceremony.

"*I* don't feel any different," she shrugs.

"I feel kind of *flat!*" he admits lethargically.

And then it's off to Wheatsylvania. No nonsense in this relationship.

To prepare Ronald Colman for his portrayal of a doctor, Sam Goldwyn engaged the services of Dr. Harry Martin, official physician to the National Boxing Commission, to teach his star the proper use of a needle for the scene in which he was to administer an injection to a dying diphtheria patient. It took Colman exactly 45 minutes to learn how to handle the hypodermic syringe deftly and correctly. Ninety minutes and three takes later, the shot was in the can, and Colman looked as if he'd been administering injections for years. Nothing was left to chance.[32]

During the early stages of production, the sensitive Britisher worried that he wasn't doing justice to the part of a midwestern country doctor, apprehensive that an Englishman couldn't portray such a recognizable American with conviction. Helen Hayes remembers that

> Ronald Colman didn't feel the part of the doctor was right for him, and he was walking through it, giving a poor performance and stinking it up in general when Sam heard about it. He came down to the set . . . sat Ronnie down in a corner, and had a long heart-to-heart talk with him. I don't know what he said, but after that Ronnie was better.[33]

Colman's fears were unfounded, for, as director John Ford remembered:

> *Arrowsmith* was already cast when I went over to Goldwyn. Ronnie and I were friends, so I was delighted. Though he was the leading star of the business then, nobody ever acknowledged what a superb actor he was. They just accepted him as Ronald Colman. He did everything so easily. He never played drunken scenes or grew a beard or did any of those things which get Academy Awards, but he was the greatest actor I have every known.[34]

Colman's work was accorded high praise by the critics, but the rave notices were saved for Helen Hayes, who was making only her second screen appearance. Her stirring death scene was one of the most sustained pieces of dramatic acting the cinema had seen to date, and her similarly restrained performance as she lay in bed after losing her baby at birth while Martin was away—tears coursing down her cheeks as she consoles her distraught husband with whispered promises—was so moving that a visitor on the set reported: "Ford looked misty-eyed when he finally called 'cut.' Hardened electricians coughed apologetically."[35] Curiously, neither Colman nor his co-star was nominated for an Academy Award for their work in *Arrowsmith,* although Miss Hayes did win the Best Actress award that year — for her performance in M-G-M's *The Sin of Madelon Claudet,* her very first film effort.

Ronald Colman, in his most challenging role since *Beau Geste,* acquitted himself with sincerity and conviction as the young doctor who dedicates his life to science, and turned in one of his finest performances to date. With his English accent, debonair manner, and wry sense of humor, he might not have been the ideal prototype of a small-town, midwestern American physician, but the character traits of dedication and sacrifice were tailor-made for the Colman image.

His finest moments come in scenes in which the frustrations of the fight struggle against the elation of the challenge. In South Dakota, he returns home late at night after failing to save a young girl dying of diphtheria. The silhouetting darkness intensifies his sense of loneliness, remorse, and failure as, slumped in a chair, he mutters over and over that he should have operated. But Leora urges him on. This scene dramatically parallels a later one in New York when, after two years of research have failed to produce a cure for disease, he despondently confesses that he's made a worse researcher than he did a doctor. Again his wife is by his side, urging him to press on. And finally, in one of Colman's most magnificent scenes, grief-stricken by personal tragedy and drinking heavily, he staggers through his clinic in the West Indies, roaring that he'll inoculate anybody he can get his hands on. But this time, although he had held the means of salvation in his very hands, his beloved Leora is gone.

Colman's crowning achievement of the early thirties, *Arrowsmith* quickly erased all traces of the ill-fated *Unholy Garden.* For his efforts he was awarded London's coveted *Film Weekly* Gold Medal and the first *Picturegoer Annual* Award. The first of his talkies to fully showcase the Colman image and the virtues with which his finest performances were so closely identified, *Arrowsmith* remained his own favorite until *A Tale of Two Cities* came along to displace it. At the age of 40, Ronald Colman found himself just entering the peak of his artistic career: the best was yet to come.

Cynara

1932. *Production:* Samuel Goldwyn, Inc. *Distribution:* United Artists Corporation. *Producer:* Samuel Goldwyn. *Director:* King Vidor. *Screenplay:* Lynn Starling, Frances Marion (from the play by H.M. Harwood and Robert Gore Browne and the novel *An Imperfect Lover* by Robert Gore Browne). *Cinematographer:* Ray June. *Musical Score:* Alfred Newman. *Art Director:* Richard Day. *Film Editor:* Hugh Bennett. *Running Time:* 80 minutes. *New York Premiere:* December 25, 1932. Reissued in 1945 as *I Was Faithful.*

Cast: Ronald Colman (Jim Warlock), Kay Francis (Clemency Warlock), Phyllis

Barry (Doris Lea), Henry Stephenson (John Tring), Viva Tattersall (Milly Miles), Florine McKinney (Gorla), Clarissa Selwyn (Onslow), Paul Porcasi (Joseph), George Kirby (Mr. Boots), Donald Stewart (Henry), Wilson Benge (Merton), C. Montague Shaw (Constable), Charlie Hall (Court Spectator), Halliwell Hobbes (Coroner).

Ronald Colman sidesteps his customary image in playing respectable English barrister James Warlock, a man with a brilliant future and a beautiful wife, in *Cynara*, King Vidor's sensitive study of marital tragedy. The drama begins and ends in Naples, where, with his career smashed and his marriage in ruins, Jim Warlock tells his wife, Clemency (Kay Francis), the story he had hoped to spare her. . . .

The camera takes us back to Clemency's departure for Venice, a four-week jaunt which commences on the eve of her seventh wedding anniversary. During her absence, her husband accompanies his friend John Tring (Henry Stephenson), a roguish old bachelor with a wandering eye, to a restaurant in Soho, where they chance to meet two attractive young shopgirls, Doris Lea and Milly Miles (Phyllis Barry and Viva Tattersall, respectively). At Tring's insistence, the four attend the cinema after they sup together.[36] After escorting Miss Lea home to her flat, Warlock promptly forgets the entire incident.

But John Tring has other ideas. In his designing eyes, there's no color in Jim Warlock's life, no variety. Deciding that his friend should kick over the traces of his straitlaced existence, Tring arranges for Warlock to judge a swimming contest, in which one of the lovely contestants is the endearing Miss Lea. The choice is difficult, but England expects of every man, and Warlock bestows the grand prize upon Doris. Against his will but nonetheless intrigued, he is enticed into an affair. It can't last, he warns her, and she in turn vows to forget him once he and Clemency are reunited. Moreover, she adds, this isn't the first time: she'd had a similar involvement once before.

Jim and Doris spend a brief idyll in a rustic cottage, but when Clemency returns, Warlock attempts to end the relationship. Fog and a dreary drizzle enshroud Hyde Park as Jim and Doris meet for the last time. Unable to face the thought of terminating their brief encounter, the girl has been neglecting her work and has been discharged. When Warlock offers to send her away on holiday, she insists he meet her the following Wednesday; she'll be in the park at five o'clock. He promises to try.

"I'll never forget you, Doris," Warlock murmurs as he puts her into a cab and Alfred Newman's "Blue Skies" motif takes on a darkening hue.

When Warlock cannot meet Doris on Wednesday, he dispatches an explanatory letter, but soon thereafter Milly Miles descends upon the barrister's residence, demanding that he settle the account with acceptable financial compensation. At this moment, a police officer arrives to ask Mr.

The moment of truth arrives as distinguished barrister Jim Warlock (Ronald Colman) decides to go through with his adulterous affair with shop-girl Doris Lea (Phyllis Barry). Cynara caused a temporary crisis in Colman's career, as audiences refused to accept him as an unfaithful husband.

Warlock whether he's acquainted with a Miss Doris Lea. It seems the young lady has committed suicide, and his letter has been found in her rooms.

At the coroner's inquest, the galleries are thronged with spectators. Thoughtful and tense, Jim Warlock looks on as Miss Miles delivers damaging testimony. When his turn comes, the barrister is asked whether any action of his was calculated to make this innocent child take such a desperate step. How did she react to his decision that they could not go on meeting? Had she had a similar relationship with any other man? Warlock refuses to admit that he had not been Miss Lea's first lover, leaving the authorities to draw the conclusion that he had used her and then discarded her—conduct for which he cannot, unfortunately, be held criminally responsible.

The story glides out of the past and brings us once again to Naples, as Jim Warlock completes his narrative. Why, Clemency asks him, didn't he tell the court that he had not been the first?

"I couldn't," he replies simply. "It was her secret."

Assuming that Clemency cannot possibly be expected to forget, Warlock leaves for the ship that is to take him to South Africa and a new life.

But Clemency does find it in her heart to forgive. Jim's been an upright barrister, and now he's a disgraced outcast who has suffered for his transgression. What if he never reaches South Africa? After all, the girl ended *her* life. Realizing that, despite all, she still loves him, Clemency rushes to join her husband on board just as the boat pulls out. Together they sail, ready to begin life anew.

Following the success of *Arrowsmith*, Sam Goldwyn toyed with the idea of starring Colman with Russian actress Anna Sten in an adaptation of *The Brothers Karamazov*, but soon assigned Arthur Hornblow the task of locating a more suitably attractive, romantic vehicle for his star. In London, Hornblow saw Gerald du Maurier in a stage version of Robert Gore Browne's novel *An Imperfect Lover*, which had been inspired by Ernest Dowson's memorable lines, "I have been faithful to thee, Cynara, in my fashion."[37] He found the role ideally suited to Colman's talents, and urged Goldwyn to acquire the rights. Colman, however, questioned the advisability of his portraying an adulterer, but when Hornblow insisted it would broaden his dramatic range, the producer decided to film it and the matter was settled.

Facing the toughest characterization of his career to date, Ronald Colman was ideally cast as the honorable gentleman who falls from grace, only to redeem himself in the witness stand. Sensitive, sympathetic, and sincere, protective of his marriage and reluctant to stray from the path of fidelity, he willingly sacrifices his career rather than reveal Doris' past. "If there are two things you can depend on," Clemency's sister Gorla (Florine McKinney) had once remarked, "they're the Church of England and Jim Warlock." Vulnerability had always been a part of the Colman mystique, but, highlighted here among the other distinctive, guiding traits which link one Colman portrayal to another, it makes this performance uniquely fascinating.[38]

It took courage to risk alienating his public by offering a characterization so different from what it had come to expect, but Ronald Colman was building a career, not merely consolidating a sudden popularity. To proclaim in 1932 that adultery need have no lasting effect upon marriage was an idea decidedly ahead of its time, and if the picture's morality and dialogue seem to creak a bit today, it is because contemporary attitudes toward infidelity have changed. Despite Colman's performance, Kay Francis' detached allure, Alfred Newman's haunting musical score, and King Vidor's tastefully restrained direction, this story of a man, his wife, and his mistress failed to impress audiences. As Colman's daughter puts it,

. . . they were simply not ready for their handsome hero to be an adulterer. They were not ready to accept him as an actor if it detracted from his personality as a star.[39]

Cynara was a prime example of the price often paid when a star contradicted any part of the image his public treasured—and, indeed, paid for . . . because his millions of fans felt they could not have misplaced their faith in him as a true gentleman of integrity and honor, and because of this were certain that Ronald Colman could not possibly be an adulterer, *Cynara* did not stand a chance. In the public's opinion it had been cheated of its money's worth of Ronald Colman. The established image was needed. . . .[40]

But although audiences largely ignored it, reviewers lavished praise upon *Cynara*. The *Los Angeles Times* called it

One of the most distinguished features of this or any other year . . . presented here recently to no great popular acclaim . . . a fine, serious and absorbing study . . . with Ronald Colman at his very best . . . a microscopic study of psychology and emotion with characters well-nigh perfectly drawn and situations that rise to rare reality and touch deep poignancy.[41]

Perhaps best of all, this analysis explains the appeal of *Cynara* today.

The Masquerader

1933. *Production:* Samuel Goldwyn, Inc. *Distribution:* United Artists Corporation. *Producer:* Samuel Goldwyn. *Director:* Richard Wallace. *Screenplay:* Howard Estabrook, Moss Hart (from the play by John Hunter Booth and the novel by Katherine Cecil Thurston). *Cinematographer:* Gregg Toland. *Musical Score:* Alfred Newman. *Art Director:* Richard Day. *Film Editor:* Stuart Heisler. *Sound:* Vernon Vinton. *Running Time:* 75 minutes. *New York Premiere:* September 3, 1933.

Cast: Ronald Colman (John Chilcote and John Loder), Elissa Landi (Eve Chilcote), Juliette Compton (Lady Diana Joyce), David Torrence (Fraser), Claude King (Lakely), Halliwell Hobbes (Brock), Helen Jerome Eddy (Robins), Eric Wilton (Alston), Montagu Shaw (Speaker of the House), Charlie Hall (Man in Park [deleted]).

A chance meeting in the London fog plummets Ronald Colman into a nightmarish, Jekyll-and-Hyde dual role as a drug-ravaged member of Parliament and the elegant double who takes his place in the House of Commons.

England is in crisis. Hunger strikers and police clash, and mob violence threatens the commonweal as the government valiantly attempts to protect the nation from disaster. Parliament's only hope lies in John Chilcote (Colman), its finest speaker but a man obviously unwell. Addicted to alcohol and morphine, the politician has just collapsed during a speech in the House of Commons. Following this disgraceful exhibition, Chilcote steadies his nerves by taking a leisurely stroll through Hyde Park. A dense, gray fog, creeping up from the Thames, has settled over London, thickening as the darkness deepens. Here Chilcote literally bumps into a man who is astonishingly similar in appearance: his cousin it turns out, an obscure journalist named John Loder (Colman again). Their faces match, feature for feature, and the seed is planted; Chilcote beholds a means of escaping the constant pressure of his parliamentary duties.

Having received an urgent call in Paris from her husband's loyal servant Brock (Halliwell Hobbes), informing her that Chilcote has suffered another breakdown, the politician's estranged wife, Eve (Elissa Landi), returns to London at once and persuades his closest party associates, Fraser and Lakely (David Torrence and Claude King, respectively), to allow Chilcote to deliver an all-important speech in the House of Commons.

But Chilcote's condition is beyond repair. Only John Loder can save the situation now.

"I know—get someone else—met him in the fog," Chilcote mumbles unsteadily. "Face—voice—everything. They'd never guess—make fine speech."

To Loder's residence at 13 Clifford's Inn, Chilcote stumbles, proposing that the journalist take his place in Parliament that afternoon. Brock, having followed his master, prevails upon Loder to impersonate the politician. A mad scheme, to be sure, but it means the end of Chilcote's career if he fails to appear in Parliament this time. Prompted by a clear consideration of duty to the Crown, Loder quickly dons Chilcote's clothes and, coached by Brock, assumes the politician's identity. The sole danger signal in this desperate move is that the journalist bears a pronounced scar on his left wrist; he'll have to keep it carefully concealed under his cuff.

To all men come portentous moments, difficult moments, triumphant moments. All three come to John Loder when, posing as Chilcote, he delivers a great, stirring speech in the House of Commons ("The only political party to whom we owe allegiance now—is all humanity!"), reasserting his position as a central figure in troubled times. Spontaneous cries of "Hear! Hear!" mark his exit from Parliament; Fraser and Lakely, congratulating him on his finest speech ever, swiftly guide him home, where a reception committee awaits him. So far the deception has worked, but can it succeed in the unfamiliar surroundings of Chilcote's own home? Smoothly exhibiting all the peculiar Chilcote mannerisms ("Nerves, nerves; just nerves, that's all!"), Loder pulls if off with perfect aplomb, managing to convince both Chilcote's mistress (Juliette Compton) and his wife with a flawless performance. The presence of both women complicates matters significantly, for Loder at first mistakenly assumes that Lady Diana Joyce, Chilcote's mistress, is his wife. In an especially delightful sequence, Alfred Newman's score takes on a light, Chaplinesque touch as the imposter,

The usually debonair Ronald Colman always sought roles that allowed him greater range. Here, in The Masquerader, *Halliwell Hobbes, as Brock, tries to pacify him, for to John Chilcote's drug-crazed mind, every shadow has become a phantom, every friend an enemy.*

fearfully assailed by doubts, beats a hasty retreat, tries on several bowlers in superb Laurel-and-Hardy fashion, then runs pell-mell into the garden, where the victory celebration is in full swing. Finally managing to reach the relative security of Chilcote's study, Loder gazes through a window at the party on the terrace.

"I'd *better* leave now," he tells Brock. "I'm making mistakes in wives!" Lady Joyce, his servant quickly explains, is "the other one!"

"Brock, who's that lovely girl out there?" Loder inquires.

"That's your wife, sir."

Unable to revive the stricken politician, Brock insists that Loder continue the masquerade, but informs him that Chilcote is not on very good terms with his wife. The door which separates Mrs. Chilcote's bedroom from her husband's has been locked for several years. But Eve's affection is soon rekindled for the man she believes to be her husband; she finds him a changed man. Replacing Chilcote's formality and disdain with gentleness and warmth, Loder falls in love with Eve, somewhat against his will.

Ignored and jealous, Lady Joyce hires a private detective, who trails Loder to the mysterious dwelling at 13 Clifford's Inn. Armed with the damaging information that Chilcote has employed a double, she confronts Loder at the posh River Club, to which the real John Chilcote is on his way.

"Do you suppose it's possible for one person to look *exactly* like another?" she taunts. "Same face, voice, expression, everything? I was just wondering if a man could vanish in the fog—walk completely out of life."

Having spotted his scar, Lady Joyce accuses Loder of being an imposter. In an effective but somewhat improbable scene, Loder backs out of the room just as Chilcote happens to enter. Asked to bare his wrist, the annoyed politician does so, but fails to exhibit a scar.

John Chilcote dies soon thereafter in Loder's flat, moments before Brock arrives with a doctor. The physician asks for the deceased's name.

"John—John Loder!" the servant replies.

Later, in Chilcote's study, Brock informs the imposter that he can never go back. The death certificate reads that John Loder, journalist, died an hour ago. There are so many great things to be done, and Chilcote had been too weak. When Loder insists he can't go on trading on another man's reputation, Brock gently reminds him that his grandfather was a Chilcote: there's more than mere chance involved.

Eve descends the stairs just as Loder prepares to depart. "It would be so easy to stray off into the fog and not come back, and I want you to stay— John Loder!"

She knows. Brock's told her.

"You've been so splendid," she pleads. "You've protected me; you've been loyal to him. You haven't a single thing to regret."

Chilcote's associates arrive. They want him to depart at once for an important summit meeting in Geneva.

"It rests," he says meaningfully, "entirely with—my wife!"

Katherine Cecil Thurston's 1904 novel of twin identities and political valor had already been the basis for two earlier dramatizations. Originally a Broadway stage hit in 1917, it was later filmed in 1922; Guy Bates Post played the dual role in both treatments. When the superbly acted Colman remake was released 11 years later, critics found much that was praiseworthy: Gregg Toland's rich, atmospheric rendering of fog-shrouded London; Moss Hart's delightfully humorous dialogue; sympathetic performances by Elissa Landi and the always impressive Halliwell Hobbes; and, of course, Ronald Colman's expert handling of the dual role.

After serving his apprenticeship with Goldwyn's ace cameraman, George Barnes, Gregg Toland was just now beginning to receive recognition as a pioneering cinematographer in his own right. His experiments here with deep-focus photography, shadowed lighting, and exaggerated low ceilings, in the stormy scenes which take place in Loder's flat, clearly prefigure his later work in *Mad Love* (1935) and *Citizen Kane* (1941). Through the use of rear projection and superimpositions, he managed perfectly to convey the illusion that Colman was conversing with his other self.

In the original novel, it was pure ambition which prompted John Loder to impersonate his distinguished cousin. The film, on the other hand, was carefully tailored to fit the Colman image, for here the supreme motivation is duty. Colman seized his opportunity and made the most of it, deftly sketching two entirely dissimilar personalities. As the debauched politician, the actor turned in a bravura performance. He appeared pale, wild-eyed, and unsteady; his staccato delivery was low-pitched, bitter, and strained. Disheveled locks of hair fell across his forehead as he stirred repeated over-doses of morphine into his whiskey. With the exception of his grief-stricken drunk scene in *Arrowsmith*, Colman had never been as flamboyant before. For most of the picture, however, he remained his self-assured, affable, jaunty self as John Loder.[42]

Besides the dual performance, *The Masquerader* bears other striking similarities to *The Prisoner of Zenda*, one of Colman's most distinctive films, on a more important level. In both pictures, he portrays a man whose pas-sion is rendered impossible through an inevitable conflict between love and honor. Always the clear course of honor wins out. Clearly, Eve has loved Loder from the moment he entered her life, presaging Princess Flavia's similar reaction to another imposter in the later film. Long before she knew he was Loder and not Chilcote, she says,

> "I never loved you as much as I love you now. Since the new John has come back to me, I don't think I really loved the old John at all.... You're a different man, someone — I seem never to have been with before, and yet I love you more than ever."

Aware that Eve loves him, Loder knows that he could have her, but he won't, for she is another man's wife. Here the similarities with *The Prisoner of Zenda* end, for Chilcote dies and Loder is not forced to renounce the woman he has come to love. Rising above convention, he and Eve carry the masquerade over into their "married" life, a dramatic conclusion which caused Sam Goldwyn untold difficulties with the censors, who complained of the apparent immorality of Eve Chilcote's living with a man who was not her husband. But the producer adamantly insisted that this was the only possible denouement, and the matter was eventually dropped.

The Masquerader was Ronald Colman's last picture for Samuel Goldwyn. Although it had been filmed shortly after *Cynara* in 1932, Goldwyn chose not to release it until the fall of 1933, sensing that he would never produce another Colman film. For, in the intervening months, the actor had sued Goldwyn and left the studio, after the producer had chosen to publicize his latest release by claiming that Colman merely condescended to lend his presence to the studio, and that he coped with the Chilcote half of his personality by belting down whiskies and sodas on the set. Always protective of his privacy and reputation, Colman had stated, as early as 1927: "If I am remembered at all, I hope I shall be remembered for what I may do on the screen, not for some publicized eccentricity, very likely not mine at all."[43]

As he wrote to Al Weingand,

> A dirty business, as you say, but if you knew the details, you would agree it had to be done. I tried every other way to try and stop them supplying such material to the press. We squawked often, but they persisted. Crazy and incredible I know. Other things behind it of course. I am confident it will come out all right, however, and pretty soon, and I believe with honour to myself.[44]

And, in a December 1932 interview, Colman added,

> I realize that nobody can be in a public business like making motion pictures without arousing a certain amount of public interest in one's affairs. I realize that there must be publicity, but it is only the kind of publicity to which I object.[45]

V

The Image of a Star

Following his dispute with Sam Goldwyn, Ronald Colman sailed for Spain with Al Weingand. After spending two months there, they crossed the Pyrenees into France. During their stay in Paris, Colman learned that his wife, Thelma, after hounding him for a decade with her battery of attorneys, had finally agreed to his terms. Their divorce was granted on August 1, 1934, with a minimum of publicity—and a substantial alimony settlement. Heady with his long-sought freedom, Colman celebrated, as Al Weingand later remembered:

> In Paris, I used to cut off at night. I was thirteen years younger than he and had not traveled extensively, so I'd go round to the night spots and he'd be very happy in the hotel after dinner, just settling down to read. Every now and then, I'd find something that looked pretty good, and if there were two of them, I'd invite them home, knock on his door and say, "Got somebody here, put your robe on and come in." And every now and then, they would stay the night. It wasn't very often, but if it was someone pretty and nice, he joined in. He was never promiscuous; it was not in his nature, only when something tickled his fancy.[1]

Relaxed and reinvigorated, they motored through Germany and Switzerland in the new Cadillac Colman had bought in Paris. After another month in a rented villa near Bayonne on the Basque coast, where their night life continued to be busy, they headed for Genoa, coursed through Suez, and boarded a Dutch ship bound for Sumatra. Java, Bali, the Celebes, and Manila followed; then across the Pacific to Seattle, a leisurely excursion down the coast by rail, and home.

Tanned and traveled after his ten-month jaunt, Colman returned to Hollywood. He was disappointed to learn that, in his absence, M-G-M had tried without success to locate him to play opposite Garbo in *Queen Christina*, a role which John Gilbert eventually got. On the brighter side, however, every major studio was eagerly bidding for his services.

Although Sam Goldwyn had wisely decided to settle Colman's damage suit out of court, the problem of contractual obligations remained. Rumors circulated that Colman would make films in England for Alexander Korda. Finally the impasse was resolved when Colman's friend Joseph M. Schenck, who had just formed Twentieth Century Pictures with Darryl F. Zanuck, persuaded Goldwyn to release the actor from his contract. Playing it safe, Twentieth Century starred him in a reprise of his first talking role in *Bulldog Drummond Strikes Back*. Reunited with lovely Loretta Young and supported by humorous sidekick Charles Butterworth, Colman outsmarts a gang of kidnappers in a delightful comedic thriller which paid off handsomely at the box office.

In his second effort for Twentieth Century, Colman appeared as lonely British empire-builder Robert Clive in an ambitious historical set piece, *Clive of India*. Loretta Young again co-starred. Despite its sweep and grandeur and a solid Colman performance, the film was ponderous, weak on action, and somewhat unsatisfactory.

Following the release of *Clive of India*, Twentieth Century merged with the Fox Film Corporation to form Twentieth Century–Fox, for which Colman made a diverting, lightweight comedy, *The Man Who Broke the Bank at Monte Carlo*. As an impoverished Russian emigré, he wooed another former leading lady, Joan Bennett, and traded quips with Nigel Bruce, but the critics pounced with sharpened claws, deeming the film unworthy of Colman's talents.

Yet they could not find enough praise for his next picture, the magnificent *A Tale of Two Cities*, made on loan-out to M-G-M. Produced by David O. Selznick, it offered elaborate costumes and sets; and an able supporting cast, headed by Elizabeth Allan, Edna May Oliver, Reginald Owen, Basil Rathbone, Blanche Yurka, Henry B. Walthall, Donald Woods, Claude Gillingwater, and Walter Catlett, made it a worthy successor to M-G-M's *David Copperfield*, released the previous year. As Sydney Carton, doomed hero of Charles Dickens' saga of the French Revolution, Colman gave a glowing, understated performance which perfectly balanced the turbulence of the film's setting. This was a role he had long wanted to play, and it remains one of his most memorable screen portrayals.

M-G-M had approached Colman at this time about co-starring with Garbo in *Anna Karenina*. Intrigued by the opportunity but aware that Garbo's role would necessarily be dominant, Colman doubled his normal fee of $150,000, and the studio promptly withdrew its offer.

During the filming of *A Tale of Two Cities*, co-star Elizabeth Allan introduced Colman to young English actress Benita Hume. The two had, in fact, met briefly three years before, when Miss Hume tested for the female lead in *The Masquerader*, an audition made necessary by the temporary illness of Colman's co-star, Elissa Landi. Attracted to each other immediately, she and Colman soon became inseparable, despite the actor's reluctance to become emotionally involved. Recently divorced herself, Benita quickly became a permanent fixture at Colman's home, both privately and as hostess for a growing number of dinner parties.

It was at this time that Colman sold his home on Mound Street and the beach house in Malibu and bought a more palatial Beverly Hills residence on Summit Drive not far from the legendary Pickfair, where his nearest neighbors, besides Mary Pickford, included Charlie Chaplin, Fred Astaire, and director William Wyler. The house boasted a large screening room, where guests frequently watched either silent films or the newest releases. There was also an extensive library, of which Colman was justly proud, that included the works of Shakespeare, Hugo, Stevenson, Wilde, Shaw, Carroll, Priestley, Conrad, and Walpole; the plays of ancestor George Colman; and especially the works of Dickens, for whom the actor held a particular fondness. His collection contained many rare first editions and signed presentation copies.

With Al Weingand, Colman also purchased San Ysidro Ranch, a 525-acre property just south of Santa Barbara, clustered with guest cottages, riding stables, tennis court, and swimming pool. A resort since 1893, it offered its own beach facilities a few miles away. Colman suddenly found himself in the hotel business, and among the celebrities who stayed there in the years to come were Aldous Huxley, John Galsworthy, Bertrand Russell, Adlai E. Stevenson, and, in 1953, Senator and Mrs. John F. Kennedy, who spent their honeymoon there. Colman used San Ysidro as he had Malibu, on weekends and between pictures, reserving for himself both a house and a studio, for his hobbies of painting and photography.

His final investment during this period was the *Dragoon*, a well-appointed, 67-foot yacht which sported a Norwegian skipper and cook, and aboard which he began taking Benita on lengthy cruises. The press soon started the rumor that they had been married on board by the skipper.

The years 1935 to 1940 found Colman at one of his highest levels of creative output. Although in his mid-forties, he always managed to look a good ten years younger, both on screen and off. In 1936 he donned French Foreign Legion attire for the first time since *Beau Geste* and returned to Twentieth Century–Fox for *Under Two Flags,* which co-starred him with Claudette Colbert, Victor McLaglen, and Rosalind Russell. Despite solid performances and suspensefully mounted battle sequences, many critics found it slow-moving and dull, and Twentieth Century–Fox chose not to renew his contract.

Every story has certain dates which rise like marble monuments above all others. A key year in the career of Ronald Colman was 1937, the year in which he gave two of his finest performances — as Robert Conway in *Lost Horizon* and as Rudolf Rassendyll in *The Prisoner of Zenda*, "the two films for which — together with *A Tale of Two Cities* — Colman is chiefly remembered."[2]

> There was now an element in Colman's acting style which suggested a vein of sadness under the surface of his roles — a world weary, *déjà vu* attitude . . . combined with a maturer, more intelligent concentration of detail. . . . Colman began to reveal facets of character whose bittersweet quality verged on a mystic awareness of the after life. His screen personality during this later period began to take on a heightened degree of spiritual changeability. Although his physical appearance never altered, and the olde worlde courtesy and charm were as much, if not more, a part of him as ever, his performances were becoming subtly different in texture. . . .[3]

Boasting a stunning visual momentum and a superlative supporting cast which included Jane Wyatt, Edward Everett Horton, Thomas Mitchell, Isabel Jewell, H.B. Warner, and Sam Jaffe, Frank Capra's *Lost Horizon* still enthralls as freshly as the day it was first released, having lost none of its prestige, popularity, or magic in the intervening years. As British diplomat Robert Conway, Ronald Colman surpassed himself; never again would he portray *himself* to such an identifiable degree, and in many ways this achievement went beyond anything he had done before or would do later.

Colman's performance in *Lost Horizon* was equaled in David O. Selznick's *The Prisoner of Zenda*, which, for sheer dazzling swashbuckling energy and excitement, ranks tops on any list of the finest films produced in Hollywood during the thirties. Colman excelled in his greatest dual role, and Madeleine Carroll, David Niven, C. Aubrey Smith, Raymond Massey, and Mary Astor lent solid support to a glittering production; Douglas Fairbanks, Jr., with his cool insolence and sparkling wit, was every bit Colman's equal as the wicked Rupert of Hentzau.

Inexplicably, neither film brought Colman an Academy Award nomination for Best Actor in 1937. Nominees were Charles Boyer for *Conquest*, Fredric March for *A Star Is Born*, Robert Montgomery for *Night Must Fall*, Paul Muni for *The Life of Emile Zola*, and the winner — Spencer Tracy for *Captains Courageous*.

Following the phenomenal success of *The Prisoner of Zenda*, Selznick put Colman under a seven-year contract, but although many projects were discussed, Colman never appeared in another Selznick picture. The role of Max de Winter in Alfred Hitchcock's first American production, *Rebecca*, was originally intended for Colman, but he declined to play a suspected murderer, remembering the public's reaction to his portrayal of an adulterer in *Cynara*. Leslie Howard and William Powell were other possibilities for the part, but it finally went to Laurence Olivier, who once said that Ronald Colman had always been among "the unwitting subjects of [his] avid imitation."[4] Colman was mentioned for the role of Anthony Keane in Hitchcock's *The Paradise Case,* but the part went to Gregory Peck, while the role of Rochester in *Jane Eyre,* eventually filmed by Twentieth Century–Fox, went to Orson Welles. Both Colman and William Powell rejected the lead in *Intermezzo,* and the part went to Leslie Howard. Colman was Selznick's first choice for Rhett Butler in *Gone with the Wind,* and they even discussed the matter of Colman's acquiring a southern accent.[5] Clark Gable was eventually signed, Vivien Leigh played Scarlett O'Hara, and the rest is history.

In 1937, Colman signed a contract for two pictures with Paramount. The first was another costumer, *If I Were King,* which chronicles the swashbuckling escapades of fabled French Renaissance poet and rogue François Villon. Preston Sturges' witty, literate script enlivened the action, and Colman was at his dashing, impudent best, courting lovely heroine Frances Dee and outwitting the schemes of Basil Rathbone's Spider King, Louis XI.

By this time, Benita Hume had made up her mind to return to London. She had been drawn to Colman, initially, because he was hard to get to know well, and because his quiet and gentle manners were thoroughly open and honest. But now, discouraged that the man she loved seemed no more interested in remarrying than when they first met, Benita left on a New York–bound train. She got as far as Albuquerque, where she found a telegram awaiting her in the train station: "Come home and let's get married."[6]

On September 30, 1938, two days after the release of *If I Were King,* they were married at San Ysidro Ranch.

"Imagine!" Benita later quipped. "I not only have that beautiful man, but that voice!"[7]

Colman was far more relaxed and social after he and Benita were wed. She was successful in drawing him out, breaking down his English restraint, and ending once and for all his reputation as a notorious Hollywood recluse. They began to live in a large, hospitable way and entertained frequently. Director Frank Capra and his wife had become close friends of the couple after *Lost Horizon,* and often attended dinner parties at the Colman residence on Summit Drive, where the most frequent guests included William Powell, Richard Barthelmess, Warner Baxter, Charles Boyer, Herbert Marshall, Col. Tim McCoy, Brian Aherne, and Richard Dix. A newcomer to the group was David Niven, whom Sam Goldwyn had signed as a Colman replacement because the Britisher spoke like Colman and was similarly moustached. Niven quickly became one of Colman's closest friends and soon graduated from the tennis regulars to the more exclusive supper group.

Newlyweds Ronald Colman and Benita Hume, married at San Ysidro Ranch on September 30, 1938.

Colman's second picture for Paramount, *The Light that Failed*, contained one of the finest performances of his career. Under William Wellman's expert direction and ably supported by Walter Huston and Ida Lupino, Colman played his usual heart-wrenching role as a tragic painter in this relentlessly faithful adaptation of Rudyard Kipling's first novel.

One of the screen's legendary partnerships, that of Basil Rathbone and Nigel Bruce as Sherlock Holmes and Dr. Watson, is celebrated by British colony friends Ronald Colman and Heather Thatcher at a party in the summer of 1939, after completion of The Hound of the Baskervilles *and* The Adventures of Sherlock Holmes.

During the filming of *The Light that Failed*, ex-wife Thelma fired one last, vindictive volley by opening a novelty shop in nearby Laguna Beach, intending to call it "The Original Mrs. Ronald Colman." She also threatened to publish a sensational memoir, but friends fortunately persuaded her to drop both ideas. Colman, happily married to Benita, ignored a potentially embarrassing situation.

His two-picture deal with Paramount completed, Colman signed a distribution arrangement with RKO, which resulted in two light comedies, both directed by veteran Lewis Milestone. *Lucky Partners*, a delicious romp which co-starred plucky Ginger Rogers, deserves more attention than it has received; *My Life with Caroline*, co-starring British newcomer Anna Lee, was less satisfying.

Thus ended a period in which Colman had made four of the finest films of his career. The forties had dawned, a decade that would bring years of diversification for Ronald Colman.

Bulldog Drummond Strikes Back

1934. *Production:* Twentieth Century Pictures, Inc. *Distribution:* United Artists Corporation. *Producers:* Joseph M. Schenck, Darryl F. Zanuck. *Director:* Roy Del Ruth. *Screenplay:* Nunnally Johnson (from the characters created by Herman Cyril McNeile ["Sapper"]). *Adaptation:* Henry Lehrman. *Cinematographer:* Peverell Marley. *Musical Score:* Alfred Newman. *Art Director:* Richard Day. *Costumes:* Gwen Wakeling. *Associate Producers:* William Goetz, Raymond Griffith. *Film Editor:* Allen McNeil. *Running Time:* 83 minutes. *New York Premiere:* August 15, 1934.

Cast: Ronald Colman (Captain Hugh Drummond), Loretta Young (Lola Field), Warner Oland (Prince Achmed), Charles Butterworth (Algy Longworth), Una Merkel (Gwen Longworth), C. Aubrey Smith (Inspector Alfred Reginald Nielson), Kathleen Burke (Lady Jane Sothern), Arthur Hohl (Dr. Owen Sothern), George Regas (Singh), Ethel Griffies (Mrs. Field), Mischa Auer (Hassan), Douglas Gerrard (Parker), Halliwell Hobbes, E.E. Clive, Yorke Sherwood (Policemen), William O'Brien (Banquet Servant), Pat Somerset, Vernon Steele, Creighton Hale (Wedding Guests), Gunnis Davis (Harsh-voiced Man), Charles Irwin (Drunk), Wilson Benge (Nielson's Valet), Olaf Hytton (Hotel Clerk), Charles McNaughton (Hotel Manager), Lucille Ball (Girl), Bob Kortman (Henchman), Doreen Monroe (Woman in Hotel Room), Billy Bevan (Man in Hotel Room).

A thick, gray fog has settled over London as Bulldog Drummond (Ronald Colman) returns home after attending the wedding of longtime hindrance Algy Longworth (the engaging Charles Butterworth). Soon lost in the impenetrable mist, he gropes his way into the first well-lit house he manages to stumble upon, hoping thereby to regain his sense of direction. Within this seemingly deserted mansion, a horrifying sight awaits him: sprawled upon a couch before a roaring fireplace lies the corpse of a man who died in frightful agony. Drummond rushes back into the fog and summons a policeman (Halliwell Hobbes).

"Officer, I've found it for you!"

"Found what, sir?"

"The *body!*" he announces triumphantly.

Together they retrace steps taken only moments ago, but this time the front door is locked, and when they do gain entrance, Prince Achmed, an Oriental of decidedly menacing countenance (Warner Oland), greets them with well-oiled courtesy. To make matters worse, the body on the sofa is no longer the same body, but merely a man awakening from a nap, claiming to have been there for the past two hours. Apologizing for the intrusion, Drummond leaves, after being urged by the patrolman to go home and sleep

Swedish-born actor Warner Oland (right) *plays Prince Achmed, an Oriental villain in* Bulldog Drummond Strikes Back. *He was at the same time also portraying Earl Derr Biggers' Chinese sleuth, Charlie Chan. Also seen* (left) *are George Regas and Halliwell Hobbes.*

it off. Does he do so? Not Bulldog Drummond. He returns, only to be warned by the sinister prince that if he places the slightest value on his life, he'll forget the entire incident.

No sooner does Drummond arrive home than a beautiful visitor invades the premises. Miss Lola Field (Loretta Young) has been looking for Colonel Nielson of Scotland Yard (crotchety old C. Aubrey Smith) in the flat above, but, learning that amateur detection is Captain Drummond's most amusing hobby, she relates a fantastic tale: She and her aunt and uncle had just arrived this morning from the East Indies, aboard the cargo ship *Bombay Girl*. Running into some sort of quarantine, they went straight to a hotel near the docks. Her uncle left to make a report, and that's the last they've seen of him; he's disappeared. The owner of the ship had instructed him to sell everything he owned in the Indies, purchase a priceless cargo of furs, and ship it to England. En route, however, they received a mysterious radiogram in code, from Port Said on the Suez Canal, where they had stopped to take a sick deckhand ashore. Miss Field has been to the owner's home, but was assured that her uncle had never arrived. The ship-owner's name: Prince Achmed!

A dark and gloomy house in the fog, a body that disappears, an evil Oriental prince, and now a young woman in distress, a lost uncle, and a coded radiogram. Drummond takes charge and motors with Miss Field and Algy, whom he has interrupted from wedding-night festivities, to the East India Hotel. But the desk clerk and hotel manager claim they've never seen the lady before; neither she, her aunt, nor her uncle is registered. Drummond inspects Lola's suite, occupied now, of course, by new tenants, but every-thing—the wallpaper, the furniture—has been changed.

"Goodnight, Captain Drummond," the manager bids them as they take their leave.

"Drummond. Why do you call me Captain Drummond?"

"You told me that was your name, sir."

"Oh, no, no, no, you're mistaken," he reproaches playfully. "I never told you my name. Matter of fact, my name is Fortesque. Mortimer P. Fortes-que. Remember that."

Leaving Algy the task of deciphering the coded message, Drummond returns to his flat with Lola, runs upstairs, and fetches Colonel Nielson out of a sound sleep. In his absence, Achmed's hirelings kidnap the girl.

"May I go to bed now?" Nielson scowls. "Drummond, you found a body; it disappeared. You found a girl; *she* disappeared. She had a hotel room; *it* disappeared. Why is it my blasted luck that everything and everybody can disappear except you?" he splutters, storming out.

Drummond regains the upper hand by snatching the heavily drugged aunt from captivity at Achmed's residence, but she too is soon spirited away by hired thugs. Enough is enough. Drummond sets out to turn the tables, after instructing Algy to bring his translation of the radiogram to Achmed's within the hour. Moments before the Bulldog reaches the prince's lair, Lola is informed that her uncle has indeed been murdered, and that her life positively depends upon the recovery of that radiogram. The doorbell rings, and Drummond interrupts Achmed's carefully prepared scenario.

"More or less open house tonight, isn't it," he grins urbanely. "Well, there seems to be a certain *charm* about this lovely old mausoleum. Now listen, my good-natured friend; perhaps we can reach some agreement. If you'll stop kidnapping people from *my* house, I'll promise to stop breaking into *yours;* otherwise, this sort of thing might keep up all night!"

Overpowered and disarmed, Drummond evaluates his predicament: "As awkward a situation, your Highness, as any I can remember. Empty-handed, entirely surrounded by villains armed to the teeth and thirsting for my blood. May I have a cigarette? You'll notice that, uh, in spite of my danger, I still remain calm and collected, keen and alert for the next move. What will it be?"

The radiogram, of course, for it means half a million pounds to Achmed. But after Algy shows up, is threatened with a revolver, and retaliates by swallowing the decoded dispatch, both he and Drummond are escorted to a heavily locked basement dungeon. Here, Algy divulges the contents of the carefully guarded radiogram: the sailor put ashore at Port Said died of cholera!

Drummond and Algy escape in time to reach the dock just before the infected cargo is unloaded. In a fast-paced scene, Drummond races up the gangplank of the *Bombay Girl* and sets the hold ablaze. Realizing that he has lost, Achmed commits suicide.

Several hours later, as the early-morning rays of sunlight begin to stream through the disappearing fog, Algy is once more prevented from exercising his marital obligations when the telephone rings: it's Hugh Drummond. Miss Field, it seems, has caught Drummonditis; the nuptials will take place as soon as Algy and his bride, Gwen (Una Merkel), can get over.

"His marriage?" Gwen asks. "To whom?"

"Some girl he met in the fog last night," Algy replies. "I never did catch her name."

These sinister doings in a fog-shrouded house marked the return of Ronald Colman to the role of Captain Hugh Drummond, with which he had launched his talkie career five years earlier. Directed with panache by Roy Del Ruth, the film offered a witty Nunnally Johnson script, handsome sets, exquisite lighting and photography, a robust musical score by Alfred Newman, and delightful performances throughout.

Like its predecessor, *Bulldog Drummond Strikes Back* is a tale of strange encounters, daring rescues, hairbreadth escapes, and glorious battles. The plot itself, centering upon a dramatically altered hotel room and an emphatic denial that Miss Field's uncle ever existed, stemmed not from the H.C. "Sapper" McNeile stories but from a supposedly true incident in which all traces of a visitor to the Paris Exposition of 1880 were systematically obliterated when it was discovered that she suffered from bubonic plague.[8] This yarn was novelized in 1936 by Ethel Lina White in *The Wheel Spins* and later filmed, in a much-altered version, by Alfred Hitchcock as *The Lady Vanishes* (1938),[9] but its basic premise was brought to the screen first in *Bulldog Drummond Strikes Back*.

More exuberant and freewheeling than the earlier treatment, the picture was studded with running gags which enlivened the action: the frequent appearances of E.E. Clive as a flummoxed bobby, mirthfully solving every crisis by crying, "Orders is orders"; the exasperation of C. Aubrey Smith, superb as the Scotland Yard inspector constantly rousted out of bed by Drummond, glowering as he repeatedly urges this "born disturber of other people's sleep" to give everybody a break by retiring to Sussex to raise hollyhocks; and, of course, the cliché of assorted disappearing bodies — one dead, two alive—who vanish with alarming frequency. But most hilarious, certainly, is Drummond's continual disruption of Algy's honeymoon activities, insisting that he drop everything at once and heed the call to adventure.

This time around, Algy Longworth is a forlorn little chap with the face of a frightened rabbit, and Charles Butterworth has ample opportunity to prove that providence looks after infants, inebriates, and idiots of the Algy stamp. Early on, Drummond congratulates him on his marriage.

"Thanks, Hugh; they say I'll be very happy," confides Algy with an open mind.

"Don't forget to telephone," he reminds Drummond moments later, "even if it's just a postcard!"

Butterworth is clearly reminiscent of Stan Laurel in his comedic touch, as vacant stare quickly gives way to thoroughgoing bewilderment.

"Oh, Algy, I'm the happiest woman in the *world!*" Gwen gushes upon their arrival at the bridal suite.

"Oh, no, darling; *I* am!"

Hours later, Algy returns to his anxious bride after having rushed off with Drummond.

"Darling, you'll never leave me again, will you?" she implores.

"Never, my love, never, and I'll be right back, too!"

Ronald Colman's lighthearted flair for comedy and his unruffled polish were as readily apparent as before. All of the little comedic nuances that had defined the Drummond character in 1929—especially the wisecracks—we now find developed and perfected in his 1934 incarnation. With its amusing, satiric zest, *Bulldog Drummond Strikes Back* received a warm welcome from both public and critics. Although "less remarkable a film in the context of its year . . . than the original had been in 1929, by all other standards it was that rarity, a sequel superior to its original."[10]

Clive of India

1935. *Production:* Twentieth Century Pictures, Inc. *Distribution:* United Artists Corporation. *Producers:* Joseph M. Schenck, Darryl F. Zanuck. *Director:* Richard Boleslawski. *Screenplay:* W.P. Lipscomb, R.J. Minney (from their play and the biography *Clive* by R.J. Minney). *Cinematographer:* Peverell Marley. *Musical Score:* Alfred Newman. *Art Director:* Richard Day. *Costumes:* Omar Kiam. *Associate Producers:* William Goetz, Raymond Griffith. *Assistant Director:* Ben Silvey. *Film Editor:* Barbara McLean. *Running Time:* 90 minutes. *New York Premiere:* January 17, 1935.

Cast: Ronald Colman (Robert Clive), Loretta Young (Margaret Maskeleyne), Colin Clive (Captain Johnstone), Francis Lister (Edmund Maskeleyne), C. Aubrey Smith (Prime Minister), Cesar Romero (Mir Jaffar), Montagu Love (Governor Pigot), Lumsden Hare (Sergeant Clark), Ferdinand Munier (Admiral Charles Watson),

Gilbert Emery (Mr. Sullivan), Leo G. Carroll (Mr. Manning), Etienne Girardot (Mr. Warburton), Robert Greig (Mr. Pemberton), Mischa Auer (Suraj Ud Dowlah), Ferdinand Gottschalk (Old Member), Doris Lloyd (Mrs. Nixon), Edward Cooper (Clive's Butler), Eily Malyon (Mrs. Clifford), Joseph Tozer (Sir Frith), Phyllis Clare (Margaret's Friend), Leonard Mudie (General Burgoyne), Phillip Dare (Captain George), Ian Wolfe (Mr. Kent), Herbert Bunston (First Director), Wyndham Standing (Colonel Townsend), Ann Shaw (Lady Lindley), Vernon Downing (Mr. Stringer), Neville Clark (Mr. Vincent), Peter Shaw (Mr. Miller), Pat Somerset (Lieutenant Walsh), Keith Kenneth (Second Director), Desmond Roberts (Third Director), Connie Leon (Ayah), Charles Evans (Surveyor), Vesey O'Davern (Assistant Surveyor), Lila Lance (Mango Seller), Harry Ernest (Boy Bugler), John Carradine (Drunken-Faced Clerk), Emmett O. King (Merchant), Olaf Hytten (Parson), Don Ameche (Black Hole of Calcutta Prisoner).

Appearing without his famous moustache for the first time since *Handcuffs or Kisses?* (1921), Ronald Colman starred in *Clive of India,* Twentieth Century's impressively costumed screen biography of England's eighteenth-century empire-builder, Robert Clive.

India in 1748 . . . rich in jewels, spices, and precious metals . . . where French, Dutch, Portuguese, and British entrepreneurs attempt to outwit one another in establishing exclusive trading rights over this vast paradise of wealth. At Fort St. David, headquarters of the British East India Company, we meet Robert Clive (Colman), an impetuous young man who had arrived years before as a clerk for the company. Sensing that he is destined to play a major role in securing British rule over India, Clive joins the British army when French forces seize an English outpost. At Trichinopoly, the entire British force stumbles into a trap and faces almost certain annihilation. Quickly displaying an astute military talent, Clive is given unreserved authority. He relieves Trichinopoly by capturing the capital city of Arcot, and in less than a year becomes the conqueror of Southern India.

Clive weds lovely Margaret Maskeleyne (Loretta Young), and together they return to England, where the next step is Parliament and real power. For six years he wages one successful election battle after another, always being returned to his seat in the House of Commons. But in 1756, destiny again chooses Robert Clive: war has broken out, and the East India Company implores him to sail immediately. Despite the serious illness of their newborn son, Margaret accompanies her husband to India, leaving the child behind in England, where he soon dies.

British forces have been expelled from Calcutta, and when Colonel Clive demands the release of all prisoners, local Moslem ruler Suraj Ud Dowlah (Mischa Auer) consigns them to the suffocating hell of the Black Hole; not more than a handful out of the entire 146 survive. Clive determines to drag this madman from his throne and replace him with Mir Jaffar (Cesar Romero), a potential ally who is not unwilling to serve British interests. If Suraj wants death to the last man, he shall have it.

In a rare moustacheless appearance, Ronald Colman plays British Empire–builder Robert Clive, seen here consulting with the treacherous Mir Jaffar (Cesar Romero). Francis Lister stands at left.

Clive and Mir Jaffar arrange a secret treaty assuring England's right to trade in peace, but Clive's nominal superior, a blundering elephant of an admiral named Watson (Ferdinand Munier), refuses to sign it. With nothing less than an empire at stake, Clive unhesitatingly forges the officer's signature on the document and prepares to meet Suraj on the field of battle, pausing only to bid his wife good-bye:

> "Margaret, tell me; it may happen soon that I shall stand at the crossways. Yet to go on and fail may mean the death of us all. *If* I fail, Suraj will have no mercy on man, woman, or child. I—I—I may *want* to go on, if my work is to endure. Tell me, if I find myself at that crossway, would you give me *leave* to go on, even then?"

Whatever happens, she'll stand by him. "Bob, I'm a very simple woman, but I *know* that a man like you will do what he must."

Clive's small force of British and sepoys reaches Plassey, where Mir Jaffar has promised to join them with 30,000 troops. But will he? Once Clive crosses the river and engages Suraj's army, he'll be stranded, with no assurance that Jaffar will fulfill his part of the bargain. Governor Pigot (Montagu Love) urges him not to take the risk, but Clive, anxious to launch his sudden attack, dismisses him with a simple message for Margaret: "Tell her—I stand at the crossways. She'll understand."

In a superbly mounted montage sequence, aurally enhanced by the howling wind and Alfred Newman's pounding musical score, Clive pushes across the river as raging monsoon winds rend the air. Like a whirlwind, the British begin the piecemeal destruction, until Suraj hurls into the battle India's most fearsome weapon: armored elephants. This frightful tangling of men and brutes leads to a full-scale withdrawal of Suraj's obliterated troops at the moment when all had seemed lost: Mir Jaffar keeps his promise and launches his force of 30,000 into the fray. Robert Clive emerges the victor of Plassey, which will forever live as a monument to one man's courage.

After accepting a grateful gift from Mir Jaffar, Clive returns to England with his wife. India is at peace, Jaffar is crowned king, and trade prospers. Clive's work is done, and Margaret's dreams are realized: her husband retires from public life and settles down to the life of a country gentleman on their estate at Walcott. The quietude of pastoral splendor, however, is soon shattered by the arrival of Governor Pigot. Only Clive can salvage the Indian situation now, says the governor; it's as bad as if he had never won the battle of Plassey.

"I implored His Majesty," says Clive with vehemence. "I begged the Prime Minister that the government should take it over. India should be a sacred trust!"

India is in ruins, and he's been promised an absolutely free hand, but this time Clive departs alone. He's already lost one child, and another's on the way, but this one will be born in England. "Meg, I must keep faith." The camera takes us to a wind-driven shot of Robert Clive en route to India, wistfully gazing at a miniature of Meg clutched in his hand.

In his absence, British newspapers start a campaign of scandal, averring that Clive's gift from Mir Jaffar was a bribe. He returns to England to scotch these malicious rumors, only to find Parliament prepared to strip him of his fortune, his reputation, and his honor. Against enormous odds, he's founded and solidified an empire, given England three new provinces, and received not a word of thanks. In the House of Commons, the broken empire-builder is indicted for illegally acquiring his vast fortune to the dishonor and detriment of the state. Alleging that a forger would hardly stop at accepting a bribe, his opponents demand a vote of censure and the confiscation of his ill-gotten gains. Mustering all his remaining strength, Clive attempts to explain:

> "You can name a thousand things out of the past—of any public man, that can be twisted, warped, and changed to suit the purpose of an inquiry, an

inquiry which takes the form of an inquisition. What I have done, I have done for India, and for my country, to the best of my ability. By this vote tonight, you can take my wealth, my honor, my reputation—just as—India has already taken from me the thing I hold most dear. But after all these years, to be called to account, to be stripped of everything I possess, is unwarrantable. It is unworthy of the British people. Gentlemen, I have a conscious innocence, and before I leave this House I have one request: that when the members come to decide upon the question—of my honor, they will not forget their own."

It is perhaps a great mistake for a soldier to live too long, Clive muses as he returns to his old home in Queen's Square to face the verdict alone, his glory departed perhaps evermore; better to be buried with honor as a fallen warrior than this. But Meg, knowing his need, returns to his side, and together they await word of what may be the end. Finally, the prime minister (C. Aubrey Smith) arrives to announce that the House has condemned Clive's conduct, nonetheless conceding that he has rendered a great service to his country. King George, in private consultation with the prime minister, has decreed that, whatever the verdict, Robert Clive's wealth and honor will remain intact.

Impressed by the London stage hit *Clive of India*, Twentieth Century's Darryl F. Zanuck quickly acquired both the film rights and the services of the play's authors, W.P. Lipscomb and Rubeigh James Minney, whom he brought to Hollywood to write a screenplay for Ronald Colman. After discovering basic similarities between his own career and that of Robert Clive (both had been clerks in their youth; both remained reserved men after later achieving fame and fortune), Colman began to devour all the literature he could find on Clive, in an attempt to work more effectively from within the character. Evidently it was this research that led to Colman's separation from his trademark moustache. Scenarist R.J. Minney recalls the day he discussed his plan:

> While we talked Ronnie Colman began stroking his moustache. I could see what was on his mind.
> I said: "You know, Ronnie, there is no reason why you should sacrifice it."
> Ronnie said: "I'm afraid I have no alternative. Clive never had a moustache. You yourself have said so."
> I said: "But Ronald Colman also owes something to his public. They know that moustache. It is something familiar. They are extremely fond of it. It is part of the architecture of that well-known face."
> "But—"
> "Wait a minute. For every one person in the audience who knows that Clive didn't wear a moustache, there will be a thousand who only remember that Ronald Colman did."
> Ronnie stroked it a fond farewell. The next morning when I saw him at the studio, it was gone.[11]

Colman's clean-shaven character inspired Jeffrey Richards to observe that with the removal of the moustache, Colman's "suave, serenely confident man about town vanishes. . . . [H]is face seems to become longer and thinner, his eyes seem to reflect a melancholy and worldweariness."[12]

Despite the research involved, the picture actually offered a highly romanticized account of Clive's life, glossing over the established historical fact that Clive *did* line his own pockets by extorting huge reparations after the Battle of Plassey in 1757, and simply ignoring his ultimate suicide in 1774 at the age of 49. Given his most challenging assignment since *Cynara,* Colman wisely sidestepped the megalomaniacal, self-aggrandizing aspects of Clive's nature, and by emphasizing his devotion to duty, made the role more appealing, thus earning the immediate sympathy of his audience. As André Sennwald commented,

> Ronald Colman, suppressing the debonair manner which has made him one of our finest light comedians, enacts the title role with vigor and conviction, providing a touching portrait of a man with a consuming passion for power. Certainly this is one of his best screen achievements.[13]

Scenarist Minney, author of the definitive biography of Robert Clive, later said, "I don't think I ever wanted anyone else for the part but him, because he was so exactly right."[14]

But despite Colman's sensitive performance and the film's success, *Clive of India* fails to hit the mark on at least two levels. The first is that Colman's portrayal is marred by an occasional fuzziness in characterization. The glow of an unquenchable patriotism causes Clive to sacrifice the life of his child, the love of his wife, and, ultimately, his reputation. We see it, we hear it, as he first arrives in England ("It's such a good country, that — one wonders — how we ever left it"), and as he later defends his actions in the House of Commons, but the well from which his imperialistic fervor springs is never made manifest; the film simply presents Clive as a driven man and milks the conflict between love and duty for all it is worth, without ever revealing *why* the lust for territorial acquisition drives him on.

At the second level, this sprawling epic is so excessively preoccupied with its subject's domestic life that it often dismisses his truly heroic exploits with intrusive intertitles which merely describe the action and adventure that audiences had paid to see. Left to our imagination, for instance, is the great siege of Arcot: how Clive struck, and how the enemy resisted, is never shown. Reportedly a costly picture, very little of the expense is evident. Many of the sets have a cramped, budget-conscious look, and the skimpy exteriors provide further evidence that most of the money was spent on the costumes. Even the thundering Battle of Plassey, the only scene which offers real action, shows every sign of a small group of extras desperately pretending to be a crowd. Paramount's *Lives of a Bengal Lancer* (1935) and RKO's *Gunga Din* (1939) were similarly lavish Hollywood yarns which celebrated the glory of British rule in India; they, too, were shot in the California hills, but they managed to look as though they had been filmed in India. *Clive* doesn't, for very little of it was shot outdoors.

With its serious flaws in emphasis, the film remains a worthwhile effort that just doesn't catch fire. No wonder, then, that André Sennwald called it

> ...a dignified and impressive historical drama which misses genuine distinction by a comfortable margin.... The military drama attains its richest expression by dropping the time-honored sex motif and concentrating on the sheer excitement of physical action.[15]

The Man Who Broke the Bank at Monte Carlo

1935. *Production and distribution:* Twentieth Century–Fox Film Corporation. *Producer:* Darryl F. Zanuck. *Director:* Stephen Roberts. *Screenplay:* Nunnally Johnson, Howard Smith (from the play *Monsieur Alexandre, Igra, Lepy, and the Gamble* by Illie Surgutchoff and Frederick Albert Swann). *Cinematographer:* Ernest Palmer. *Musical Director:* Oscar Bradley. *Incidental Music:* Bert Kalmar, Harry Ruby. *Running Time:* 66 minutes. *Release Date:* November 14, 1935.

Cast: Ronald Colman (Paul Gallard), Joan Bennett (Helen Berkeley), Colin Clive (Bertrand Berkeley), Nigel Bruce (Ivan), Montagu Love (Casino Director), Frank Reicher (Assistant Director), Lionel Pope (Assistant Director), Ferdinand Gottschalk (Office Manager), Charles Fallon (Croupier), Sam Ash (Guard), Vladimir Bykoff (Helen's Guide), Leonard Snegoff (Nick the Chef), Charles Coleman (Head Waiter), John Pecora (Patron), Lynn Bari (Flower Girl), Georgette Rhodes (Check Room Girl), Ramsey Hill, Milton Royce (Ushers), Bruce Wyndham (Excited Man), Frederic Sullivan (Pompous Man), Alphonse Martel (Chasseur), John Spacey, William Stack (Directors), Don Brodie (Photographer), E.E. Clive, Bob De Coudie, Joseph De Stefani (Waiters), Will Stanton (Drunk Waiter), Christian Rub (Gallard's Guide), I. Miraeva (Singing and Dancing Cook), Tom Herbert (Man at Table), Torben Meyer, Maurice Cass, Ferdinand Munier.

Monte Carlo! Croupiers and gaming tables, millions of francs changing hands. The spin of the wheel, the roll of the dice, the toss of the cards. The bigger the risk, the greater the thrill.

To Monte Carlo comes Parisian taxi driver and expatriate Russian aristocrat Paul Gallard (an elegantly attired Ronald Colman), determined to risk his own savings and those of his fellow emigrés—and break the bank as well. After a terrific run of 15 straight wins at the baccarat table, he wagers his entire stack—and wins again. The house surrenders and withdraws. He's broken the bank! Victory and cash: to live again like a Romanov. Cramming his millions of bank notes into a battered suitcase, Gallard exits grandly the following morning and returns to Paris, despite the insistence of the casino management that he try his luck a second night.

To lure him back to the tables, the villainous casino director (Montagu Love) engages the nefarious services of lovely Helen Berkeley (Joan Bennett) and an accomplice posing as her brother (Colin Clive). Miss Berkeley and Gallard share a romantic interlude in picturesque Switzerland, where she concocts an elaborate ruse designed to land him solidly in the clutches of the Monte Carlo gambling syndicate. But complications arise when Miss Berkeley falls hopelessly in love with her ardent gambler, and he with her.

Cautioned not to return to Monte Carlo by his faithful valet Ivan (the ever-delightful Nigel Bruce), whose non-existent Sherlockian abilities have deduced that Helen Berkeley is a money-hungry adventuress, heavily financed with Monte Carlo gold and prepared to throw him away like an empty vodka bottle once he's lost his millions, Gallard places his tongue firmly in cheek and protests with mock sincerity:

"Don't worry, old friend. I understand what going back to Monte Carlo may mean. I give you my word I fought against it. I fought a good fight, a hard fight. But fortunately," he grins, "I have a very weak character."

Word quickly circulates through the crowded casino: the man who broke the bank is back. Tension mounts as he begins to win. And win. And win. The house is down to its last tray of cash. Again Gallard bets his whole stack — 4,000,000 francs — but this time he loses. Everything. The law of averages, you know.

Discovering Miss Berkeley's part in the plot, but unaware that she regrets her shabby behavior, the once-prodigal son heads for Paris with a jaunty exterior but a disillusioned heart.

A year later, still a Paris cabbie with nothing to his name but 15 francs, one melancholy valet, and an unquenchable capacity for living in the past and dreaming of the future, Gallard encounters Helen Berkeley on his own turf. This time she's a cabaret chanteuse, of all things.[16] After some difficulty, she manages to convince him that she does love him, and all ends on a happy, if slightly poverty-stricken, note.

One could have guessed it would. Somewhere in the Swiss Alps, Miss Berkeley had remarked that this was, after all, melodrama, not romance. She was right: it was. And pretty silly stuff at that.

With two straight successes behind him since his departure from Goldwyn (*Bulldog Drummond Strikes Back* and *Clive of India*, both made for Twentieth Century), Ronald Colman decided to remain within the friendly embrace of the newly merged Twentieth Century–Fox organization for his next picture. Sporting the famous clipped moustache once again, he starred in this diverting if not particularly outstanding light comedy, "chiefly distinguished for the length of its title."[17]

Colman's attempt to portray a Russian would have been an embarrassment, were it not for the fact that he doesn't make the attempt at all. With his light, debonair manner, we either accept him as one — English accent and all — or we don't. Period. What the film lacks in verisimilitude, however, is offset by some pretty brisk dialogue, much of it from Colman's gloomy playmate Ivan, as benevolent a buffoon as ever Nigel Bruce portrayed:

"I never held with gambling, sir," he intones at one point. "During the war, your excellency's losses at cards prevented your paying me for about five years, which has left me with a rather lukewarm attitude towards games of chance. The only way to cure a gambler, sir, is to kill him."

In contrast to such morose insights, Colman displays his typical savoir faire when, reclining on a mountain ledge in the Swiss Alps, he blandly looks up, perceives Joan Bennett dangling from the end of a safety rope a foot or so off the ground, and whimsically refrains from disengaging her:

"You don't know anybody by the name of Marshwater, do you?" he asks playfully.

"No."

"No, neither do I, though I must say I've always wanted to."[18]

Charming and nonchalant though Colman's performance was, the critics expected something rather more substantial than this gay, entertaining trifle. André Sennwald found Colman "handsome and debonair, though somewhat less sprightly than is his custom,"[19] and Miss Bennett (given ample opportunity to prove herself no more plausible than she had been six years earlier in *Bulldog Drummond*) "badly miscast, her wooden charm and vocal monotony having almost nothing to do with the lady of mystery that she is pretending to be."[20] Pulling no punches, he added: "Commonplace in its plot workings and meager in gayety, the film misuses a promising comic idea."[21]

The Man Who Broke the Bank made a killing at the casino but broke very few box-office records. The film was only a moderate success. Despite Colman's avowed preference for light comedies, one suspects that he was consciously marking time while awaiting a better script. As one observer remarked, "It added little to Colman's stature, but at the same time did him no harm."[22] Nor could it, for *A Tale of Two Cities* was just around the corner.

A Tale of Two Cities

1935. *Production and distribution:* Metro-Goldwyn-Mayer Pictures Corporation. *Producer:* David O. Selznick. *Director:* Jack Conway. *Revolutionary Sequences Directors:* Val Lewton, Jacques Tourneur. *Additional Scenes Directors:* Robert Z. Leonard, W.S. Van Dyke (uncredited). *Screenplay:* W.P. Lipscomb, S.N. Behrman (from the novel by Charles Dickens). *Bibliography:* Thomas Carlyle's *The French Revolution*, M. Clery's *Journal of the Temple*, Mlle. des Escherolles' *Memoirs*, M. Nicholas' *Memoirs*. *Cinematographer:* Oliver T. Marsh. *Musical Score:* Herbert

Stothart. *Christmas Carols:* Father Finn's Paulist Choristers. *Art Director:* Cedric Gibbons. *Associate Art Directors:* Fredric Hope, Edwin B. Willis. *Wardrobe:* Dolly Tree. *Film Editor:* Conrad A. Nervig. *Sound:* Douglas Shearer. *Running Time:* 121 minutes. *New York Premiere:* December 25, 1935.

 Cast: Ronald Colman (Sydney Carton), Elizabeth Allan (Lucie Manette), Edna May Oliver (Miss Pross), Reginald Owen (C.V. Stryver), Basil Rathbone (The Marquis St. Evremonde), Blanche Yurka (Madame Therese de Farge), Henry B. Walthall (Dr. Manette), Donald Woods (Charles Darnay), Claude Gillingwater (Jarvis Lorry), Walter Catlett (Barsad), H.B. Warner (Gabelle), Fritz Leiber (Gaspard), Lucille LaVerne (The Vengeance), Mitchell Lewis (Ernest de Farge), Isabel Jewell (Mlle. Fontaine, the Seamstress), Tully Marshall (Woodcutter), Billy Bevan (Jerry Cruncher), E.E. Clive (Judge in Old Bailey), Robert Warwick (Judge at Tribunal), Eily Malyon (Mrs. Cruncher), Lawrence Grant (Prosecutor), Ralf Harolde (Prosecutor), Fay Chaldecott (Lucie, the child), John Davidson (Morveau), Tom Ricketts (Tellson, Jr.), Donald Haines (Jerry Cruncher, Jr.), Barlowe Borland (Jacques 116), Boyd Irwin, Nigel de Brulier, Sam Flint, Winter Hall (Aristocrats), Ed Peil (Cartwright), Edward Hearn (Leader), Richard Alexander (Executioner), Cyril McLaglen (Headsman), Frank Mayo (Jailer), Walter Kingsford (Victor, the Jailer), Rolf Sedan (Condemned Dandy), Dale Fuller, Tempe Pigott (Old Hags), Montagu Shaw (Chief Registrar), Chappell Dossett (Priest), Forrester Harvey (Joe, the Coach Guard), Jimmy Aubrey (Innkeeper), Billy House (Border Guard).

 Of all the children of his fancy, Ronald Colman had in his heart of hearts a favorite child, and his name was Sydney Carton. An assiduous reader of Dickens, Colman practically knew *A Tale of Two Cities* from memory, and had waited years for the opportunity to portray the ill-fated English advocate in that immortal tale of love and sacrifice during the French Revolution.[23] At last his chance came in 1935, when producer David O. Selznick obtained his services from Twentieth Century–Fox and starred him (moustacheless) in M-G-M's big-budgeted Dickens spectacular.

 England in 1775 . . . the Dover Road in the thick of night. A lone horseman approaches the Dover mail coach at a gallop, with a message for one of its occupants, Jarvis Lorry (Claude Gillingwater), trust officer of Tellson's Bank in London. He's to wait at the Royal George in Dover for Mam'selle.

 "Recalled to life," is Lorry's cryptic reply.

 At the inn in Dover, Lorry informs Lucie Manette (Elizabeth Allan) that her father, a client of Tellson's branch in Paris, who has been buried alive for 18 years in the Bastille, still lives. Recalled to life from his dreadful incarceration, he awaits them in Paris.

 Lorry and Miss Manette journey to a narrow street in the slum quarter of Paris, where the daughter greets a father she has never known. Dr. Manette (Henry B. Walthall), a small frail, pathetic fright, stooping under the burden of his years, looks up at them through a cobweb of tangled hair, and is soon whisked off to London.

Ronald Colman's supreme achievement of the thirties, and his own personal favorite, was as the brooding, alcoholic Sydney Carton in Dickens' A Tale of Two Cities.

Into our drama steps the Marquis St. Evremonde (Basil Rathbone), a hawk-faced gentleman of baleful countenance and one of the most hated aristocrats in all France. All the more dangerous because he wields such power, this obscene vulture plots to frame his nephew, Charles Darnay (Donald Woods), for treason when the young Frenchman emigrates to England rather than tolerate the squalor, sickness, and want to which his uncle has subjected the French peasantry. On board the ship bound for London, Darnay befriends Dr. and Lucie Manette, but Evremonde's paid hireling, Barsad (Walter Catlett), a horrid, weaselly little man, plants incriminating lists of His Majesty's forces on him, and Darnay is arrested for espionage.

The Frenchman is to be defended by the celebrated C.V. Stryver (Reginald Owen) of King's Bench Bar, at whose quarters we meet his associate, Sydney Carton (Colman), a sometimes brilliant, often intemperate, always disillusioned English advocate. When Carton identifies Barsad's name as one that's been involved in treason cases before, he seeks him out and, over drinks, tricks him into revealing his involvement in the Darnay business.

Darnay comes to trial at Old Bailey. After Barsad, principal witness for the prosecution, testifies that the prisoner had the treasonable documents in his possession, Stryver, well coached by Carton, asks him if he doesn't know a certain French Marquis. Could he not have mistaken Darnay for someone else he might have seen on the Dover boat—his learned assistant, Carton, perhaps? Carton stands up and winks heavily at Barsad, as if to convey acknowledgment of a difficult situation.

"Well, sir, come to think of it," blusters the unwitting Barsad, recognizing his former drinking companion, "as a matter of fact, it was *not* the prisoner at all, sir!"

Darnay is acquitted, and an envious Carton watches forlornly as the radiant Lucie Manette congratulates the freed prisoner. When the advocate and Darnay dine together later, Carton, under the influence, becomes belligerent.

"You are *smug*, Mr. Darnay, when you ask why people *drink*, but I'll tell you. So that they can stand their fellow men better," he chuckles. "After a few bottles, I might even like *you*."

Carton proposes a toast to Miss Manette. "There's a fair young lady to be pitied by and wept for by. Ah, must be worth being tried for one's life to be the object of such sympathy and compassion. Tell me, Mr. Darnay," he adds, "do you think I particularly *like* you?"

Insulted, Darnay settles for the dinner and bows out gracefully. Carton, a bit unsteadily, studies his own reflection in a mirror on the wall. "Why treat the fellow like that? Is it because—he shows you what *you* have fallen away from? What you might have been? Change places with him. Would *you* have been looked at by those blue eyes as *he* was? Ah, come on, Carton, you're jealous!"

On Christmas eve, as Sydney Carton sits drunk in a good old English tavern, Charles Darnay visits Dr. Manette and confesses that he is the nephew of the wicked St. Evremonde who consigned him to the Bastille so many years ago. Meanwhile, Lucie and her faithful companion, Miss Pross (Edna May Oliver), are trudging through the snow on their way to church, when they unexpectedly meet Sydney Carton on a street corner. The advocate readily accepts Miss Manette's invitation to join them for the service, and, once they are there, the camera lingers on Carton's face as Lucie lights a candle for him. Beneath a furrowed brow, his perturbed eyes restlessly search the unfamiliar surroundings, until at last they turn inward and reflect self-evaluation and regret.

After church, Carton escorts the women home and, when Lucie asks him in to celebrate, gratefully promises to come another time. In one of the film's most moving moments, he stands wistfully in the snow after they retire within. Christmas carolers pass by, singing "O Come, All Ye Faithful," but Carton's sorrowful face is hardly "joyful and triumphant."

The following spring, in the Manette garden, Carton, reticent as always, attempts to tell Lucie that he's fallen in love with her.

"It's only now, after knowing you, that I've told myself that, perhaps, it's not—too late," he tells her. "I wonder if you know how *much* your happiness means to me."

But Lucie reveals that she and Charles Darnay plan to marry. In the lowest depths of despair and dejection, Carton fails to attend the wedding and stays home drunk.

Coming events cast their shadows. In Paris, the Marquis St. Evremonde is assassinated, boldly heralding the revolution which is to sweep away four centuries of tyranny.

Years roll by. Darnay now has a job at Tellson's Bank in London, and he and Lucie have a young daughter. One night, Carton pays them a visit and ventures upstairs to bid good night to little Lucie (Fay Chaldecott). In one of the picture's most memorable scenes, he and Lucie step out onto a moon-splashed balcony overlooking the child's bedroom, where Carton shares his innermost feelings.

"Oh, I admit that once, when—when I first knew you," he begins, "the sight of you and your home stirred old shadows that I thought had died out of me. I had unformed ideas of—striving afresh, beginning anew, fighting out the abandoned fight; a dream that ended in nothing. But you inspired it."

"Must it end in nothing?" she asks.

"I'm afraid so. But for that inspiration, and for that dream, I shall always be grateful to you, Lucie."

"I feel in you still such—possibilities."

"No, they'll never be realized," he scoffs. "I'm like one who—died young. But—this I know, too," he adds softly. "I would embrace *any* sacrifice for you, and for those dear to you. Will you hold me in your mind as being ardent and sincere in this one thing? Think now and then that there is a man who would give his life to keep a life you love beside you."

"Thank you, Sydney," she replies, a bit uncomfortably. "God grant it may—never be necessary."

The rumbling of distant thunder seems to echo footsteps in Parisian streets, where, on July 14, 1789, the oppressed rise to avenge themselves. In an impressive set piece, the revolutionary mob storms the Bastille, engulfing Paris in a cataclysm of destruction. The prison falls, and a message of hate rings forth: "Death to all Aristos!"

Grim shadows of death hover over France for three years. A decree is passed which abolishes hereditary nobility, consigning family escutcheons to the rubbish heap of things no longer to be tolerated. Nobles flee abroad or die at home as revolutionary justice unleashes the Reign of Terror upon innocent and guilty alike.

Charles Darnay is tricked into returning to Paris, where he is arrested under a new law which forfeits the lives of all aristocrats who return to France. Dr. Manette, who suffered at the hands of an Evremonde, now tries to save one, and delivers an eloquent plea in his son-in-law's behalf, but Darnay's trial is a grotesque mockery of justice. When the fanatical Madame de Farge (Blanche Yurka) denounces him before the tribunal, Darnay is quickly condemned to Mme. Guillotine: "Death within forty-eight hours!"

When Carton arrives in Paris and learns that Darnay is to be executed shortly after sunrise, he resolves to make good the promise he once made to Lucie. Having discovered that Madame de Farge, who has sworn vengeance on the Evremondes to the last of their kin, knows of little Lucie's existence, he persuades Mr. Lorry to leave Paris the following morning with Lucie, Dr. Manette, little Lucie, and Pross, no matter what. Wait for nothing, he insists, but to have his (Carton's) place occupied on the coach.

"You don't wish to tell me anything more?" asks Lorry.

"Yours is a long life to look back on, Mr. Lorry," Carton replies wistfully. "Long life. Useful one. Tell me, if you looked back on that long life and saw that you had gained neither — love, gratitude, nor respect of any human being, it would be a bitter reflection, wouldn't it?"

"Why, yes, surely."

"Don't let *anything* she may say — change your plans."

"I hope to do my part faithfully."

"And I hope to do mine."

Aware that Barsad is now a minor official at La Force prison, where Darnay awaits his end, Carton waylays him in the night and threatens to expose him as a former paid spy of the Marquis St. Evremonde unless he gets him into La Force to see the prisoner. His plan works. Except for a candle on a small table, the cell is shrouded in darkness. Carton promptly urges Darnay to write what he dictates: "You will remember the words that passed between us on a certain occasion. I am grateful the time has come when I can prove them. That I do so is no subject for regret or grief. I said that if ever I could do anything for you or those dear to you — "

Carton quickly overpowers Darnay with a powerful narcotic, takes up the pen, and completes the letter himself: "In the long night that is approaching, I shall be guided by the memory of your kindness. God bless you for your sweet compassion."

Carton scrawls his signature, summons Barsad, and together they dress Darnay in the advocate's overcoat and hat. Barsad, instructed to have Darnay at Mr. Lorry's by eight o'clock, assists "Carton" from the prison, explaining that he'd fainted when he saw his friend.

And thus another is "recalled to life."

Carton stands by a small window in his cell as the sun rises, alone with his thoughts. Not long thereafter, a coach bearing Jarvis Lorry's party rumbles out of Paris. One of its occupants is Sydney Carton's gift to Lucie Manette.

Carton is taken to a dungeon where those marked for execution await their conveyance to the public square where the sentence is to be carried out. As he sits in shadow, lest his identity be discovered, a little seamstress (Isabel Jewell), who was convicted the same day as Darnay for consorting with an enemy of the Republic, approaches him in tears.

"My poor child," he consoles. "It isn't understanding we need now; it's courage."

Seeing that he is not Citizen Evremonde, she sobs, "You're going to die in his place. Why?"

"He is my friend."

"When we go to the guillotine, will you let me hold your hand? That might give me courage, too."

"Yes, I'll hold it—to the last."

Soon they are paraded through crowded streets in a tumbril bound for the Place de la Revolution. As drums roll, the blade falls with a sickening thud, and a brutalized mob gloats in frenzied approval. Carton and the seamstress stand at the foot of the scaffold.

"You're not afraid," she whispers. "The others are only pretending, but you—it's almost as if you welcomed it."

"Perhaps I do," he replies thoughtfully. "Perhaps in death I receive something I never had in life. I hold a sanctuary in the hearts of those I care for."

He kisses her good-bye when her number is called. Moments later, Sydney Carton mounts the steps and goes to his death. The camera rises above the guillotine to a cloudy sky, as we hear him deliver those most courageous of all famous last lines: "It's a far, *far* better thing I do than I have ever done; it's a far, *far* better rest I go to—than I have ever known."

Charles Dickens' stirring tale of revolution, resurrection, and renunciation had been staged and filmed many times since its initial serialization in 1859. By far the most successful Sydney Carton who trod the boards was

Sir John Martin-Harvey, whose Byronic good looks led him from a London opening on February 16, 1899 (in an adaptation entitled *The Only Way*), through the provinces, America, and Canada, a run which lasted some 36 years. J. Stuart Blackton produced the first film treatment for Vitagraph in 1911, starring Maurice Costello and Norma Talmadge. A 1917 William Fox remake featured William Farnum, and Martin-Harvey recreated the role for the cameras in the 1926 United Artists release, *The Only Way*.

In the early thirties, Paramount considered it as a vehicle for Gary Cooper, and Warner Bros. contemplated filming it with Leslie Howard, but nothing came of either project. When M-G-M's *David Copperfield* became a smash hit in 1935, producer David O. Selznick, anxious to bring another Dickens novel to the screen, immediately turned to *A Tale of Two Cities*.[24] Brian Aherne was cast but not yet signed as Sydney Carton, when at the last minute Selznick learned that Ronald Colman, his first choice for the part, was available.[25] Colman insisted that he not play a dual role, maintaining that although Carton and Darnay resemble each other, Dickens never suggested that they were identical in appearance. Selznick finally agreed, deciding that "it would be very difficult to get an audience excited about Ronald Colman going to the guillotine to save Ronald Colman playing Charles Darnay."[26]

While most of the distinguished cast turned in delightful performances, Elizabeth Allan made little more than a pretty ingenue as Lucie Manette, while Donald Woods' Charles Darnay was wooden, over-virtuous, and rarely convincing.

Using authentic settings and costumes, director Jack Conway stunningly brought to the screen the magnitude of the French Revolution. Visually, however, the most striking scene in the picture was the result of second-unit work by directors Val Lewton and Jacques Tourneur, who staged the spectacular storming of the Bastille. At the beginning of the sequence, the Parisian rabble, pained by cold, ignorance, and want, hungrily eye slabs of meat being tossed to the royal hounds, as Madame de Farge screams, "*Why* do you endure it?" Conway effectively employs an abstract use of cinema here, flashing the word "Why?" across the screen and through the gutters and garrets of the Parisian slums four times in succession, each time in larger lettering, to the dissonant accompaniment of trumpet blasts. Moments later, an answer sears the screen as the camera pulls back to reveal a tumultuous mob filling the streets, rushing headlong toward the Bastille. Throughout this frenzy, Lewton and Tourneur utilize sweeping montage techniques, cutting again and again from close-ups of one desperate, cadaverous face to another. There is something in these haggard faces beyond reproof: the outraged spirit of justice.[27]

Any version of *A Tale of Two Cities* ultimately stands or falls by its Sydney Carton. The role would have been a heaven-sent gift to any romantic

On the set of A Tale of Two Cities. *With Edna May Oliver and Claude Gillingwater (reflected in mirror) looking on, director Jack Conway discusses the role of Sydney Carton with Ronald Colman. (Note tape indicating Colman's "mark" for this shot.)*

actor, but in Colman's hands it became the quintessence of all the innumerable gallant roles he had played since *The Dark Angel* and *Beau Geste*. He was always at his best when he loved and sacrificed in vain, forcing a smile to hide his broken heart. Sydney Carton is, perhaps, the most unheroic of heroes, yet strong enough to accept himself and walk to the guillotine to ensure Lucie's happiness. His longing for an ideal love that might flower in domestic warmth, his fear that he might never find it, his deep sense of remorse for all that he could have been, his need to atone for the errors of his wasted life, his growing awareness that redemption can be achieved only through death, and his anguished sense of the grandeur of self-sacrifice — all are shut away within Carton's breast, yet readily observed in Colman's deeply suffering face and eyes. Colman appeared without his thin but famous moustache only twice in his Hollywood career (the first time was in *Clive of India*); without it, his face seemed leaner, more sensitive, drawing attention to the bemusement and melancholy in those haunted eyes.

Carton's need for motivation to live and his willingness to die have been subtly apparent almost from the beginning, but are gradually fulfilled within the context of a Biblical allusion, "I Am the Resurrection and the Life." This inscription is first seen emblazoned upon a plaque in Lucie's quarters, as Carton stands before it and decides to substitute himself for Darnay; later it is superimposed across the screen at the close of the film, after he has gone to the guillotine. Coupled with this is another religious motif, the musical refrain "O Come, All Ye Faithful," which further reinforces the theme of rebirth. We first hear it outside the Manette residence on Christmas eve, as Carton, sensing that the time has come to mend his ways, stands alone in a scene full of the tang of snow and cold air, crisp green holly leaves, blazing hearths, and human hearts; it soon reappears to underscore four of the picture's most memorable moments: as he makes his vow to Lucie on the balcony, as he stands in front of the "Resurrection" plaque and seals his fate in Lucie's lodgings, as he completes Darnay's letter in La Force prison, and finally, after he has made his rendezvous with destiny at the scaffold. Acting in the image of Christ, Carton becomes, through his splendid sacrifice, the embodiment of the best achievement in man; the guillotine becomes what the cross was formerly: a sign of regeneration.

At the start of the production, Selznick wrote: "Bear in mind that we have Colman playing the role and that there is the difficulty of getting him as anything but a rather gay, casual Colman—as he has always been."[28] The producer's fears were unfounded. More relaxed and unselfconscious than ever before, Colman revealed the fullness of his power and turned in more than a good role well acted: it was a work of mature reflection, a penetrating and compassionate study of the growth of a human mind molded by the pattern of destiny. Other actors govern scenes in which he does not appear, but Colman, who is not introduced until the film has been running nearly 25 minutes, so thoroughly dominates the picture that one realizes only later that he has been on screen for relatively little of its two hours. He played his early scenes as a hard drinker with tousled hair and slurred speech, yet consummate restraint combined with whimsy and a charming deference to Lucie Manette; and later, a gentle protectiveness and sympathetic treatment of the poor little seamstress. Finally, with a look not of satisfaction or pleasure, but of unregretting acquiescence, he mounts the steps to the guillotine and recites his last line ("It's a far, *far* better thing I do . . . .") with heavily mournful nobility—the most haunting, lingering impression in the Colman oeuvre. "No film actor of his era, or indeed any subsequent era, could have been delivered the most famous of all last words. . . ."[29] How many pictures have even one scene of such power?

If a film classic can be defined as one that survives passing tastes and fashions, is independent of the conditions under which it was produced, and imparts a message for future generations, then *A Tale of Two Cities* qualifies. One of the most moving stories ever filmed, it was told with a strikingly lyric simplicity that gives it the timeless universality of a fable; its pervading atmosphere is one of melancholy, if only because the tragic wistfulness of Colman's eyes so constantly commands our attention. As John Baxter put it,

> Nobody has captured so accurately Carton's melancholy fatalism or the moral necessities which can drive a man to self-destruction. If only for the scene where Carton waits in the snow at Christmas time and watches the carollers and the church-goers hurry past to the warmth of the home which he does not possess, *A Tale of Two Cities* must be considered one of the most successful films of the period.[30]

After five months in production, *A Tale of Two Cities* opened at New York's Capitol Theatre on Christmas day, 1935. The critics turned handsprings, and audiences flocked to see it for months. *Boston Herald* reviewer Elinor Hughes commented that

> No one can maintain the position that he has without starting some sort of dispute concerning his ability. We had engaged upon them upon occasions, feeling more than once that Mr. Colman was getting away with polite murder and walking through his roles with an agreeable smile and a display of personal charm that was not precisely a substitute for acting. British reticence, we could not help but feel, was being carried too far. With the release of *Two Cities*, the actor in Mr. Colman got the better of his policy of understatement and he offered the best screen portrayal we have ever seen him do.[31]

Julian Fox later wrote: "The film was at once a culmination of Colman's star position, and a suggestion that there were depths in Colman which had as yet been untapped."[32]

The picture was nominated for an Academy Award as Best Picture (M-G-M's *The Great Ziegfeld* won), but Colman, unaccountably, failed to receive a nomination for Best Actor.[33] Colman considered it his finest performance, and it remained his favorite film. Together with his later portrayals of Robert Conway in *Lost Horizon* and Rudolf Rassendyll in *The Prisoner of Zenda*, Sydney Carton is the role for which Colman will always be remembered. He had had something enduring to say, and how unforgettably he said it.

A Tale of Two Cities was made again in England, by J. Arthur Rank, in 1958, with Dirk Bogarde as Carton. His performance was solid and affecting, but *The Dickensian*, that prestigious, leading authority on Dickens, found him curiously subdued and remarkably clear-eyed for an inebriate. "Even after twenty years," remarked Leslie C. Staples, "the exaltation of the closing scenes of the Ronald Colman version remain vivid in the memory, and the new film cannot match them."[34] A 1980 British television production featured astute performances by Peter Cushing, Kenneth More, Barry Morse, and Flora Robson, but Chris Sarandon's unsympathetic portrayal of both Carton and Darnay was a major disappointment. An ambitious 1989 adaptation, coproduced by England's Granada Television and France's Dune Television for the bicentennial of the French Revolution, starred James Wilby as Carton, and was unique in its use of British and French casts for their respective parts.

Under Two Flags

1936. *Production and distribution:* Twentieth Century–Fox Film Corporation. *Producer:* Darryl F. Zanuck. *Director:* Frank Lloyd. *Screenplay:* W.P. Lipscomb, Walter Ferris (from the novel by Ouida). *Cinematographer:* Ernest Palmer. *Battle Photography:* Sidney Wagner. *Musical Score:* Louis Silvers. *Director of Battle Sequences:* Otto Brower. *Technical Advisor:* Jamiel Hasson. *Ballistics Expert:* Lou Witte. *Associate Producer:* Raymond Griffith. *Assistant Directors:* Ad Schaumer, A.F. Erickson. *Film Editor:* Ralph Dietrich. *Running Time:* 110 minutes. *Release Date:* April 30, 1936.

Cast: Ronald Colman (Sergeant Victor), Claudette Colbert (Cigarette), Victor McLaglen (Major Doyle), Rosalind Russell (Lady Venetia Corona), Gregory Ratoff (Ivan), Nigel Bruce (Captain Menzies), C. Henry Gordon (Lieutenant Petain), Herbert Mundin (Rake), John Carradine (Cafard), Lumsden Hare (Lord Seraph), J. Edward Bromberg (Colonel Ferol), Onslow Stevens (Sidi-Ben Youssiff), Fritz Leiber (French Governor), Thomas Beck (Pierre), William Ricciardi (Cigarette's Father), Frank Reicher (French General), Francis McDonald (Husson), Harry Semels (Sergeant Malinas), Nicholas Soussanin (Levine), Douglas Gerrard (Colonel Farley), Louis Mercier (Barron), Frank Lackteen (Ben Hamidon), Jamiel Hasson (Arab Liaison Officer), Gwendolen Logan (Lady Cairn), Hans von Morhart (Hans), Tor Johnson (Bidou), Marc Lawrence (Grivon), Geroge Regas (Keskerdit), Rolfe Sedan (Mouche), Hector Sarno (Arab Merchant), Gaston Glass (Adjutant), George Ducount (Soldier).

Into the ranks of "God's Forgotten" steps Ronald Colman, returning to the French Foreign Legion in Twentieth Century–Fox's *Under Two Flags* for the first time since *Beau Geste*, made ten years earlier. The fourth screen adaptation of Ouida's famous 1867 novel of adventure and romance in the desert, it swept Colman into the panoramic world of action and glamour so typical of Hollywood productions in the thirties.[35] As Sergeant Victor, the mysterious soldier of fortune whom fate has consigned to the shelter of the all-concealing Legion, Colman shoulders the blame for a crime he did not commit and becomes a fugitive from English justice. A man without hope, without refuge, he chooses the desolation of flight and the desert, disguised in the uniform and lost in the crowd.

In a small garrison town on the edge of the Sahara, a cheery, roisterous bustle announces that the troops are back, celebrating their few hours of freedom. Here the mischievous Mademoiselle Cigarette (Claudette Colbert), a curvaceous, impudent little friend of the French flag, chances to meet Sergeant Victor and loses her heart forever.

Her jealousy is aroused when Victor falls in love with Lady Venetia Corona (Rosalind Russell), an elegant Englishwoman to whom he presents a perfect statuette of a famous English thoroughbred which he has just finished carving. Perhaps out of homesickness, as if letting his memory drift back to a time when he had known another world than that of Africa, he has carved the name of the stallion on its base. How does this melancholy legionnaire come to know of Forest King, she wonders, sensing that it must be from memory. Sergeant Victor guides Lady Venetia through the narrow, crooked alleyways of the Arab quarter to a rendezvous at a moonlit desert monastery, where the two become lovers.

The following morning, dangerous rebel chieftain Sidi-Ben Youssiff (Onslow Stevens) raids the town. Major Doyle (crusty Victor McLaglen) is ordered to defend the Tricolor by preventing the juncture of Youssiff's three tribes. But, since he is in love with Cigarette himself, his jealousy prompts him to dispatch Victor on the dangerous mission, confident that he'll never return. Before he leaves, Victor discovers that his beloved is the niece of Lord Seraph (Lumsden Hare), whom he had known intimately in England. He must retrieve that carving before Seraph uncovers his true identity. The legionnaire stealthily searches Lady Venetia's chambers; when she unexpectedly confronts him, he confesses that only a prison cell awaits him in his homeland.

After the troops march out, Lord Seraph spies his niece's statuette and at once suspects the truth.

> "He was a young friend of mine. One of the most popular officers in the Guards. Haven't seen him for years. Disappeared. Ugly scandal. He'd been shielding his younger brother. Last summer, his younger brother met up with a nasty accident. Before he died, he cleared Rafe completely."

Seraph promises to clear "Sergeant Victor" of all charges immediately.

Later, as scores of wounded are returned to town, Cigarette and Lady Venetia search for the same man among the dead and dying. Though she knows that, by saving Victor, she will lose him to her rival, still Cigarette makes the only possible choice. Doyle, too, proceeds into the desert to rescue Victor and his men from the scourge of Sidi-Ben Youssiff. The simple, unsung code of honor among comrades-in-arms prevails.

The Arabs close in on the besieged legionnaires, and the attack begins. Down they stream like the wind, the dust of death hovering low over the desert fort. Exhausted, Sergeant Victor commands the last defense, hoping

Director Frank Lloyd ponders the next move in the war between legionnaires and Arabs in Under Two Flags, *as Claudette Colbert and Ronald Colman aid his thoughts.*

only that they can hold out until relief arrives. With four squadrons of Chasseurs on the way, Victor effects a daring plan designed to buy needed time. Under cover of darkness he creeps through the Arab ranks, determined to confront Sidi-Ben Youssiff himself. For, improbable though it may seem, they had once studied together at Oxford.

Old classmates meet in the heart of the desert as enemies, while Cigarette directs the relieving forces toward the beleaguered fortress. As the avengers swoop down to pierce through the Arab lines like the closing jaws of a huge steel trap, the Tricolor is hoisted high, but at a terrible price. Mortally wounded and cast from her horse to a hot bed of sand, Cigarette lies immobile until Sergeant Victor arrives to cradle her in his arms. She smiles up into his eyes.

"I've seen so many men die, I know what this is," she whispers. "She said—the English lady—she said, if I loved you, I would save you. Tell her I tried."

One last kiss; then the Queen of the Legionnaires lies dead. Victor's face turns skyward, achingly.

Once more the small garrison town. The hot Arab sun streams down on the folds of the Tricolor as legionnaires assemble to pay honor to a soldier of France killed in action. In the annals of the French Foreign Legion,

On the set of Under Two Flags, *Ronald Colman and Rosalind Russell gaze out beyond the lights at director Frank Lloyd and cameraman Ernest Palmer.*

the name Cigarette will long be remembered. But Sergeant Victor is not among the ranks, for his work here is done; he will return to England to begin life anew with the lady, not the girl. He watches intently, knowing that in his heart, Cigarette will live forever.

Fresh from his critical success in *A Tale of Two Cities,* one of the most haunting landmarks of his career, Ronald Colman strode with confidence into the scorching Arizona desert to shoot the exteriors for *Under Two Flags.* Two months later, filming was completed, and the picture did extremely well at the box office. Many reviewers, however, found the film exasperatingly slow paced, despite director Frank Lloyd's attempt to keep the action moving with increasing acceleration toward the crashing final battle sequence. These combat scenes were effectively photographed and boasted both deft direction and taut editing, but elsewhere the picture suffered from bad process shots and obvious studio backdrops. Especially disappointing was the moonlit scene in which Colman and Rosalind Russell sat in a blatantly artificial Moorish ruin, beneath a typical Hollywood version of an African moon.

In view of its many technical flaws, much of the film's popularity was undoubtedly attributable to its fine cast. Rosalind Russell was decorative and bewitching as the aloof patrician who wins the heart of Sergeant Victor. The virile Victor McLaglen (who had starred with Colman in *Beau Geste*) turned in a stalwart performance as the rugged commandant who gives his men full marching orders simply to make them eat dust. The role of Victor's sidekick, Captain Menzies, was excellently served by the blissfully obtuse Nigel Bruce. In one exchange, for instance, Cigarette shamelessly cheats Menzies by selling him a fine stallion, changing saddles, and promptly offering him the same horse as its perfect mate.

"Chap's gotta keep his wits about him with these Arabs," he chortles. "Turn your back for one minute and they'll swindle you."

Claudette Colbert was a last-minute substitution, replacing French actress Simone Simon, whom illness prevented from playing Cigarette. As the temperamental darling of the Legion, who loved Victor but couldn't have him, Miss Colbert was exceptionally touching, capricious, and fiery.

Colman's daughter chronicles a particularly harrowing incident on the set of *Under Two Flags:*

> Along with his leading players, Ronnie was insured for $5,000 against camel bite during the production, but since he always made a point of avoiding them anyway, no misfortune occurred. However, he did have an unfortunate experience with a Yaqui Indian knife-thrower.
>
> The plot required Claudette/Cigarette to throw the knife at Ronnie, which narrowly misses him and lands instead in a wooden post. Doubles were never used as this particular knife-thrower (at $250 a throw) had been infallible in all his twenty years in the business. Nobody thought twice about Ronnie doing the scene himself. Even for Yaqui Indians, however, there is a first time for everything. Afterward claiming that his attention had been distracted by a bystander looking at his eyes when he threw, the Yaqui missed the post, and his heavy knife, going at full tilt, struck Ronnie sideways....[36]

Rosalind Russell recalled an amusing, if embarrassing, experience:

> He wouldn't kiss me on the mouth. I kept trying to push my face around, but he just wouldn't kiss me. Between takes I'd go in and swallow half a bottle of Listerine and spray myself with perfume. The scene went on and on. It started to get late; some of the crew were restless and beginning to giggle. Finally the director said, "Maybe we'll just have to put this off until tomorrow morning."
>
> Oh my God, I thought, I won't sleep. By now I'm reeking of Arpege and mouthwash, and I'm desperate. I finally just grabbed Ronnie, clung to him, would not let him go, and kissed him until he was purple in the face and the director was yelling, "Cut! Cut! Cut!"
>
> What I didn't know was (a) that a kiss full on the mouth doesn't photograph as pleasingly as an off-center buss, and (b) that they'd been doing a glass shot, a form of dissolve. The camera wasn't even on us most of the time, it

was on the camels, the desert, the sun going down, the sun coming up again to indicate that we've spent the night together. Colman, of course, was aware of the camera (he knew cameras like Wernher von Braun knows rockets), but all the time we were supposed to be standing apart making small talk . . . while they're shooting the camels and the sunrise, he's had this maniacal female clutching him to her fevered lips.[37]

The first screen adaptation of *Under Two Flags* was a three-reeler produced in 1915 by Biograph, nearing the end of its long, pioneering existence. Theda Bara vamped her way through the 1917 remake, and four years later Priscilla Dean and James Kirkwood starred in still another version. All three had one thing in common: the story was Cigarette's. The Colman account reversed this tradition; designed to showcase Sergeant Victor's unspoken code of honor and self-sacrifice, the plot concentrated on him, and his role was tailor-made for the Colman image. Displaying a strong family likeness to the earlier *Beau Geste*, this rendition featured another nobly born legionnaire who instinctively follows a brave, simple creed of loyalty in order to protect family honor from disgrace. To no one's surprise, Colman splendidly conveyed all the qualities for which he was justly famous. But despite its merits, *Under Two Flags* cast a smaller shadow than the already legendary *Beau Geste*. Instead of giving audiences desert hardships and sweltering heat, the studio chose to emphasize romance and Hollywood glamour. As a result, the film fails to hold up today as well as it might.

Under Two Flags was Ronald Colman's last picture under his Twentieth Century–Fox contract. He struck out as an independent from this point on, rarely appearing in more than one film a year, and earning between $150,000 to $200,000 per picture for his efforts.

Lost Horizon

1937. *Production and distribution:* Columbia Pictures Corporation. *Producer and director:* Frank Capra. *Executive Producer:* Harry Cohn. *Screenplay:* Robert Riskin (from the novel by James Hilton). *Cinematographer:* Joseph Walker. *Aerial Photography:* Elmer Dyer. *Special Camera Effects:* E. Roy Davidson, Ganahl Carson. *Assistant Cinematographers:* Al Keller, William Jolly. *Musical Score:* Dimitri Tiomkin. *Musical Director:* Max Steiner. *Voices:* Hall Johnson Choir. *Technical Advisor:* Harrison Forman. *Art Director:* Stephen Goosson. *Set Decorations:* Babs Johnstone. *Costumes:* Ernst Dryden. *Assistant Directors:* C.C. Coleman, Milton Carter. *Film Editors:* Gene Milford, Gene Havlick. *Sound:* Edward Bernds. *Running Time:* 132 minutes (road-show engagements); 118 minutes (general release); 107 minutes (1942 rerelease entitled *Lost Horizon of Shangri-La*). *New York Premiere:* March 3, 1937.

Cast: Ronald Colman (Robert Conway), Jane Wyatt (Sondra Bizet), Edward Everett Horton (Alexander P. Lovett), John Howard (George Conway), Thomas Mitchell (Henry Barnard/Chalmers Bryant), Margo (Maria), Isabel Jewell (Gloria

Stone), H.B. Warner (Chang), Sam Jaffe (High Lama/Father Perrault), Hugh
Buckler (Lord Gainsford), David Torrence (Prime Minister), Leonard Mudie
(Foreign Secretary), Boyd Irwin (Assistant Foreign Secretary), John Miltern
(Carstairs), John Burton (Wynant), John T. Murray (Meeker), Max Rabinowitz
(Sieveking [deleted]), John Tettemer (Montaigne), David Clyde (Steward), Val
Durand (Talu), Noble Johnson (Leader of Porters), Chief Big Tree (Porter), Milton
Owen (Fenner), Dennis D'Auburn (Aviator), George Chan (Chinese Priest),
Richard Loo (Shanghai Airport Official), Eric Wilton (Englishman), Lawrence
Grant (First Man), Neil Fitzgerald, Darby Clark (Radio Operators), Willie Fung,
Victor Wong (Bandit Leaders), Wyrley Birch, Carl Stockdale, Ruth Robinson,
Margaret McWade (Missionaries), Beatrice Curtis, Mary Lou Dix, Beatrice Blinn,
Arthur Rankin (Passengers), Delmer Ingraham, Ed Thorpe, Harry Lishman
(Porters).

Frank Capra's fantasy classic *Lost Horizon* gave audiences Ronald Colman as British diplomat Robert Conway, who, fleeing from a world of
hatred, greed, and strife, discovers the utopian paradise of brotherly love
and peace, Shangri-La, hidden among the highest uncharted reaches of the
Tibetan Himalayas. The film captivated a Depression-ridden world increasingly alerted to the threat of another shattering war.

> "In these days of wars—in the bitter struggle against oppression—haven't
> you ever dreamed of a place where there was peace and security, where liv-
> ing was not a struggle but a lasting delight? Of course you have. So has every
> man since Time began. Always the same dream. Sometimes he calls it
> Utopia—Sometimes the Fountain of Youth—Sometimes merely 'that little
> chicken farm.' One man had such a dream and saw it come true. He was
> Robert Conway—England's 'Man of the East'—soldier, diplomat, public
> hero—"

Thus begins *Lost Horizon*, a soaring, fantastic poem of flight from chaos to
tranquility.
     From the minute director Frank Capra read James Hilton's best-
selling 1933 novel, he decided to film it, realizing instinctively that this
ageless tale of adventure and idealism, with its utopian theme of man's eternal quest for peace within himself, would faithfully reflect the yearnings of
peace-loving audiences throughout the world. It was all there, he
reflected—poetry, fantasy, spectacle, high adventure. Determined to bring
these qualities to the screen, Capra persuaded Harry Cohn to advance the
unprecedented sum of $2,000,000 and launched Columbia's most lavish
and ambitious project. While Robert Riskin, Hollywood's highest-paid
scenarist, wrote the screen adaptation, Capra and famed Tibetan explorer-
photographer Harrison Forman undertook an exhaustive one-year study of
Tibetan books, documents, engravings, and photographs. They meticulously
researched lamaseries, language, and customs; clothing, architecture, and
furniture; wildlife, weapons, and musical instruments. Ten property men

labored for ten months to create 700 articles used in daily Tibetan life, while armies of technicians built a total of 65 sets. Shangri-La rose spectacularly above Columbia's Burbank ranch, as art director Stephen Goosson supervised the construction of what would become the film's centerpiece: the breathtaking lamasery, one of the largest and costliest sets ever constructed in Hollywood, rivaling in its scope and grandeur D.W. Griffith's towering Babylonian set for *Intolerance* (1916) and Douglas Fairbanks' massive medieval castle for *Robin Hood* (1922). And when all was done, the homework showed in every shot, right down to the last flawless detail.

From the beginning Frank Capra knew that only one actor could portray Robert Conway—man of action, guardian of the Empire, dreamer, idealist, mystic; the man who always wanted to see what was on the other side of the hill; the man who had once written, "There are moments in every man's life when he glimpses the eternal." That actor was Ronald Colman, about whom Capra has said:

> Had the High Lama been able to scour the whole world for a man to carry on his vision of Shangri-La, he would have selected Ronald Colman. Beautiful of face and soul, sensitive to the fragile and gentle, responsive both to poetic visions and hard intellect. . . .[38]

"Above all," writes Colman's daughter, "he was an idealist with a tough mind."[39]

Colman enthusiastically accepted the part, for if Shangri-La was Conway's hope come true, *Lost Horizon* was Colman's—he shared Conway's dreams.

The film begins on the night of July 7, 1937, in the war-torn Chinese city of Baskul, where Robert Conway has been dispatched to evacuate 90 white residents before they are slaughtered by raging Chinese hordes. Battling his way through surging mobs of panic-stricken Chinese, Conway— cool, dependable, fully in control—resourcefully supervises the massive rescue effort, until only he and four others remain at the beleaguered airfield, awaiting the arrival of one last plane. Finally it appears; Conway clears the runway, sets the hangar ablaze, and the five scramble aboard just in time. With a Chinese patrol in pursuit, machine guns blazing, the plane skitters down the runway and lurches off into the night toward Shanghai. The chaotic density of these opening shots is reinforced by Capra's proficient manipulation of crowds and his expert coupling of rapid-cutting devices with feverishly intense music, dramatically evoking an ambience of tension, menace, vertigo, and delirium.

As the plane soars, we meet Conway's four companions in adventure. George, Conway's headstrong younger brother, an "Englishmen-fear-nothing" type, is played by John Howard. Gloria, an American prostitute dying of tuberculosis, is superbly portrayed by Isabel Jewell. With his customary aplomb, Thomas Mitchell plays the brassy American industrial magnate, Barnard, who is on the run for having mishandled his stockholders' funds. In a comedic tour de force, the inimitable Edward Everett Horton portrays the fainthearted and fussbudgetty paleontologist, Alexander P. Lovett.

A careworn Conway slumps indulgently into his seat; though steady and serenely confident after years of dedicated consular service, his eyes reflect the intrinsic wistfulness of unfulfilled dreams. He begins to drink, quickly becomes inebriated, and then tells George:

> "Just you wait till I'm Foreign Secretary. Ha, ha. Can't you just see me, Freshie, with all those other shrewd little foreign secretaries? You see, the trick is to see who can outtalk the other. Everybody wants something for nothing. If you can't get it with smooth talk, you—send your army in. But I'm going to *fool* them, Freshie. I'm not going to *have* an army. I'm going to disband mine. I'm going to sink my battleships; I'm going to destroy every piece of warcraft. Then when the enemy approaches, we'll say, 'Come in, gentlemen. What can we do for you?' So then the poor enemy soldiers will stop and think. And what will they think, Freshie? They'll say to themselves, 'There's something wrong here. We've been *duped.* This is not acccording to *form.* These people seem quite friendly and why should we shoot them?' Then they'll lay down their arms. You see how simple the whole thing is? Ha. Centuries of tradition kicked *right* in the pants. Ha, ha, ha, ha. And I'll be slapped right into the nearest insane asylum. . . . Don't worry, George. Nothing's going to happen. I'll fall *right* into line. I'll be the good little boy that everybody wants me to be. I'll be the best little Foreign Secretary we've ever had. Just because I haven't the *nerve* to be anything else."

"Ever notice the sunrise in China, George? Ah, you should," he tells his brother, adding in a fragile whisper, "It's beautiful."

Hours later, as the first rays of dawn break through the opaque mist, Barnard discovers that the plane is off its course; Shanghai is to the east, but they are heading west. Approaching the cockpit, Conway is confronted by a sinister and singularly uncommunicative Oriental pilot who, with a significant flourish of his revolver, terminates the discussion before it can begin.

Conway retreats without arguing the point: "Charming chap!"

The party's plight is now abundantly clear: they have been hijacked. George recklessly suggests beating the pilot's brains in, but Conway sensibly inquires whether anyone else knows how to fly a plane. Since apparently no one can, that settles that.

Suddenly they begin to descend; the plane swoops down at a tremendous speed toward an immense sun-scorched desolation, where swarms of hastily assembled and heavily armed Mongolian warriors surround the craft and refill the nearly empty tanks, regarding its dazed prisoners with grotesque stares and menacing gestures. Its refueling completed, the plane pitches forward toward the hazy vapors of the Tibetan frontier. Once again Capra's skillful handling of large masses of extras and his masterful use of shock-editing techniques, aurally reinforced by the dissonant booming of music, dialect, and wind, perfectly convey an almost fevered atmosphere with devastating intensity.

The camera takes us to the London Foreign Office, where an official orders a massive search for Conway and postpones an impending Far East Conference.

"We can't afford to meet those nations without Conway," he intones.

Meanwhile, the anxious captives begin to suspect that their abduction was planned: the fuel was there, waiting for them. Relentlessly the plane drones for hours over range upon range of glacier-covered snowpeaks — jagged, uncompromising, majestic. As desperation mounts — George becoming increasingly petulant, Gloria sobbing and screaming hysterically — the plane sputters out of fuel and begins to lurch dangerously toward the vast abyss below. Conway quickly orders everyone into the tail — they are going to crash. During tense seconds of straining and snapping, crashing and swaying — the camera jerking upon impact from Conway to the snowy vastness into which they have plunged — the howling wind mounts in merciless ferocity. Chilled and shivering, with no sound in their ears save the infernal gusts of wind, they are lost, a thousand unexplored miles from the edge of the world, their pilot dead, their craft smashed.

Conway resolves to set out in the direction of India, hoping sooner or later to run into some native tribe. But then, inconceivably, they spot the remote figures of men, clad in sheepskins, fur hats, and yak-skin boots, approaching them through a dense blanket of snow from a distant slope.

"Do you think they're cannibals?" Lovett asks fearfully.

The elderly leader of the patrol, played by that fine, sensitive actor of soft-spoken grace, H.B. Warner, introduces himself in English: he is Chang, from a nearby lamasery. Conway, ever correct and urbane ("You've no idea, sir, how unexpected and *very* welcome you are"), relates the bewildering series of events which has brought them to the wilds of Tibet.

"At the mercy of a mad pilot!" Lovett adds gratuitously.

Chang replies that he would consider it an honor to escort Conway and company to his lamasery, a journey, he adds, that is "not particularly far, but quite difficult."

The expedition slowly but inexorably begins its steep ascent toward the snowy pyramids which loom above. Capra's cutting is unerringly rapid and terse, the music somber and relentless, the atmosphere raw, yet appropriately majestic. Inching their way single-file along perilously narrow ledges hacked into unscalable icy cliffs, half frozen in the face of brutal windswept sleet, and finally finding it impossible to climb any higher, they pass through a narrow mountain defile, leaving the raging blizzard behind. Ahead, only a short distance away, lies a strange and incredible sight: Shangri-La, in the hidden Valley of the Blue Moon.

Sheltered by lofty ranges on every side and perched on a barren aerie, the palatial lamasery is exquisite: majestic colonnades, magnificent sweeping stairways, imposing courtyards, sun-drenched walls, radiant fountains, flower-strewn paths, the dream-landscape of a warm verdant valley hazily distant some 3,000 feet below. Conway absorbs it all in silent wonder, his face quizzical and half-unbelieving, his eyes reflecting a glow of satisfaction that such a place could still exist in this world—inaccessible, sheltered, as yet uncontaminated by civilization. Perhaps he had always known in his heart that Shangri-La was there somewhere, beckoning to him. Conway had always wanted to see what lay on the other side of the hill; staring from a plane window toward infinity, his eyes had often been drawn toward the horizon. Now he was there.

Some hours later, refreshed and attired in embroidered silk gowns, the newcomers are joined for an excellent supper by the distinguished Chang. For Conway, perhaps the nightmare has turned into a beautiful dream, but the others are not of the same opinion, and George demands immediate means to get them back to civilization.

"Are you so certain you are away from it?" the Lama searchingly inquires.

He informs them that, regrettably, they are cut off from the outside world entirely, without any means of communication, but assures them that "if there is a prolonged delay, Shangri-La will endeavor to make your stay as pleasant as possible."

In the gently shadowed moonlight of the terrace garden, the Conways discuss the mystery of their arrival at Shangri-La. Far from being the senseless act of a lunatic pilot, the flight had been planned by some shrewd guiding intelligence: the plane had been expected, the patrol had been waiting for them; clearly, they had been deliberately brought here as virtual prisoners. Chang, for all his courtesies, is uncommonly vague and noncommittal: there are too many things that he deeply regrets he may not discuss. Conway exerts a restraining influence on his hot-tempered young brother:

> "Oh, I'm feeling far too peaceful to be concerned about anything. I *think* I'm going to like it here. Something happened to me when we arrived here, George, that, well—did you ever go to a totally strange place and feel certain you'd been there before?"

Conway, for all his reputation, had never been one of those resolute, empire-building representatives of the British Government. Let the world charge about in a perpetual state of fever-heat; here in this hidden kingdom of contentment, the secret of Shangri-La was beginning to exercise over him a rather soothing fascination.

The following morning Chang escorts Conway to the interior museums which house the lamasery's rare and abundant treasures—ceramics, porcelains, tapestries, paintings, music, the world's great literature—and then relates the amazing story of the remarkable Belgian priest responsible for this vast collection of cultured wealth. Father Perrault, the first European to stumble into the valley, had arrived some 200 years ago; one leg being frozen, he amputated his own limb, but despite the infirmity remained very vigorous at the age of 108 when he finished building Shangri-La.

In fact, Chang explains, "it is quite common here to live to a very ripe old age"; the absence of struggle may indeed prolong life indefinitely:

> "A perfect body in perfect health is the rule here. In your countries, on the other hand, how often do you hear the expression, 'He worried himself to death' or 'This thing or that killed him'? Your lives are therefore, as a rule, shorter, not so much by natural death as by indirect suicide."

Conway's face reflects astonishment.

"Why, Mr. Conway, you surprise me," his soft-spoken host admits. "I could have understood it in any of your companions; but you, who have dreamed and written so much about better worlds—or is it that you fail to recognize one of your own dreams when you see it?"

That evening Chang brings his guests "the most amazing news"—the High Lama has sent for Robert Conway. Now perhaps the mystery will be unlocked: why they were kidnapped, why they are being kept here against their will, and why no porters have been furnished to escort them out of Tibet. This first audience with the extraordinary Master of Shangri-La is worth recalling in detail for its treatment of the film's theme.

Ushered into the High Lama's chambers, Conway perceives a small, ghostly, seated figure, illuminated only by the haloed glow of a solitary candle which leaves one side of his wrinkled face in deep, motionless shadow. His outline grows less vague as Conway's eyes become accustomed to the gloom.

"Sit here, near me," a soothing, melancholy voice whispers. "I'm an old man and can do no one any harm."

Conway starts to speak when, suddenly, he notices the crutch propped against the Lama's chair, sees only one leg, and realizes the impossible.

"It's astonishing and incredible," he stammers, shaken with emotion. "You're the man. You're the first who—two hundred years ago! *You're still alive, Father Perrault!*"

Seconds pass and the whisper resumes:

One of the film's most important performances, by which Lost Horizon *would either stand or fall, went to 38-year-old Sam Jaffe, who movingly portrayed the 200-year-old High Lama.*

"You may not know it, but I've been an admirer of yours for a great many years. Oh, not of Conway the Empire builder and public hero. I've wanted to meet the Conway who in one of his books said, 'There are moments in every man's life when he glimpses the eternal.' That Conway seemed to belong here. In fact it was suggested that someone be sent to bring you here. We need men like you here, to be sure that our community will continue to survive."

But what possible reason can there be for prolonging the future, Conway asks, when life itself seems so pointless? The whisper continues, touched by a shadow of emphasis:

"We have reason.... Look at the world today. Is there anything more pitiful? ... A scurrying mass of imbruted humanity, crashing headlong into each other, propelled by an orgy of greed and brutality. The time *must* come, my friend, when this orgy will spend itself.... When that day comes, the world must begin to look for a *new* life, and it is our hope that they will find it here .... When that day comes, it is our hope that the brotherly love of Shangri-La will spread throughout the world."

Conway's face, hauntingly etched in shadowed close-up, indicates surrender to the comforting whisper that matches the peace of his own
thoughts.

"I understand you, Father," he murmurs softly, and leaves, promising
to come again.

Special mention must be made of Sam Jaffe's remarkable performance
as the frail and failing prophet who passes on his benevolent vision of harmony to Robert Conway. With snow-white hair, suffering face, frenzied
eyes, and an almost inaudible whisper, his is a truly moving presence.

Shangri-La has even more to offer Conway: Sondra, an orphan brought
up since childhood by Father Perrault himself, played by young Jane Wyatt
in one of her first film roles. Conway had seen her before in the valley forest,
swimming in a deep, unrippled lotus pool which lay in a dense net of moist,
glistening leaves. Now they are together. In the aviary where she keeps her
pigeons, she reveals that it had been her idea to bring him to Shangri-La.
She too had read his books, and in them she'd seen a man who was accomplishing nothing, going nowhere—a man whose busy life was empty.

"You're absolutely right," he agrees. "And I had to come all the way to
a pigeon house in Shangri-La to find the only other person in the world who
knew it. May I congratulate you?"

Conway tells her he has experienced the sensation of having been here
before, the sense of belonging in Shangri-La:

> "I can't quite explain it, but everything is somehow familiar. The very air I
> breathe; the lamasery with its feet rooted in the good earth; this fertile
> valley. All the beautiful things I see—these cherry blossoms; you—all look
> somehow familiar. Why? Can you tell me why?"

"Perhaps because you've always been a part of Shangri-La without
knowing it," Sondra replies. "I'm sure of it. Just as I'm sure there's a wish
for Shangri-La in everyone's heart. I've thought about it for years," she murmurs, turning her face toward his for another kiss. "I knew you'd come, and
I knew when you did, you'd never leave."

It was perfectly true; Conway just rather liked being here. The
stimulating challenge of Father Perrault's glorious concept was most grati-
fying. Fate had brought him to the Valley of the Blue Moon, and here he
would remain.

But can Conway's companions be persuaded of their good fortune? It
would appear that the crisp mountain air of Shangri-La has exerted its subtle fascination over the others too. Barnard unburdens himself and reveals
his true identity: he is Chalmers Bryant, notorious Wall Street swindler,
hounded by the police for more than a year.

"I knew it!" shrieks Lovett, his eyes widening as he drops his spoon.
"I *knew* I had a reason for hating you!"

Here Barnard feels he can be of great service, and enthusiastically busies himself by installing a fully modernized plumbing system (a worthy sentiment, if a mixed blessing). Gloria removes her makeup to reveal a wholesome beauty that had lain hidden behind a mask. Lovett appears to be enjoying himself fully, for he not only sets about reorganizing the village school, but no longer even objects to Barnard's addressing him as "Lovey." Their reaction to the prospect of leaving is most extraordinary: they, like Conway, decide to stay. Barnard, with his newly acquired social consciousness, has his plumbing business; Gloria, her health restored, has Chalmers Bryant; "Lovey" has a new nickname and his geology classes ("I never for a moment believed that *ridiculous* kidnapping story. Simply preposterous!"). They have all been reborn, their real potential emerging for the first time in their lives, under the tranquil primacy of Shangri-La. All except brother George, a singularly hopeless case who, refusing to become reconciled and determined to leave, porters or no porters, runs amok with a loaded revolver.

Conway seeks the advice of the High Lama, not knowing that it is to be their last visit.

"Your brother is no longer my problem," the aged voice whispers. "He is now your problem, Conway."

He tries to reply, but fails, as the voice murmurs its last prophetic words:

> "Because, my son, I am placing in your hands the future and destiny of Shangri-La, for I am going to die . . . . My friend, it is not an arduous task that I bequeath, for our order knows only silken bonds: to be gentle and patient, to care for the riches of the mind, to preside in wisdom while the storm rages without. You, my son, will live through the storm. You will preserve the fragrance of our history, and add to it a touch of your own mind."

Conway stares at the ghostly silhouette in silence as a soft breeze extinguishes the candle, whispers through the snowy hair, and cradles the ancient spirit into eternity. The glow has faded. The High Lama is dead.

Through the courtyards and up the massive staircases the solemn, torchlit funeral procession winds single-file. Conway is at the window, staring out at all the beloved things that are now his, when George bursts in with urgent news: porters are waiting just beyond the pass, ready to accompany them on the long journey back to civilization. Very softly and with great compassion, Conway explains what he has found and why they must never leave the valley:

> "Something grand and beautiful, George. Something I've been searching for all my life. The answer to the confusion, bewilderment of a lifetime. I've *found* it, George, and I can't leave it. It's weird and fantastic and sometimes unbelievable, but *so* beautiful."

Conway tells his brother the whole story of Shangri-La, exactly as he had heard it from the High Lama. But George cares not a whit for the utopian schemes of "loose-brained fanatics"; he is leaving and taking the young Russian girl Maria with him. Conway knows that this cannot be allowed, for Chang has told him that the youthful-looking Maria (played by Mexican dancer Margo) came to Shangri-La in 1888, and was then 20 years of age; take her out of the valley, and she would quickly revert in appearance to her actual age. Maria, desperate to leave, joins George in a passionate appeal: the High Lama has been insane for years; she was kidnapped and brought here just as they were, only two years ago. Conway faces the disquieting realization that his dream is not meant for everyone. George could never be happy here, nor could he ever get through that country alone—it would be suicide. But is this glorious vision not bigger than brotherly love? To leave a world of such incomparable refinement and harmony? To return to a world in which the storm is already brewing, where every precious thing is sooner or later doomed to destruction? Conway's moment of indecision passes; he makes his choice and agrees to leave the outstretched arms of Shangri-La, pausing only momentarily before the secret mountain pass for just one last look. The lamasery, the valley floor beneath, the surrounding mountains in all their inaccessible purity, all float after him through the haze—all these are his, yet he is leaving. It comes to him that a dream has dissolved.

The porters leave them farther behind each day, until the merciless fury of an avalanche claims all but Conway, his brother, and their youthful companion. Suddenly and dramatically the lovely Maria crumbles away like old wood, until nothing is left but a shriveled mask—an unforgettable, hideous moment of truth. In horror and confusion, George runs screaming into the blizzard and plummets to his death over an icy precipice. A grief-stricken Conway plunges on alone—a pale shadow against the snow—through the most terrifying mountainscape in the world. On and on he pushes, never giving up, toward that overwhelming goal which haunts his half-crazed dreams, until finally—lost, blinded by sun and snow, lungs bursting—oblivion consumes him, and he topples unconscious into a remote tribal village.

"CONWAY FOUND ALIVE IN CHINESE MISSION," the newspaper headline screams, and a certain Lord Gainsford (Hugh Buckler) is immediately dispatched to return the amnesia-stricken diplomat to London. But Conway recovers his memory, tells Gainsford a fantastic story about a mysterious place in Tibet, insists upon returning there at once, and jumps ship at Singapore. For the greater part of a year Gainsford pursues Robert Conway, never overtaking him, always missing him by inches. Returning to London, Gainsford relates half-unbelievable tales of Conway's grim determination during ten long months:

The Lost Horizon *camera crew sets up a shot during Conway's amnesiac flight from* Shangri-La.

"He learned how to fly, stole an army plane, and got caught; put into jail; escaped. He begged, cajoled, fought, always pushing forward to the Tibetan frontier. Till eventually, I trailed him to the most extreme outpost in Tibet. His memory will live with those natives for the rest of their lives. 'The man who was not human,' they called him. They'll never forget the devil-eyed stranger who six times tried to go over the mountain pass that no other human being dared to travel, and six times was forced back by the severest storms. . . . And finally, he disappeared over that very mountain pass that they themselves dared not travel. And that, gentlemen, was the last that any known human being saw of Robert Conway."

Asked what he thinks about all this talk of Shangri-La, Gainsford lifts his glass and replies, "Yes, I believe it. I believe it because I *want* to believe it. Here's my hope that Robert Conway will find his Shangri-La; here's my hope that we *all* find our Shangri-La."

Lost Horizon enjoyed a considerable popular success when first released in 1937. Its simple but ageless story of one man's love affair with life struck a responsive chord in a Depression America which, like Lord Gainsford, believed it because it *wanted* to believe it. Oddly enough, its Santa Barbara preview was a disaster, and after almost two years of preparation and production *Lost Horizon* was, in the words of its director, "an unshowable, unreleasable motion picture."[40] Then Capra had a brainstorm, and simply excised the first 20 minutes — the film now began with the rescue operation at Baskul. That was all it took. At its second preview, the audience was spellbound, prompting Capra to remark, "When something goes haywire with a film, try burning the first two reels."[41] Reissued shortly after America's entry into the Second World War, by which time "Shangri-La" had become something of a household word, its box-office appeal was phenomenal. It has subsequently become one of the top money-makers of all time, capturing the imaginations of audiences throughout the world.

Six factors combine to make *Lost Horizon* one of the most impressive films of both Colman's and Capra's careers: compelling performances, marvelous script, richness and authenticity of production, flawless direction, inspired treatment of theme, and—most important—the magnetic presence of Ronald Colman.

A farsighted casting decision on Capra's part led him to select fairly well-known actors as Conway's hijacked companions, for, since they had come from the "real" world, their faces had to be easily recognizable (John Howard, Isabel Jewell, Thomas Mitchell, Edward Everett Horton). The characters from Shangri-La, inhabitants of an unknown world, had to have correspondingly less well-known faces, requiring the selection of actors whose film exposure had been in most cases fairly limited (H.B. Warner, Sam Jaffe, Jane Wyatt, Margo). The contrast was simple, subtle, and effective.

The casting of the High Lama gave the director a chronic headache. In all, some two dozen actors were tried for the part. Most failed; others died.

"Our first thought," Capra writes, "was to find some very old and forgotten stage star whose face had never been filmed. We found one, in nearby San Gabriel Valley."[42]

The 90-year-old ex-stage actor was quickly screen tested. Capra continues:

Next morning we saw the test on the screen. He was perfect. Just as he was. No make-up. We phoned his home to announce he had been chosen. His

Left–right: *Director Frank Capra, Ronald Colman, and composer Dimitri Tiomkin take a break during the filming of* Lost Horizon.

housekeeper wept with joy. An hour later she called us back. She wept in sorrow. The old gent had died—right after he heard the news. Died peacefully, with a smile on his face. The long-hoped-for Hollywood call had come.[43]

Next to get the nod was old screen favorite Henry B. Walthall, the "Little Colonel" in Griffith's *The Birth of a Nation* (1915) and kindly Dr. Manette in *A Tale of Two Cities*. But death again intervened, before the frail old gentleman could be tested.

The search continued, until Capra remembered 38-year-old Shakespearean actor Sam Jaffe, whose Broadway successes had included *Grand Hotel, The Jazz Singer*, and *A Doll's House*.[44] Snowing up Jaffe's wild hair and applying a layer of parchment to his face, Capra filmed a test. He knew instantly that he had found his High Lama, but Columbia chief Harry Cohn disagreed, objecting that Jaffe exuded weirdness rather than the benign fatherliness of a priest. So Capra reshot the scene with another distinguished stage actor, Walter Connolly, and when Cohn saw the results, Capra won the day and Jaffe got the part.

Robert Riskin's literate script, while extremely faithful to its source, markedly strengthened the original through the inclusion of several major departures, the most important being the motivation for the Baskul kidnapping. In the novel the abduction had been a somewhat clumsy plot device intended merely to furnish Shangri-La with new blood, since they did not know they were getting Robert Conway. It was only later that the High Lama discovered he had found a worthy successor, whereas in Riskin's adaptation the Lama specifically sought out the man who had "glimpsed the eternal," just as, centuries before, he himself had. A similar improvement was the transformation of Conway's assistant, Mallinson, into his younger brother, rendering more forceful Conway's decision to leave Shangri-La, as a self-sacrifice motivated by family obligation. The addition of the Lovett character (in the novel, Conway had only three companions) was inspired, and resulted in some of the wittiest dialogue sequences Robert Riskin ever wrote.

Stephen Goosson's magnificent lamasery sets, for which he won an Academy Award, were criticized in 1937 on the grounds that his unsuitable mixture of Mandarin and Frank Lloyd Wright was both insightly and unimaginative.[45] But despite contemporary disparagement, the massive palace, when viewed today, evokes a singularly appropriate mixed quality befitting neither East nor West but rather the disparate cultures brought together in Shangri-La: a Christian philosophy, founded by a Belgian monk, in an Oriental setting—a perfect rendering of a timeless, otherworldly atmosphere reflected visually through its architecture. Similarly reinforcing is Dimitri Tiomkin's musical score, which, through its sparing use of a haunting monastic vocal chorus, conveys perfectly the fragile ambience of a place apart.[46]

Besides using footage of the Himalayas as well as Elmer Dyer's shots of the Sierra Nevadas, Capra conjured up the vast, rolling Arctic rigors of snowbound Tibet in a fully equipped cold-storage warehouse. Nothing was faked—it was all real snow, real icy breath, real frosty eyebrows, real subfreezing temperatures, all contributing to an authenticity never surpassed in the celebrated German mountain films of Arnold Fanck and Leni Riefenstahl.

The stark contrast between the outside world of turmoil and brutality and the fantasy world of serenity is due in large part to Capra's unerring sense of narrative construction and rhythmic contrast editing. The mounting

As this Lost Horizon *publicity display shows, some parts of the Shangri-La set had been constructed in miniature for use in process shots.*

series of dramatic crises which begins with Baskul is shot in rapid short sequences, the mood harsh, dazzling, starkly oppressive. When the threshold is crossed, the fever pitch dissolves with the howling wind, the sequences become longer, the mood contrastingly lyrical, befitting the poetic dignity of Shangri-La. Capra, completely in control and fully aware of what moves audiences, accompanies the change in narrative mood with a corresponding change in the tempo and pace of his editing style, giving the film a dynamic thrust out of which the climax of Robert Conway's struggle to regain his lost dream flows like a river through a burst dam. Similarly suggestive of the stark contrast between two worlds is the silhouetted secret mountain pass—gateway to another world, its shadowy presence graphically obliterates the boundaries between the real and the unreal.

 Lost Horizon is a classic anti-war film in a fantasy format, preaching peace and love for all mankind at a time when the rest of the world was gearing for war. Within a framework of immense scope and spectacle, Capra used the story to project an abstract idea, to which the story, although important in its own right, was subordinate. This type of film stands in marked contrast to those which merely tell a story, illustrative of nothing beyond the story itself. On its most profound level, *Lost Horizon* is one continuous, dramatic, philosophical argument, its dynamism dependent upon the intensity of its ideas and ideals: they possess the power to haunt. Capra considers it his best film.[47]

Lost Horizon was in every way Ronald Colman's most inspired performance, in a role which might almost have been written specifically for him. Why is Colman so memorable as Robert Conway? Ultimately it is a matter of restraint as well as the depth of his identification with the character.

The bittersweet qualities which had by now become so much a part of the Colman image — the lacing of charm, integrity, and dedication with wistfulness and melancholy — were all expressed with each fragile modulation of his voice and, even more tellingly, through the subtle and silent art of pantomime. Those slightly quizzical, seemingly trifling traits, stemming in large part from his expressive eyes, all contributed to reveal his innermost thoughts without the necessity of uttering a word. Three prime examples of Colman's magnetic ability to evoke intensity through restraint come toward the end of the picture. First, weary, full of deep, conflicting tenderness, and wavering between two worlds, Conway makes the decision to leave Shangri-La and accompany his brother back to civilization. No words are needed: his expression changes, and his eyes tell us that duty has triumphed. Second, pausing at the narrow mountain defile, he turns back for one wistful moment; hat pulled low, collar turned up, the most sublime close-up we shall ever have of Colman's face — yearning, beautifully etched with awe, losing the dream of a lifetime; then he heads into the wind and whatever lies beyond. His is an anguish that bleeds. And finally, the stunning visual momentum of the film's last moments builds toward Conway's return to the Valley of the Blue Moon. Perhaps after ten months he no longer believes it still exists or had ever existed until, in that last shot, he sees the secret crevice in the mountains. Hauntingly photographed in extreme close-up, we see his bearded, haggard face — exultant, possessed of great beauty, idealism, and strength. The horizon has lifted like a curtain, and Conway is home at last!

Colman did not so much portray Robert Conway as he in fact became Conway. Writing of her father's identification with the character's values, Juliet Benita Colman observes that the role was

> a classic example of both perfect and natural casting. It was Ronald Colman stepping into his own image. Not only did Robert Conway fit the public image of Colman, he was also the embodiment of a great deal of Colman's character: his idealism, mystique, intelligence, gentleness. . . . They had a great deal more in common than the initials of their names. Ronnie effortlessly expanded the role of Conway by opening doors within himself.[48]

Frank Capra remembers that Colman

In a scene cut from Frank Capra's Lost Horizon, *amnesiac Robert Conway (Ronald Colman) plays an unpublished and unknown Chopin piece he learned from one of Chopin's own pupils. Chopin expert Sieveking (Max Rabinowitz) reminds Conway that a person who studied under Chopin would have to be over a hundred years old. This framing device is long lost, and this is all we are ever likely to see of the film's opening sequence.*

felt he was revealing himself on the screen in *Lost Horizon* more than he ever had done—or would do again. He shared Conway's dreams. He always talked about the Conway part later on. I'd say he was quite sure he had played himself in it.[49]

The story of Columbia's butchering of *Lost Horizon* in successive repackagings is a disquieting reminder of Hollywood's apparent disinterest in preserving its most valuable treasures.

As originally filmed, the picture opened with a framing device in which the amnesia-stricken Conway, returning to London by steamship with Lord Gainsford, meets the renowned pianist and Chopin scholar Sieveking (Max Rabinowitz), and insists that he has recently met one of Chopin's pupils. When the pianist objects that such a student would have to be well over a century old, Conway—his memory jogged—jumps ship and sets out for Shangri-La. When a preview audience found this 16-reel, 150-minute version too tiring, Capra eliminated the prologue and, for its road-show engagements, the film was released in a 14-reel, 132-minute format. Never again would *Lost Horizon* be unfolded in flashback. For its general release, it was shortened to 118 minutes, and when Columbia reissued the picture in 1942 under the new title *Lost Horizon of Shangri-La*,[50] an additional 11 minutes were scissored.[51] Nine more minutes were trimmed in the late forties, and in 1952, when Columbia again rereleased the film, the cutting shears were wielded with a vengeance: it clocked in at just about 90 minutes—powerful, moving, and majestic still, but mutilated nonetheless.[52]

Sequences added to the discard pile included the significant conversation between the Conway brothers on the plane, Gloria's hysterical outburst, Lovett's diverting adventure in the Valley of the Blue Moon, parts of scenes between Conway and Sondra, and all of their well-publicized aviary scene.

The original nitrate negative deteriorated in 1967. In 1973, the American Film Institute began a 12-year restoration project, an exhaustive search through the world's film archives in an effort to locate all surviving versions of *Lost Horizon*. A partially restored print was premiered at Hollywood's famous Chinese Theatre in 1979, with Frank Capra, Sam Jaffe, Jane Wyatt, and cinematographers Joseph Walker and Al Keller in attendance. This reconstruction ran 122½ minutes, several minutes longer than the general release, and contained sequences from the original road-show version.[53] In 1986, the AFI sponsored the release of a nearly complete print: it ran 125 minutes, and the entire 132-minute soundtrack had been restored. The seven minutes of footage still missing were deftly reconstructed through the use of stills and freeze-framed images.

Of the 1973 color musical remake of *Lost Horizon* which starred Peter Finch in the Conway role, the less said the better; rather, let Frank Capra have the last word: "I never have been tempted to do a remake in wide screen and color and everything. Frankly, I felt we had done it. Besides, where could one find another Ronald Colman?"[54]

The Prisoner of Zenda

1937. *Production:* Selznick International Pictures, Inc. *Distribution:* United Artists Corporation. *Producer:* David O. Selznick. *Director:* John Cromwell. *Screenplay:* John L. Balderston. *Adaptation:* Wells Root (from the novel by Anthony Hope and the play by Edward Rose). *Additional Dialogue:* Donald Ogden Stewart. *Cinematographer:* James Wong Howe. *Musical Score:* Alfred Newman. *Art Director:* Lyle Wheeler. *Set Decorations:* Casey Roberts. *Special Effects:* Jack Cosgrove. *Technical Advisors:* Prince Sigvard Bernadotte, Colonel Ivar Enhorning. *Costumes:* Ernst Dryden. *Assistant to the Producer:* William H. Wright. *Assistant Director:*

Frederick A. Spencer. *Assistant Directors (uncredited):* W.S. Van Dyke, George Cukor. *Film Editors:* Hal C. Kern, James E. Newcom. *Sound:* Oscar Lagerstrom. *Running Time:* 101 minutes. *Release Date:* September 2, 1937.

Cast: Ronald Colman (Rudolf Rassendyll and King Rudolph V), Madeleine Carroll (Princess Flavia), Douglas Fairbanks, Jr. (Rupert of Hentzau), C. Aubrey Smith (Colonel Sapt), Raymond Massey (Black Michael), Mary Astor (Antoinette de Mauban), David Niven (Fritz von Tarlenheim), Byron Foulger (Johann), Eleanor Wesselhoeft (Cook), Montagu Love (Detchard), William von Brincken (Krafstein), Philip Sleeman (Lauengram), Ralph Faulkner (Bersonin), Alexander D'Arcy (De Gautet), Torben Meyer (Michael's Butler), Ian MacLaren (Cardinal), Lawrence Grant (Marshal Strakencz), Howard Lang (Josef), Ben Webster (British Ambassador), Evelyn Beresford (British Ambassador's Wife), Boyd Irwin (Master of Ceremonies), Emmett King (von Haugwitz, Lord High Chamberlain), Charles K. French (Bishop), Al Shean (Orchestra Leader), Charles Halton (Passport Officer), Otto Fries (Luggage Officer), Florence Roberts (Duenna), Spencer Charters (Porter), Russ Powell, D'Arcy Corrigan (Travelers), Francis Ford (Man), Nigel Bruce, Halliwell Hobbes (Men in Club [deleted]), Henry Roquemore, Lillian Harmer, Pat Somerset, Leslie Sketchley.

The swashbuckling adventure classic, so abundant in the twenties through numerous adaptations of Rafael Sabatini's novels and the ever-popular Douglas Fairbanks costume spectacles, had lain dormant after the invasion of the talkies and during the early Depression years. But the mid-thirties saw a revival of lavish period costumers with the filming of such classics as *Treasure Island, The Count of Monte Cristo, Mutiny on the Bounty,* and *Captain Blood.* Swashbucklers—old-fashioned "moving" pictures— were in again, and the stage was set for the richest of them all: *The Prisoner of Zenda.* This aggressive yet lighthearted romp combined thrill, spectacle, acrobatic agility, irrepressible humor, and delicate romance with such panache and style that its flow of images remains unsurpassed among classics of the genre. Its direction by John Cromwell is crisp, its editing flawless, its cinematography and lighting exquisite, its production sumptuous, its script brilliant, its musical score unforgettable, and its supporting cast so magnificent that one can hardly imagine the parts having been written for any other actors. Moreover, it boasts Ronald Colman at his most dashing in one of his most distinctive and irresistible performances, his last and decidedly best dual role. No wonder then that *The Prisoner of Zenda* opened to universal popular and critical acclaim.

"Toward the close of the last century, when History still wore a Rose, and Politics had not yet outgrown the Waltz,"[55] Europe shimmered in the sunset of its years, a mythical universe that never was and yet exists—a world of dark, gloomy castles, dungeons, and moats; royal intrigue, dirty dealing, and the clash of cold steel. Into this myth steps Ronald Colman as Major Rudolf Rassendyll, on a fishing expedition to the peaceful kingdom of Ruritania. Rumors of political unrest in the capital of Strelsau, where the new king is to be crowned the following day, hold no interest for Rassendyll, for he has trout in mind, not coronations. Making his way to the Royal Game Preserve in the Province of Zenda, he decides the fish can wait; sleep comes first, for the journey has been long and tiring.

He awakens to find two men regarding him with much curiosity and more amazement.

"Shave him and he'd be the king!" exclaims the elder of the two, an old soldier with a bristly, gray moustache (played with crusty authority by C. Aubrey Smith).

Colonel Sapt's companion is a slender, handsome chap, Captain Fritz von Tarlenheim (a very young David Niven). Both are in the service of His Majesty the King, which makes their uninvited guest, not so long ago in the service of Her Britannic Majesty Queen Victoria, a kindred spirit.

"Then we're all brethren of the sword," proclaims Fritz with a broad grin.

King Rudolph, fifth of the Elphberg line, played by Colman in his second role, enters the clearing, and for an instant he and Rassendyll stand motionless, staring at one another. Except for the Englishman's beard, the two men look astonishingly similar. For these challenging scenes, James Wong Howe's superb special effects, split-screen techniques, and superimpositions not only permit Colman to converse with his other self convincingly, but also allow him to shake hands with himself with detection-defying perfection. Rassendyll is "by way of being a relative" of the king; it seems that their mutual ancestor, Rudolph II, effected a liaison with one of the more sportive representatives of the Rassendyll clan, and every now and again the Elphberg face reappears to betray that most scandalous of royal indiscretions, the same offence for which the present Rassendyll admits himself guilty: fishing in forbidden waters.

The king invites Cousin Rudolf to his hunting lodge, where the wine is plentiful and beyond all price or praise. They do it justice, and are soon as full of spirits as they have any right to be. Tomorrow, in the cathedral, Rudolph shall be proclaimed king, and king he shall be for the rest of his life. But tonight he drinks with his friends — well, perhaps just his friend, for young Fritz, hilariously drunk and continually muttering "Toast!" until at last he mercifully passes out, is no longer in the running. The elderly Sapt paces back and forth angrily, his unpleasant scowl darkening the festivities, for it is always a disagreeable task to be a reminder of duty:

"I question your freedom, Sire, to drink youself into a condition in which you will not be fit to be crowned tomorrow."

Having earned himself a royal slap across the face, Sapt takes his leave. Rassendyll soon nods off, leaving only the king to consume the contents of the new flagon proffered by the servant.

"Everybody sleeps but the king," Rudolph mutters as he sips the wine that will shortly alter the destiny of his kingdom.

As the early rays of dawn silently announce that the great day is at hand, Rassendyll awakes with a start and a shiver—his face, hair, and clothes dripping with water, Sapt scowling at him, an empty pitcher in his hand. Fritz sits opposite them, as pale as a ghost. Before them on the floor lies the inert form of the king, drugged and breathing heavily. Who would perform such a foul deed? Who else but Black Michael, the king's half-brother, who wants the throne for himself and will stop at nothing to get it. The colonel sits glowering, realizing what must be done: Rudolf Rassendyll is the right man in the right place at the right time.

"If he's not crowned today," Sapt tells him, "he'll never be crowned. Then Michael sits on the throne tonight, and the king lies in prison—or his grave."

By tonight, Rassendyll can be dispatched safely across the border, but this morning he must take the king's place at the coronation—a terrible risk against an even more terrible certainty.

"Englishman, I'm much older than you," Sapt says grimly. "As a man grows old, he begins to believe in Fate. Fate sent you here. Fate sends you now to Strelsau!"

Sapt appeals to his sense of duty, and Rassendyll shaves off his beard and becomes the future sovereign. The king is hidden in the wine cellar, and it's off to Strelsau.

"Sleep well, Sire," Fritz intones. "We go to see you crowned."

At this moment Black Michael is busily assuming the regency of the kingdom and proclaiming a state of martial law. Our first glimpse of the would-be usurper, impeccably attired in black and portrayed with all the malevolence and sadism which only Raymond Massey could bring to the role, provides an ominous foreboding of dastardly things to come. This personification of everything unspeakable is joined by his equally cunning but decidedly more charming second in command—the wicked young Rupert of Hentzau. Arrayed from head to toe in an immaculate black uniform, this rakish devil is most dashingly brought to life by Douglas Fairbanks, Jr., in what is unquestionably his finest role.

The time grows near, for at any moment the coronation ceremonies are to be cancelled. Amidst the towers and spires of a great city, the deadly game begins. As scores of trumpets triumphantly proclaim the arrival of His Majesty's train, Rassendyll and company alight to thundering cheers of "God save the King!"

Barely audible in the bustle, the confusion, and the magnificent honor guard is Sapt's stalwart whisper: "God save 'em both; steady, lad!"

As the long procession enters the cathedral, the sudden imposing sense of the audacity of it all nearly overcomes them—Rassendyll, resplendent in a magnificent white uniform; Sapt following grimly, his great craggy face and ramrod posture masking the mounting tension; poor young Fritz, near

Colonel Sapt (C. Aubrey Smith) and Fritz von Tarlenheim (David Niven) watch nervously as their imposter-king (Ronald Colman), about to be crowned, is confronted by Black Michael (Raymond Massey), the sneering half-brother of the real king, in The Prisoner of Zenda.

fainting with fright, bringing up the rear. Michael and Hentzau are predictably less then overjoyed by the king's unexpected appearance.

"If only he'd drunk what *I* wanted to put in the bottle!" Hentzau insolently hisses, as he leaves for Zenda to find out what went wrong.

With the pealing of the great organ in their ears, Rassendyll looks his enemy squarely in the eye. An unsuspecting Michael—lips parched, flesh sagging, mouth frozen in a perpetual ghastly sneer—bows formally, offers his arm, and escorts his "brother" to the altar. So the likeness serves, a new king is proclaimed, and an ideal and exquisite princess, soon to be Rudolph's bride and queen, kneels to pledge her fidelity. She of the glorious golden hair and flowing bridal raiment is Princess Flavia, portrayed with fragile "porcelain beauty"[56] by Madeleine Carroll. As Black Michael glowers in disgust and barely restrained jealousy, Fritz and Sapt heave final sighs of relief. The masquerade is over—or so they think.

Hours later, Rassendyll and the princess share an intimate moment at the palace.

"You seem an entirely different person," Flavia smiles, her face alight with devotion. "I can't understand it."

"Don't try," he whispers.

Her life has been spent preparing for an empty marriage of state. "But now I don't have to tell you how different it is," she says gently.

Promising to see him tomorrow, she takes her leave.

"Tomorrow," he murmurs, his eyes growing troubled, his face etched with longing for the lovely princess who by tomorrow will have become, for him, a haunting memory.

Rassendyll prepares to take quiet leave of his friends. What a day to remember! For one brief, shining moment, he has been a king, preserving the dignity of a crown, meeting the most beautiful princess in all of Europe, and enjoying the camaraderie of men who live, as he does, by the unspoken code of honor and integrity.

Sapt and Rassendyll leave the palace, spur their horses to a gallop, and ride out to get the real king. The hunting lodge is shrouded in darkness and ghostly silence. In the wine cellar, they find the king's murdered servant, a note pinned to his bloodied breast: "One King is enough for any Kingdom." This can only be the work of that impertinent young Hentzau: he's abducted the king.

Upstairs, Sapt lights his pipe and smokes for a moment in silence. By now Michael knows all, but dare he risk an open conflict? With Rassendyll in Strelsau, Michael cannot murder the king without exposing his own treachery. It's a wild and desperate wager, but the crown must remain on Rassendyll's head until the king is saved, for if Michael kills the king and becomes regent, he will force Princess Flavia to marry him.

"But you *can't* let that happen to her!" Rassendyll insists.

"Can *you*?" the old man searchingly inquires, aware of the Englishman's feelings for the princess.

Thus, the clever soldier invokes once more his companion's sense of obligation and chivalry. And so the masquerade continues and the challenge is met, but it comes to them that they are now pawns in a new game—this one played according to Black Michael's rules.

In the palace garden, aglow with fretted light and rippling shadows, Rassendyll and his princess savor the gentle quality of emotions freely given.

"I love you more than truth, or life, or honor," he says softly, drawing her close.

"Why is it that I love you now," she asks breathlessly, "when I never even *liked* you before?"

"*Never* before?"

"It was at the coronation. I looked at you and—"

"And *that* was the first time you loved me?" he asks with delicacy.

"I wanted you to be different from the Rudolph I didn't love, and you are, and yet you aren't," she replies, her upraised face close to his.

"Flavia, if I were different—" he begins hesitantly, his face half hidden in shadowed close-up, as if silently exposing the king who is really not a king, "could you still love me if I were not the king?"

"In my heart there is no king, no crown, only you," she murmurs gently, her eyes seeking his.

"Flavia," he whispers, after a short pause, "I am not—"

"Your Majesty!" Sapt's stern voice interrupts harshly, emerging from the shadows as a ghostly reminder of a secret which must be kept. Thus a glorious night comes to an abrupt end.

Inside the palace, Rassendyll protests the continuation of this deception, insisting that the king be found without further delay. And find the king they do, for an unexpected ally joins their cause—Antoinette de Mauban, Black Michael's bewitching mistress, played by the ravishing Mary Astor. Preferring exile with her lover to the role of resident courtesan, she arranges a shadowy tryst with Rassendyll. They meet, but she warns him that three men are on their way to kill him. The king is hidden in the dungeon of Michael's castle at Zenda, but if the castle is attacked, the king will be murdered instantly.

Sudden footsteps outside—it's Hentzau and two assassins. The other thugs are unwilling to enter the dark cottage.

"Shoot with a lady present?" Count Rupert smirks as he draws his pistol. "In England, old boy," he assures his cohorts, "it simply *isn't* done!"

As Hentzau forces the door and fires, Rassendyll braces himself, shields his head and body with a tea table, and springs through the doorway. Battering his way through a tangle of arms, legs, and revolvers, Rassendyll leaps up and over the courtyard wall in a flash, and is off to rescue the king.

The next night, long before the cold light of dawning day begins to steal in, Rassendyll and his comrades cross the valley. Michael's looming castle frowns at them in the haze as the moat twinkles in the darkness. Without a splash, Rassendyll lowers himself into the black water, swims the moat, and scales the moist, moss-covered masonry which leads to the welcoming window of Antoinette de Mauban. Her servant (Byron Foulger) will lower the drawbridge, but Rassendyll alone must reach the dungeon and hold off the guards until the others can cross the bridge and get below.

As Rassendyll creeps stealthily down the passageway to the dingy hole where the king lies chained, Antoinette de Mauban lures Count Rupert into her room and away from the action. Moments later Michael burst in to discover the flirtatious decoy in a compromising embrace.

"I was only apologizing for your absence, Your Highness," taunts Rupert with a smug grin.

Prisoner of Zenda director John Cromwell, with pipe, sets up the hunting lodge confrontation between Rupert of Hentzau (Douglas Fairbanks, Jr., left) and Rudolf Rassendyll (Ronald Colman). Legendary cinematographer James Wong Howe is seen at the camera.

A fight ensues, Hentzau's knife flashes, and Black Michael breathes his last. The servant's turn comes next; before he can untie the drawbridge rope, Hentzau finishes him off with a stout length of pipe. Rassendyll, meanwhile, has dispatched both guards, but before he can unchain King Rudolph, the murderous count intervenes.

There follows one of the most dazzling, and certainly the most satiric, of climactic duels in all cinema.[57] Scenery, props, and shadowed lighting are used to good effect as hero and villain slash their way up the winding staircase. As Rassendyll inches his way ever closer to the drawbridge rope, gigantic shadows of the two figures loom menacingly on the damp, glistening wall. The agile derring-do is constantly punctuated by lighthearted banter, as the deadly rivals pause during the clash of steel to exchange witty thrusts and parries.

> *Hentzau:* I just killed one man for trying that.
> *Rassendyll:* An unarmed man, of course.
> *Hentzau:* Of course! You English are a stubborn lot.

Rassendyll: Well, England expects of every man, you know.
Hentzau: Why don't you let me kill you quietly?
Rassendyll: Oh, a little noise adds a touch of *cheer!*

Rassendyll's blade steals toward the drawbridge rope and, after several thwarted attempts, severs it. A score of mounted soldiers thunders across the bridge.

"This is getting too hot for me. Au revoir, play-actor!" Hentzau cries as he turns and leaps from a high window into the moat to escape his thoroughly well-deserved fate.

Old Sapt rushes to Rassendyll's side.

"The king lives," the wounded Englishman says softly.

This time the masquerade *is* over.

Anthony Hope's popular 1894 tale of high adventure and *l'amour royal* had been a perennial favorite on the stage prior to the first of its numerous screen adaptations. James K. Hackett, who had starred in the play, recreated the dual role in the 1913 four-reeler directed by American film pioneer Edwin S. Porter. Rex Ingram's 1922 production featured Lewis Stone as Rudolf/Rudolph and Ramon Novarro as Count Rupert, and a sequel, *Rupert of Hentzau*, was filmed in 1923. These early versions were handsomely mounted action programmers — nothing more, nothing less.

John Cromwell's 1937 *Prisoner of Zenda* is, however, classic escapist entertainment at its best: showcasing the swashbuckling agility of Ronald Colman and Douglas Fairbanks, Jr., the film has a zest and sheer exuberance of spirit which are exultantly free from the weight of everyday reality. The collaborative efforts of producer David O. Selznick, director John Cromwell, scenarists John L. Balderston and Donald Ogden Stewart, cinematographer James Wong Howe, art director Lyle Wheeler, and composer Alfred Newman produced an overwhelmingly sparkling, swashbuckling triumph. Purely with regard to art direction, script, music, and perfect casting, the film is an unsurpassable achievement. The costumes and sets glitter with beauty; the spectacular set pieces (the coronation and the grand ball) dazzle with elegance and verve. The script, while a model of fidelity to the novel, laces the heroics with gaiety and a quick and ready wit reminiscent of the Douglas Fairbanks, Sr., swashbucklers of an earlier decade. The musical score splendidly captures the sweep of romance, intrigue, and adventure, and the subtle identification of each major character with his or her own musical motif neatly underscores the action without ever becoming obtrusive. The teaming of dark, dashing Ronald Colman and willowy, blonde Madeleine Carroll was enchanting, and the marvelous support given them by C. Aubrey Smith, David Niven, Raymond Massey, Mary Astor, and especially Douglas Fairbanks, Jr., adds immeasurably to the film's charm.[58] What makes it more than a mere escapist fantasy, and one of the most

*On the eve of the coronation of King George VI, on a sound stage at Selznick Interna-
tional Pictures, prominent members of Hollywood's British colony gather to broadcast
their radio tribute to king and country. With American master of ceremonies Douglas
Fairbanks, Jr., are Madeleine Carroll, Ronald Colman, David Niven, and C. Aubrey
Smith. By presenting the broadcast from the sound stage, it was possible for the
quintet to step away from* The Prisoner of Zenda *set to deliver their messages.*

impressive Hollywood films of the thirties, is its incomparable visual stylization, its profound treatment of major themes, and—most important—the
extraordinarily inspired performance of Ronald Colman.

James Wong Howe's lustrous cinematography rivals the films of Josef
von Sternberg in its mastery of shadowed, atmospheric lighting, meticulous
composition, and glossy chiaroscuro. Because of his remarkably sensuous
pictorialism, there is always something to intrigue, excite, and bewitch the
eye. In most entertainment pictures, a shot is appropriate because it is
beautiful; for Howe, a shot is beautiful because it is appropriate. Technical
bravura and dazzling contrast lighting are not ends in themselves, for style
is the servant of meaning. There is not a shot nor a shadow which does not
tell in itself some essential incident of the story.

At the more general level, shadowy stylization is employed for abstract
and decorative purposes to create a fantasy world of light, with darkness
serving only as a foil for that light—a perfect rendering of a dreamworld
which has just enough contact with reality to give substance to the delicate

shadows. On a more specific level, suggestive atmospheric lighting is used for subjective and symbolic purposes to emphasize dramatic details. A striking example occurs during the imposing coronation ceremony in the great cathedral. As the newly proclaimed king rises to deliver his stirring oath, Howe stabs a shaft of light from a high window down onto him, graphically evoking a solemn mood of exalted sovereignty.

The two scenes which best illustrate Howe's enlightened use of expressive spotlighting appear in tandem when, moments after discovering that Princess Flavia loves *him* and not the king, Rassendyll stands before a huge fireplace and listens as Sapt tells him he has struck a good blow for the king.

"What's to prevent me striking a blow for myself?" the imposter storms, struggling with the terrible temptation to let the king die and keep the princess to himself.

"You're bound *in honor* to play the king's part!" Sapt grumbles, frowning heavily.

"Have you *left* me any honor? I'm a man in love with a woman who loves *me*—you *saw* tonight, you *heard* tonight! Then why should I ever leave the throne?" he snaps, his dark eyes blazing in the reflected glow of the roaring fire. "I could marry the princess, and send Michael and the king to—"

"You could do that," Sapt grunts with a sour yet sad look of understanding, "but you wouldn't." For the old soldier knows that honor is the cornerstone of this Englishman's character—it's written on his face; having pledged his word to serve the king, integrity prevails, as they both know it must. In this classic scene of love and honor in conflict, Howe deflects the full glow of the fire directly onto Rassendyll's face, subtly and effectively underscoring both the passion and the moral conflict. Meanwhile Black Michael and Count Rupert, comfortably ensconced in plush armchairs before a similarly roaring fireplace, concoct a new piece of villainy: the assassination of the king's double. As the sinister blackguards puff away on their cigarettes, Howe skillfully employs the dense smoke which curls about them to conjure up a satanic ambience of the fires of hell; the imagery is vivid, simple, and unmistakable.[59]

Howe was not the only perfectionist on the set. Douglas Fairbanks, Jr., had this to say about David O. Selznick:

> David was a great but maddening producer. Although John Balderston, author of *Berkeley Square*, had done the original adaptation and Donald Ogden Stewart, one of our best writers, had submitted an excellent screenplay, every few days a whole pile of pages, rewritten by David, would be sent to the set, and whole scenes would have to be relearned. This so angered director Cromwell that he and David had a showdown. In the end, John was relieved of his assignment and a good deal of the film was reshot with W.S. Van Dyke replacing Cromwell as director.[60]

Nigel Bruce and Halliwell Hobbes listen to the reminiscences of an elderly Rudolf Rassendyll (Ronald Colman), in the deleted opening scene of The Prisoner of Zenda.

Shortly after the release of *The Prisoner of Zenda*, Selznick discussed the picture and its star:

> . . . I frankly would not have purchased the material if I hadn't had Ronald Colman under contract, and if I hadn't determined in advance that Colman would play the role. One of the thousand-and-one functions of the producer is to make sure that the star is happy with his assignment, or face the prospect of losing him when the contract expires. Colman and I talked at great length about the picture, about its drawbacks, about what I saw in it and his fears concerning it. . . .
>
> The big discussion with Colman was whether he should play the dual role. He has a dread of dual roles, based upon a picture he made some years ago, called *The Masquerader*. . . .[61]

Selznick went on to reveal that a framing device had originally been filmed, but was later scrapped. In a prologue set in England, an elderly, lonely Rassendyll was pictured sitting in his club. The story was then told in flashback, and ended with an epilogue in which the old man received a rose from Flavia, and with it a note from Fritz telling him that the queen had died.[62]

The Prisoner of Zenda, a landmark of cinema romanticism and "one of the purest and noblest fables of Love and Honour ever put on film,"[63] gave audiences Ronald Colman in his most memorable and universally praised dual role. His King Rudolph was, at the start, an irresponsible wastrel whom Princess Flavia had always found repugnant, while his Rudolf Rassendyll, the king's likeness in physical appearance only, embodied a personal nobility perfectly tailored to the Colman image. As the dedicated Englishman who saves a kingdom at the expense of his own happiness, Rassendyll is the perfect incarnation of all the qualities which made the definitive Colman screen personality so overwhelmingly popular in the thirties: sincere and reliable, determined and resilient, affable and witty, yet somehow always bearing just a touch of the "broken wing" which so arouses female sympathy and affection.[64] This inner fragility, the vague sadness under the surface which was reflected both facially and through the sensitive, restrained delivery of that exquisite voice, had by now become the most distinctive element of Colman's style. It is this bittersweet alchemy which makes his portrayal of Rudolf Rassendyll so compelling, irresistibly attractive, and one of the classic performances for which he is most fondly remembered.

At the close of the film, Rassendyll makes ready for his immediate departure. No one must ever know that, for a time, there were two kings. Entering his cousin's bedchamber, he returns the royal ring he has worn with such distinction.

> *Rassendyll:* I've tried not to dishonor it, Sire.
> *Rudolph:* I wanted to keep you with me, and tell everyone what you have done. You would have been my best and dearest friend, Cousin Rudolf. But Sapt says the secret must be kept.
> *Rassendyll:* Let me go. My work here is done.
> *Rudolph:* Yes, it's done, but no one but you could have done it. I don't know when I'll see you again—
> *Rassendyll:* If I can ever serve you, Sire—
> *Rudolph:* You could never serve me better, Cousin. You taught me how to *be* a king.

When all was said and done, Rassendyll had borne himself as a wise and brave king, had done what was expected of him quietly and with humility, and had set a standard of excellence for Rudolph V to emulate. It was perhaps inevitable that Princess Flavia would fall in love with him, and he with her, but fate has decreed that he must leave her to the man in whose place he has stood. As thoughts of their exalted love arise to stab him, Rassendyll hesitantly enters the chamber where Flavia awaits him. Radiant sunlight streams in, highlighting her blonde hair and matchless beauty. This classic renunciation scene underscores the themes of honor, duty, and self-sacrifice with such perfection that it is worth recalling in detail.[65]

"I sent for you to thank you for the service you've done this kingdom and its king," the princess begins, with some discomfort. "No one can know better than *I* how *conscientiously* you've played your role!"

"I love you. With my *whole* heart and soul, I love you. In *all* else, I've been an imposter, but *not* in that," Rassendyll replies. "From the first moment I saw you in the cathedral, you've been the *only* woman in the world for me. As I stand here now, I know there never can be any other."

"It would have made no difference if I'd known. It was *always* you and *never* the king," she reassures him with a smile, and then asks, with worry in her eyes, "Is it true that you're going home to England?"

"Tonight. Come with me!" he cries eagerly, a sudden blaze of passion stirring in him as he takes her in his arms. "I won't give you up! I won't let them stand in the way of our happiness! *Come with me!*"

"Oh, if I could!" she exclaims, a flush on her cheeks as they embrace and kiss.

"There's a *world* outside," he tells her with tenderness and a warm smile, "our world. And a throne for you—a woman's throne, in my heart."

"I want that!" the princess cries out with great emotion, her eyes aglitter.

"Ah, my love, think. You'll be free—free of all these cares and duties, and live your own life as freely and joyously as—"

Her face suddenly clouded with pain, Flavia realizes why their dream can never be. "I was *born* to those cares and duties, Rudolf. *Help me* to do what I was *born* to do! Help me to do what I *must!*" she pleads.

"My dear, how can I?" his conflicting emotions prompt him to ask. "I love you!"

"But is love the *only* thing? If love were all, I could follow you in rags to the end of the world. If that *were* all, you'd have left the king to die in his cell. Honor binds a woman too, Rudolf. My honor lies in keeping faith with my country and my house. I don't know *why* God has let me love you," she sobs, "but I *know* that I must stay!"

"I was mad to ask you," he says softly.

"For one lovely moment, I too was mad," she murmurs.

"Never to *see* you again, never to *hold* you, never—"

"You'll always be in my heart, and the touch of your lips on mine," her voice gently whispers, as the camera pulls back from the parting lovers and frames them in long shot. The composition emphasizes an awesome sense of departure and loss, as Rassendyll kneels and bids his princess farewell—"his honour satisfied, his heart broken."[66]

Colonel Sapt and Fritz escort Rassendyll to the frontier and bid their faithful friend adieu.

Rassendyll: We'll meet again, Fritz.
Fritz: Fate doesn't always make the right men kings.
Rassendyll: Good-bye, Colonel. We've run a good course together.
Sapt: Good-bye, Englishman. You're the finest Elphberg of them all!

Spurring his horse forward, Rassendyll pauses at the crest of the hill. Silhouetted against the awakening sky, he turns, salutes his comrades, and then, as the music swells to a stirring crescendo, disappears over the horizon.

When still another version of *The Prisoner of Zenda* was released in 1952, this time in color, with Stewart Granger in the dual role and James Mason as Hentzau, its critical reception was mixed. To call it a mechanical, scene-for-scene remake, as some critics averred, does the film an injustice. Although certainly overshadowed by its predecessor, it possesses great visual beauty and excels in every respect. The fact that the same script, musical score, and camera angles were used merely indicates its producers' realization that the excellence of the Colman version was going to be impossible to beat. It was. A Peter Sellers comedy remake of 1979 prompted *The New Yorker* to remark that Ronald Colman remained the only prisoner of Zenda worthy of the name.

If I Were King

1938. *Production and distribution:* Paramount Pictures, Inc. *Producer and director:* Frank Lloyd. *Screenplay:* Preston Sturges (from the play by Justin Huntly McCarthy). *Cinematographer:* Theodor Sparkuhl. *Special Photographic Effects:* Gordon Jennings. *Musical Score:* Richard Hageman. *Musical Director:* Boris Morros. *Art Directors:* Hans Dreier, John Goodman. *Set Decorations:* A.E. Freudeman. *Costumes:* Edith Head. *Associate Producer:* Lou Smith. *Assistant Directors:* William Tummel, Harry Scott. *Film Editor:* Hugh Bennett. *Sound:* Harold C. Lewis, John Cope. *Running Time:* 100 minutes. *New York Premiere:* September 28, 1938.

Cast: Ronald Colman (François Villon), Basil Rathbone (Louis XI), Frances Dee (Katherine de Vaucelles), Ellen Drew (Huguette du Hamel), C.V. France (Father Villon), Henry Wilcoxon (Captain of the Watch), Heather Thatcher (The Queen), Stanley Ridges (René de Montigny), Bruce Lester (Noel de Jolys), Walter Kingsford (Tristan l'Hermite), Alma Lloyd (Colette), Sidney Toler (Robin Turgis), Colin Tapley (Jehan le Loup), Ralph Forbes (Oliver le Dain), John Miljan (Thibaut d'Aussigny), William Haade (Guy Tabarie), Adrian Morris (Colin de Cayeulx), Montagu Love (General Dudon), Lester Matthews (General Saliere), William Farnum (General Barbezier), Paul Harvey (Burgundian Herald), Barry Macollum (Watchman), May Beatty (Anna), Winter Hall (Major Domo), Francis McDonald (Casin Cholet), Ann Evers, Jean Fenwick (Ladies-in-Waiting), Russ Powell (Ruffian),

Harry Wilson (Beggar), John George (Dwarf Beggar), Stanley King (Captain of Archers), Henry Brandon (Soldier), Ethel Clayton (Old Woman), Judith King, Cheryl Walker (Girls).

Ronald Colman swashbuckles his way across the screen in Frank Lloyd's *If I Were King,* a frothy tale of adventure, intrigue, and romance in fifteenth-century France, and one of Paramount's most lavish projects for 1938. The slash of his sword and the passion of his poetry help save the city of Paris, rout the Burgundians, and win the affection of a lovely lady-in-waiting.

Paris under siege: throughout a long winter of starvation, the skeletal hand of famine takes a firm grip on the city, as its beleaguered inhabitants, surrounded by the invading Burgundians, cry out, "Who will deliver us?" While the poor perish from want in their miserable hovels, an answer rings forth from that densely populated, vice-infested sewer of Paris, the Court of Miracles: François Villon! This scholar, gutter poet, and companion of rogues, thieves, and cutthroats (Colman) can usually be found drinking, wenching, and writing questionable verse at his favorite tavern, except for the night he and his band of brigands break into the king's royal storehouse and make off with enough food to nourish half the starving populace. Pursued by the king's troops after the robbery, Villon finds refuge in the home of his foster father (C.V. France), an elderly priest who insists upon dragging the thief to church to repent of his sins. There Villon observes Katherine de Vaucelles (Frances Dee), one of Her Majesty's ladies-in-waiting, deep in prayer. When this vision of loveliness rises to leave, he follows her down the church steps.

"I was afraid you'd gone!" Villon cries.

"Why—why, I've never seen you before in my life."

> "Ah, but you've forgotten—my dreams. I've dreamed of you always. Each night we've roamed the starry way together; each morning I wake with despair in my heart, to realize no mortal could be so fair. Yet here you are, the loveliest lady this side of Heaven. . . . Of course, if I had better manners, I'd keep you all to myself, but, you see, I have no manners."

Villon is apprehended by the king's soldiers while reciting a love poem, but when Katherine intercedes, claiming that a gentleman seen at prayers could not possibly have robbed His Majesty's storehouse, he is promptly released. The culprit quickly steals back into church and kneels beside Father Villon, who, oblivious to his son's temporary absence, has just finished his prayers.

"Now, François, admit it," he smiles benevolently. "You feel better for it, don't you."

"I do, Father, I do!" Villon agrees.

"You see, my son, time spent in church is not wasted."

"Oh, indeed not, Father. She—she smiled at me."

Meanwhile, the Burgundians continue their advance, the royal army falters, and wily King Louis XI (Basil Rathbone in a comedic tour de force) indulges in a bit of imperial espionage. Informed that a nest of Burgundian spies frequently foregathers at the sordid Fircone Tavern in the Court of Miracles, King Louis, disguised in a hooded robe, joins the wanton rabble in that boisterous den to observe the goings-on. Villon and his roistering band arrive to devour their storehouse plunder, and the vagabond does his best to insult the stranger by calling him a "juiceless mold" and "Brother Long-nose." When Villon, never suspecting that the victim of his ribald tongue is the king himself, launches into a denunciation of the "nincompoop" who sits on the throne, Louis asks "this cockroach" what he would do, if *he* were king. To begin with, the poet boasts, he'd rid himself of the vermin who inhabit the palace, and try to earn his subjects' devotion and loyalty, instead of their loathing.

> "By abolishing despair and substituting hope, by knowing the longings in their hearts, as a man of the people would. Seeing them as they are, and admitting that their vices are as deep-rooted as their virtues, I'd treat them as my children, instead of as my enemies. So, by knowing the worst in them, I bring out the best in them."

The king's grand constable (John Miljan), who is also a paid Burgundian spy, enters the tavern to arrest Villon, but in the brawl which follows, the rhymster kills him. At this point, King Louis reveals his identity. ("Who are you to interfere with the king's justice?" "I *am* the king's justice!") He arrests Villon and his cohorts and has them thrown into the palace dungeon. But the monarch is soon faced with the perplexing task of both punishing and rewarding Villon for the same offense. In view of the favor he inadvertently rendered the Crown by ridding the king of his chief traitor, Louis informs Villon that he has decided not to hang him just yet. With perverse slyness and a generous royal cackle, he dubs him the Count de Montcorbier and names him grand constable of France.

Very well, then; grand constable it shall be, and Villon, shorn of his beard and outfitted in suitably regal splendor, proceeds at once to fulfill one of his chief duties, that of trying all prisoners. In one of the comic highlights of the film, he sits hidden behind a lectern and listens to his own comrades' impassioned pleas of innocence.

"I was home in bed," one insists.

"So was I," agrees Huguette (Ellen Drew), a pretty tavern wench and Villon's lover. "We were *all* in bed!"

"It is becoming more and more evident that a grave injustice has been committed," Villon intones, struggling to conceal his mirth. "Since you were

Scruffy street poet François Villon (Ronald Colman) is hauled before France's Spider King, Louis XI (Basil Rathbone), in If I Were King. *Walter Kingsford stands by, center. Rathbone, on the eve of his most famous performances in two 1939 Sherlock Holmes pictures, has been credited with having stolen the film.*

all home in bed, you can't possibly have robbed His Majesty's storehouse. Probably this *Villon* did it all by himself."

"That's a lie!" blurts Huguette. "He was with me, I tell you!"

"I won't ask you where!" the grand constable quickly adds.

Relishing his new power, Villon frees them all and, since they have obviously suffered false imprisonment, awards them seven gold pieces each. Jubilant cheers of "Long live the king!" ring out, for His Majesty's new policy of extreme leniency has quickly turned rebellious hatred into staunch loyalty. Observing the proceedings from a concealed position is Louis himself.

"You have just seen my new method of dealing with habitual criminals," he remarks to an aide in shocked disbelief. "We don't hang them; we cover them with *gold!*"

Later, a herald from the Duke of Burgundy (Paul Harvey) arrives at the palace under a flag of truce and demands an immediate, unconditional surrender. The new grand constable, in the presence of the assembled court, takes charge before the king or his timorous generals can reply:

"You have bad manners, my friend, and you rate yourself too highly! You're not the envoy of a conquering hero, but the servant of a group of *shabby* little vassals, rebellious serfs of a noble lord! Now, go back and tell them this: kings are great in the eyes of their people, but the people are great in the eyes of God, and it is the people of France who are speaking to you now! . . . We give you one week to disband and get out. If at the end of the week you are still cluttering up the outskirts of our city, we will *attack and destroy you to the last man!* Now, we don't wish to be annoyed further."

But the generals refuse to fight. With the army demoralized and Burgundian forces assembled in overwhelming numbers outside the walls of Paris, they urge prompt surrender. To make matters worse, Louis informs Villon that his term as grand constable is to last but one week, at the end of which he fully expects the Count de Montcorbier to erect a fine gibbet out of the stoutest oak on which to hang Master François Villon!

A virtual prisoner within the palace walls, Villon swiftly mounts the winding staircase which leads to the chambers of Katherine de Vaucelles. Never suspecting his true identity, she'd fallen in love with the grand constable from the moment she first set eyes on him. Finding her lover despondent, Katherine suggests that the generals would *have* to fight if they didn't have enough food in their fat bellies. That's it! Villon escapes from the palace and orders the contents of all His Majesty's storehouses distributed among the starving poor. The following morning, revelry reigns in the streets as long-suffering commoners unite in surfeited cries of "Long live the king!"

When Villon returns to the palace and cheerfully informs His Majesty that the "royal" goodwill mission has been a complete success, the king asks him what can be done, now that they are without food.

"France is *full* of food," Villon replies. "The country outside is growing with grain. Mountains of flour mildew in the mills. The pigs beseech you to accept their fattest hams! All we have to do is go and get them."

"Hah! And to do so," inquires Louis with no little disdain, "I suppose you suggest we *fly* over the Burgundian lines?"

"Oh, no, not at all, Your Majesty. We can *fight* through them. Don't you think so, General," he says, playfully jabbing the officer's ample abdomen.

Meanwhile, with the French army on the verge of defeat, the Parisian rabble spread the word that the king is merely attempting to buy their loyalty through their stomachs as he fattens them for the kill. As the city streets throng with confused commoners, Katherine joins the concerned grand constable on the palace ramparts. His week ends tonight, he tells her, asking if she has ever wondered where the Count de Montcorbier came from.

"Katherine," he confesses, "I am François Villon!"

Aware that the Burgundians have just broken through the west gate, the generals suggest that the rebellious army might be pacified by the immediate hanging of the noble lord who gave away their food. A desperate Villon escapes once again and dashes to the Court of Miracles in a reckless attempt to prevent the rabble from sacking and looting the city. He leaps from his horse and addresses the incited mob with words of flame:

> "We all know there is no honor among thieves," he shouts, "so I'm not going to talk to you about honor. And I'm not appealing to any patch of decency I know you never had. Now, as you stand there, the city is falling, falling to thieves like ourselves; cutthroats who have come all the way from Burgundy to take what belongs to us. . . . . Are we going to let these poachers move in on *our* preserve? These country *louts* show *us* how it's done? Are they going to starve us to death? Then I tell you this: there's no city that can be conquered unless it wants to be, and whether they like it or *not, we are part of the city*, the part that knows how to *fight! Or don't we?*"

Furious agreement greets his impassioned plea. "Good!" he cries. "Then let's *fight. I say let us fight! On to the west gate!*"

In a fast-paced montage sequence, an enraged human torrent pours into the streets and, led by François Villon, soon has the invaders in full retreat.

The king's generals claim credit for the victory, but Louis is informed by Katherine that the same grand constable he plans to hang has saved the city. Faced with a difficult decision, Louis commutes Villon's sentence to life imprisonment — except for Paris, from which he is banished forever, the noble vagabond is confined to the rest of France. Into exile he trudges, down a long, lonely, dusty road, but one cannot help feeling that his banishment will be somehow sweetened, for Katherine de Vaucelles follows in discreet pursuit.

After signing a two-picture deal with Paramount, Ronald Colman was reunited with director Frank Lloyd, and turned in one of his most stylish performances as the devilishly resourceful François Villon. The public's appetite for swashbuckling epics had been whetted by *The Prisoner of Zenda* and, earlier in 1938, *The Adventures of Robin Hood;* when *If I Were King* was premiered in New York, unprecedented crowds lined up to see it and caused traffic jams for weeks.

Justin Huntly McCarthy's 1901 play, staged with E.H. Sothern in the Villon role, was first filmed in 1920, and starred William Farnum.[67] John Barrymore, co-starring with German actor Conrad Veidt as Louis XI, portrayed *The Beloved Rogue* in 1927, and in 1930, Dennis King and Jeanette MacDonald were featured in *The Vagabond King,* a musical remake based on Rudolf Friml's 1925 operetta.[68] What made the Colman version such a critically acclaimed success was something which none of the earlier pictures possessed: the talents of witty scenarist Preston Sturges. Rapidly

Director Frank Lloyd puts Ralph Forbes and Ronald Colman through their paces as they prepare to shoot a scene from If I Were King.

emerging as one of Hollywood's foremost satirists, Sturges streamlined this old-fashioned romance with his pungent wit and crackling verbal rhythms, perhaps best showcased in the following encounters:

"I was saying, Your Majesty," says General Dudon (Montagu Love), when presented to the new grand constable for the first time, "I'm not familiar with the name of de Montcorbier, though heraldry's my dearest hobby."

"Well, I can't say the same for the name of Dudon, General," taunts Villon. "Ever since you won the Battle of Mont lhéry, I have watched your success with increasing enthusiasm."

"But I—I did not win the Battle of—of Mont lhéry!"

"Oh, yes, yes, of course. Yes, you lost it, yes. But there was the siege of Liège."

"We lost that one too, my dear count," a bemused king hastily explains.

"Forgive me. I'm so sorry," Villon exudes with false warmth. "We must talk about your battles some other time, General."

Later, when the generals insist that France must surrender immediately, Villon calmly suggests that they simply break through the Burgundian lines and surround the enemy.

"Hah!" harrumphs General Dudon.

"Very interesting opinion, General," Villon assures him suavely, "but it leaves me in the dark!"

"It's quite apparent that you have no knowledge of military maneuvers," asserts Dudon.

"You're right, General," Villon agrees regretfully. "I've only studied yours, and I've learned *nothing* from them! My only wonder is that you chose the sword, when you care so little for fighting."

Insistent upon not taking the story too seriously, Sturges armed Colman and Basil Rathbone with deliciously satiric dialogue. The comic touch made all the difference.

Film historian Robert Milton Miller chronicles Sturges' preproduction tribulations:

> He went into seclusion with an armload of books about Villon, Paris in the 1400's, the French court, and King Louis XI. He emerged with a gleam in his eye and went to work on the script.
>
> He worked furiously, sometimes going for twenty-four hours without sleep, laboring on what had become for him a truly inspired project. Lloyd was serving as his own producer and was therefore allowed to pass on Sturges' work. He received the completed script in piecemeal fashion, examining a few pages each day. At first he was delighted, then he became disturbed. He called Sturges in for a conference, explaining that the part of Villon was going to be played by Ronald Colman. . . . Why, Lloyd wanted to know, were the best lines in the script going not to Villon, but to his rival, King Louis? Sturges explained to the disgruntled director that Louis was verified by history as a much more worthwhile and noble character. The writer had come to the conclusion that while Villon was a good poet, he was still basically a vagabond, a cutpurse, a haunter of back alleys, and a thorough rascal. King Louis, on the other hand, was a ruler with the common touch, one dedicated to the unification and aggrandizement of his kingdom. . . . Lloyd, however, could see box-office disaster awaiting anyone who drastically altered so popular a piece of historical fiction. He threatened to get another writer. Sturges sulked. Eventually they reached a compromise. Lloyd assumed that Sturges would go back and revise the script as he had been told. What the writer really did was to reinstate Villon as a major character, but one whose exploits carried with them a faint air of tongue-in-cheek. . . .
>
> Sturges fought still another uphill battle with his suggestion that the superb villain, Basil Rathbone, be cast as the king. Lloyd objected at first, calling the part too "spindle-legged" to merit a true swashbuckler. At last he relented, allowed Rathbone to be tested, and cast him.[69]

Although the limited historical data available suggest that François Villon was nothing more than a thoroughgoing rogue, his poetry (which has come to be highly regarded) gives evidence that he also possessed a more delicate, chivalrous nature. *If I Were King* accepted the romanticized legend of the dashing vagabond king and presented Colman as the most lighthearted, street-worn charmer who ever cheated a hangman. As *Newsweek* opined,

> Colman's Villon is still the roistering cock of the Paris underworld, the Robin Hood who feels for a starving proletariat. . . . But the actor plays him with a hint of tongue-in-cheek blandness that is one of the film's saving graces.[70]

Even with bedraggled, curly locks, an unkempt beard, and a rakish cap, this rhyme-spouting, ragged poet managed to exhibit more than a jaunty trace of the Colman mystique. "Who else but Colman," writes Jeffrey Richards, "could have pronounced the little love poem . . . with such wistfulness and such affection?"[71]

> "If I were king—ah love, if I were king!
> What tributary nations would I bring
> To stoop before your sceptre and to swear
> Allegiance to your lips and eyes and hair.
> Beneath your feet what treasures I would fling;
> The stars should be your pearls upon a string,
> The world a ruby for your finger ring,
> And you should have the sun and moon to wear
> If I were king."

Once he sheds his dusty rags, dons a splendid uniform of silk and velvet, and assumes the role of the Count de Montcorbier, he sets a standard of nobility for Louis to emulate, just as Rudolf Rassendyll had done in *The Prisoner of Zenda*. As Frank S. Nugent wryly observed,

> Mr. Colman . . . invests the role with dignity and virtue. Perhaps too much virtue. His confession that he has been the associate of cutthroats, thieves and wantons carries no conviction at all. Secretly he knows, and we know, that he always dresses for dinner.[72]

And then there is Basil Rathbone's fey impersonation of the sly, scheming Spider King, the high point of many scenes. Rathbone hammed it up for all he was worth. With a senile cackle, croaking voice, and doddering, slithering shuffle, he stole the picture and won an Academy Award nomination for Best Supporting Actor.

Nonetheless, the Colman magic reigned triumphant, and the actor reestablished his position as the only rival to Errol Flynn, by now the screen's preeminent romantic swashbuckler.

The Light that Failed

1939. *Production and distribution:* Paramount Pictures, Inc. *Producer and director:* William A. Wellman. *Screenplay:* Robert Carson (from the novel by Rudyard Kipling). *Cinematographer:* Theodor Sparkuhl. *Musical Score:* Victor Young. *Art Directors:* Hans Dreier, Robert Odell. *Set Decorations:* A.E. Freudeman. *Second Unit Director:* Joseph O. Youngerman. *Film Editor:* Thomas Scott. *Sound:* Hugo Grenzlock, Walter Oberst. *Running Time:* 98 minutes. *New York Premiere:* December 24, 1939.

Cast: Ronald Colman (Dick Heldar), Walter Huston (Torpenhow), Muriel Angelus (Maisie), Ida Lupino (Bessie Broke), Dudley Digges (The Nilghai), Ernest Cossart (Beeton), Ferike Boros (Madame Celeste Binat), Pedro de Cordoba (Monsieur Binat), Colin Tapley (Gardner), Fay Helm (Red-haired Girl), Ronald Sinclair (Dick as a boy), Sarita Wooton (Maisie as a girl), Halliwell Hobbes (Doctor), Charles Irwin (Soldier Model), Francis McDonald (George), George Regas (Cassavetti), Wilfred Roberts (Barton), Colin Kenny (Doctor), Clyde Cook, James Aubrey, Harry Cording (Soldiers), Major Sam Harris (Wells), Connie Leon (Flower Woman), Cyril Ring (War Correspondent), Barbara Denny (Waitress), Pat O'Malley (Bullock), Clara M. Blore (Mother), George Chandler, George H. Melford (Voices), Leslie Francis (Man with Bandaged Eyes), Barry Downing (Little Boy), Harold Entwistle (Old Man with Dark Glasses).

Colman's second film for Paramount (following *If I Were King*), under his two-picture contract, cast him as Victorian artist, adventurer, and dreamer Richard Heldar in William Wellman's vigorous adaptation of Rudyard Kipling's first novel, *The Light that Failed*.

A British encampment deep in the Sudan: under a shadowless sky and the scorch of a blazing desert sun, fierce Fuzzy-Wuzzy warriors stage an unexpected attack, and the sands run red with blood. While saving the life of his war-correspondent friend Torpenhow (Walter Huston), British trooper and newspaper illustrator Dick Heldar (Colman) is slashed across the forehead and collapses with an ugly, bloody gash over his right eye. In the weeks that follow, Torpenhow nurses the delirious soldier back to health. Heldar recovers from his wound and is invalided back to London, where he shares Torpenhow's bachelor quarters and soon finds his battle paintings much in demand. Equipped with his own studio across the hall from Torp's flat, he quickly tastes success when his "Sudan Campaign" sketches are exhibited in galleries and lionized in the press.

A chance meeting in Regent's Park throws Dick into constant companionship with his childhood sweetheart, Maisie (Muriel Angelus), an over-ambitious lass who tries to pursue a similar career as an artist but with no degree of success. Despite Heldar's repeated protestations of love, she puts him off. Choked with envy after beholding his *Break of Day* (depicting a rearing charger whose master has just been shot down), she welcomes his friendship and advice, but refuses to marry him.

Dick comes to like the fame, the fuss, and especially the fortune, but

Torpenhow and their old comrade in arms, the Nilghai (Dudley Digges), take him to task for his smug willingness to "prettify" his pictures. The coarse brutality of war never looked like that: he's slicked it up, made it too heroic and dashing. His works, they complain, are disgraceful potboilers, done without conviction to please a fashion-driven, undiscriminating public.

As a last bid for artistic recognition, Maisie resolves to paint a *Melancholia*, the sorrowful woman who suffered until she could suffer no more, and then began to laugh at it all. Dick, irritated by Maisie's stubbornness, decides to tackle the same subject. Returning to his studio, Heldar discovers a young street waif (Ida Lupino) whom the kindhearted Torpenhow has brought home, after he'd found her faint from hunger. Dick sees the perfect model for his new painting; her face registers all the terror, futility, and sorrow he needs for his *Melancholia*. The cockney wench, who answers to the name of Bessie Broke, agrees to pose, but soon accuses Dick of coming between her and Torpenhow, whom she openly adores. Someday, she threatens, she'll get even.

Heldar begins to experience searing flashes which torture his forehead: the light's getting bad, he's seeing double, and heavy drinking only partially restores his vision. When at last he consults an oculist (Halliwell Hobbes), he learns that the sword stroke he had sustained years ago damaged the frontal bone, which is causing pressure on the optic nerve. If he avoids all strain and worry, he'll have about a year; otherwise, his sight will go at any time and without warning.

As he leaves the doctor's office, Heldar shares his despair with Mr. Binkie, Torp's little black terrier:

"We've got it badly, little dog," he murmurs. "Just as *badly* as we can get it."

Later, in the loneliness of his studio, he continues:

"All the Torpenhows in the world can't save me. We must be calm, Binkie. This isn't nice at all. What shall we do? We must do something. Time is short."

Aware that this will be his last effort, he vows to throw all his talent and energy into the one portrait by which he will be remembered, summing up all the grief of mankind before blindness and fate deprive him of his working light.

"Allah, Almighty, help me through my time of waiting," he whispers, "and I won't whine when my punishment comes."

Fighting against time and drinking for clearer vision as the pain grows worse than ever, Heldar stirs Bessie into a smoldering rage:

"Come on, Bessie, throw back your head and laugh. *Laugh, Bessie, laugh!*" he commands. "Why, you little fool, I'm giving you something you never had

One of Colman's most successful roles was as Rudyard Kipling's blighted painter, Dick Heldar, who must complete his masterpiece before going blind, in The Light that Failed.

before. A soul — a soul on canvas! I'm making you *immortal*! A hundred years from now they'll be looking at you when you're dust and water, and a whisper of the wind, and saying, '*That* is sorrow. That is *every* sorrow. That's sorrow so *deep*, it's — it's laughter!' Come on, Bessie, throw your head back and laugh! Come on," he shouts, "*laugh, Bessie, laugh!*"

Bessie's screams and tears dissolve into hysterical laughter, and when the painting is finally finished, it's a masterpiece of *real* feeling. After Bessie flees the premises, sobbing uncontrollably, Torpenhow enters the studio and Dick displays his portrait.

"I'm drunk and everything's *blurred*, and there's no more hope, but it's *good* work," he cries; "it's *great* work!"

Heldar confesses that he is going blind. Suddenly tired and spent, he is tucked into bed by the faithful Torp. While he sleeps, the vindictive Bessie takes her revenge, sneaks back into the studio, and viciously destroys the *Melancholia* with turpentine and a palette knife. All that remains is a formless, scarred muddle of color.

In a great, moving scene, Dick awakens to find that he is totally blind. Torpenhow, who has discovered the defaced painting and knows that his friend's affliction is the direct result of that heroic rescue years ago in the Sudan, answers Heldar's cry for help and rushes to his side.

> "I'm all in the dark. In the dark, I tell you. Torp, old man, don't go away," he pleads. "Don't leave me. You wouldn't leave me alone now, would you? It's black, quite black, and I feel as if I were falling through it all. My God, I'm *blind*, I'm *blind*, and the darkness won't go away! Would you mind — letting me hold onto you? One drops through the dark so."

He clings like a terrified child to his friend's arms, waiting for the darkness to lift. Torp holds him close as men sometimes do a fallen comrade in the hour of death, to ease his suffering.

But the thick night has come to stay, and as Dick gradually adjusts to the weight of his dark prison, Torpenhow cannot bring himself to mention the ruined masterpiece. He does, however, inform Maisie of Dick's condition. When she arrives unexpectedly at the studio, Heldar attempts to dismiss his malady by explaining that he's had a little bother with his eyes, and then unveils his disfigured portrait. In a shattering, dramatic moment, Maisie covers her face with her hands and stares at the defaced travesty in horrified disbelief.

"There she is! What do you think of her?" he asks with proud, unknowing confidence.

"It — it's magnificent," she gasps. "It's wonderful."

"Is it *that* good?" he inquires, sensing that she is deeply moved. "I think you've looked at it long enough," he adds, covering the remnant of his work with a cloth. "It's not a thing you can look at *too* long. It seems to strike everybody *that* way."

She wants to stay; things have changed, she tells him. "Isn't there anything I can do?"

The sightless eyes turn toward her. "Yes," he replies, aware that her offer is prompted by pity. "You can — you can give me my pipe. It's on the mantlepiece."

Maisie leaves moments later. "Good-bye, Maisie," he intones with ominous finality, as she rushes from the room, unable to hold back her tears any longer.

Torpenhow, about to return to the Sudan, enters the studio.

"Did, uh, did it come out all right?" he inquires, assuming that Dick and Maisie will soon be married.

"Oh, yes, yes, fine," Heldar says, trying to evade the issue.

"Tell me about it," Torpenhow insists.

"Torp, you mustn't stay here on my account. I don't need you — *now*," he replies, unselfishly letting his old friend continue in optimistic ignorance.

"Then it's all settled."

"Yes. Yes, it's all settled," he says with ambiguous truthfulness.

"I'm awfully glad, Dick. Every man needs a wife."

"Only after he divorces his Torpenhow!" quips Heldar with forced cheer.

"Want to help me pack?"

"No, thanks, I'll stay here with Binkie. If I get my hands on some of that field equipment, I might want to go with you."

"You don't talk much like a newly engaged man."

"Oh, I have a lot of life to forget. By the way, Torp, she liked the picture."

Torpenhow swallows his emotion. "You've got a good girl, Dick."

Weeks later, Heldar and his landlord, Beeton (Ernest Cossart), stroll along a fog-shrouded embankment, and meet Bessie. Beeton informs her that Heldar is blind. Dick asks her to visit him at his studio, and when she arrives, he takes her in his arms, kisses her, and asks her to keep house for him. Caught off guard, Bessie confesses that she'd destroyed his painting. Stunned beyond belief, Heldar realizes that it's all over: his career, his hopes, even his masterpiece. There's nothing left. And then, through his crushing disappointment, he sees a way out. He determines to return to the Sudan, that limitless, desolate kingdom of drifting sand, to be with Torp for the last time and come as near to the old life as he possibly can.

Moved by the chance for one last, great adventure, he cries, "East, out of the mouth of the river, then west, then south, then east again, all along the underside of Europe, then south again to the end of the world! *Oh*, it's good to be alive again!"

Later in the Port Said, Heldar is assisted by his old friend Madame Binat (Ferike Boros), whose husband had taught Dick everything he knew about color, light, and motion before he began to mix his own colors with gin and died. In a Spartan hotel room, Heldar dons his uniform with meticulous care. And then, when everything is perfectly correct, he's off into the desert with a guide.

The battle is at full pitch, but Dick can only hear the rapid fire and smell the gunpowder. Poised on his horse, he finally finds Torp, who yields to his impassioned plea to turn his mount toward the charge. Heldar gallops forward into the fray, inspired to exaltation by the immanence of death. The end is merciful and swift. A bullet throws Heldar from his horse. The animal gallops on, then circles back to paw at the ground where Heldar lies—a touching evocation of the artist's most celebrated painting, *Break of Day*. Torp and Nilghai race to the scene.

Looking solemnly at the body of his fallen friend, Torpenhow intones, "Nilghai, God has been very good; he's dead."

Kipling was only 25 when *The Light that Failed* was published in 1891. When an over-squeamish editor rejected the original denouement, in which Richard Heldar finds the death he had sought on a battlefield in the Sudan, the author was forced to provide a less sorrowful ending, wherein the painter regains his sight and finds happinesss with Maisie. But in later years, readers agreed with Kipling that the happy conclusion negated the novel's underlying mood and theme, and destroyed its dramatic unity. Nevertheless, when Pathé filmed *The Light that Failed* in 1916 with Robert Edeson in the lead, and Paramount starred Colman's friend and fellow English actor Percy Marmont in a 1923 remake, the typically Hollywood happy ending was favored. The Colman version, one of the most remarkably faithful adaptations of a novel ever produced on film, restored the tragic, final scene as its author had written it. Unfortunately Kipling never saw it, for he died in 1936.

The cast was beyond reproach. Walter Huston, a last-minute replacement for Thomas Mitchell in the role of Torpenhow, turned in a fine, stalwart performance as Heldar's compassionate comrade in arms, the staunchest friend there ever was. Colman had insisted that Vivien Leigh be cast as Bessie, but director William Wellman chose ingenue Ida Lupino, who desperately wanted the part. Wellman's decision was justified and Miss Lupino responded with an intensely florid, cockney portrayal that made her a star. With Muriel Angelus as the selfish Maisie and the always impressive Dudley Digges as Nilghai, the supporting roster was as "right as right can be."[73]

William Wellman was one director with whom Colman experienced temperamental differences. In one of his last interviews, Wellman recalled the cause of the friction:

> I was a kind of wild guy. I'm housetrained now and have been for some years; however, the time during which I directed *Light* was my wildest time of all. A lot of people didn't want to work for me, nor did I want to work with them.
>
> Now we come to Mr. Colman. He and I didn't like each other from the very start. When they called me in and said they wanted to do this film with him, I said I loved the idea of doing *Light* but I thought Wellman and Colman wasn't such a good idea. It was a most unusual combination! I was a crazy guy, and he was very much the gentleman. . . .
>
> He was a funny guy, to me he proved very hard to know. Now, Frank Capra and he were great friends, but Frank was such a nice guy and I wasn't. He was accustomed to someone that took great pains; I took great pains too, but I probably printed more first takes than anyone in the business. I know the business of being a director. . . . I often found that you could get a certain inspiration from a first take that you could never get again . . . [but] I know that I had the weakness of impatience. . . .
>
> Ronnie . . . never blew his lines. . . . Come Lupino's big scene, where she has to work herself up into a state of hysteria while he is painting her portrait,

he forgot his lines right in the middle of it, right in the middle of her hysteria. So I said, "Cut!" and I thought that maybe he had been as affected by her performance as I. So we rested for a few minutes and I started again and he forgot again. Then I got mad. I cut and went up to him and said, "Let's you and I take a little walk together." So we got away from the others. "Look, Mr. Colman, I know there is a reason behind this. I don't give a goddam what the reason is. My reason for anything good or bad is to try and make a good picture. Nothing else means anything to me, but I've got to tell you this, if you do it once more, I'm going to make a character man out of you. I'm not kidding, that lovely face of yours is not going to look the way it does right now!" And I walked away. Now he is not that kind of a screwball; we did the scene again and it was done beautifully.

From then on, we spoke to each other as Mr. Colman and Mr. Wellman. . . .

Later on we had several dinners and we got to know each other and became friends, so it ended beautifully. I don't think he would have wanted to do another film with me though.[74]

William Wellman's restrained, stately paced direction was perfectly consonant with the leisurely flow of Kipling's fatalistic narrative. It is a very masculine film, made in an era when the screen could depict close companionship between men without fear of misunderstanding. Coursing through the pictures of Wellman, Howard Hawks, and John Ford is the common theme of men thrown together in battle, and the strong bonds they develop for one another. *The Light that Failed* is a story of such comradeship, perfectly evoking the spirit of the old Arabian proverb cited in Colman's earlier (as well as Wellman's later) *Beau Geste:* "The love of a man for a woman waxes and wanes like the moon — but the love of brother for brother is steadfast as the stars, and endures like the Word of the Prophet." It's not that the film lacks romantic interest, but that there is precious little romantic love, for despite his hopes, Heldar knows, as we do, that his passion for Maisie will forever be unrequited. Instead, "there is a fine tweedy, tobaccoey, stout-booted air to it," as Frank S. Nugent remarked.[75] The perfume we seem to smell most strongly is gunpowder smoke and pipe tobacco, and although very little of the picture takes place in the Sudan, the ever-present field equipment is a constant, subtle reminder that the desert is still there — always pulling, always beckoning.

With little flamboyance but much serenity, introspection, and quiet pathos, Ronald Colman delivered one of the most memorable, affecting performances of his career.

Apart from his success in disguising the fact that he was now forty-eight years old, the star had always been at his best with characters whom fate has singled out for a tragic end — Sydney Carton, Robert Clive, Beau Geste. He was, like Garbo, one of the few stars for whom audiences did not necessarily expect a happy-ever-after.[76]

Understatement had always been a mainstay of the Colman style, and when blindness destroys Heldar's world, he accepts his fate, deals with his despair, and manages to retain just the right measure of good-natured humor, without which the hero would have emerged rather dour and maudlin. As the *New York Times* put it,

> Mr. Colman has rarely handled a role with greater authority or charm, manfully underplaying even the sure-fire melodramatics of the sequence in which he goes blind — a heaven-sent infirmity for 99 out of 100 hard-pressed actors.[77]

Melancholy is there, to be sure, in his despairing face, but during his hours of mental clarity he summons up hidden reserves of dedication and resourcefulness and pursues his great quest, aware that he must not waste any of the precious moments left. When he gallantly renounces the woman he has loved since childhood (as he had done in *The Dark Angel*), knowing that her gesture is prompted by pity, he is also motivated by a firm belief in himself, his art, and his destiny. And when audiences saw him meet that destiny in the desert, "there wasn't a dry eye in the house."[78]

Critics called *The Light that Failed* a "letter-perfect edition,"[79] and the public adored it, with good reason. Combining integrity and taste with a heart-tugging sensitivity, and featuring Ronald Colman in one of his strongest dramatic portrayals, it was an unforgettable picture indeed.

Lucky Partners

1940. *Production and distribution:* RKO Radio Pictures, Inc. *Producer:* George Haight. *Director:* Lewis Milestone. *Screenplay:* Allan Scott, John van Druten (from the short story "Bonne Chance" by Sacha Guitry). *Director of Cinematography:* Robert de Grasse. *Special Photographic Effects:* Vernon L. Walker. *Musical Score:* Dimitri Tiomkin. *Art Director:* Van Nest Polglase. *Associate Art Director:* Carroll Clark. *Set Decorations:* Darrell Silvera. *Miss Rogers' Gowns:* Irene. *Executive Producer:* Harry E. Edington. *Assistant Director:* Argyle Nelson. *Sound:* John E. Tribby. *Film Editor:* Henry Berman. *Running Time:* 98 minutes. *New York Premiere:* September 5, 1940.

Cast: Ronald Colman (David Grant/Paul Knight Somerset), Ginger Rogers (Jean Newton), Jack Carson (Freddie Harper), Spring Byington (Aunt Lucy), Cecilia Loftus (Mrs. Sylvester), Harry Davenport (Judge), Hugh O'Connell (Niagara Clerk), Brandon Tynan (Mr. Sylvester), Leon Belasco (Nick No. 1), Eddie Conrad (Nick No. 2), Walter Kingsford (Wendell), Lucille Gleason (Ethel's Mother), Helen Lynd (Ethel), Billy Gilbert (Waiter), Otto Hoffman (Clerk), Alex Melesh (Art Salesman), Dorothy Adams (Maid), Frank Mills (Bus Driver), Billy Benedict, Murray Alper (Bellboys), Al Hill (Motor Cop), Robert Dudley (Bailiff), Grady Sutton (Reporter), Nora Cecil (Club Woman), Harlan Briggs (Mayor), Olin Howland (Tourist), Benny Rubin, Tom Dugan (Spielers), Fern Emmett (Hotel Maid), Lloyd

Ingraham (Chamber of Commerce Member), Edgar Dearing (Desk Sergeant), Jane Patten (Bride), Bruce Hall (Bridegroom).

After filming two pictures for Paramount (*If I Were King* and *The Light that Failed*), Colman set up a distribution arrangement with RKO and turned out two quickly produced light comedies. The first, *Lucky Partners,* was a lively tilt which had him splitting a sweepstake ticket with madcap Ginger Rogers.

While wandering casually one day in Washington Square, Greenwich Village artist David Grant (Colman) passes bookshop employee Jean Newton (Miss Rogers), a total stranger, and jauntily wishes her luck. Why? For no good reason at all. He merely does it. The charm works, for, moments later, a series of unexpected events results in Miss Newton's receiving a very expensive gown — a hand-me-down from a wealthy customer at the Book Nook. This *is* her lucky day, she realizes, wondering whether her good fortune is a result of her happy encounter with David Grant, whose studio is just across the street from the bookshop.

Playing a hunch, she pays the painter a visit and invites him to the Nick & Nick Cafe, where she makes a proposition. Let us admit that Mr. Grant has an open mind, for when she proposes that they go halves on a sweepstake ticket, hoping that he'll bring her more luck so that she can get married and have a proper honeymoon, he readily agrees — provided that, should they win, she agree to go off with *him* on a "platonic" honeymoon before settling down in Poughkeepsie. Insulted, Miss Newton rushes off to find her fiancé, insurance salesman Freddie Harper (Jack Carson), a huge, prototypical American go-getter and a sterling nitwit. Some say his mind has never wandered for lack of room, while others maintain that he's never had one to lose. Into the cafe they march, and Jean asks David to repeat his proposition. He does, whereupon Freddie challenges Grant to step outside. Out into the alley they go, but, somehow, fisticuffs are avoided and they return in full agreement. Freddie urges Jean to accept David's offer, for they'll simply travel as brother and sister. If it weren't for his big Poughkeepsie promotion, he adds with expansive enthusiasm, he'd go with her himself. Besides, Freddie gushes, David's quite harmless. The camera cuts to a delightful shot of Grant, who instantly assumes a pose of demure and wistful innocence.

Their horse loses, but Freddie had already sold Jean's half of the ticket, netting the tidy sum of $6,000. David and Jean take the money and set out on their glorious spree, in an automobile Grant has purchased in her name. First stop: Niagara Falls, and a quick succession of switched hotel rooms and amusing hijinks. Meanwhile, Freddie, who, for the first time in his life, has had a second thought, jealously follows them and barges into Jean's suite, demanding that she return at once to Poughkeepsie and marry him. She

Successful artist David Grant (Ronald Colman) makes a pass at a pretty girl, Jean Newton (Ginger Rogers). In this screwball comedy, Lucky Partners, *the script calls for them to win a sweepstake ticket and go on a honeymoon—even though they're not married.*

refuses, by now realizing that she and David have fallen in love, and throws Freddie out.

"Jean, I'm afraid the experiment's got a little out of hand," David tells her later. "I apologize."

"What for?"

"For letting it. I promised it should be—strictly impersonal. Jean, either we must go back to being as we were and forget all this happened, or else we can't go on with the trip."

"David, do you want to go on with it?" she inquires frankly.

"Very much," he assures her.

"Okay, then."

From this point on, things get more complicated, for at 2 A.M. Freddie, determined to restore Jean to her senses, bursts into the wrong room like gangbusters. Finding his fiancée in the suite he presumes to be Grant's, he promptly batters down the door to the adjoining room, only to discover that David has checked out. Always the perfect gentleman, Grant has politely bowed out, feeling that he has unjustifiably intruded into their relationship.

Eventually they all land in court—David for the apparent theft of Miss Newton's auto, Jean for possession of an apparently stolen painting by one Paul Knight Somerset (which Grant had given her), and Freddie for a certainly busted hotel-room door. A kindly old parrot of a judge (Harry Davenport) listens intently as Freddie insists he's engaged to Miss Newton (who's registered at the hotel as Miss Grant), she insists she is most definitely not engaged to anyone, and David testifies that his name isn't Grant at all—it's Paul Knight Somerset, the long-missing famous artist! Newspaper photographers swarm in to snap his picture, and their morning editions blare forth the news that the wealthy, renowned painter has been found.

The courtroom is packed the following morning, as Somerset reveals that he had rented his own painting from a gallery because he wanted Miss Newton to see it. Freddie (anxious to get Somerset's autograph on one of his insurance policies) testifies that he had initially disapproved of the trip, but now realizes that, with Paul being such a celebrity, he was mistaken. Miss Newton swears it was all meant as an experiment.

"I was to be a guinea pig," she blurts, as the courtroon dissolves in laughter. "He was going to show me things."

The old judicial parrot, on his perch above, convinced that they've all been running a racket, opens a wizened eye and inquires whether Mr. Somerset kept his word.

"Not entirely, your Honor."

"Did he kiss you?"

"Yes," she peeps almost inaudibly.

Under the judge's disapproving glance, Somerset takes the stand. Did he take Miss Newton, an engaged woman, on a trip, make love to her, and then desert her in an automobile bought with her money? Acting as his own defense counsel, Somerset cross-examines himself.

"When did you fall in love with Miss Newton?" he asks, addressing an empty chair.

"I think," he replies, as he quickly takes the stand, "it must have been when she called a sweepstake ticket a 'swoopsnake swicket.'"

Miss Newton's testimony discloses the fact that Paul Knight Somerset had been one of America's finest painters until three years ago, when he was sent to prison for illustrating a so-called "indecent" volume of folklore and legends, now recommended at universities for classroom use. Because of this injustice, he stopped painting and hasn't let the world see his work since.

The judge sums up the case: Mr. Harper is clearly a dope; Miss Newton was much wronged—a little trusting, perhaps, but in no way to blame; Mr. Somerset, on the other hand, acted without principle. At this point Jean explodes in protest, insisting that the old bird apologize to Paul Knight Somerset in the name of American justice. After determining that he loves her and she loves him, the sympathetic judge expresses his profound regrets for the disservice Somerset has suffered.

"And if you'd send me a copy of that classical book," he adds with a knowing grin, "I'd appreciate it."

Shot rather hurriedly in less than two months on the RKO lot just to keep Colman's new production company active, *Lucky Partners* was a clever, diverting bedroom farce which became an immediate hit with audiences and reviewers alike. A lighthearted mood prevails, and Colman bounces through the film with an infectious zest reminiscent of his performance in *The Devil to Pay*. At Niagara Falls, for instance, he and Miss Newton enjoy a meal in the hotel lounge.

"I didn't quite visualize it like this," Jean remarks, aware that she's fallen for him.

"Did you think we'd never eat or drink?" he asks, feigning innocence.

Cute stuff. The *New York Times* called it an effervescent comedy "that is dry and sparkling and bubbles till the last drop," loaded with "impudent charm and rippling wit."[80] To be sure, director Lewis Milestone could have pruned his material more carefully, for the wishing-well scene is a bit cloying in its romantic sweetness, and the courtroom denouement, despite its gaiety, is fairly predictable. But with its witty script, fine comic portrayals by debonair Ronald Colman and romantic Ginger Rogers, and a superb supporting cast (including Jack Carson as the annoyed lunkhead of a fiancé, Spring Byington as the aunt with a passion for racy French novels, and Harry Davenport as the bewildered judge), *Lucky Partners* emerges as a thoroughly delightful romp. A little picture by any standards, and curiously underrated when contrasted with Colman's previous half-dozen efforts, it merits closer inspection than critics have accorded it in recent years.

As one reviewer put it, "Only a misanthropist would refuse to take a chance on 'Lucky Partners.'"[81]

My Life with Caroline

1941. *Production:* United Producers. *Distribution:* RKO Radio Pictures, Inc. *Producer and director:* Lewis Milestone. *Screenplay:* John van Druten, Arnold Belgard (from the play *Train to Venice* by Louis Verneuil and Georges Berr). *Director of Cinematography:* Victor Milner. *Special Photographic Effects:* Vernon L. Walker. *Musical Score:* Werner Heymann. *Art Director:* Nicholai Remisoff. *Set Decorations:* Darrell Silvera. *Gowns:* Edward Stevenson. *Executive Producer:* William Hawks. *Assistant Director:* Edward Donahue. *Film Editor:* Henry Berman. *Sound:* John L. Cass. *Running Time:* 81 minutes. *New York Premiere:* October 29, 1941.

Cast: Ronald Colman (Anthony Mason), Anna Lee (Caroline Mason), Charles Winninger (Mr. Bliss), Reginald Gardiner (Paul Martindale), Gilbert Roland (Paco del Valle), Katherine Leslie (Helen), Hugh O'Connell (Muirhead), Murray Alper (Jenkins), Matt Moore (Walters), Robert Greig (Albert, the Maitre d'), Richard Carle (Dr. Curtis), Clarence Straight (Bill, the Pilot), Dorothy Adams (Rodwell), Nicholas Soussanin (Pinnock), Jeanine Crispin (Delta), James Farley (Railroad Conductor), Billy Mitchell (Railroad Porter), Gar Smith (Radio Announcer), Jack Mulhall (Man).

Colman's second comedy for RKO (following *Lucky Partners*) was *My Life with Caroline*, which teamed him with young British actress Anna Lee. It proved a sad embarrassment to all concerned, for it was one of the actor's weakest efforts. The Caroline in question (Miss Lee) is the neglected wife of wealthy publisher Anthony Mason (Colman), whose frequent and prolonged business trips provoke marital indiscretions of the flightiest sort. Although the details are hardly worth unraveling, this rather aimless and uneven confection takes us to an airport in Idaho, where Caroline, bored as usual, has fallen in love again — this time with rakish Argentinian Paco del Valle (Gilbert Roland), who wants to marry her so they can ride the pampas forever after. In his gaudy, studded bandolero outfit, he looks like he's just stepped off the set of one of Ronald Colman's late-twenties swashbucklers with Vilma Banky. Mason flies to the fashionable ski resort to break up his wife's latest affair. After he observes Caroline and Paco snuggling up to one another in the airport lounge and overhears his wife pondering whether this hasn't all happened to her before, Mason turns to the camera and speaks directly to the audience:

> "The pampas. That's what it is this time. Five minutes with a man who gives her a new line on herself, and over she goes. But once it was politics, once it was palmistry, now it's the pampas. . . . And when she's away from me like this, and I get an urgent wire saying she's coming up to see me, then I drop everything and go and see her. That's — that's my life with Caroline. . . . But you heard her say just now that she thought this had all happened before in some former life. She *has* lived this scene before, but not in any other life. It was just another airport, that's all. It was two years ago — "

The camera takes us back in time to a similar scene, only this time they're in Florida and Caroline's involved with their neighbor, Paul Martindale (Reginald Gardiner), a wealthy sculptor struggling along on an income of about $100,000 a year. When the publisher surprises his flirtatious wife with an unexpected visit at the airport and is introduced to Martindale, he asks the sculptor if he's married.

"No, not yet," his rival intones stiffly, "but I hope to be shortly."

"My dear fellow, you must hurry up," Anthony exclaims with gleeful irony. "You don't know what you're missing!"

Ronald Colman gives a reassuring grin to Anna Lee, who is about to meet Hollywood critics for the first time. The two were currently filming My Life with Caroline.

Caroline plans to elope that evening with Paul, begins to regret her decision when she falls in love with her dashing husband all over again, then changes her mind and keeps her end of the bargain by going to meet Paul on the night train. Martindale, however, misses the train, a misfortune for which Mason is entirely to blame. After a series of complicated plot twists and mirthful moments, the film lumbers headlong to its conclusion — an encounter among husband, wife, and lover which results in Caroline's reconciliation with Anthony.

We return to the present and the Idaho airport, where Mason suavely cures his wife of her infatuation with Paco, signaling—one hopes—that his life with Caroline will be more tranquil in the months to come. But from what we've seen, we're left with the disquieting notion that it won't be long before she's at it again.

My Life with Caroline went into production almost immediately after the completion of *Lucky Partners,* and, like the earlier picture, was quickly filmed in only six or eight weeks on the RKO lot. It's not that the film's premise was a bad one, for it looked sophisticated and promising enough on paper. But it turned out to be an absolutely uninspired dud on the screen, and its tedious script, a flimsy affair to begin with, had the approximate weight and consistency of a summer breeze. All of it was directed into incoherence by Lewis Milestone, who barely manages to rouse himself now and then, only to sink right back into quicksand. The line between genuine originality and mere technical competence is a difficult one to draw, especially when one's work is not patently individual, pioneering, or brilliant. Although Milestone's *The Front Page* (1931) remains one of the finest-paced early-talkie comedies, and his work on *Lucky Partners* sparkled, one cannot escape the conclusion that a director with a more gifted flair for comedy could have made *Caroline* a better film.

One must grant that the picture does have occasional moments of bright dialogue, and that the supporting players offer some clever comic portraits. Reggie Gardiner is effective as Colman's gloomy rival, and Charles Winninger provokes a chuckle or two as Caroline's fortune-hunting father, Mr. Bliss. In the film's most amusing scene, Caroline exchanges heated words with Paul and vociferously demands an explanation for his failure to meet the train. The camera cuts back and forth from Martindale's picture window to Anthony's garden next door, where Mason and Bliss witness the encounter and parrot the lovers' dialogue verbatim. Anthony, of course, is well-equipped for the task, for it's merely a repeat of a scene he's observed many times before.

When the picture was released, audiences ignored it and the critics had a field day: finding it vapid and frivolous, they unanimously turned thumbs down. The resulting box-office failure merely confirmed the fact that Colman had made one of the biggest mistakes of his career. Anna Lee failed to make a hit with the public in her Hollywood film debut, for the hollow, dizzy heroine she portrayed cried out for an actress of the Jean Arthur stamp. As Bosley Crowther put it,

> Things have come to a pretty pass, certainly, when Ronald Colman . . . has to work to hold onto his lady as laboriously as he does in RKO's "My Life with Caroline" . . . either Mr. Colman is slipping or his writers are.
> Frankly, we think it's the latter, for a duller lot of nonsense you never heard. . . . And we use the word "heard" advisedly, because this is one of

those deadly static films in which the poor actors try hard but vainly to put a comedy across with small talk. . . .

There must be some logical explanation why . . . Mr. Colman, Mr. Gardiner and Miss Lee . . . should be wasted on such obvious frippery. But it's too much for our comprehension.[82]

Colman, clearly coasting on his charm, turned in another cheerful performance filled with self-assured irony, wit, and detachment, and almost managed to make us forget our woes. But, as Jeffrey Richards observes,

At the most superficial level, he could play effortlessly debonair, lighthearted charmers, in frothy, inconsequential comedies, and it is these which are his least successful films, for they clearly indicate that his potential is not being utilised.[83]

Colman considered *Caroline* his poorest picture since *The Unholy Garden*. It was an example of what a clever actor could do under discouraging circumstances, but is best left strictly for the staunchest of Colman fans, for he, at least, almost made it worth the wasted time. Fortunately it did his career no permanent damage, for *The Talk of the Town* and *Random Harvest* were waiting in the wings for 1942.

VI

Years of Diversification

In the early days of Ronald Colman's screen appearances, it became an obvious advantage to develop an established character rather than essay a new one in each picture. Readily recognized as he first flashed across the screen in roles which were tailored to fit his image, Colman found this immediate identification a tremendous help and advantage in the twenties and thirties, but it created difficulties as well. Audiences, sitting in judgment, silently commanded that Ronald Colman had best be himself, and do the job he was expected to do — no more, no less. The fate of *Cynara* proved that public tastes were often rigid, allowing little leeway for development, not to mention inspiration. By the early forties, Colman had determined that the mold must be broken, and sought to broaden his range by selecting parts which would expand his screen personality.

In the meantime, dissatisfied with *Lucky Partners* and *My Life with Caroline,* he decided to devote his energies to radio broadcasting until a really good film script turned up. Immediately following the outbreak of the Second World War, Colman threw himself into fairly exclusive work for the Franco-British War Relief Fund, which he established with Douglas Fairbanks, Jr., and Charles Boyer. After the fall of France, he founded and became president of the British War Relief Association of Southern California, which raised prodigious sums in the film colony.[1] Colman's deep-rooted love for England surfaced during the war, and he contributed nearly a third of his income during these years to various war charities. When America entered the conflict in 1941, Colman, then 50, volunteered for war service in any capacity, but was told he could best serve the war effort by continuing to lend his voice to broadcasts and appeals. Despite his phobia regarding public appearances, he traveled all over the United States and Canada and gave of his time willingly, as did many other stars during this

231

Left–right: *George Sanders, Rod La Rocque, Mischa Auer, and Ronald Colman appear at a benefit performance of "Cad's Chorus." La Rocque was enjoying one of screenland's longest marriages, to Colman's former silent screen co-star, Vilma Banky; and Sanders would later wed Colman's widow, Benita. That's Hollywood.*

period of crisis. Among the public activities with which he associated himself were the Hollywood Victory Committee, the American Red Cross, and numerous bond drives for the Treasury Department.

One of the first major Hollywood stars to conquer radio, Colman had made his debut on the air with George Arliss and Constance Bennett in 1934, when they celebrated the first anniversary of Twentieth Century Pictures. In 1939, he hosted a series called *The Circle*, an hour-long, star-studded talk show for NBC which featured Carole Lombard, Cary Grant, Basil Rathbone, and Lawrence Tibbett. On hand to provide touches of insanity were Groucho and Chico Marx. The show failed to catch on, and Colman quit five weeks into the series. As his screen appearances became less frequent in the forties, he began to devote more of his time to radio, starring in episodes of such popular broadcasts as *Lux Radio Theatre, Screen Guild Theatre, Everything for the Boys, Favorite Story,* and *Suspense.* Reprising many of his most popular film roles, such as *Lost Horizon* and *Random Harvest,* he quickly became a top favorite in shows transmitted to the troops overseas. He recreated *The Dark Angel* (with Merle Oberon), *A Tale of Two*

Fredric March and Ronald Colman were among many of Hollywood's top stars to lend their voices to radio. Here they appear, in the mid-thirties, on NBC's Lux Radio Theatre.

Cities, If I Were King, The Light that Failed, and *The Prisoner of Zenda* (with Benita Hume as Princess Flavia). New roles came in *The Petrified Forest* (with Susan Hayward); *Rebecca* (with Ida Lupino, in the part he had turned down for the movies); *Around the World in Eighty Days* (as Phileas Fogg); James Hilton's *Good-bye, Mr. Chips;* Victor Hugo's *Les Misérables;* W.F. Harvey's "August Heat"; and H.P. Lovecraft's "The Dunwich Horror."

Colman's first "older" screen role came in George Stevens' *The Talk of the Town,* made for Columbia in 1942. He played a stuffy but good-natured law professor, whose efforts to finish writing a weighty criminological tome are constantly interrupted by two irresistible screwballs, Cary Grant and Jean Arthur. Their sparkling comic entanglements set all America roaring with laughter.

Random Harvest came later that year for Mervyn LeRoy at M-G-M, and

Colman was back in full force as the struggling amnesiac victim who winds up marrying Greer Garson twice without realizing it. A smash hit, the film was nominated for Best Picture of 1942 and earned Colman his third Academy Award nomination for Best Actor. He was 51 years old, and women were falling for him all over again.

M-G-M retained his services for William Dieterle's 1944 remake of *Kismet,* Colman's first picture in color. Lavishly staged and expensively budgeted, this Arabian Nights fantasy co-starred Marlene Dietrich at her most exotic, but despite a warm reception by wartime audiences, one wonders why Colman ever bothered to make it. The film is almost unbearable and cannot be recommended except to those who might wish to suffer through it as Carlyle said he read the Koran: out of a sense of duty.

Following the release of *Kismet,* Colman discussed his future with Edwin Shallert, drama editor of the *Los Angeles Times:*

> It's twenty-two years since I made *The White Sister,* and that's a long time. I'm not ambitious to make too many pictures today, but I have never put any actual restriction on the number. I am guided entirely by the character of the stories which come to me from the studio. Of necessity, one thinks in terms of a picture a year, or at the most three pictures every two years under those circumstances, but as far as I am concerned I would have no antipathy toward more if the subject were obtainable. A director might be something to consider for the future, but I am quite satisfied to remain the actor as long as there seem to be assignments at fairly regular intervals.[2]

On July 24, 1944, daughter Juliet Benita was born; her father was 53, her mother 37. Her godfathers were Tim McCoy and Warner Baxter; her godmothers were Benita's sister and Lady Sylvia Ashley (Douglas Fairbanks' widow).[3]

After the war, Colman's filmic pace slackened considerably, but frequent radio appearances kept him busier than ever. In December 1945, he and Benita were guests for the first time on *The Jack Benny Program* for NBC, playing the comedian's next-door neighbors. Often mentioned during episodes in which they did not appear, the Colmans soon discovered that these riotous skits led many to believe that they really did live next door. In fact, they lived eight blocks away. Colman also hosted and occasionally starred in *Favorite Story,* a syndicated dramatic series that reached 223 stations and paid him $156,000 a year for his efforts. Another lucrative field opened up when he began making 78 rpm recordings of such favorites as *A Tale of Two Cities, Lost Horizon,* and *A Christmas Carol.*

Colman returned to the screen in 1947 to play a snobbish but likeable Boston patriarch in Twentieth Century–Fox's *The Late George Apley.*

Ronald and Benita Colman would soon begin to appear regularly as guests on Jack Benny's radio show. Here Colman and Benny make a 1944 broadcast with Lionel Barrymore.

Richard Haydn, Edna Best, Percy Waram, and Mildred Natwick were also on hand, and the picture bubbled with good humor and sparkling wit.

Later that year, he made *A Double Life* for George Cukor at Universal-International, the film that finally brought him his long-deserved Academy Award for Best Actor. (His first two nominations, for *Bulldog Drummond* and *Condemned!* in 1929–1930, had been primarily for his facility with dialogue; his third, for *Random Harvest* in 1942, finally recognized his true dramatic abilities, but he lost to James Cagney for *Yankee Doodle Dandy*.) An uncompromising foray into psychological realism, this brisk, gritty melodrama showcased Colman as an obsessed Broadway idol who commits murder while portraying Othello. Austerely indifferent to all considerations of glamour, it was in no way a "star" vehicle, and it tested Colman's acting abilities as had no previous role.

No one was surprised when Colman received his Oscar at the annual Academy Award ceremony, held in Hollywood on March 20, 1948. Backstage following the formalities, journalist Ruth Waterbury jostled her way to the victorious actor: "I ran straight into him. He was holding his

Colman's fabled reserve is finally supplanted by open jubilation as he holds his coveted Oscar after being chosen as Best Actor for 1947, for his role in A Double Life, *on March 20, 1948.*

Oscar. He almost gasped, 'Oh, Ruth!' and then he began to cry. That dignified, handsome man."[4] Colman began sorting through the congratulatory telegrams that were pouring in, among which he found the following from Sam Goldwyn: "An award well deserved for an unusually fine performance. I'm particularly pleased for nostalgic reasons. You are getting better all the time."[5]

Awaiting the jubilant Colmans were the London and Brussels premieres of *A Double Life*. Accompanied by Edna Best and her husband, Nat Wolf, Colman's agent, they headed for New York and sailed on the *Queen Elizabeth*. It was Colman's first trip abroad in over a decade.

After *A Double Life*, Colman made few screen appearances, devoting the bulk of his energies to radio, television, and recordings. In 1950, he returned to the screen and starred with Vincent Price in an energetic spoof of radio and television quiz-show programs, *Champagne for Caesar*. The same year, a *Variety* poll of film workers voted Colman and Laurence Olivier runners-up to Charles Chaplin as "best actor of the half-century." That summer, the Colmans took daughter Juliet on her first extended family outing; sailing to Naples, they joined Rex Harrison and his wife, Lilli Palmer, in Portofino, and went on to Venice and the south of France before returning to Hollywood.

Colman had his own radio series from 1950 to 1952. In *The Halls of Ivy*, first heard on NBC on January 6, 1950, he played Dr. William Todhunter Hall, the kindly, whimsical president of Ivy College, and Benita co-starred as his wife, Vicky, a former musical-comedy actress. Colman had total control over material and casting, and the series quickly became immensely popular. When presidential candidate Adlai E. Stevenson was criticized for speaking over the heads of most voters, he told an audience at the University of Wisconsin, "You may be right; but you see, my favorite radio show is *Halls of Ivy*, and I was speaking to that public!"[6] The series finally lost its sponsor in 1952, but it later resurfaced on television for 39 episodes, premiering October 19, 1954, on CBS. Slow-paced and static, it had worked better on radio; nonetheless, the 63-year-old Colman was as debonair as ever and a delight to watch. The Colmans appeared occasionally on Jack Benny's television show, once again playing his neighbors; Colman also filmed episodes of *G.E. Theater* and *Four Star Playhouse*, the latter a series produced by Dick Powell, Charles Boyer, Joel McCrea, and David Niven.

In 1953, the Colmans sold their home on Summit Drive and moved permanently to San Ysidro Ranch, something Colman had wanted to do for years. Apart from narrating an educational short subject, *The Globe Theatre*, he appeared but twice on cinema screens in the fifties, both times in all-star epics. A brief cameo in Mike Todd's *Around the World in 80 Days*, released in 1956, was the first of the two roles which would mark his farewell to the cinema. Colman's final screen appearance came the following year in *The*

The Colmans at home in 1956, at San Ysidro Ranch, with close friend Brian Aherne, who contributed the foreword to the present volume. Note that the room is decorated with oil paintings by Colman, an enthusiastic amateur artist. (Photograph courtesy of Brian Aherne)

Story of Mankind, an unintentional "disaster" picture with producer-director-scenarist Irwin Allen, king of disaster films, at his crudest. Despite the towering absurdities of Allen's dizzy casting decisions, Colman and arch-antagonist Vincent Price were worth watching. Although encased in clichés, Colman turned in a fine farewell performance as the Spirit of Man, defending mankind and its achievements before a heavenly tribunal.

One of movieland's most durable stars had made his last picture. Even at the end, with almost snow-white hair, he was an unmistakable thorough-bred—tall, erect, and dignified. But by now he was in failing health, and thus decided to forgo writing his autobiography. The Colmans made one last trip to England, however, after which he did manage to record all 157 of Shakespeare's sonnets.

Forever prone to colds and chills, Colman contracted pneumonia, was hospitalized, and on May 19, 1958, he died peacefully in his sleep. He had had emphysema for some time. With Benita at the simple funeral service were Juliet, Bill Powell, and Dick Barthelmess.[7] The world mourned the passing of a friend.

He left us just at the moment that his type was going out of fashion —
dignified, suave, and debonair, ever gracious and dependable, the epitome
of all that was best in an English gentleman.

The Talk of the Town

1942. *Production and distribution:* Columbia Pictures Corporation. *Producer
and director:* George Stevens. *Screenplay:* Irwin Shaw, Sidney Buchman. *Adaptation:* Dale Van Every (from a story by Sidney Harmon). *Cinematographer:* Ted
Tetzlaff. *Montage Effects:* Donald Starling. *Musical Score:* Frederick Hollander.
Musical Director: M.W. Stoloff. *Art Director:* Lionel Banks. *Associate Producer:* Fred
Guiol. *Assistant Director:* Norman Deming. *Film Editor:* Otto Mayer. *Running Time:*
118 minutes. *New York Premiere:* August 27, 1942.
    Cast: Cary Grant (Leopold Dilg), Jean Arthur (Nora Shelley), Ronald Colman
(Professor Michael Lightcap), Edgar Buchanan (Sam Yates), Glenda Farrell (Regina
Bush), Charles Dingle (Andrew Holmes), Emma Dunn (Mrs. Shelley), Rex Ingram
(Tilney), Leonid Kinskey (Jan Pulaski), Tom Tyler (Clyde Bracken), Don Beddoe
(Chief of Police), George Watts (Judge Grunstadt), Clyde Fillmore (Senator James
Boyd), Frank M. Thomas (District Attorney), Lloyd Bridges (Donald Forrester),
Max Wagner (Second Moving Man), Eddie Laughton (Henry), Billy Benedict
(Western Union Boy), Pat McVey (First Cop), Ralph Peters (First Moving Man),
Harold "Stubby" Kruger (Ball Player), Lee "Lasses" White (Hound Keeper), William
Gould (Sheriff), Edward Hearn (Sergeant), Ferike Boros (Mrs. Pulaski), Dewey
Robinson (Jake), Mabel Todd (Operator), Don Seymour (Headwaiter), Gino Corrado (Waiter), Frank Sully (Road Cop), Lee Prather (Sergeant at Arms), Clarence
Muse (Doorkeeper), Leslie Brooks (Secretary), Alan Bridge (Desk Sergeant), Joe
Cunningham (McGuire).

A fugitive with a fondness for borscht seeks refuge in the home of a
slightly daft schoolteacher. She's rented the house to a stuffy law professor
who's about to be nominated to the Supreme Court. When the young lady
becomes attracted to both men, sparks are bound to fly. And fly they do as
Cary Grant, Jean Arthur, and Ronald Colman become *The Talk of the Town*
in Columbia's delightfully satiric comedy hit of 1942.
    It never would have happened if Nora Shelley (Miss Arthur) hadn't hidden Leopold Dilg (Grant) in her attic. But she has, for she believes that the
accused arsonist is innocent. She's also leased her cottage for the summer
to Professor Michael Lightcap (Colman), bearded bard of the commonwealth's most prestigious law school and possessor of the state's most
distinguished legal mind. And that's where the trouble — or the fun, depending upon your point of view — starts. Lightcap wants nothing more than a
well-deserved rest and reasonable solitude in which to finish writing his
definitive treatise on "The Relation of Literature to Legislation in the
Eighteenth Century in England." But no sooner does he arrive and attempt
to settle in than his privacy is invaded. A host of unwanted worthies

Top stars Cary Grant, Ronald Colman, and Jean Arthur combined forces with direc-
tor George Stevens to create one of Hollywood's most delightful comedies of the forties,
The Talk of the Town.

suddenly appear, including Dilg's distressed attorney, Sam Yates (Edgar
Buchanan); a newspaper reporter (Lloyd Bridges) anxious to solicit the professor's opinion on the Dilg case; and finally the police, who are conducting
a house-to-house search for Dilg. It's a clear case of arson, all right, Yates
tells Lightcap, but the perpetrator of the act (which resulted in one man's
death) was Andrew Holmes (Charles Dingle), the town's big political boss
and owner of the factory which burned. Dilg, the only man with gumption
enough to stand up to Holmes, had predicted that the mills would be
torched. When Holmes did it for the insurance money, he framed Dilg,
rigged the evidence, and staged a phony trial after placing his own man on
the bench as presiding judge. Dilg broke out of jail because he knew he
didn't stand a chance. But the professor refuses to become involved in little
local affairs and shows them all the door, for his only concern lies in the
abstract principles of the law, not in their application. Little does he know
that he's got a major local affair lurking upstairs in the attic, or that Nora
Shelley has already determined to enlist his support, whether he's willing
or not.

Lightcap settles down to a good morning's work on his book. Eighteenth-century legislators, he contends, built the law on firm principles of reason and fashioned an instrument of pure logic entirely immune to considerations of petty emotion and greed.

"Impossible," Leopold Dilg cuts in sharply as he casually saunters out onto the terrace where the professor is dictating his manuscript to Miss Shelley. "What is the law? It's a gun pointed at somebody's head."

Nora quickly passes him off as her gardener, Joseph. "Uh, how are the zinnias getting along, Joseph?" she blurts when he persists in his impertinence.

"Dying!" he sneers with a bitter note of sarcasm.

Later that morning, Lightcap learns that the president has nominated him for a Supreme Court justiceship. In six weeks his name will be submitted to the Senate for approval. The dream of a lifetime is about to bear fruit, unless Nora Shelley succeeds in dragging his name into the Dilg scandal.

"This stuff he reads is remarkably dead," Dilg observes later. "An intelligent man, but cold. No blood in his thinking. Can't let a man like that take a seat on the highest court in our land. Bad for the country."

And so Dilg, Nora, and Sam Yates join forces to thaw the professor out. Dilg takes the initiative at the breakfast table the following morning. After a startled Nora deliberately spills two fried eggs across the front page of Lightcap's morning paper, cleverly concealing the photograph of the supposedly dangerous criminal under a headline which screams "DILG ESCAPES TRAP!" the fugitive engages the professor in a heated dispute on the philosophy of law.

"Where's the soul?" he asks. "Where's the instinct; where's the warm, human side?"

"All right, Joseph, you conduct the law your way on random sentimentality, and you will have violence and disorder," replies Lightcap imperturbably.

"And your way," Dilg says flatly, "you'll have a Greek statue: beautiful but dead."

"I see your point of view, theoretically. In fact, I—I—I respect it."

"I wish I could respect yours, Professor. All you know about the American scene is what you read in newspapers and magazines; somebody else's impressions, hashed up for lazy people. If you don't feel it yourself, you've learned nothing."

Two schools of thought clash head on: the one conservative, rigid, and immutable; the other radical, anarchistic, and equally unbending. But although the disputants disagree on the law, there's an earthy touch of the philosopher in "Joseph" that Lightcap admires, and Dilg, somewhat less willingly, is beginning to share a similar respect for the professor. Dilg challenges him to spend half a day with his books, and the other half finding out how people really live. Lightcap accepts and attends a baseball game where he discovers that the Dilg case has indeed been prejudiced: Judge Grunstadt (George Watts), a paid hireling, takes his every order from Andrew Holmes.

"What do you do about it?" Dilg asks him later.

"I? 'Tis nothing to do. Well, I can't intrude on the—on the business of the superior court of the county."

"So you just turn your face."

"Joseph, you don't understand."

"I understand this much," Dilg replies contemptuously. "You laugh at my kind of law, and wink at the other. What kind do *you* practice?"

When Holmes stages a demonstration at the site of the gutted factory to stir up public opinion against Dilg, Nora lures Lightcap to the scene. Once the townspeople are whipped into hysteria and thirsting for Dilg's blood, Holmes demands mob rule and quick justice.

At home that night, Lightcap asks Nora to come to Washington with him in the fall; he'll need someone there, more than a secretary—a lifetime position offered with decidedly romantic overtones. But the happy family atmosphere is broken when Lightcap serves "Joseph" his favorite dish— borscht—at supper, for the newspaper in which the soup is wrapped sports a front-page photograph of Leopold Dilg. In shocked disbelief, Lightcap attempts to call the police. For him, the telephone represents law and order; for Dilg, it means the final curtain in a vicious frame-up. The two schools of thought again collide, this time in action, and when the professor ignores the fugitive's warning and picks up the receiver, Dilg floors him with a quick punch. After Dilg escapes into the forest and the police arrive, Lightcap confronts Nora:

"You—you knew it was Dilg," he snaps in a harsh tone of reproof. "All those lies, attentions, just—for Dilg. You and Sam Yates—planned it all, didn't you. You had me feed and lodge a notorious fugitive from justice. You endangered a lifetime's career for a—stupid gesture."

"You were right to grow a beard," she splutters back. "You're an old man. Don't ever shave it off, Mr. Twilight. Somebody might think you were alive. That would be misrepresentation!"

Nora leaves in a huff, and Lightcap, cut to the quick, resolves to clear Dilg of the crime he did not commit. In as symbolic a gesture as there ever was, he shaves off the beard he's had for 15 years and sets out in pursuit of Regina Bush (Glenda Farrell), girlfriend of Clyde Bracken, the foreman who supposedly died in the fire. Aware that she's in thick with Holmes, Lightcap takes her to a popular watering hole, pumps her full of drinks, and discovers that Bracken is alive and well in Boston, where he picks up his mail each morning at the local post office.

Meanwhile, Dilg has returned to Nora's attic, where he and Miss Shelley realize that they've fallen for each other. Dilg knows, however, that if he hadn't intruded, Nora would very willingly have consented to accompany the professor to Washington. Lightcap arrives and informs them that Clyde Bracken is alive. Dilg decides that he'd rather face a jail cell than a lynching party, but the professor insists that they accompany him to Boston.

"That is taking the law into your own hands, Professor," Dilg remarks grimly.

"Leopold, sometimes there are—extenuating circumstances," replies Lightcap with thoughtful emphasis. "The letter of the law is sometimes wrong."

When Dilg refuses to go, Lightcap slugs him most unprofessorially, tosses him into the back seat, and off they motor to Boston. At the post office the following morning, the three allies await the arrival of Clyde Bracken, as Dilg examines his own portrait on a prominent wanted poster.

"Nobody'd recognize me from that," he chirps with self-satisfaction. "Doesn't catch the spirit."

Bracken (Tom Tyler) finally shows up and is collared by Lightcap. On the way back to Nora's house, he confesses that the mills were going bankrupt, and that Holmes' only solution was to burn them for the insurance.

"Professor, you solved this case beautifully," Dilg tells him later at home, wishing to spare him political embarrassment, "and I'm very grateful to you, but, uh, this country needs a man like you on the Supreme Court bench. I don't want to take the risk of losing that."

"Ah, that's very thoughtful of you, Leopold. I see things differently now."

"So do I," Dilg replies with gravity.

But Lightcap is insistent. "I want to see this job through. I'd sooner do that than hand down the finest piece of literature from the bench."

Events move quickly after Bracken clubs Dilg and Lightcap with a block of firewood and flees into the forest. The police arrive, Dilg is captured, and the professor is once again urged not to get involved. But he *is* involved, for a man's life is at stake.

"Listen," Lightcap cries, "my great-great-grandfather fought off a couple of dozen Indians for a whole week in 1756, and I'm a direct descendant. Now you tell that to the Senate. If it isn't good enough for the Supreme Court bench, it's just too bad!"

Grabbing a revolver, he rushes off to find Clyde Bracken.

At the courtroom, an angry mob has broken in, searching for Leopold Dilg and brandishing clubs and ropes. At the eleventh hour, Lightcap forces his way in, fires his pistol at the ceiling, and produces the supposedly murdered Clyde Bracken.

"There's the man the law is looking for," he shouts, "not Leopold Dilg. His only crime was that he had courage and spoke his mind. And you, what—what are you doing in a court of law with weapons and ropes? This is *your* law. This is your law and your finest possession. It makes you free men in a free country. Why have you come here to destroy it?"

Michael Lightcap has come a long, long way.

Dilg is freed and Lightcap is named to fill the Supreme Court vacancy. Nora journeys to Washington to be with Michael on his first day as a Supreme Court justice. In his chambers, he tells her that a dream of 20 years has come true, and that he has more happiness than any man deserves. Shouldn't someone, he asks her, take Leopold's reckless hand and offer him love and companionship? They kiss and part. Later, as Nora watches his performance before the court, Dilg enters briefly, smiles at Lightcap, and receives a benevolent beam in return. In a tight close-up, Nora winks at Mr. Justice Lightcap, and leaves the courtroom to catch up with Dilg, who's just left, assuming that she's come to Washington to join Michael. Until now, we've been kept in suspense as to whose life Nora will share, but in the final scene she marches off hand in hand through the stately court lobby with Leopold Dilg.

After making two comedies with which he was dissatisfied (*Lucky Partners* and *My Life with Caroline*), Colman returned to Columbia for the first time since *Lost Horizon* and accepted third billing in the lively comedy-drama *The Talk of the Town*. The actor had rejected most of the scripts he had been offered in the past two years, and was little concerned with the order of billing at this point in his career. What mattered was that he was to be teamed with two comedy giants, Cary Grant and Jean Arthur, the script was bright and literate, and the picture would be directed by first-rate comedy director George Stevens.

One perfectly acceptable definition of humor is that it is a détente—a release from tension. As Mark Twain put it, "Humor is only a fragrance, a decoration. . . . Humor must not professedly teach, and it must not professedly preach, but it must do both if it would live forever."[8] *The Talk of the Town* does both, for although its more important themes spring forth from wells of laughter, the film is, at its core, deadly serious. Its cheerful dress gets heightened color from sober hues. The humor is provided by Miss Shelley's attempts to conceal Dilg's true identity from Lightcap, her efforts to involve the professor in Dilg's defense, and the effects their dissimilar personalities and convictions have upon one another. Clearly opposites do attract, and the comic entanglements created by this irresistibly bizarre romantic triangle furnish much mirth and excitement, reminiscent of the previous decade's classic "screwball" comedies.[9] But it's the satirical jabs at judicial corruption which in fact represent the film's most vivid claim upon our memories. Through a series of verbal confrontations concerning the letter versus the spirit of the law, Dilg and Lightcap both come to share an understanding of each other's views. Each develops a different perspective on the law: the brash young radical gains respect for the professor and the system he represents, while the conservative theorist learns the meaning of intolerance and hypocrisy, loses his academic detachment, and discovers that there's more to justice than what he reads in his law books.

George Stevens' sprightly direction gives the picture freshness and enthusiasm without ever sacrificing its serious concerns to the comic elements. It would be difficult to imagine any thriller matching the visual flair and sheer excitement of the film's opening: a sweeping montage sequence of searing newspaper headlines superimposed across shots of the burning factory; Dilg being hauled off by the police and facing the gavel-rapping judge; then escaping and eluding the search party through the night, the rain, and the mud; until at last he arrives at Nora Shelley's doorstep — all handled with economy in an amazingly short space of time.

Immediately popular with audiences and critics, *The Talk of the Town* was one of the big hits of 1942 and received an Academy Award nomination for Best Picture (it lost to M-G-M's *Mrs. Miniver*). As the frozen legal giant who loses his smugness, his beard, and his heart when he tangles with husky-voiced heroine Jean Arthur and the delightfully fey Cary Grant, Ronald Colman did full justice to his part. Colman had always managed to look younger than his years, and the Colman mystique, now enhanced with middle-aged dignity, was as much in evidence as ever.

Random Harvest

1942. *Production and distribution:* Metro-Goldwyn-Mayer Pictures Corporation. *Producer:* Sidney Franklin. *Director:* Mervyn LeRoy. *Screenplay:* Claudine West, George Froeschel, Arthur Wimperis (from the novel by James Hilton). *Director of Cinematography:* Joseph Ruttenberg. *Musical Score:* Herbert Stothart ("She's Ma Daisy" staged by Ernst Matry). *Art Director:* Cedric Gibbons. *Associate Art Director:* Randall Duell. *Set Decorations:* Edwin B. Willis. *Set Decorations Associate:* Jack Moore. *Gowns:* Kalloch. *Makeup:* Jack Dawn. *Hair Styles:* Sydney Guilaroff. *Film Editor:* Harold F. Kress. *Sound:* Douglas Shearer. *Running Time:* 126 minutes. *New York Premiere:* December 17, 1942.

Cast: Ronald Colman (Charles Rainier), Greer Garson (Paula Ridgeway), Philip Dorn (Dr. Jonathan Benet), Susan Peters (Kitty), Henry Travers (Dr. Sims), Reginald Owen ("Biffer" Briggs), Bramwell Fletcher (Harrison), Rhys Williams (Sam), Una O'Connor (Tobacconist), Aubrey Mather (Sheldon), Margaret Wycherly (Mrs. Deventer), Arthur Margetson (Cheywynd), Melville Cooper (George), Alan Napier (Julian), Jill Esmond (Lydia), Marta Linden (Jill), Ann Richards (Bridget), Norma Varden (Julia), David Cavendish (Henry Chilcet), Ivan Simpson (The Vicar), Marie de Becker (The Vicar's Wife), Charles Waldron (Mr. Lloyd), Elisabeth

Risdon (Mrs. Lloyd), Clement May (Beddoes), Arthur Shields (Chemist), John Burton (Pearson), Alec Craig (Comedian), Mrs. Gardner Crane (Mrs. Sims), Montagu Shaw (Julia's Husband), Lumsden Hare (Sir John), Frederick Worlock (Paula's Attorney), Wallis Clark (Jones), Harry T. Shannon (Badgeley), Arthur Space (Trempitt), Ian Wolfe (Registrar), Olive Blakeney (Woman), Helena Phillips Evans (Ella the Charwoman), Hilda Plowright (Nurse), Terry Kilburn (Boy), Reginald Sheffield (Judge), Kay Medford (Wife), Cyril McLaglen (Policeman), Leonard Mudie (Old Man), Lowden Adams (Clerk), George Kirby (Conductor), Major Sam Harris (Member of House of Commons).

November 11, 1918 . . . Armistice Day. A remote and guarded building in the English midlands is Melbridge County Asylum, grimly proud of its new military wing, which shelters the shattered minds of the war that was to end war. Here, psychiatrist Jonathan Benet (Philip Dorn) treats a patient known only as "John Smith" (Ronald Colman), who was picked out of a shell hole near Arras by the Germans in 1917, close to death; when he returned to consciousness in a field hospital, he had developed a speech impediment and could remember nothing of his past. Eventually he was exchanged through Switzerland and sent to Melbridge.

At night, Smith walks through the unguarded gates and wanders from the asylum, heading past the Melbridge Cable Works into town. Caught up in a jubilant crowd celebrating the end of the war, confused and buffeted by the cheering and singing, he seeks refuge in a little tobacco shop just off the main street. Smith tries to ask for cigarettes but begins to stammer. The shopkeepr (Una O'Connor) realizes that he's from the asylum, and hastens to call the hospital authorities. At this moment, Paula Ridgeway (Greer Garson), a lovely music-hall entertainer, enters the shop. Seeing that the soldier doesn't look fit, she takes pity on him, follows him back into the din, and guides him into a pub run by ex-boxing champ "Biffer" Briggs (Reginald Owen). Then she takes him to an old English music hall to see her act. In her dressing room before the show begins, Smith slumps in a chair and confesses that he's lost his memory.

"Look here, Smithy," she says gently. "You don't mind if I call you Smithy, do you? Now how are you ever going to get better if you're not happy?"

"Perhaps I shouldn't—be very happy—anywhere, just now," he stammers, still a little bewildered.

"Have you no friends?" she asks. "No parents that you can trace?"

He struggles to get his words out. "Some—people came to see me at the hospital, but I—I wasn't their son. I'd have liked to belong to them."

Through gathering tears, Paula makes her way to the stage, where she sings and dances her way through Harry Lauder's "She's Ma Daisy," sporting a Scots dialect and wearing an abbreviated kilt. When she returns, Smith has collapsed on the catwalk above the stage.

Amnesia victim Charles Rainier (Ronald Colman) is buffeted by crowds, jubilant over the announcement of the armistice, in Random Harvest.

He wakes up in Paula's rented room and summons enough energy to speak. "I'm — all right. It's my speech. I can't — remember. I'm not like the others; I'm not like them. I'm all right. But I — I can't go back. I — I'll never come out; I'll — I'll be like the others."

Paula decides to take Smithy in and care for him. Aware that the asylum authorities are already looking for him, she quits her job and they escape to a quiet spot in Devon where they'll be safe: a small country inn owned by the charmingly eager Mrs. Deventer (Margaret Wycherly). For several months, Paula nurses him, mothers him, until finally they fall in love. In an idyllic wooded setting, Paula brings Smithy a small check from the *Liverpool Mercury* for an article he had submitted. Braced by this solid indication of his ability to make a new life, he proposes marriage, in his slow and careful way.

"Paula, it's — it's a lot of nerve," he says softly, his tone a shade eager, "but — I'm — I've fallen in love with you. I'm asking you to marry me, on a — on a check for two guineas."

"Smithy, don't ask me, please. I might take you up on it," she replies breathlessly. "I'm just that shameless. I've run after you from the very

Luminous Greer Garson would win an Academy Award for her performance in Mrs. Miniver *in 1942. Colman was also nominated, but lost to James Cagney. James Hilton's sentimental novel,* Random Harvest, *was successful on screen and was nominated for Best Picture that year.*

beginning; you know I have. I've never let you out of my sight since I first saw you in that little shop."

"Never do it, Paula."

"What?"

"Never leave me out of your sight—never again," he pleads. "My life began with you. I can't imagine the future without you."

"Oh, I better say 'yes' quickly," she cries, "before you change your mind. It's 'yes,' darling." The next moment, her lithe body is in his arms.

Soon thereafter, to the tortured strains of "O Perfect Love," played by a minimally talented group of colorful locals, Paula and Smithy are wed. Returning from the church, they enter their little country cottage, through a squeaking gate on a white picket fence and past a low-hanging bough that needs trimming. Time passes and a son is born. To commemorate the occasion, Smithy presents his wife with a necklace.

Six days later, Smithy receives a telegram from his editor at the

Liverpool Mercury, offering him a permanent position on the paper. The next morning, after Paula suggests that he stay at the Great Northern, the best cheap hotel near the station, he sets out for Liverpool, promising to return the following night.

In the morning, after leaving the Great Northern on his way to the offices of the *Mercury*, Smithy crosses a street and is suddenly struck down by a taxi. The camera cuts to a tight close-up of his face as he lies unconscious: superimposed flashbacks of his war experiences in the trenches flood the screen, aurally reinforced by deafening reports of artillery fire. He regains consciousness in a nearby chemist's shop and looks around in confusion.

"This—this is all wrong," he exclaims. "I've—no business to be in civvies."

"What should you be in?" asks the chemist.

"In uniform, of course. I'm on active service."

A policeman enters the shop and asks him his name. He identifies himself as Charles Rainier, captain of the Wessex regiment. His address?

"The trenches—Arras," he says.

"Beg your pardon, sir?" asks the puzzled bobby.

"Random Hall, North Random, Surrey," replies Smith.

The date, he is informed, is November 14, 1920. Rainier leaves the shop and wanders through the streets, his mind racing as he walks.

"1920. Three years gone. Three years. France—I remember distinctly. But after that—what after that?" he wonders. "Liverpool—what am I doing here? Where have I been? Better go home. Yes—may clear things up. Better go home—"

Back from three years in deepest amnesia, Rainier arrives at the imposing stone edifice of Random Hall. There a servant mechanically informs him that his father has recently died. The following morning, Charles greets assorted relatives who have gathered for the funeral, and tells them of his loss of memory. He had been in Liverpool the previous day. Before that he remembers nothing but a shell hole in France, three years ago. All he found in his pockets, he tells them, was some money and a house key—an elusive reminder of a lost past.

As seven more years pass, Rainier takes over his father's business, his career prospers, and the press takes to calling him "the Industrial Prince of England." He learns to cover his inner numbness with a facade of businesslike geniality, all the while absent-mindedly fingering that mysterious house key—his only link to a forgotten period he can't recapture, but it affords him no clue.

Eventually he becomes involved with Kitty (Susan Peters), a distant relative. One day, as they dine at a restaurant, Charles overhears a familiar voice at a nearby table—it's Dr. Benet from Melbridge Asylum, who is now in private practice. But the wisp of memory can't be caught before it slips away into the darkness.

Still struggling to break through the barrier which separates him from his past, Rainier returns to his office, fingers the house key again, then summons his secretary, Margaret Hanson. As she walks in, the startled audience recognizes Paula, but Rainier's amnesia prevents him from knowing that his present secretary is also his wife. She brings him a report on the Melbridge Cable Company, which might make a very valuable subsidiary, but Rainier's interests lie elsewhere. He tells her that he's soon to be married.

"I hope you won't take it into your head to—follow my example, Miss Hanson. I don't know what I should do without you."

"I—I have been married Mr. Rainier," she replies with controlled emotion. "You may remember I told you when I took the position."

"Oh, yes, to be sure. It slipped my memory. You had a child, I believe."

"Yes, a little boy. He died."

"Oh, yes, I remember. I'm sorry."

That night, Paula consults her friend, Dr. Benet, and begs his permission to tell Charles the truth. But Benet insists that the impetus must come from within; if she suddenly claims to be his wife, he still won't recognize her. At this point, we learn that Paula had failed in her efforts to locate Smithy after his disappearance, and had been seriously ill after her baby's death. Years had passed. Following an unsuccessful attempt to return to the stage, she had studied stenography. By chance she had spotted Rainier's photograph in a magazine, and applied for the position she's now held for two years. Someday, perhaps, he will remember.

A short time later, Charles and Kitty visit the chapel where they are to be wed a few days hence. As an organist plays "O Perfect Love," Rainier struggles to remember, his gaze averted and confused. Kitty, realizing that he's distracted, confesses that she's been uncertain from the very beginning; she'd had a curious feeling that she reminded him of someone else, someone he had once known and loved. She's been so very nearly the one, she tells him, but nearly isn't enough for a lifetime. Saddened, she breaks off the engagement.

Haunted by but unable to trace his lost years, Rainier journeys to Liverpool, where he had returned from the dead in 1920. Learning of his whereabouts, Paula follows him. In his hotel room, she informs him that the liberal cause has asked him to stand for election to Parliament. Extremely depressed, all he can manage by way of a reply is that he had come to Liverpool hoping to stumble onto the trail of his past and how he had come to be here some 12 years before. Perhaps he hadn't *lived* in Liverpool, suggests Paula; perhaps he had come in by train from the country. Judging from the direction in which he was walking when the accident occurred, she adds, he might have been staying at the Great Northern Hotel; perhaps he'd left unclaimed luggage. Fresh hope turns to despair when Rainier examines a battered suitcase marked "John Smith," for it fails to jog his memory.

Rainier wins his seat in Parliament. After his debut in the House of Commons, he and Paula celebrate his success, and he thanks her for her indispensable help in the campaign.

"You're staring at me, you know," she remarks.

"Oh, everyone has these feelings of having lived through certain moments before."

"You mean you have the feeling," she suggests with barely disguised eagerness, "that — you've known me before?"

"I had, for a moment," he admits. "As a matter of fact, I felt it quite strongly the first day you came into my office." Then he adds, "Forgive me, but — is there any possibility that you might marry again?"

"Not the slightest."

"I'm asking you because I have a proposal to make. I need your help in my parliamentary life."

"Social secretary," she interjects.

"Well, ah, not exactly. You and I are in the same boat, Miss Hanson; we're both — ghost-ridden. . . . We are prisoners of our past. What if we were to pool our loneliness, and give each other what little we have to give — support, friendship? I'm proposing marriage, Miss Hanson, or — should I call it a merger? A Member of Parliament should have a wife, Margaret; so I'm told on all sides. He needs a clever hostess; you have exceptional gifts. Would it interest you to have a wider field for them? You need have no fear that — I would make any — emotional demands upon you. I have only — sincere friendship — to offer. I won't ask any more from you."

Paula, though crushed, agrees, and becomes Lady Rainier.

On their third wedding anniversary, Rainier gives her a priceless emerald necklace, said to have belonged to the Empress Marie Louise. Alone, Paula opens her jewelry box, removes the string of cheap little beads that Smithy had given her when their son was born, and sobs. When her husband unexpectedly returns to her bedroom and notices what she's clutching, she loses her composure at last.

"He said they were the color of my eyes," she blurts.

Trying feebly to comfort a pain he cannot understand, Rainier asks her, "Isn't there something morbid in burying one's heart with the dead?"

"That's a strange thing for you to say," replies Paula. "Your capacity for loving, your joy in living, is buried in a little space of time you've forgotten."

"In some vague way, I still have — "

" — hope?"

"Yes, I suppose that's it."

"Have you, Charles? Do you feel that there—really is someone? That someday you may find her? You may have—come so near her, may even have brushed by her on the street."

"Yes, I've thought of that," he confesses wistfully.

"You might even have met her, Charles. Met her and not known her. It might be someone you know. Charles," she says, pausing slightly as if in emphasis, "it might—might even be *me*."

"Oh, Margaret," he scoffs, dismissing the suggestion.

When Paula decides to get away and travel, Rainier sees her off at the railroad station. She'll spend two nights at a delightful old country inn in Devon before her ship sails for South America.

That very night, a strike at the Melbridge Cable Works takes Rainier to the town where he and Paula had first met on Armistice Day. After settling the dispute in the workers' favor and accepting their grateful thanks, he and an associate (Bramwell Fletcher) enter a pub, where an elderly "Biffer" is still spinning yarns about how he gave it to "the Gunner" years ago. This seems to strike a responsive chord in Rainier's mind. They leave and mingle with the throng of laborers who fill the streets, celebrating their victory. So much noise—another random detail. Rainier offers his assistant a cigarette, but finds he's fresh out.

"Never mind," he says without hesitation. "There's a little tobacconist just around the corner."

The elderly proprietress (Una O'Connor) sells him a pack, and they leave the shop.

"I thought you said you'd never been in Melbridge," Harrison says.

"I haven't," he replies, standing in the same little alleyway where he and Paula first talked.

"But you said, 'There's a little tobacconist just around the corner.'"

"I said that?"

"That shop was off the main street. You couldn't have seen it on your way from the station."

"No!" he exclaims.

"Then—how did you know of it? You went straight to it."

"I *did* know," he says, struggling to remember. "I don't know how. Melbridge—Melbridge—let me think; there's something. That—that shop; that—that woman—"

The pieces are starting to fall back into place. The music swells ominously as they hail a cabbie and Rainier asks, "Where is the—the hospital?"

"You mean the old one or the new one, sir?"

"The old one, I think. It's on a hill; big gates—a high wall all around it."

"Don't sound much like either of them. You wouldn't be meaning the asylum, would you, sir?"

They retrace his steps of so many years ago to the asylum gates.
"There was—some excitement, and a great deal of noise. I'd been to
that shop. There was—a good deal of fog, and people shouting. I was trying
to get away from something, trying to escape. There was some danger, and
I was afraid. There was a girl—there was a girl—yes, there was a *girl!*"

Meanwhile, Paula checks out of the inn where she and Smithy first
stayed, and is told that old Mrs. Deventer has been dead for two years. Lots
of folks ask after her, the desk clerk confides. Why, there was a gentleman
asking for her just minutes ago; said he used to rent a cottage nearby years
ago. In shock, Paula knows instinctively that Smithy's been there.

The camera takes us to the cottage, where Rainier walks tentatively
through the still-squeaking front gate, past the bough that still needs trimming. He inserts his long-treasured key into the lock and opens the front
door. Memory floods back into his face.

"Smithy," Paula calls out as she arrives at the front gate. He rushes to
meet her. "Oh Smithy," she sobs; "oh, darling."

"Paula!" he cries.

They embrace and kiss. The random years are over.

M-G-M had originally purchased the rights to James Hilton's best-
selling 1941 novel, *Random Harvest,* as a vehicle for Spencer Tracy, but
quickly signed Ronald Colman when they learned that his services were
available. It was Colman's first picture for M-G-M since *A Tale of Two Cities*
seven years earlier. Co-starring with him was beautiful British actress Greer
Garson. Their teaming was unique, for Colman had given one of his finest
performances in Hilton's *Lost Horizon,* and Miss Garson had become an
overnight sensation in another Hilton adaptation, *Goodbye, Mr. Chips*
(1939).

Hilton's memorable love story is, to be sure, rather contrived and terribly implausible—heavenly romantic kitsch, panting with undying love, a
moment of idyllic bliss, and the anguish of separation. The film treatment
could have been drenched in great sheets of goo, but M-G-M managed to
pull it off. It remains harrowing and tender, an old-fashioned, tear-stained
heart-tugger, but fashioned with such elegance, taste, and discretion that
one forgets the soap at its core. And pretty rich soap at that, for it emerges
as really powerful drama, with warmth and humanity pervading every
scene. It reminds us what a versatile director Mervyn LeRoy was, able to
bring to soap opera the slick, intelligent approach that he displays here. A
sentimental near-masterpiece, in its way perfectly done—very touching
and quietly elusive.

Ronald Colman and Greer Garson both gave moving performances of
great beauty. Miss Garson's gentle compassion as Paula is fully complemented by her serene radiance later as Rainier's secretary, Miss Hanson,
who patiently helps him try to remember. But it was Colman's sensitive

portrayal of the amnesiac struggling to come to terms with his past that won most of the critical acclaim. Once again he played a character whose spiritual restlessness invites immediate audience sympathy: he always manages to exhibit a submerged but bewildering sense of loss through his confused, frightened stare—a haunting mixture of wistfulness, yearning affection, and vague anxiety. Unable to see into his past, he can only grope. His eyes dwell on Paula with soft regard, and yet seem always to pose a question; his face, despite its cheerful geniality, bears indefinable traces of a man who has passed through long periods of suffering; his voice adopts the pronounced stammer common to victims of shell shock, only gradually regaining the impeccable Colman diction that audiences had come to expect.

Although some critics found *Random Harvest* banal and aimed too knowingly at its audience (James Agee recommended it to "those who can stay interested in Ronald Colman's amnesia for two hours"[10]), most reviewers gave it glowing notices. Bosley Crowther called it "a sweep of rich romance,"[11] with *Newsweek* adding that "not since his performance in 'Tale of Two Cities' has Ronald Colman been so good."[12] The picture enjoyed an enormous popularity, became the longest-running film ever to play New York's Radio City Music Hall, and was nominated for four Academy Awards: Best Picture (along with *The Talk of the Town*), Best Actor (Colman's third nomination), Best Director, and Best Supporting Actress (Susan Peters). None won, although Greer Garson received the Best Actress Oscar for her performance in M-G-M's *Mrs. Miniver*.

It was Colman's finest role since that of Dick Heldar in *The Light that Failed*. Now in his fifties, with gray just beginning to salt his dark hair, he remained as dashing as ever. As Julian Fox comments, "*Random Harvest*, moving, beautifully mounted and supremely entertaining, is the best-remembered film of Colman's later period—his performance in it showed us an appealing veteran incapable of false emotion."[13]

Kismet

1944. *Production and distribution:* Metro-Goldwyn-Mayer Pictures Corporation. *Producer:* Everett Riskin. *Director:* William Dieterle. *Screenplay:* John Meehan (from the play by Edward Knoblock). *Director of Cinematography:* Charles Rosher (Technicolor). *Special Photographic Effects:* Warren Newcombe, A. Arnold Gillespie. *Technicolor Color Directors:* Natalie Kalmus, Henri Jaffa. *Musical Score:* Herbert Stothart. *Orchestral Collaboration:* Murray Cutter. *Songs:* Harold Arlen, E.Y. Harburg ("Willow in the Wind," "Tell Me, Tell Me, Evening Star"). *Art Directors:* Cedric Gibbons, Daniel B. Cathcart. *Set Decorations:* Edwin B. Willis, Richard Pefferle. *Costume Supervision:* Irene. *Costume Creation:* Karinska. *Assistant Director:* Marvin Stuart. *Film Editor:* Ben Lewis. *Sound:* Douglas Shearer. *Running Time:*

100 minutes. *Release Date:* August 22, 1944. Reissued in 1955 (in black and white) as *Oriental Dream.*

Cast: Ronald Colman (Hafiz), Marlene Dietrich (Jamilla), James Craig (Caliph), Edward Arnold (Mansur, The Grand Vizier), Hugh Herbert (Feisal), Joy Ann Page (Marsinah), Florence Bates (Karsha), Harry Davenport (Agha), Hobart Cavanaugh (Moolah), Robert Warwick (Alfife), Beatrice and Evelyne Kraft (Dancers), Barry Macollum (Amu), Charles Middleton (The Miser), Victor Killian (Jehan), Nestor Paiva (Captain of Police), Harry Humphrey (Gardener), Eve Whitney (Café Girl), Minerva Urecal (Retainer), Dan Seymour (Fat Turk), Cy Kendall (Herald), Dale Van Sickel (Assassin), Pedro De Cordoba (Muezzin).

Shades of Douglas Fairbanks' *The Thief of Bagdad,* as Ronald Colman dons a turban to outwit an evil ruler and win the heart of Marlene Dietrich in M-G-M's *Kismet,* a lavishly produced Technicolor Arabian Nights extravaganza.

"Once upon a time when Old Bagdad was new and shiny, there was a beggar and he was a rascal. Having convinced himself that he was a king of some kind, he would roam the streets at night, disguised as one of the princes of the empire. Now, in a great palace in the city lived a Queen—a beautiful Queen—a naughty queen and she had some great moments with this prince. She didn't know of course that he was a beggar."[14]

Magician and beggar king Hafiz (Ronald Colman) haunts the streets of Bagdad with but one purpose—besides stealing, that is: to make his lovely daughter Marsinah (Joy Ann Page) the bride of a prince. But she has eyes only for the gardener's son, who just happens to be the Caliph of Bagdad in disguise (James Craig, as convincing a caliph as the average banana split). To further his scheme, Hafiz poses as the Prince of Hassir, visits Bagdad's Grand Vizier (the always masterful Edward Arnold), and woos the wicked potentate's mistress Jamilla (Marlene Dietrich) for good measure. Exposed as an imposter and arrested for robbery, Hafiz faces the ceremonial lopping off of thieving hands, courtesy of a wrathful vizier, until he offers to murder the caliph and elevate the grand vizier to caliphdom—provided His Majesty shows proper gratitude by marrying daughter Marsinah. Eventually Kismet smiles upon the wily beggar, for after a succession of assassination plots, duels, and harem dances, Hafiz kills the vizier, sees his daughter married to the handsome young caliph, and lurches off on a camel into a desert eternity with the adoring Jamilla.

With his fine performance in M-G-M's *Random Harvest* just behind him, Ronald Colman returned to that studio and signed on as the star of this overblown and over-budgeted $3,000,000 fantasy. *Kismet* had been adapted from Edward Knoblock's celebrated play, which stage star Otis Skinner had made his own in 1911; touring the old warhorse for many years thereafter, he later starred in two film treatments (a silent version in 1920 and a talkie remake in 1930). William Dieterle, who had filmed still another early-talkie version in Germany before resettling in Hollywood, was assigned directorial chores for M-G-M's newest remake in 1944. Elaborately costumed and stunningly photographed in Technicolor (Colman's first), it was immediately greeted as a "delightful, opulent, totally disarming romp"[15] by audiences all too willing to accept any colorful diversion from the more grim realities of the Second World War. Directed with an eye mostly on the spectacle, it gave audiences what they needed: pure escapism, glamour, and romance.

Colman, sporting a closely cropped beard and arrayed from head to toe in rags, robes, and turbans, used his innate charm and mellifluous voice to good advantage as the rhyme-spouting rascal who was at once reminiscent of both François Villon (*If I Were King*) and Douglas Fairbanks' earlier thief. Lacking little of the Fairbanksian flair as he slashed his way up and down the palace staircases, Colman performed his sleight-of-hand tricks with obvious dexterity and glee. Turning scarves into knives and disappearing and reappearing at will, he hammed it up for all he was worth, playing to the gallery in everything he did and with every word he spoke.

But this is one fairy tale that doesn't hold up so well these days. The plot rambles as nonsensically as the back streets of Bagdad; the script possesses a strength approximating gossamer; and William Dieterle's meticulous sense of atmosphere, control, and Teutonic thoroughness fail him entirely, for the direction is slow-paced, uninspired, and undistinguished throughout. And despite Academy Award nominations for its cinematography, art direction, and sets,[16] it is not particularly satisfying on a visual level either, filled as it is with excesses of pictorialism that are at once its glory and ruination. With cardboard storybook castles whose exteriors are, at times, even more artificial than their interiors, the whole conceit rings false and just a bit silly, requiring little of its leading players, who all too often seem lost in the production splendor. Springing from the fertile brains of those Hollywood types whose only artistic amulet is the dollar sign, and whose sole criterion for outstanding pictures is that they make a lot of money, *Kismet* pandered to the lowest level of mob taste—and it made a lot of money. It's all a matter of what your goals are.

These are heavy debits indeed, but *Kismet* also boasts a fair amount of charm, entertainment, and overtones of undeniable beauty.[17] Chiefly remembered today as the film in which Marlene Dietrich's curvaceous legs—encased in glittering layers of shimmering gold paint—seared the screen with a sinuous, exotic harem dance, the picture received a healthy shot of adrenaline through the presence of Miss Dietrich and her sultry charms. But even here the magic backfires: mummified under far too many layers of makeup and sporting a looped and braided hairstyle which made her "about as seductive as a rosebush,"[18] La Dietrich never looked worse.

Colman, on the other hand, by accentuating the genial rakishness beneath the urbane exterior (as he had in his silent swashbucklers with Vilma Banky), once again portrayed a vagabond of the Villon stamp with delightfully lighthearted results, turning in "a terrific and wholly energetic piece of bravura acting."[19] And if this didn't save the picture, at least it made its failure less obvious.

Coming after *Random Harvest*, *Kismet* was a disappointment. One of Colman's weaker and most problematic efforts, it should never be screened by itself as an example of his work, but rather considered within the context of the actor's entire output, for although the performance brought pleasure, the vehicle was unworthy of his talents.

The Late George Apley

1947. Production and distribution: Twentieth Century–Fox Film Corporation. *Producer:* Fred Kohlmar. *Director:* Joseph L. Mankiewicz. *Screenplay:* Philip Dunne (from the play by John P. Marquand and George S. Kaufman and the novel by John P. Marquand). *Cinematographer:* Joseph La Shelle. *Special Photographic Effects:* Fred Sersen. *Musical Score:* Cyril J. Mockridge. *Musical Director:* Alfred Newman. *Orchestral Arrangements:* Maurice de Packh. *Art Directors:* James Basevi, J. Russell Spencer. *Set Decorations:* Thomas Little, Paul S. Fox. *Costumes:* René Hubert. *Makeup:* Ben Nye. *Assistant Director:* F.E. Johnston. *Film Editor:* James B. Clark. *Sound:* Bernard Fredericks, Roger Heman. *Running Time:* 99 minutes. *New York Premiere:* March 20, 1947.

Cast: Ronald Colman (George Apley), Vanessa Brown (Agnes Willing), Richard Haydn (Horatio Willing), Charles Russell (Howard Boulder), Richard Ney (John Apley), Percy Waram (Roger Newcombe), Mildred Natwick (Amelia Newcombe), Edna Best (Catherine Apley), Nydia Westman (Jane Willing), Peggy Cummins (Eleanor Apley), Francis Pierlot (Wilson), Kathleen Howard (Margaret), Paul Harvey (Julian H. Dole), Helen Freeman (Lydia), Helen Dickson (Governess), Theresa Lyon (Chestnut Vendor), William Moran (Henry Apley), Clifford Brooke (Charles), David Bond (Manager of Modiste Shop), Ottola Nesmith (Madame at Modiste Shop), Mae Marsh (Maid), Diana Douglas (Sarah), Cordelia Campbell (Child Skater), Richard Shaw (Man), Wyndham Standing, Stuart Hall (Gentlemen), J. Pat Moriarty.

There once were men who stood by their convictions. Such a man was George Apley, who, it would seem, never sat down. This is the story of a Boston Brahmin and his Beacon Street citadel—a series of faded tintypes and faint reflections which gradually reveal what life was like when the city of Boston was regarded, at least by its inhabitants, as the very hub of the universe. Here, in 1912, we meet George Apley (Ronald Colman), one of Boston's most active and eminently respected sons. Bred of financial security, social stability, and intellectual sterility, Apley is accustomed to the responsibilities of his inherited position. This loyal spirit is the self-appointed guardian of an insular society dedicated soley to the preservation of its own superiority. Fond of bird lore and given to quoting the late Ralph Waldo Emerson at every imaginable opportunity, this high-minded gentleman is willing to give, at a moment's notice, in emphatic and even dictatorial terms, any number of ever-so-reasoned suggestions concerning the social, cultural, and intellectual destiny of his native Boston. Throughout his lifetime, George Apley has formed tastes, values, and associations which have come down to him as an unaltering legacy. Pride of ancestry, place, and tradition—these mark the man, for upon his shoulders rests the future of Boston's educational and philanthropic institutions. Everything has its place, established and unvarying. That's why he's devoted his life's work to the innumerable charities, clubs, committees, and societies of which he's so inordinately proud: the Boston Waif Society, the Save Boston Society, the Tuesday Afternoon Club, the Wednesday Night Club, and the Blue Hill Bird Watchers' Society. For George Apley sees himself as a steward, as his father and grandfather were before him, and as his son will be someday. Someone, after all, must keep harmful literature from reaching Boston's libraries and one's children. That's why he's giving his son a Harvard education, and why he plans to arrange the marriages of his offspring to suitable, native Bostonians.

But Boston and the world outside have grown at a dizzying pace since George Apley's values were formed. Of the radical rumblings of a changing world, he is painfully aware. The Boston he has always loved is reaching the end of an era. And so he cries out in fervid appeal: Why can't everything remain as it has been? Apley's home on Beacon Street has changed little since the days of his grandfather, but progress is about to invade even this bastion. The younger Apleys have grown up and are ready to leave the nest: his son has fallen for an Irish girl from Worcester, his daughter for a Yale man—from New York. Horror! Circumstances are about to make harsh demands upon the Apley household. Blue-nosed bigotry is about to take a fall. George Apley is about to mellow.

In their sensible, rigorously unostentatious home on Beacon Street, Apley and his wife, Catherine (Edna Best), inspect the dinner table before their annual Thanksgiving Day feast—a holiday gathering which, within certain limits of propriety, has its own modicum of gaiety. Catherine has made the table more festive by decorating it with snapdragons and pumpkins, something she's never done before.

"Verging a bit on the radical, isn't it?" her husband inquires. But before his wife can respond, he directs the conversation to a matter of equal weight: an upcoming meeting of the Save Boston Society. "It's about allowing an electric sign on the edge of the Common."

"Is that so important, George?" asks Catherine.

"My dear," he replies with utmost gravity, "it's going to say 'Grape Nuts.'"

"I suppose we *must* put a stop to *that*," she readily agrees.

Moments later, the relatives arrive: George's sister Amelia (Mildred Natwick) and her husband, Roger Newcombe (Percy Waram); Horatio Willing (the ever-delightful Richard Haydn), his wife, Jane (Nydia Westman), and their timid daughter Agnes (Vanessa Brown), who, it has always been assumed, will someday marry George's son John (Richard Ney), who is also present. As George carves the turkey, he takes up a little family matter concerning the Henry Apleys, a very distant branch of the Apley famly (barely Apleys at all), and the burial of Cousin Hattie, who's been dead for a month.

"Do you mean to say they haven't *buried* her yet?" taunts the cynical Roger.

"They buried her at Mount Auburn, and to that I have no general objection. The family plot is *completely* democratic," Apley pontificates. "Any Apley connection, no matter how remote, is welcome to rest there. Even you, Horatio," he adds, casting an approving glance at his cousin.

"By Jove! Thank you, George," beams Horatio.

"Well, you're all fixed now, Horatio," Roger snorts.

It seems that Henry Apley has buried Cousin Hattie in George's part of the lot. George has written him a letter explaining that he must move his mother down to the bottom of the slope.

"Boston will be split into factions over this," Horatio remarks unctuously. "People will take sides. It will create—talk."

"It won't create any talk at all," growls Roger. "Who gives a hoot *where* the Apleys are buried? You know, it's possible that there are quite a few people in the world who never even *heard* of the Apleys?"

"Nonsense!" Amelia barks. "Everyone's heard of us—in Boston, anyhow."

After dinner, they all retire to the drawing room to sit in the same chairs they've occupied for the past 18 Thanksgivings. Daughter Eleanor (Peggy Cummins) arrives home with her young man, Howard Boulder (Charles Russell), who's well mannered and articulate; but he comes from New York, has a Yale Ph.D., and—worst of all—smokes cigarettes. He's also lecturing at Harvard's Emerson Hall. After asking Agnes about her forthcoming society debut, the liberated Miss Apley shocks the assemblage by observing: "The whole thing is an outmoded folk custom. Boston's full of 'em. We're—we're like a savage tribe; we suffer from ancestor worship. Thanksgiving is a *typical* tribal feast, and coming out's nothing but an old idea of introducing the virgin to the *rest* of the tribe!"

"*Really*, Eleanor!" exclaims George, acutely disconcerted. "There are some things we simply don't mention."

"If things exist," she insists, "I don't see why we shouldn't face them."

Benita Colman and two-year-old daughter Juliet visit the star on the set of The Late George Apley.

"Because we do not face virginity in the drawing room after a Thanksgiving dinner," he replies firmly.

In an attempt to divert the conversation into more appropriate channels, Apley engages Boulder in a discussion of his lectures and all the great figures—Emerson, Thoreau, Hawthorne—whom Boulder labels "the Concord Radicals."

"Did you say—*radicals*, Mr. Boulder?" Apley asks in frank astonishment. "I must confess I can't very well picture Emerson as a radical."

"But he was, sir, for his time," Boulder explains. "And so were the others. Now, take Thoreau's *Essay on Civil Disobedience*. You see, that's the point I make in my lecture: Yesterday's radical is today's stuffed shirt."

After Eleanor and Boulder depart for Cambridge and John rushes off to points unknown, Apley discovers a letter—from John's girlfriend—which has fallen from his son's pocket onto the floor. "It's postmarked Worcester," he tells his wife in shocked disbelief. "Catherine, the girl is a foreigner!"

Soon thereafter, George shows Catherine the letter he's just received from Henry Apley, informing him that Cousin Hattie has been moved. "In view of your astonishing attitude," it reads, "it is my present plan to have her buried at sea. I trust you have no prior rights in the Atlantic Ocean."

The following morning, Apley sets out for Harvard to sit in on one of Howard Boulder's lectures, determined to protect the reputation of the late Ralph Waldo Emerson. As a result, Boulder loses his position, accepts an offer from Columbia, and Apley is confronted by an irate daughter.

"You have a position in the world," he tells her, trying to express his anxious solicitude for her welfare. "You're an Apley, and you can't ever forget it."

"Well, I don't want to be an Apley. I just want to be Mrs. Boulder."

"No, Ellie," he says, envisaging the broader aspects of the situation, "you and I can't do things like that. We can't *escape* what we are. Other people may be able to, but we can't. You may as well face it, Ellie. You were born in Boston. Boston's not just a city," he purrs indulgently; "it's a state of mind. You can't run away from a state of mind."

After John tells Agnes, at her debutante ball, that he loves another, Roger approaches George on the Apley terrace and informs him that his candidacy for president of the Blue Hill Bird Watchers' Society has been rejected. Apley had had every reason to believe that he'd be elected, but his fellow members have turned him down because they feel he's been making a fool of himself—that cemetery business concerning Cousin Hattie for one thing, and forcing Howard Boulder out of his job for another.

"You know, George, those bird watchers of yours are pretty sound people," Newcombe counsels him. "At least, unlike most societies in Boston, they're interested in something that's alive. I wonder if you see yourself as other people see you. You're doing the same thing with John you do with Eleanor and Cousin Hattie: raising objections about things that don't matter—because you live in a narrow world, George."

When Roger leaves, Apley sits alone on the terrace and reflects. "Catherine, I've been thinking," he exclaims broad-mindedly after his wife joins him. "Worcester isn't Boston, but it *is* in Massachusetts!"

Further evidence of progress is displayed when George writes Henry Apley a conciliatory letter: "It has occurred to me in thinking things over," it begins, "that we can all die only once. As it happens, I still have a little time to consider where I wish to be placed in the family plot, and Cousin Hattie hasn't. Therefore, I suggest that we both adopt the motto, 'Let sleeping dogs lie,' and join our efforts in endeavoring to activate another little motto which is peculiarly our own, 'Bring Cousin Hattie back.'"

Later, in their bedroom, George confesses that he's been browsing through (and then hidden) that book by Dr. Freud, the one Eleanor praises so highly.

"It advances a theory that *frankly* never occurred to me. It's about the mind, and the human relationships that affect the mind."

"What sort of relationships?" asks Catherine.

"Well, I hardly know how to put it, Catherine," he replies, a bit uncomfortably. "I shall have to resort to a word I've never used in your presence. It seems to be very largely a book about—sex."

"Oh," she manages. "But how can he write a whole book about—that?"

"Dr. Freud does seem to pad it a little here and there," explains George. "For instance, he tells this story of a certain Mr. X. It seems that this Mr. X, when he was four years old, had an experience with his nurse that colored his *entire* life. Now, I remember my own nurse very well. . . . And I know that *neither* of us forgot ourselves even for a moment."

"Yes, but what happened between Mr. X and *his* nurse?"

"Well, that's what's so confusing. Nothing at all definite *did* happen, but ever after that he always dreamed of locomotives. It seems to be Dr. Freud's idea that emotion—that is, uh, sex—very largely governs the lives of people—in other parts of the country."

"Well, there's no reason to hide the book, George," exclaims Catherine as he attempts to do just that.

"No. *No*, I'll put it on the shelf downstairs, next to Emerson. Come to think of it, Catherine, they've more than a little in common. Dr. Freud is trying to do the same thing *with* sex that Emerson did without it!"

Apley soon has lunch at his club with Julian Dole (Paul Harvey), father of John's girlfriend, Myrtle, and quickly gets to the point:

> "I don't know what your ideas may be, yours and Mrs. Dole's, and I hope you won't mind my suggesting this, but I thought perhaps it might be better if the announcement of the engagement were to be made in Boston rather than in Worcester. . . . I was just thinking of the simplest way to explain matters here; and I thought if you and Mrs. Dole could go so far as to take an apartment in Boston, and then if the announcement were to be made from *there*, I honestly see no reason why Worcester should be brought into it at all."

It might be a shame to pass up such a gracious gesture, but Dole turns him down flat. Twenty years from now, he explains, he couldn't stand the thought of having a son-in-law as impressive as George Apley. Stunned beyond amazement, Apley has learned the lesson of his life (albeit the wrong one) and his course is clear: each to his own kind. He'll insist that John and Agnes marry, and pack Eleanor off on an extended European jaunt with Aunt Amelia.

Months later, after Eleanor returns from her trip, still very much in love with Boulder, George accompanies Agnes to New York to purchase the trousseau for her long-planned marriage to John.

"Now, remember," he cautions her as they enter the dress shop, "we mustn't tell them where we're from. We don't wnat to appear to be boasting." Later, as they leave, they unexpectedly meet Howard Boulder with a group of friends. Boulder taunts:

"Well, look who's here. Let me present *my* friends . . . all from Yale, Mr. Apley. Say, have I ever told you gentlemen about Mr. Apley? You've, uh, all heard of Boston, haven't you? The hub of the universe? Mr. Apley is the gentleman who spins the hub and makes the wheel go round. It's Mr. Apley who won't allow his fellow citizens to see your play or read your novel or admire your painting. It's Mr. Apley who kicks you off your lecture platform when you try to pump a little vitality into the carcass of the late Ralph Waldo Emerson!"

George Apley is getting the message.

The camera takes us forward in time to Boston and the wedding of John and Agnes. Before the ceremony begins, the proud father of the groom takes Eleanor outside the church, where Howard Boulder waits. It seems that Apley called him in New York, but Boulder hadn't found an opportunity to apologize for his remarks.

"Nonsense, my boy," assures George; "you were perfectly right — especially when you called Boston the hub of the universe!"

But now they must hurry, for George has arranged their elopement and hands them their steamship tickets; the captain can marry them on board.

Apley returns to the church and takes his place beside Catherine as the wedding procession starts. With his whispered remark that "in his way, Emerson was something of a radical," the picture closes on a note of gentle humor.

After concentrating on radio appearances and recordings for more than two years and turning down all the film scripts he'd been offered, Ronald Colman returned to the screen in 1947 to star in Twentieth Century–Fox's *The Late George Apley*. The picture was based on John P. Marquand's 1936 novel, which won the Pulitzer Prize in 1938 and became a Broadway hit in 1944 (with Leo G. Carroll in the lead) when Marquand and George S. Kaufman collaborated on the stage adaptation. The novel (and later the play) was a deft and devastating satire of Bostonian customs, mores, and manners; the screen version, directed by distinguished writer-producer-director Joseph L. Mankiewicz, offered polish, style, and "a splendid sense of period and locale,"[20] but critics were quick to point out that it lacked the satiric bite of the original. Bosley Crowther was especially critical:

> This stolid and dignified pillar of Beacon Street aristocracy was a muddled but irrevocable creature of a most rigid discipline, you recall. He may have wavered slightly in his inbred regard for caste when he found himself confronted by a rebellious daughter and son. . . . But essentially he was as fastened to a social system and attitude as if he had been chained. . . .
> However, the Hollywood people have managed to change all that. . . . They have pictured George Apley as a sober fuddy-dud and a gentleman of

Ronald Colman and Vanessa Brown meet John P. Marquand, author of The Late
George Apley, *on the set of the film.*

unrelenting notions — up to a certain point. . . . And he, being smitten with
conscience anyhow, takes the hint.

Some of the lines are still good — keen and swiftly revealing of a moss-
covered state of mind. But the slickness is too apparent. . . . As a comment
on Boston mores . . . it misses by a couple of thousand miles.[21]

Life echoed these sentiments:

As characterized in the book and the play, Apley and the intellectual
straight-jacket in which he lived provided some of the most biting satire
ever directed at Beacon Hill. But the 20th Century–Fox version . . . is far
gentler and often less credible, principally because the movie Apley
mellows and compromises his principles to provide a happy Hollywood
finale.[22]

Other reviewers commented that Colman's clipped British accent was
hardly Bostonian, and that, since he didn't die at the end, the picture's title
was left "several feet out on a limb."[23] In the novel, the term "late" was used
in both a literal and figurative sense; in the film, it merely suggests that, better late than never, Apley sacrifices the narrowness of his own thinking

rather than ruin his children's future for the sake of the past. And while it must be conceded that the George Apley of the book was somewhat more complex than his counterpart on the screen, he does mellow in his sunset years and faces the challenge of change with the gallantry of his kind. A more suitable title for the picture might have been *The Winning of George Apley*. Despite the critics' barbs, *The Late George Apley* was popular with audiences and soon proved its worth at the box office.

If Mankiewicz's treatment softens the satirical tone, it manages to retain much of Marquand's and Kaufman's wonderfully ironic dialogue; presents a gently satiric portrait of Bostonian family life which provides insight into the passing of an outmoded, but still warmly human, way of life; and features an unusually able supporting cast: Richard Haydn as the delightfully prissy Horatio Willing, Mildred Natwick as the unyielding Amelia Newcombe, Edna Best as the long-suffering Catherine Apley, and Percy Waram, especially good as the brandy-guzzling relative who's the only sensible one of the lot (a re-creation of the role he played on Broadway). Finally, of course, it offers Ronald Colman in a delightfully conceived performance as the not-so-late George Apley, that proud possessor of a distinguished past, whose children aren't nearly so troublesome as he is. In selecting the part, Colman made a perfect choice: suitably stuffy but exhibiting a compassionate warmth for his family, he waltzed through the film with all the grace and aplomb that had sparked his earlier forays into screen comedy. When author John P. Marquand visited the set and observed Colman's jaunty, lighthearted portrayal, he remarked that he couldn't envision anyone else in the role.

A Double Life

1948. *Production:* Kanin Productions, Inc. *Distribution:* Universal-International Pictures Company, Inc. *Producer:* Michael Kanin. *Director:* George Cukor. *Screenplay:* Ruth Gordon, Garson Kanin. *Director of Cinematography:* Milton Krasner. *Special Photographic Effects:* David S. Horsley. *Musical Score:* Miklos Rozsa. *Art Directors:* Bernard Herzbrun, Harvey Gillett. *Set Decorations:* Russell A. Gausman, John Austin. *Production Design:* Harry Horner. *Production Assistants:* George Yohalem, Jack Murton. *Assistant Director:* Frank Shaw. *Advisor (Othello sequences):* Walter Hampden. *Film Editor:* Robert Parrish. *Sound:* Leslie I. Carey, Joe Lapis. *Running Time:* 104 minutes. *Release Date:* January 6, 1948 (although shown at the Guild Theatre in Hollywood on December 25, 1947, in order to qualify for that year's Academy Awards). *New York Premiere:* February 19, 1948.

Cast: Ronald Colman (Anthony John), Signe Hasso (Brita Kaurin), Edmond O'Brien (Bill Friend), Shelley Winters (Pat Kroll), Ray Collins (Victor Donlan), Philip Loeb (Max Lasker), Millard Mitchell (Al Cooley), Joe Sawyer (Pete Bonner), Charles La Torre (Vito Stellini), Whit Bissell (Dr. Roland F. Stauffer), John Drew Colt (Stage Manager), Peter Thompson (Assistant Stage Manager), Elizabeth Dunne

(Gladys), Alan Edmiston (Rex), Art Smith, Sid Tomack (Wigmakers), Wilton Graff (Dr. Mervin), Harlan Briggs (Oscar Bernard), Claire Carleton (Waitress), Janet Warren (Beth Wellman), Betsy Blair, Marjory Woodworth (Girls in Wig Shop), Curt Conway (Reporter), Paddy Chayevsky (Photographer), Nina Gilbert (Woman), John Derek (Police Stenographer), Buddy Roosevelt (Fingerprint Man), Fred Hoose (Laughing Man), Bruce Riley, Wayne Treadway (Men at Party), Pete Sosso (Tailor), Mary Worth (Woman in Audience). In *Othello* sequences: Guy Bates Post, David Bond, Leslie Denison, Virginia Patton, Thayer Roberts, Fay Kanin, Arthur Gould-Porter, Frederic Worlock, Boyd Irwin, Percival Vivian. In *A Gentleman's Gentleman* sequence: Elliott Reid, Georgia Caine, Mary Young, Percival Vivian.

In 1947, scenarists Ruth Gordon and her husband, Garson Kanin, offered Ronald Colman an original screenplay, which they had written some years earlier, about a celebrated stage actor who becomes so obsessed with his roles that he takes on the personalities of the characters he plays behind the footlights. When he portrays Othello, he lives out the part in real life and commits murder. Thrilled with the script but apprehensive about playing Shakespeare, which he had never felt the desire or the ability to tackle, Colman wrestled with the idea, reluctant at first to accept a role which he felt should best be left to Shakespearean actors. But he soon realized that the excerpts from *Othello*, so absolutely essential to the story, presented him with a unique opportunity to step out of his star image once and for all and prove his mettle as an actor. Finally convinced that the part was right for him, Colman accepted the challenge and placed his faith in veteran director George Cukor. What was to make *A Double Life* all the more challenging was that Ronald Colman would not merely portray an actor who was portraying Othello; he would play a *mad* actor who was playing Othello!

Matinee idol Anthony John (Colman) nears the end of his long-running Broadway engagement as a debonair butler in Robert E. Sherwood's *A Gentleman's Gentleman*. Having always wanted to prove himself capable of turning in really top-notch dramatic performances but fearing that he's become typecast in light, frothy comedies, he is persuaded by his producer and director (Philip Loeb and Ray Collins, respectively) that his next venture should be *Othello*. To be an actor — a real actor — after a thousand and one one-night stands, to strangle Desdemona with a kiss — his contribution to Shakespeare — that's the thing.

But Tony's lovely leading lady and former wife, Brita (Swedish actress Signe Hasso), resists the suggestion that they take on *Othello*. Still in love with her husband two years after their divorce, she's always hoped they might make a go of it again. When he's doing something light and gay, he's wonderful to be with; but when he attacks the dark, heavy numbers, he can't leave the role at midnight. It stays with him. The pacing, the brooding, the black moods, the long disappearances. If he sticks to comedy, it might work for them; if they do *Othello*, it would be the end.

Manhattan past midnight. Dim and quiet in the dead of night. Shadows lie heavily upon the streets as Tony wanders aimlessly, his mind grappling with the *Othello* project. He knows what such parts did to his marriage. A shop window catches his eye and reflects his own image as he moves closer and spots the travel poster within—Venice! The Moor of Venice! But the reflection peering back at him—swarthy, bearded, bejewelled, and arrayed in rich white robes—not Tony John: Othello, proud and stern! The street no longer New York, but Venice!

"Oh, beware, my lord of jealousy . . . rise black vengeance. . . ."

The tricks one's mind can play.

More wandering. Finally he comes to an Italian restaurant in Greenwich Village. Waitress Pat Kroll, an aggressively delectable former masseuse anxious to try the modeling game (sultry newcomer Shelley Winters in her screen debut), engages him in conversation, with obvious implications.

He accepts her tempting invitation to join her at her apartment following work, and after wandering about for several hours with little awareness of his whereabouts, he finds his way to her shabby lodgings. In a scene filled with just the right kind of sexual tension, the seductive creature finally gets around to asking his name.

"Which one?"

"Your real name. The one you were born with."

"Ah, it's not my real name," he assures her. "Look, if I could find out who I am I'd be a happy man, you know it? You want to know my name? Martin. Also Ernest and Paul. Hamlet and Joe. And maybe—Othello! Yes, and I'm French and Russian and English and Norwegian—"

"I got mixed blood too!"

"All right, darling, but are you rich and poor, and brave and cowardly, and in love and not, and trusting, and *jealous*? Are you?"

"What am I mixed up with here?" she blurts with a worried frown. "Some kinda nut?"

With a sudden movement, Tony reaches for a discarded earring, holds it up to his ear, and casts an appraising glance into the mirror. Half-growled quotations from *Othello* tumble from his lips.

". . . impudent *strumpet*!"

"You're talkin' so funny, like you're somebody else almost."

"I was."

"Don't talk funny no more. In fact, don't talk at all," she urges hungrily.

As the days and weeks follow, *Othello* is launched and rehearsals begin. A skillful manipulation of montage techniques transports us through weeks upon weeks of preparations—the sights and sounds, the hopes and frustrations—with economy and dispatch. And through it all strides the

Newcomer Shelley Winters got her first screen role opposite Ronald Colman in his Academy Award–winning performance as the mentally unstable Anthony John in A Double Life.

robed and hooded figure of Anthony John, his face darkened and strongly bearded, his superimposed voice echoing uncontrollable inner torments:

> ". . . trying to make someone else's words your own, thoughts your own, over and over and over. You whip your imagination into a frenzy. Key to the character—jealousy. You dig for it within yourself. What does it feel like—*real* jealousy? Try to remember jealous moments in your own past. Jealousy. Jealousy. Find it, hold it, live it—*jealousy!* The part begins to seep into your life, and the battle begins. Imagination against reality. Keep each in its place—that's the job—if you can do it. And all at once, it's opening night. And you look at the audience—terrifying monster with a thousand heads. You're in a kind of trance. Try to hang on desperately. You're two men now, grappling for control. You—and Othello."

Othello opens on Broadway. Anthony John scores a sensational triumph as the Moor; Brita shines as Desdemona. But after some 200 performances, Tony has begun to carry his raging and storming backstage. The ordeal is getting to him, one maddening step at a time. A poster announces

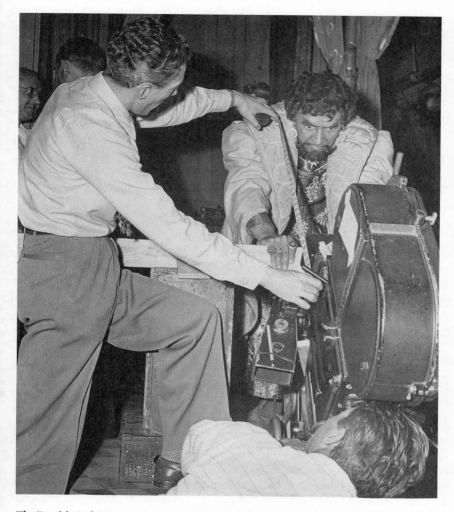

The Double Life *camera crew makes final preparations for a tight close-up of Ronald Colman garbed in his Othello costume.*

the play's 300th performance—a milestone, and with it, near-tragedy and an unexpectedly grisly climax. Othello crushing Desdemona's soft body to his, clamping his dark beringed hand tightly round her throat. The death-kiss—his mouth forced upon hers, crushing away her life. *Jealousy! Jealousy!* Brita struggling breathlessly, feebly. Flinching gasps from an audience shrinking in horror. It all seems so real.

A choking, whispered moan: "Tony, please, you're hurting me—"

He draws her closer, tightening the kiss of death.

A sudden crash of thunder. A vigorous knock on the chamber door. Desdemona's maid. The camera cuts quickly to an extreme close-up of Tony's face as the deadly trance is broken, a contorted mask of fury, dazed, sightless, uncomprehending. An actor grappling for control—and losing.

Othello enters its second year, and with it, the green-eyed monster of jealousy casts Tony John into a bottomless abyss of violence and pain. Convinced that press agent Bill Friend (Edmond O'Brien) is playing off-stage Cassio to Brita's Desdemona, the actor stalks the damp, glistening streets of moonlit Manhattan, brooding—tormenting himself to insanity. Infidelity! Jealousy! Revenge! Brita, Bill; Brita, Bill!

"Yet she must die...."

Overhead a tram shrieks by, screaming as if to underscore the unintelligible terror of creeping madness.

"Help me, Pat. Desdemona, Brita...."

Desperate going until he reaches Pat's apartment. Rudely awakened, but there she is, soft and eager in a revealing negligee.

Why does he look so different, she pouts; where has he been?

"*Venice!*" he sneers, his tone a shade ominous.

He glances quickly at his reflection in the mirror, as another tram hurtles past just outside, filling his ears with its howling.

"How many fellas you got, Pat? Any press agents? Any named *Bill?*"

"You wanna put out the light?" she asks huskily.

"Put out the light," he murmurs, searching his memory. Where has he heard—of course, now he remembers. Put out the light—Desdemona! Infidelity! Put out the light! Fierce and frightening, half-garbled lines from *Othello* pierce the air.

"Seen *Bill* lately?" he snaps, seizing her with arms hard and unyielding. His lips hold hers greedily, mercilessly.

"Out, *strumpet!*"

The terrors of the night world have taken control.

Newspapers quickly pick up the angle that the murdered girl was the victim of "a kiss of death." It makes big, sensational, attention-grabbing headlines. Bill Friend, aware that Tony frequently disappears at night, puts two and two together and goes to the police. An elaborate scheme is concocted to test the theory that Anthony John is the murderer. Assuming Pat's position in the restaurant is a young model who bears a striking resemblance to the murdered girl—the face, the voice, the body, the disarranged blonde hair, even the earrings are deadly accurate. Observed by a police detective, Tony joins Bill, and as the waitress bends over him to take his order, the actor's startled face gives him away. Shaken, he hastily departs.

And so the curtain prepares to descend on Anthony John's final performance as the Moor of Venice. Desdemona has been murdered once again.

Exhausted, unstrung, spent in body and spirit, he regards her lifeless corpse. As detectives wait in the wings, lightning and thunder reinforce the realization that a terrible dream has become reality, confronting him in its full horror. Distractedly and in a faltering voice he begins to mumble his lines, face dripping with sweat. Staggering a few steps as he hears the momentary rumble of a distant tram, he whips his dagger from its sheath—

"And *smote* him—"

A gleaming blade held at arm's length...

"—*thus!*"

The knife drives home, full to the hilt. Stumbling to his knees, he drags himself to his beloved Desdemona, slumps beside her, and moves no more.

Carried backstage, Tony dies with Brita's name on his lips. Anthony John's *Othello* has run its glittering course.

Of all Ronald Colman's films, *A Double Life* is the darkest and the most terrifyingly claustrophobic. The fact that Colman was playing a mad actor who was portraying Othello called for a singularly overshadowed approach not only to his interpretations of Anthony John and the Moor but to the visual and aural mood of the picture as well. Colman's schizophrenic double identity, which makes it in essence another dual-role performance, lends itself to an ever-increasing Jekyll-and-Hyde atmosphere—an eerie, hallucinatory, almost surrealistic netherworld of the mind. Anthony John, steeped in his own coagulated horror, represents a prodigious achievement of imaginative energy. Colman reveals Tony John's talent as dreadfully fragile, frightening, and ultimately grotesque, breathing into the role an increasingly terrifying power, and an even more terrifying powerlessness. Few actors have captured more poignantly the aching sense of cumulative madness or the brutality of insanity in its closing stages.

A madman's world screams out for a madman's eyes and ears. Appropriately reinforcing the ever-gloomier side of Anthony John's existence are Milton Krasner's sparkling cinematography and Miklos Rozsa's superb underlying musical score, which make an immediate appeal to the visual, auditory, and emotional senses by shunning the "real" world and conjuring up an introspective nightmare of dim shapes and strange apparitions, twisted shadows and intimidating sounds. Obliterating the boundaries between the real and the unreal, this subjective stylization is highlighted by distortions of perspective, tilted camera angles, collisions of light and shadow, and shrill screechings. And as the final desperation of madness slowly engulfs the mind of Anthony John, we *see* it closing in, *hear* it overtaking him. It lurks in the labyrinthine streets he walks night after night, growing, creeping. It's there, whispering its warnings to him at the opening-night party—strange disembodied voices which can't be real and yet are.

A chilling, recurrent motif is the mirror image, those demonic reflections of the second soul within Anthony John's breast which threaten to

Scenarists Ruth Gordon and Garson Kanin visit Ronald Colman, in Othello makeup, on the set of A Double Life.

consume what had been his "real" self. The symbolism is discreet but persistent. Swallowed whole by Othello, the actor finally succumbs, and the mirror image devours what is left of Tony John.

As Shakespeare's *Othello* builds wondrously toward the final mad outbursts in the last scene of the last act, Colman's rendering of Anthony John develops along strikingly parallel lines of suspense and inevitability. Like Othello, Anthony John is, at the end, hopelessly undone, unhinged by mounting confusion and weariness, but finally aware of what jealousy has wrought. Building up both roles with enormous skill and power, Colman projects the struggling inner compulsions through both verbal nuances and a telling, subtle uses of pantomime. His dialogue gravitates more and more toward percussive punctuation, clipped jerky sentences, and staccato phrases; his physical movements toward increasingly broad gestures and flamboyance. In both instances, Colman abandons his accustomed style of restraint and understatement and incorporates elements common to German Expressionism. He had to. For both Tony John and Othello, the nightmare stage had been reached. It is significant that the only *Othello* scenes we see Colman perform are those last, desperate moments when the

Moor, finally driven to belief in Desdemona's infidelity and convinced of his own duty to avenge it, commits murder and suicide. For both characters, the last act brings widening, though still disordered, horizons of self-awareness; murder wrenches release from aching depths. All this—the agony and the exhaustion, the anguish and the peace—Colman registers visually, facially, during Anthony John's last minutes. He lies backstage, uncertain of his identity no longer. A smile for Brita and Bill, a long shuddering breath, and then:

> "I'm—I'm—all right. Never better. So are you—now—and Bill. We're all—all right. Funny the things you think about, you know? Bill, you know, 'way back—yes—an actor once, old-time actor, name of Kirby. 'Way, 'way back. Famous for death scenes. Th—th—this Kirby, he'd finish, and from the gallery, they'd shout, 'Die again, Kirby, die again,' and he'd—he'd get up and bow and—die agan. Ever hear of him—Kirby? Tonight—things that go through one's head. Suddenly I thought, no one shouts—'Die again'—'cause—I couldn't have. The things that go through one's head. Doesn't feel bad now. Peaceful, really. It's in my *mind* that I feel bad. Pat—that unfortunate Pat. I'll apologize to her up there—or down there. Yeah, down there—Bill? Don't let 'em say I was a bad actor—Brita? Brita—Brita...."

A shadow passes gently over his face, darkening it as he dies. Tony John has missed his last curtain call.

Director George Cukor recalls the extraordinary effect of this scene:

> For the death scene, I was shooting from a high angle, and I told him, "When you die, all your life, everything that's happened, should come into your eyes for a brief moment." Well, he did it—or told me he did it—but I couldn't see it when we shot it. Next day, in the rushes, it was all there. He knew how to let the quality of *thought* come out.[24]

Shabbiness and glamour, darkness and light. An arresting demonstration of controlled scriptwriting, solid direction, remarkable cinematography and scoring, and superb casting.[25] But it was Ronald Colman's bravura performance which dominated *A Double Life*. The challenge and the complexities of the split personality inspired him to turn in one of his finest creative efforts. Striving since the early forties to prove that he was more than just a star personality, he had found the ideal vehicle in this uncompromising psychological melodrama. It seemed a safe bet that Ronald Colman would finally win his long-overdue Academy Award.

The rave notices poured in. Bosley Crowther called it *the* role of Colman's lengthy career: "The only question is whether Mr. Colman is more spectacular as the mentally distressed star of Broadway or as the bearded Venetian Moor."[26] *Time* judged it "a wonderfully rich present . . . an actor's dream. His performance is a pleasure in itself, but the real delight is to watch his delight in his job."[27] *Newsweek* added that "it provides a field day for Ronald Colman, and the actor responds with one of the most impressive performances in his career."[28] "A top actor and a great star at the peak of his powers and achievement," echoed still another reviewer.[29]

His first prize was the Golden Globe Award of the Hollywood Foreign Correspondents Association. The second, his most cherished, came as no surprise. On March 20, 1948, at the twentieth annual Oscar ceremony, held at the Shrine Auditorium in Los Angeles, Ronald Colman received the Academy Award for Best Actor—his only one, although he had received nominations earlier for *Bulldog Drummond, Condemned!,* and *Random Harvest.* The competition had been stiff—John Garfield for *Body and Soul,* Gregory Peck for *Gentleman's Agreement,* close friend William Powell for *Life with Father,* and Michael Redgrave for *Mourning Becomes Electra*—but Colman carried the night.[30] Ironically, Colman's only Oscar had come for a performance which flaunted uncharacteristic flamboyance and elaborate makeup. Casting his customary reserve to the winds, Colman stepped out of his image, and it paid off.[31] At the age of 57, he had reached the pinnacle of his career.

For the *Othello* sequences in *A Double Life,* which were meticulously rehearsed and then shot in continuity, apart from the rest of the picture, Ronald Colman was coached for ten days by distinguished Shakespearean actor Walter Hampden.[32] It was well worth the effort, as George Cukor remembers:

> He played Othello the way he saw it, within his vision, his strengths and his limitations. In *A Double Life* he wasn't playing Othello for the camera, he was performing as though he were doing it in the theater. He wore stage makeup as opposed to screen makeup; Signe Hasso did so as well. The contrast was deliberate. He would have played Othello quite differently had he acted it for the screen. He also indicated that the line between the reality of life and the reality of the theater was blurred.[33]

But would Colman have made a great Othello? Cukor put it this way:

> Colman had so much equipment for a screen actor, he was photogenic, he could move, he could give the impression of movement and yet remain perfectly still, he had this plastic quality, he'd studied Chaplin and Fairbanks. . . . But, yes, I question whether he had the danger and the madness for a great Othello, on the stage or in real life. Some can be scary, some can't, and Colman was a most gifted actor who didn't have a sense of the demonic.[34]

When interviewed, Colman commented:

Having done so many pictures, it becomes monotonous unless I can find something inspired like this, that I can get my teeth into. This was almost too much for me, but the hard work itself made the whole thing worthwhile.[35]

It was the most satisfying role I ever had, though there were others I found fulfilling. It tested my total range, and all my resources. And it came at a time in my career when I needed a recharging of my creativity. And certainly receiving the Academy Award for it was a great moment, a capstone of all I had striven for in my work for so many years.[36]

"Now," as Bosley Crowther asked, "what does Mr. Colman do for an encore?"[37]

Champagne for Caesar

1950. *Production:* Cardinal Pictures, Inc. *Distribution:* United Artists Corporation. *Executive Producer:* Harry M. Popkin. *Producer:* George Moskov. *Director:* Richard B. Whorf. *Screenplay:* Hans Jacoby, Fred Brady. *Director of Cinematography:* Paul Ivano. *Musical Score:* Dimitri Tiomkin. *Art Director:* George Van Marter. *Set Decorations:* Jacques Mapes. *Costumes:* Maria Donovan. *Furs:* Al Teitelbaum. *Makeup Artists:* William Knight, Ted Larsen. *Hair Stylist:* Scotty Rackin. *Technical Assistants:* John Claar, Robert H. Forward (By Arrangement with CBS and KTTV). *Associate Producer:* Joseph H. Nadel. *Assistant Directors:* Ralph Slosser, Leon Chooluck. *Film Editor:* Hugh Bennett. *Sound:* Hugh McDowell, Mac Dalgleish. *Running Time:* 99 minutes. *New York Premiere:* May 11, 1950.

Cast: Ronald Colman (Beauregard Bottomley), Celeste Holm (Flame O'Neil), Vincent Price (Burnbridge Waters), Barbara Britton (Gwenn Bottomley), Art Linkletter (Happy Hogan), Gabriel Heatter, George Fisher (Announcers), Byron Foulger (Gerald), Ellie Marshall (Frosty), Vici Raaf (Waters' Secretary), Douglas Evans (Radio Announcer), John Eldredge (Executive #1), Lyle Talbot (Executive #2), George Leigh (Executive #3), John Hart (Executive #4), Mel Blanc (Caesar's Voice), Peter Brocco (Fortune Teller), Brian O'Hara (T-Man Buck), Jack Daly (T-Man Scratch), Gordon Nelson (Lecturer), Herbert Lytton (Chuck Johnson), George Meader (Mr. Brown).

Beauregard Bottomley (Ronald Colman) not only knows a lot; he knows everything—everything, that is, except how to make a buck. This brilliant, unemployed Ph.D. lives with his sister in Hollywood, where, in the constant pursuit of knowledge, he reads, and reads, and reads—and waits for the perfect career opportunity. He and his sister, Gwenn (Barbara Britton), are the proud guardians of an alcoholic, ribald-tongued parrot named Caesar, who'll drink to anything. They had found him one night, leaning up against a lamp post; how he'd gotten there is anybody's guess.

It's hard, as they say, to get a job when one knows everything, but one bright day our mild-mannered genius applies for a position that's right up his intelligent alley: conducting a research survey for Milady Soap Company

Vincent Price as Burnbridge Waters, head of Milady Soap Company, in Champagne for Caesar, *a satire on American corporate pretensions as well as radio and television quiz programs.*

("The Soap that Sanctifies"). A hopeful, determined Bottomley, bewildered by his preposterously surreal surroundings, which appear to have been created on Mars by Frank Lloyd Wright, is ushered into the inner sanctum of Milady's chief executive, Burnbridge Waters (Vincent Price), only to find that gentleman enthroned in a plush swivel chair, gazing off into space with profound intensity: he is, in fact, in a trance.

"Mr. Waters is not with us," an official explains matter-of-factly. "He's concentrating; he's on a higher plane. We must wait. But it won't take long," he adds with conviction; "he'll be back."

Suddenly snapping back to reality, Waters swivels to his guest and gets briskly to the point:

> "How do you do. My time is extremely valuable. Seconds tick away into minutes, minutes become hours, hours disappear into days and weeks, weeks suddenly form months, and months have a habit of becoming years. You are a dreamer; I am a doer. I have an idea. I want to find out what the average man thinks of it; then when we find out what he thinks of it, we'll, uh, change his thinking. What I am about to tell you now is very top secret.

It ranks with the discovery of electricity and the invention of the wheel. I am thinking of putting on the market an all-purpose cake of soap that will also be used to clean teeth."

"I see," Bottomley chuckles. "Sort of, uh, foam-at-the-mouth approach, eh?"

"You would have started tomorrow morning," Waters replies stiffly.

"That would have been fine, but aren't we using rather a strange tense — 'would have'?"

"No, sir, we are not. I loathe humor, and you are humorous. This is a deadly serious world, this world of business. You are the intellectual type. I *despise* intellectual types. You are an improvident grasshopper, and I am an industrious squirrel. Nothing personal."

"If you are a squirrel," Bottomley snaps, "you're a very nutty one! You are also an unmitigated, pompous ass, *and* an expensive moron!"

However, the squirrel hears not, for, suddenly, he is once again no longer on the same plane, and the annoyed grasshopper takes his leave, but not before the great idea is born. Milady Soap sponsors the hit television and radio quiz program, *Masquerade for Money,* a double-or-nothing game show on which each contestant appears in a costume representing his or her favorite person or object. With Milady worth $40,000,000 Bottomley sets out to soak the company for every chunk of stock, every factory, every bar and flake of soap it owns.

He succeeds brilliantly. Introduced by that "joyful, jolly, jestful, jivy joker" quiz-master, Happy Hogan (Art Linkletter), Bottomley appears on the program dressed as a huge, leather-bound book.

"What are you supposed to be," the obnoxious knuckle-knob host inquires, "a bookie?"

"I am the encyclopedia."

"And the monocle?"

"Britannica," Beauregard smiles with benign self-assurance.

"Well, uh, may I ask your name?"

"You may."

"Well, well, what is your name, then?"

"Beauregard Bottomley."

"Would you — would you mind repeating that again?"

"I would mind, very much."

The walking encyclopedia unerringly answers question after question.

"You have five seconds to tell us the Japanese word for 'good-bye.'"

"'Sayonara,'" replies Bottomley, smiling confidently as he feels himself inspired by a gratuitous witticism: "Not to be confused with 'cyanide,' which is, of course, 'good-bye' in any language."

Bottomley calmly refuses to take his $320, insisting he'll come back the next week to double his winnings. Week after week he returns, soon becoming the hero of both television and radio. Backstage before one broadcast, he is introduced to the mighty Waters himself.

"Oh, yes, I've met Mr. Waters, in the well-upholstered torture chamber where he practices witchcraft over a bar of soap."

"Mr. Bottomley, I would like to thank you," the executive gushes. "Through you, we have (a) increased our ratings, (b) gotten quite a bit of publicity, and (c) we have doubled our sales!"

Bottomley regards Waters earnestly as he replies, "(d) I couldn't hear better news; (e) I hope the sales increase even more; and (f) it would *frighten* you if you knew why I feel this way!"

Beauregard's winnings soon hit the $40,000 mark, and the following week he'll be shooting for $80,000. In a desperate move, Waters cancels *Masquerade for Money*, but Bottomley, having no intention of ending the contest, refuses to accept a check for $40,000 and confidently predicts that both he and the program will soon be back on the air. And back they are, for when hundreds of Beauregard Bottomley fan clubs arise in protest, Milady's profits sink to a stunning $36. Beauregard soon increases his winnings to $10,000,000, decides it's time to acquaint himself with his future holdings, and pays a visit to Milady's main processing plant. With difficulty, Waters resists the homicidal impulse to shove his nemesis into a scalding cauldron of soap, and instead offers him the firm's vice-presidency.

"I've just had the greatest idea since the discovery of fire. I will bathe the world physically, and you will cleanse it mentally. Together we will bring about a spotless, sparkling world."

No soap. Bottomley rejects the proposal.

"Beauregard," coos Waters with utter insincerity, "it's terrible to have money. It's frightening to be wealthy. It's disastrous to be loaded. It is my sincere conviction that the only way to be happy is to be poor."

"My dear Burnbridge," Bottomley responds thoughtfully, "I see your point. I am about to make you the *happiest* man in the world!"

Enough is enough. Burnbridge Waters has tried to be fair, but it's time to live up to the nickname he earned in college: no, not "Sky Blue Waters" but "Dirty Waters" (now we see why he went into the soap racket in the first place). He determines to bore from within, reach in and twist, and *find* Bottomley's Achilles' heel. Happy Hogan, in this mess right up to his options, has already been assigned the task of romancing Gwenn, and discovers that her brother does have one weakness: he's always searched for the perfect woman. If that's what he wants, that's what he'll get: Flame O'Neil (Celeste Holm), a "corn-fed Mata Hari" with a mind as sharp as a razor, a woman who has everything — except a heart. Posing as a nurse sent by his fan club in Billings, Montana, to care for him when word leaks out

Barbara Britton, Ronald Colman, and Vincent Price discuss their next scene with scenarist Fred Brady and director Richard Whorf on the set of Champagne for Caesar.

that he's caught a slight cold, the elegant Miss O'Neil has been commissioned to drive Beauregard Bottomley to a disorganized state of bewildered confusion.

She lavishes her treacherous charms with a vengeance, and Bottomley soon falls hopelessly in love, scattering his erudition, logarithms, and Greek translations to the winds. Sister Gwenn takes a similar shine to that wisecracking moron, Happy Hogan, and by the time they all arrive at the studio for the next broadcast, Bottomley's mind is twisted, his nerves shot. Terribly distracted, he is asked the question on which $20,000,000 rides: "How does Einstein regard the space-time continuum?" His response is absolutely . . . wrong! The studio audience groans in dismay and disappointment.

Like a soaring eagle, triumph alights on Waters' face as he watches the proceedings from the control booth, until, moments later, he receives a long-distance telephone call.

"Hello?" he says, filled with self-congratulatory warmth. "What? Princeton, New Jersey? Who's calling? Oh, yes, a Professor Einstein for Happy Hogan. Have this switched to the stage phone." Brief pause as Price does a masterfully slow take. Then, as understanding dawns, he shrieks: "*Einstein?*"

That's right; the professor has called to affirm that Beauregard's answer was indeed correct! Amid tumultuous applause, Bottomley is hoisted onto the shoulders of his admirers and transported through the studio audience. Next week he'll be back for the entire cake of soap: $40,000,000. Dimitri Tiomkin's jubilant refrain quickly dissolves into a funeral dirge as Burnbridge Waters, who has collapsed, is borne out, like Hamlet's corpse, by executive-assistant pallbearers.

After the show, Bottomley heads straight for Flame's apartment. Suspecting that she had set him up, he had earlier confessed to her that his trouble with Einstein's theory had almost led to a mental and physical collapse. What he hadn't revealed was that he later spent an entire summer with the professor and finally mastered it. He arrives, finds his winsome temptress on the phone with Waters, snatches up a hairbrush, and turns her over his knee. Moments later, he sees the phone off the hook and picks up the receiver.

"Miss O'Neil is having Bottomley trouble!" he quips, hanging up the phone and kissing her harshly. Flame O'Neil has received her comeuppance, and has also fallen irretrievably in love.

Meanwhile, at his Milady headquarters, Burnbridge Waters is preparing to go down in a blaze of glory, and books the Hollywood Bowl for the final showdown. With appropriate fanfare and pageantry, it'll be the Twilight of the Gods! Valhalla!

"And like Romeo and Juliet," he murmurs to his secretary, "you and I will die together."

"You're *nuts!*" she screams, and flees the premises.

The big night arrives, with Gwenn fearful that Hogan simply wants to marry into $40,000,000, and Beauregard similarly apprehensive, despite Flame's insistence that now she truly loves him. The Hollywood Bowl is packed, and tension mounts as the historic event begins. Burnbridge Waters brings down the house: "May the best man — *lose!*" And then the big moment. Will Beauregard Bottomley be worth $40,000,000 — or nothing? The question he is asked couldn't be simpler — his own social security number — but this time his answer is legitimately wrong!

At home later, Bottomley can well afford to accept his "defeat" with dignity, for the doorbell soon rings: it's Burnbridge Waters with the beginning of a lifelong supply of champagne.

"Champagne for Caesar!" exclaims Beauregard.

"'Dirty Waters'!" Caesar squawks as the executive enters. "Champagne! Let's get loaded!" The mystery of Caesar's dark past is explained at last: Waters and the dissipated fowl had been roommates in college together.

Happy Hogan calls for Gwenn, and Flame arrives moments later, thus proving that neither of them had been interested in the money after all.

Flame and Beauregard drive off in a brand new convertible, a wedding gift from an exultant — and very generous — Burnbridge Waters. Moreover, Bottomley will also get a bit of stock and his own radio program. He had, we discover, made a deal with "Dirty Waters" and deliberately answered the final question incorrectly, to find out if Flame wanted him merely for his money. Oddly enough, he *hadn't* known his social security number.

After making no screen appearances for two years, Ronald Colman chose *Champagne for Caesar* as the best of many scripts he had been offered since his Academy Award–winning performance in *A Double Life*. With quiz programs flooding America at the beginning of the television age, he found the makings of a comedy hit in this delightfully charming spoof. Ably assisted by Vincent Price, Colman settled in, got down to business, and delivered some of the wittiest dialogue of his career.

Critics agreed that Colman's urbanity and lighthearted, bantering style were quite irresistible, but otherwise found the picture a heavy-handed misfire. To be sure, the film would have been more successful had the script been carefully pruned and tightened. Although Art Linkletter, for instance, was perfectly cast as the imbecilic quiz-show host, he fails miserably as a romantic lover, and why Barbara Britton falls for him is anybody's guess; their scenes together seem rather drawn out, intended merely to pad the length of the picture.

But there is no question that Vincent Price stole the show from Colman with his devastatingly flamboyant performance as the mad merchandizing giant whose style fluctuated between catatonic trance, calm assurance, and wildly gesticulating outbursts. When Waters' secretary, for example, suggests that they simply refuse to allow Bottomley on the program, the High Lama of Lather launches into an initially composed explication:

> "Let me explain something to you, my dear. If we take Mr. Bottomley off the show, the people who listen to our show wouldn't like the idea. If they don't like the idea, they won't listen to our show. If they don't listen to our show, *our sales will drop to nothing, and we will lose MONEY!* . . . I hope I — didn't upset you, my dear."

Champagne for Caesar was rather oddly distributed. Independent producer Harry M. Popkin paid his stars a flat fee when the film went into production, and promised them a second installment after the picture had been released. Following a brief theatrical release through United Artists, the film was quickly sold to television, and neither Colman nor any of his fellow performers ever received another penny for their efforts. Colman's daughter recalls that whenever her parents drove past Popkin's home in Beverly Hills, "Ronnie and Benita would shake their fists and we'd all join in with, 'That's where that son-of-a-bitch-Harry-Popkin-with-all-my-money used to live.'"[38]

Champagne for Caesar was decidedly ahead of its time. Its satiric thrusts at the questionable ethics of the business community—with its deadly serious charts, graphs, and production statistics—were largely unappreciated in 1950. But times have changed and, when seen today, despite its flaws in construction, the picture emerges as one of Colman's finest comedies. *The Devil to Pay* and *The Talk of the Town* were better crafted, but also decidedly less hilarious.

Around the World in 80 Days

1956. *Production:* Michael Todd Company, Inc. *Distribution:* United Artists Corporation. *Producer:* Michael Todd. *Director:* Michael Anderson. *Screenplay:* S.J. Perelman, James Poe, John Farrow (from the novel by Jules Verne). *Cinematographer:* Lionel Lindon (Todd-AO Process and Eastman Color). *Todd-AO Consultant:* Schuyler A. Sanford. *Special Effects:* Lee Zavitz. *Musical Score:* Victor Young. *Art Directors:* James W. Sullivan, Ken Adams, Julio Molina. *Set Decorations:* Ross Dowd. *Costumes:* Miles White, Anna Duse, M. Cottin, Mme. Rey. *Choreographer:* Paul Godkin. *Documentary Unit Director:* Sidney Smith. *Parisian, Middle Eastern, and Asian Unit Director:* Kevin O'Donovan McClory. *Unit Manager:* Frank Fox. *Screen Credits:* Saul Bass. *Associate Producers:* William Cameron Menzies, Kevin O'Donovan McClory. *Executive Assistant:* Samuel Lambert. *Film Editor:* Paul Weatherwax. *Sound:* Joseph Kane. Prologue contains sequences from the 1902 Georges Méliès version of Jules Verne's *A Trip to the Moon. Running Time:* 175 minutes. *Release Date:* October 17, 1956.

Cast: David Niven (Phileas Fogg), Cantinflas (Passepartout), Shirley MacLaine (Princess Aouda), Robert Newton (Inspector Fix). With cameo appearances by Charles Boyer (M. Gasse), Joe E. Brown (Station Master), Martine Carol (Girl in Railroad Station), John Carradine (Colonel Proctor), Charles Coburn (Steamship Office Clerk), Ronald Colman (Great Indian Peninsular Railway Official), Melville Cooper (Steward), Noël Coward (Roland Hesketh-Baggott), Finlay Currie (Member of the Reform Club), Reginald Denny (Police Inspector), Andy Devine (First Mate), Marlene Dietrich (Saloon Owner), Luis Miguel Domingúin (Bullfighter), Fernandel (Coachman), Sir John Gielgud (Foster), Hermione Gingold (Tart), José Greco (Dancer), Sir Cedric Hardwicke (Sir Francis Cromarty), Trevor Howard (Fallentin), Glynis Johns (Tart), Buster Keaton (Train Conductor), Evelyn Keyes (Tart), Beatrice Lillie (Revivalist Leader), Peter Lorre (Japanese Steward), Edmund Lowe (Chief Engineer), A.E. Matthews (Billiard Player), Mike Mazurki (Drunk), Tim McCoy (U.S. Cavalry Commander), Victor McLaglen (Helmsman), John Mills (Cabby), Robert Morley (Ralph), Edward R. Murrow (Prologue Commentator), Alan Mowbray (British Consul), Jack Oakie (Captain), George Raft (Bouncer), Gilbert Roland (Achmed Abdullah), Cesar Romero (Henchman), Frank Sinatra (Piano Player), Red Skelton (Drunk), Ronald Squire (Member of the Reform Club), Basil Sydney (Member of the Reform Club), Harcourt Williams (Hinshaw).

The most star-studded entertainment extravaganza ever unleashed on mankind, *Around the World in 80 Days* was the bombastic brainchild of gambler, con man, and master showman Mike Todd. With the ambition and brashness of D.W. Griffith and Cecil B. De Mille combined, this colossal Hollywood phenomenon decided to produce a high-flying, earth-shaking rendition of Jules Verne's 1873 novel concerning the singular global undertakings of that intrepid adventurer, Phileas Fogg, and his antic manservant, Passepartout.

No back lots for Mike Todd: he intended to follow them literally around the world. During the next 12 months he spent $6,000,000; employed 68,894 people and 33 assistant directors; traveled 4,000,000 miles to 13 different countries; shot 680,000 feet of color film; conned, cajoled, and prodded 42 internationally renowned actors and actresses into appearing in bit parts which he called "cameos"; and shot the works in the magnificent Todd-AO process, the revolutionary wide-screen format which he himself had pioneered in the early fifties.[39] And what made this prodigious array of wonder and splendor all the more impressive was the fact that this was his first motion picture.[40]

Genial Englishman David Niven (for years one of Ronald Colman's closest friends) heads the cast as Phileas Fogg, that elegant gentleman of noble countenance who attempts to win a bet of 20,000 pounds by circling the globe in the miraculously short span of 80 days. Witty, urbane, and imperturbably British, Niven makes the perfect Fogg, full of abundant good humor and diverting charm. Mexico's beloved Cantinflas, that magnificent actor, comedian, pantomimist, and matador, was lured to Hollywood to portray Passepartout, Fogg's loyal valet. Whether burlesquing bullfighting in Spain or getting soused and shanghaied in Hong Kong, Cantinflas' performance is one of the cinema's great comedic ballets, reminiscent of Chaplin at his best. His zany antics make Passepartout the most unlikely, and funniest, soldier of fortune in recent screen history. Gifted English actor Robert Newton shines as Inspector Fix, the indefatigable Scotland Yard sleuth who, convinced that Fogg has robbed the Bank of England, shadows the pair to the ends of the earth. As their comic nemesis, Newton — with booming laughter, a wink, and a leer — turns in his finest performance. Shirley MacLaine shares the bill as the beautiful Princess Aouda, whom the sojourners rescue from being burned at the stake in an Indian suttee ceremony, and who joins them for the rest of their journey. The whimsical, pixieish nature of this lovely newcomer gives her co-stars a run for their money.

David Niven had never met Mike Todd before the legendary theatrical impresario offered him the leading role in *Around the World in 80 Days.* As Niven recalled it, their conversation was as follows:

"Ever heard of Jules Verne?" Todd glibly inquired.

"Yes, of course."

"Ever read *Around the World in Eighty Days?*"

"I was weaned on it."

"I've never made a picture before, but I'm gonna make this one. . . . How'd you like to play Phileas Fogg?"

"I'd do it for nothing," the overeager actor blurted, his heart bounding.

"You gotta deal," Todd boomed, grasping Niven's hand.

It took Niven several weeks to get money tossed into the contract, he remembers with a twinkle in his eye.[41]

Niven urged Todd to hire Robert Newton for the part of Inspector Fix, but warned the producer that Newton's heavy drinking might create a problem, begging him not to relate the source of the information. Todd interviewed Newton in Niven's presence and went into his routine.

"Ever heard of Jules Verne?"

"Ah, dear fellow," Newton bubbled, "what a scribe!"

"*Eighty Days Around the World?*"

"A glorious piece, old cock."

"How'd you like to play Mr. Fix?"

"A splendid role," Newton replied, rolling his eyes. "Do I understand you are offering it to me, dear boy?"

"I might," said Todd, "but your pal Niven, here, says you're a lush."

"Aah! My pal Niven is a master of the understatement."

Newton was immediately hired, and gave his word of honor that he would not touch a drop until the picture was finished. The promise was kept, but Newton went on a bender immediately thereafter, and dropped dead of a heart attack a month later.[42]

Ronald Colman was offered the choice of a token check or a new yellow Cadillac for his afternoon's work. Colman already had enough money; he took the Cadillac. When a woman later asked him whether he had received the automobile for working just half a day, Colman cocked an eyebrow and replied, "Not at all, madam, for the work of a lifetime!"[43]

The story of Phileas Fogg's frantic race against time is so well known that a catalogue of his adventures is unnecessary. One incident, however, bears close scrutiny here. Fogg, Passepartout, and a stuffy brigadier general, Sir Francis Cromarty (Sir Cedric Hardwicke), are coursing through India, when their train screeches to an abrupt halt in the thick of the jungle. Alighting, Fogg approaches a railway official attired in a spotless white uniform and asks wherein lies the difficulty.

"Difficulty?" the official replies, turning around and revealing himself to be Ronald Colman. "None whatever. This is the end of the line. There is still fifty miles of track to be laid between here and Allahabad."

"But the London newspapers announced the opening of this railway throughout," Fogg insists.

"Must have been the *Daily Telegraph*," the official laughs. "Never would have read that in the *Times.*"

The travelers inquire about some other possible form of conveyance — an elephant, perhaps.

"Well, I do happen to know of one, but I doubt if the owner would part with her. She sleeps in the house with the family . . . a pet."

Colman, appearing for but one minute as a gentlemanly British official of the Great Indian Peninsular Railway, could not have been more appropriately cast, for all his gifts of charm, presence, and characteristic good humor are showcased in that scant 60 seconds. His brief cameo arouses "feelings of nostalgia combined with the deepest respect,"[44] for this was indeed the end of the line. In a symbolic sense, Colman's appearance marks not only the end of the line for the British Empire, with which his many roles had often been so closely associated, but also for the type of picture he had contributed so richly to for more than a generation and the kind of gentlemanly characterization he had personified for as many years. Thus his brief stint here serves as a fitting farewell to his own screen career, for it seemed to symbolize those qualities with which he made his mark on screen history.

"The style of what I used to do is gone," Colman remarked in one of his last interviews, "the old Romantic film, the classics."[45] And, "My kind of picture is gone. Romance on the screen seems to have gone into an eclipse; so has noblesse oblige, the tradition of the gentleman, the scholar, the poised, elegantly styled adventurer whose heart is essentially in the right place."[46]

The cinema is the dwelling place of wonder, and *Around the World in 80 Days* proved it in a big way. Among the staggering number of "firsts" with which Mike Todd shattered records and precedents are the following: it sported the most stars ever to appear in a film — 46; the most people photographed in separate world-wide locations — 68,894 in 13 different countries; the most miles traveled to make a picture — 4,000,000 (5,500,000 including passengers and freight); the most sets — 140 actual location sets, in addition to the stages of six major Hollywood studios as well as studios in England, Hong Kong, and Japan; the most camera set-ups — 2,000; the most costumes — 74,685; the most assistant directors — 33; and more species of animals photographed in their natural habitats — 34 different species, a total of 7,959 in all.[47]

Stories of the bulldozing tactics that netted Todd 42 top name stars for cameo appearances are legion. Marlene Dietrich, George Raft, Red Skelton, and Frank Sinatra, for instance, appear together in a San Francisco honkytonk, and the crew of Jack Oakie's Liverpool-bound merchant steamer includes Victor McLaglen, Edmund Lowe, and Andy Devine. And so it goes. When a Screen Actors' Guild representative learned what Todd had pulled off, he exclaimed, "Good heavens, Todd! You've made extras of all the stars in Hollywood. There's no precedent for it."[48] He was right; there wasn't.

Mike Todd's solid showmanship paid off handsomely at the box office, making it one of the biggest money-makers of all time, and it was the hit of the year with the critics as well, who unfurled in its praise every superlative they could find. Full of variety and excitement, it appealed to lovers of just about anything because it had just about everything in it. Nabbing no fewer than five Academy Awards—Best Picture, Best Adapted Screen Play, Best Color Cinematography, Best Music Score, and Best Film Editing—in addition to nominations for Best Direction, Best Costumes, and Best Art Direction, it was also named best picture of the year by the New York Film Critics, the National Board of Review, and the Associated Press.

Clean, clever, and classy; the super-spectacle to end all super-spectacles. It was, undeniably, quite a show. But was it cinema magic at its best?

Seen today, it is clear that the use of famous stars in cameo roles amounts to little more than a gimmick, a running recognition game designed to keep viewers on their toes, if not on the edges of their seats, and that the giant-screen panoramics were inserted primarily to exploit the more spectacular aspects of the new Todd-AO process, giving the picture the quality of a somewhat glorified, eccentric travelogue. Most critics seemed not to notice; few cared. One who did was Bosley Crowther, who complained that Todd's "unities of content and method are not detectable in his splattered form."[49] Five years later, Ezra Goodman called it "a circus on celluloid with little film-making finesse."[50]

Gigantism run amok, perhaps. Still, the cast was superb, and S.J. Perelman's script was witty and nimble throughout. So although the picture may not be a masterpiece any way you take it, that it provided thrilling entertainment brooks no denial.

The Story of Mankind

1957. *Production:* Cambridge Productions. *Distribution:* Warner Bros. Pictures, Inc. *Producer and director:* Irwin Allen. *Screenplay:* Irwin Allen, Charles Bennett (from the book by Hendrik Willem van Loon). *Director of Cinematography:* Nick Musuraca (Technicolor). *Technicolor Color Consultant:* Robert Brower. *Musical Score:* Paul Sawtell. *Art Director:* Art Loel. *Set Decorations:* Arthur Krams. *Costumes:* Marjorie Best. *Research:* Jean McChesney. *Technical Advisor:* Ruth K. Greenfield. *Associate Producer:* George E. Swink. *Assistant Director:* Joseph Don Page. *Supervising Film Editor:* Roland Gross. *Film Editor:* Gene Palmer. *Sound:* Stanley Jones. *Running Time:* 100 minutes. *Release Date:* November 8, 1957.

Cast: Ronald Colman (The Spirit of Man), Vincent Price (Mr. Scratch), Sir Cedric Hardwicke (High Judge), Hedy Lamarr (Joan of Arc), Groucho Marx (Peter Minuit), Harpo Marx (Isaac Newton), Chico Marx (Monk), Virginia Mayo (Cleopatra), Agnes Moorehead (Queen Elizabeth), Peter Lorre (Nero), Charles

Coburn (Hippocrates), Cesar Romero (Spanish Envoy), John Carradine (Khufu), Dennis Hopper (Napoleon), Marie Wilson (Marie Antoinette), Helmut Dantine (Antony), Edward Everett Horton (Sir Walter Raleigh), Reginald Gardiner (William Shakespeare), Marie Windsor (Josephine), George E. Stone (Waiter), Cathy O'Donnell (Early Christian Woman), Melville Cooper (Major Domo), Henry Daniell (Bishop of Beauvais), Francis X. Bushman (Moses), Franklin Pangborn (Marquis de Varennes), Jim Ameche (Alexander Graham Bell), Nick Cravat (Apprentice), Dani Crayne (Helen of Troy), Anthony Dexter (Christopher Columbus), Austin Green (Abraham Lincoln), Alexander Lockwood (Promoter), Melinda Marx (Early Christian Child), Bart Mattson (Cleopatra's Brother), Don Megowan (Early Man), Marvin Miller (Armana), Nancy Miller (Early Woman), Leonard Mudie (Chief Inquisitor), Reginald Sheffield (Julius Caesar), Abraham Sofaer (Indian Chief), Bobby Watson (Adolf Hitler), Major Sam Harris (Nobleman in Queen Elizabeth's Court), David Bond, Richard Cutting, Toni Gerry, Eden Hartford, Burt Nelson, Tudor Owen, Ziva Rodann, Harry Ruby, William Schallert.

This embarrassing, pseudo-historical monstrosity begins somewhere in outer space, and it should have stayed there.

The fate of mankind hangs in the balance, for a heavenly tribunal has been convened up in the clouds to decide whether to allow the human race to perish by its own sword—the newly invented Super H-Bomb, set to destroy the earth at any moment.

A billowing puff of scarlet smoke heralds the arrival of Mr. Scratch, a rude and improper individual of many talents and traits—all bad—played with superb, flamboyant malevolence by Vincent Price. If this satanic emissary has his way, the earth will be blown to smithereens.

Chosen to speak in mankind's behalf is a wanderer through time, a combination of all men of all times—"the pious and the fallen, the bold and the meek, the dreamers and the builders, the chaste and the guilty, the great and the small"—all represented by one, who comes to speak for all: the Spirit of Man, embodied in Ronald Colman. With no fanfare save his eloquence, this compassionate, honorable defender of man's potential argues that mankind should be granted one last chance to avoid the final nuclear holocaust:

"Man was created in the image of God. But there the similarity ends. Mortal, not immortal, are we. Of the flesh, not of the spirit, are we. Human, not godlike, are we. But whatever our sins, whatever our shortcomings, we believe the good deeds done by man on Earth far outweigh the bad, thereby earning him the right to survive. If goodness be its own reward, let there be a tomorrow on the planet Earth."

And so it comes to pass that these adversaries, observed from above, journey to Earth to review the course of human development during all periods of time since the world began. The evidence they present will determine whether man shall further inherit the earth through Heaven's intervention, or whether he shall be permitted to blast himself to eternity.

The colorful panorama unfolds.

From the violence of the earliest caveman to the horrors of twentieth-century global war, Mr. Scratch presses his case unremittingly, highlighting the evil of the human race since the beginning of time: villainous, twisted minds have begat endless orgies of hatred and destruction, from the bloody victories of ancient Egypt and the tormented lunacies of Nero to the darkened madness of Attila the Hun and the despotism of Napoleon and Hitler—a chilling indictment of mankind's bigotry and fratricidal wickedness through the ages; a criminal cruelty the likes of which even the venerable Mr. Scratch himself could not have surpassed. Instant annihilation is man's most fitting reward. Surely he has earned it.

But the Spirit of Man listens to other voices than Nero's depraved ramblings, and traces the birth of reason, progress, and social consciousness:

> "We inherited the earth, and were blessed with certain rare gifts—the capacity to speak, to think, to reason; the ability to walk erect, on two solid arches. We were fruitful; we multiplied. We were resourceful; we replenished the earth and subdued it. These were the covenants; these we fulfilled."

After an infinity of groping in the darkness came the first dawning of hope: the ancient world produced Moses, a simple man of God who set his people free from the land of the godless, and the Golden Age of Greece with its great philosophers—Socrates, and his doctrines of universal humanity; Plato, with his love of beauty, truth, and justice; Aristotle, the first great scientist; Hippocrates, the Father of Medicine. After hundreds of years of lawlessness, a miraculous recovery at Runnymede: the Magna Carta, cornerstone of law, order, and the sacredness of civil liberties. Then came the Renaissance and a great burst of human expression—the classic writings of Dante, Boccaccio, and Petrarch; the architecture and art of Titian, Michelangelo, and Leonardo. Columbus and a new spirit of adventure. Men of honor in a new land—Washington, Jefferson, Franklin, Adams, Lincoln, Bell, and Edison; the internal combustion engine and the brothers Wright.

"Man's inherent goodness is strong enough to rise above the bad," the Spirit of Man concludes, "even if both are born in the same place."

As the great heavenly clock ticks away, warring armies already move against one another on Earth. Having carefully weighed the good of man against the bad, the celestial judge (Sir Cedric Hardwicke) determines that the scales are balanced much too evenly, reserving final judgment in order to allow mankind more time to set its house in order.

Eternal life or Super H-Bomb oblivion? By this time, who cares? An intriguing premise indeed, but one which unfortunately betrays the heavy-handed effort of co-author, producer, and director Irwin Allen to convey an edifying message while making as much money as possible.[51] Producers had been addle-headed before, and this one was well up to form. Letting his wildest fantasies rip, Allen assembled a battery of famous stars to appear in cameo roles as the great personalities of history, "which for the sheer inspired lunacy of its casting deserves a place in cinema annals."[52] Stumbling through this pompous charade are the likes of Hedy Lamarr as Joan of Arc, Peter Lorre as Nero, Edward Everett Horton as Sir Walter Raleigh, and Dennis Hopper as Napoleon. And sandwiched in for good measure is enough stock footage of battle and carnage scenes lifted from old Warner Bros. historical extravaganzas to choke the Roman Empire — bathetic, wearisome, and all the more killingly monotonous when contrasted with the elevating, literate encounters between Messrs. Colman and Price. Nothing was cut, but almost everything in this mindless mess should have been; rambling and trivial, plodding from one dumb scene to another, the result is intellectually about as deep as a cookie sheet.

Occasionally the eccentric casting works. Harpo Marx's harp-strumming portrayal of Isaac Newton, featuring a malicious apple which bonks him on the head and produces the Great Idea, is marvelous stuff, as is brother Groucho's swindling of the Indians out of Manhattan:

"How!" the chief greets him.

"Three minutes, and leave 'em in the shell!" Pilgrim-Groucho shoots back.

"What?"

"No, not what; how!"

And in a diverting aside, Colman effectively capitalizes on Vincent Price's reputation as a well-known connoisseur of art when he regards Leonardo's *The Last Supper* and remarks:

"The trouble with you, Mr. Scratch, is that you know nothing about painting."

"I've never pretended to be an art expert," is the bemused reply.

But although the film was accepted as amusing nonsense by those who saw it, audiences were unable to decide whether this ambivalent confection was drama, comedy, or simply horror. Not knowing how to take it, the public simply didn't. It bombed at the box office and produced a spiritual shudder from the critics as well, who found it a long-winded, tasteless pastiche, "lacking in punch, sophistication and a consistent point of view."[53] It has not aged well in the intervening years, and when seen today it is as apt to produce a succession of groans and guffaws as anything else.

The whole venture was so witless under Allen's non-direction that it would be kinder to say no more and merely let it sleep, were it not for the fact that there were good things in it. Ronald Colman acquitted himself with distinction as the Spirit of Man, though he was terribly disappointed in the finished film. Already familiar with Hendrik van Loon's popular account of man's past, he had optimistically embraced the role which was to mark his final appearance on the screen. But after battling it out before the celestial court of history with close friends Vincent Price and Sir Cedric Hardwicke, he saw the completed product and its mountains of wildly incongruous, puerile stock footage—a vulgarized travesty of what had begun as a thoughtful, uplifting production. Perhaps realizing that, had it been carefully pruned, it might have found a higher place among his works than it obviously would, Colman succinctly summed up the problem when asked whence the story came: "From the jacket of the book by the same name by Hendrik van Loon."[54]

While one regrets that the abilities and energies of an actor of the Colman stamp were wasted upon such a project, there is no denying that his performance, together with that of Vincent Price, improved the film considerably. Ever youthful in appearance and carrying his 66 years as easily as most men carry 46, Colman was ideal and inspiring as "the poised, urbane and eminently distinguished Spirit of Man—a role which fitted Colman like a glove, since in almost every respect he was playing himself."[55] It seemed appropriate that the image should meet the man in this final screen appearance, for it showcased all the archetypal qualities which the durable star had personified in his many portrayals for nearly four decades. Gentlemanly, virtuous, and honorable to the last, Ronald Colman was truly the spirit of man as he bade his faithful public a grateful farewell. With his past achievements to recommend him, and the reminder of past successes after which to strive, he didn't let himself or his reputation down.

VII

Of Shadow and Substance —
The Legacy of Ronald Colman

"He represented to filmgoers all over the world all that typified the English gentleman."[1] His name alone on a marquee gathered crowds, the title of the picture almost irrelevant. Ronald Colman expressed in his films, as he did in his private life, faith in a system of values that has all but evaporated over the last third of a century. His was a voice which cried out for an earlier, simpler era in which honor, chivalry, and gentility supplied order and grace to the world. His standards provided reassurance that such things were still possible. The virtues of uncompromising integrity, strength of purpose, and generosity of mind defined his character, sustained his popularity, and made him one of the cinema's chief attractions for nearly 40 years.

Colman became a hero in the less cynical twenties, thirties, and forties. But, unlike Clark Gable and Humphrey Bogart, he failed to become a "cult" figure in the sixties, seventies, and eighties, because his *type* had gone quite out of fashion in an essentially anti-heroic age. The English gentleman, whose ranks include David Niven, Laurence Olivier, Brian Aherne, Clive Brook, Leslie Howard, and even Douglas Fairbanks, Jr. (an American), still evokes an affectionate nostalgia for older viewers, but younger movie enthusiasts do not as readily accept the qualities of courteous, soft-spoken heroes. Gable and Bogart, if not exclusively anti-heroic, present a sharper, more brittle edge which makes them more adaptable to today's tastes.

Colman was without question the leader of that small but select band of "gentleman" heroes, and, while retaining a strong following in Europe, became the most famous Englishman on American screens since Charlie Chaplin. In part, his mystique was

291

RONALD COLMAN
1891 — 1958

OUR REVELS NOW ARE ENDED.
THESE OUR ACTORS.
AS I FORETOLD YOU.
WERE ALL SPIRITS.
AND ARE MELTED INTO AIR.
INTO THIN AIR.
WE ARE SUCH STUFF
AS DREAMS ARE MADE ON;
AND OUR LITTLE LIFE
IS ROUNDED WITH A SLEEP.

Ronald Colman's tombstone in Santa Barbara, California. (Photograph by R. Dixon Smith)

an "Englishness" peculiar to the silver screen, and specifically to the Hollywood silver screen. Whether Englishmen ever existed in real-life with quite Colman's brand of good looks, derring-do, olde worlde courtesy and saleable mysticism is altogether another story....[2]

An actor's star quality is the stuff of cinematic myth, and the list of Hollywood stars who were influenced by Colman's physical appearance and who grew Colman moustaches is long: Niven, Flynn, Olivier, and a host of others come immediately to mind. But if Colman's conviction and sincerity were the essence of his stardom and made him the movies' greatest gentleman hero, how are we to regard his accomplishments today? Most actors enjoy ten-year spans of popularity, only to level off as tastes change and the world moves on; Colman continued to deliver for 40 years, rarely suggesting severe self-discipline, always exhibiting a confirmed indifference to the trappings of stardom. Many proclaimed him one of the most polished actors of his time; others insisted that he simply portrayed Ronald Colman in whatever part he played. As Raymond Massey commented,

> Ronnie had a genuine acting talent which received far too little recognition from the critics. His performances seemed so smooth and effortless that his acting was taken for granted. But this naturalness and ease were the result of meticulous preparation and technical skill. He always reminded me of Gerald du Maurier; both men made acting look so easy. One had only to see untalented imitations of their style to realize how good they were.[3]

Vincent Price agrees:

> When I first became a part of his profession, I was sent to a drama coach to study his and Charles Boyer's technique, for according to her, they were able to convey everything with the greatest economy and to resolve most of the problem of motion picture acting in the eyes. . . . So Ronnie became not just an actor for me, but a way of life.[4]

Colman's general air of uncontrived elegance and jaunty self-assurance contributed to the creation of characters consistently and immediately recognizable as Colman "types," beyond the unique variations he brought to each role. As Brian Aherne observed,

> There are two kinds of actors. There are those who, like Ronald Colman, Gary Cooper, Clark Gable, James Stewart, John Wayne, and Cary Grant, play themselves and continue to do so in every part, to the great delight of the producers, the stockholders, their fans, and their bank managers. There are also those, like Paul Muni, Laurence Olivier, Alec Guinness, and Rex Harrison, who are not interested in projecting their own personalities but in trying to look and sound like the characters they have to play. . . .[5]

Because Carton, for instance, was so well drawn, audiences already knew what to expect from Conway, Rassendyll, Heldar, and Rainier. The effect was cumulative: Carton's pain is felt in Heldar; his lightheartedness in Rassendyll; his depth in Conway.

Colman's flair for comedy has been widely touted, yet when it is overemphasized, one underestimates his dramatic range. Certainly the comic ability exists, but it is only the frosting on the cake. In *The Devil to Pay,* for example, he alights from a cab, spots an elderly woman, and grasps her elbows. "Have no fear for the day," he assures her; "you look divine!"

Yet such lightheartedness and charm, even coupled with good looks and a smooth stream of faultless English, simply do not explain Colman's enduring popularity. Consider, for instance, Herbert Marshall, another Englishman whose similarly modulated voice failed to make him a Colman-level star, though he did very well in his way.

What, then, is the cake? Restraint, understatement, and subtlety, in conjunction with personal charisma. It was the light and unselfconscious way he carried himself that made him so appealing and which made his conflicts so much more deeply felt by his public. It was easy for men to feel that he was within their reach as a model—smooth and suave, yet able to suffer the same self-doubts and pangs of love that every sensitive man experiences. And for women, he represented the best of all possible lovers: physically devastating and adroit, yet revealing a sense of romantic incompleteness, that sad but uncomplaining look in his eyes which made every female on the block want to protect him. Perhaps the most recurrent motif which shaped the Colman image was the perpetual struggle between love and honor and duty—what one *wants* to do versus what one *ought* to do. In *Beau Geste* and *Under Two Flags*, he is driven into exile and adventure because honor and duty demand it; in *The Masquerader* and *The Prisoner of Zenda*, he is willing to renounce the woman he loves because he has filled another man's shoes; in *A Tale of Two Cities*, he goes to the guillotine to fulfill a promise he had made to another man's wife. Passion thus repressed by alternative drives made women viewers feel deliciously frustrated—if only someone like *him* loved *me* like *that*!

Like Fairbanks and Flynn, Colman graced the silver screen as the gallant knight-errant who, with complete aplomb, tilted against dragons, rescued damsels in distress, righted wrongs without count of gain or cost, and, in general, did fine deeds finely. Forever faithful to the trust, he epitomized the romantic hero as ultimate salvation. Rarely does an audience get to see an actor's soul at work, but one can if one watches Colman's face and eyes and listens to his soft-spoken words; one can almost touch the thought that has been transposed into cinematic terms. Within his pictures, one discovers some of Hollywood's most unforgettable moments: Beau's death in the desert, Carton climbing the scaffold steps, Conway battling through the snow, Rassendyll's farewell to Flavia,[6] Heldar going blind, Rainier reunited with Paula, Anthony John's final performance and suicide.

The past becomes legend, and Colman's genial, well-mannered earnestness passes from the scene. And yet, his style doesn't become dated. If one sifts the world's cinema of romance and adventure, Colman remains; sift Colman, and *A Tale of Two Cities* remains; sift *A Tale of Two Cities*, and Sydney Carton's closing lines remain. His films have been remade, but the original magic has never been recaptured; *Beau Geste, A Tale of Two Cities, Lost Horizon,* and *The Prisoner of Zenda* have been copied, duplicated, imitated, and simulated, but rarely equaled, never surpassed. Although the most famous of his pictures are occasionally reissued, both theatrically and on television, Ronald Colman is less well remembered today than he ought to be, but his work will continue to attract cineastes as long as motion pictures hold any attraction. As a young man of 25, struggling with the conflicting options of either entering the diplomatic service or becoming an actor, Colman dreamt, as do most young men, of becoming a hero, a beau ideal — and then he lived it out through his films.

As an indication of the extent to which Colman's brand of poetic romanticism is still capable of enthralling younger audiences, the author recalls a Minneapolis screening of *The Talk of the Town* several years ago. As he left the theatre after watching Colman cavort with Cary Grant and Jean Arthur, he overheard a teenaged girl remark, "Oh, Mother, wasn't Ronald Colman wonderful."

She was right.

He was.

Notes

I. Before the Films Beckoned

1. Cited in David Niven, *The Moon's a Balloon* (New York: Putnam, 1972), p. 147.
2. Walter Kerr, *The Silent Clowns* (New York: Knopf, 1975), p. 11.
3. Roland Wild, *Ronald Colman* (London: Rich & Cowan, 1933), p. 7.
4. *Ibid.*, p. 5.
5. Cited in Edward R. Sammis, "The Dark Angel of the Films," *Paris and Hollywood Screen Secrets* (Vol. 4, No. 35, February, 1928), p. 49.
6. Juliet Benita Colman, *Ronald Colman: A Very Private Person* (New York: Morrow, 1975), p. v. The claim has been made that Colman was severely gassed at the time he sustained his wounds, and that "this gave rise to the lung complaint which was to remain with him until the end of his life—certainly it contributed to the singular 'fragility' of the famous Colman voice." See Julian Fox, "Colman," *Films and Filming* (Vol. 18, No. 6, March, 1972), p. 27. The actor's daughter, however, reports that the gassing incident is a myth. See Colman, p. 11. Gas was not used, of course, until later in the war.
7. Cited in Colman, p. 13.
8. Cited in Sammis, p. 49.
9. Cited in Fox, p. 27.

II. The Early Silents

1. Approximately 75 percent of all silent films are presumed lost. Until the early fifties, the chemical base of the emulsion which reproduces the photographic image on the celluloid was nitrate, which is both highly inflammable and unstable; it decomposes and disintegrates, first to jelly and then to dust, if not properly stored in temperature-regulated vaults with proper exposure to air. Most studios, through neglect or plain destruction, have allowed prints and master negatives to smoulder away or be incinerated, once a picture has made its profit.

2. Cited in Fox, p. 27.

3. Colman had seen his first motion picture in 1907 at the age of 16, in a carnival sideshow at the Earl's Court Exhibition.

4. British pictures were invariably inferior to the American product which flooded the British market during these years. (It is hoped that this will not arouse growls from the British side.)

5. Cited in Colman, p. 25.

6. Cited in Fox, p. 28.

7. Colman later credited Harding with teaching him a great deal about the art of acting. Harding, like Colman, also emigrated to America and finally landed in Hollywood.

8. Cited in Sammis, p. 49.

9. Cited in Fox, p. 28.

10. Cited in Colman, p. 31.

11. *Ibid.*, p. 34.

12. *Ibid.*, p. 35.

13. *Ibid.*

14. Lillian Gish with Ann Pinchot, *The Movies, Mr. Griffith, and Me* (Englewood Cliffs, N.J.: Prentice-Hall, 1969), p. 253.

15. Henry King was to direct four more Colman pictures: *Romola, Stella Dallas,* and two Colman-Banky vehicles, *The Winning of Barbara Worth* and *The Magic Flame.*

16. Cited in Lawrence J. Quirk, *The Films of Ronald Colman* (Secaucus, N.J.: Citadel, 1977), p. 16.

17. Cited in Fox, p. 28.

18. *Ibid.*, p. 27.

19. Cited in Colman, p. 19.

20. Cited in Quirk, p. 26.

21. *Ibid.*, pp. 26–27.

22. According to one source, the murder victim was the lover's uncle. See *ibid.*

23. Cited in *ibid.*

24. Cited in *ibid.*, p. 28.

25. Cited in Colman, p. 26.

26. Cited in Quirk, p. 28.

27. Cited in *ibid.*, p. 29.

28. Cited in Fox, p. 28.

29. Cited in Quirk, p. 29.

30. *Ibid.*

31. Fox, p. 28.

32. Cited in Quirk, p. 30.

33. Cited in *ibid.*, p. 33.

34. *Ibid.*, p. 34.

35. Cited in Kevin Brownlow, *The Parade's Gone By* (New York: Knopf, 1968), p. 112.

36. *Ibid.*, p. 110.

37. *Ibid.*, pp. 109–110.

38. Cited in Colman, p. 38.

39. Cited in Gish, p. 252.

40. *Ibid.*

41. *Ibid.*, p. 256.

42. Cited in Colman, p. 43.

43. Cited in Quirk, p. 48.
44. *Ibid.*
45. *New York Times,* June 10, 1924, p. 24.
46. *New York Times,* December 2, 1924, p. 13.
47. Cited in Lillian Gish, *Dorothy and Lillian Gish* (New York: Scribner's, 1973), p. 132.
48. *Ibid.*
49. See Edward Wagenknecht, *The Movies in the Age of Innocence* (New York: Ballantine, 1971), p. 246.
50. The new, highly sensitive panchromatic stock, used effectively by Overbaugh for the exteriors of *The White Sister,* was used exclusively on *Romola,* with even more spectacular results.

III. The Early Goldwyn Years—The Image Is Shaped

1. Cited in Sammis, p. 50.
2. Fox, p. 30.
3. Cited in Colman, pp. 61–62.
4. *Ibid.,* p. 98.
5. *Ibid.,* p. 74.
6. Fox, p. 28.
7. Cited in Colman, p. 72.
8. She made *The Awakening* with Walter Byron and then *This Is Heaven,* which paired her with James Hall, but after a desultory talkie with Edward G. Robinson in 1930, she drifted comfortably into semi-retirement and finally faded out of sight forever soon after the onset of the talkie era. Goldwyn tried to correct her faulty English, but the thick Hungarian accent wouldn't budge, and the producer finally gave up and settled her contract by paying her a reported $1,000,000. Vilma Banky remained happily married to Rod La Rocque until the actor's death in 1969, her romantic legend still intact.
9. Cited in Colman, p. 80.
10. President of the Motion Picture Producers and Distributors Association since 1922, Will H. Hays, former Postmaster-General under President Warren G. Harding, was the industry's self-imposed censor and moral arbiter.
11. Also in the cast was William Boyd, destined to gain fame a decade later as Hopalong Cassidy.
12. *New York Times,* October 13, 1924, p. 21.
13. Cited in Alvin H. Marill, *Samuel Goldwyn Presents* (New York: Barnes, 1976), p. 47.
14. Still another Talmadge sister, Natalie, was married to Buster Keaton.
15. While in production, the film was tentatively titled *Heart Trouble.*
16. Quirk, p. 60.
17. Cited in Quirk, p. 59.
18. *Ibid.,* p. 60.
19. Mordaunt Hall in the *New York Times,* January 26, 1925, p. 14.
20. Cited in Quirk, p. 66.
21. Interview, Blanche Sweet with author, December 26, 1979.
22. Cited in Quirk, p. 73.
23. Interview, Blanche Sweet with author, December 26, 1979.

24. *New York Times*, May 11, 1925, p. 14.
25. Mordaunt Hall in the *New York Times*, April 13, 1925, p. 24.
26. *Ibid.*
27. *Ibid.*
28. Interview, Blanche Sweet with author, December 26, 1979.
29. Cited in Quirk, p. 78.
30. Cited in Colman, p. 55. So convincing was Colman's performance that he soon found himself deluged with Braille texts and sympathy cards from well-wishing fans.
31. *Ibid.*, p. 54.
32. *Ibid.*, p. 55.
33. *Stella Dallas* became in fact a popular NBC radio soap-opera series which began on October 25, 1937, and ran for more than 18 years.
34. For a dissenting opinion, see Robert E. Sherwood's review in *Life*, December 10, 1925, pp. 24–25: "Then there is the trite ending. . . . This same conclusion has been arrived at dozens of times before. It is stale." Sherwood's evaluation is an apt description of the novel's conclusion, but unduly harsh with respect to the cinematic treatment. With all its clichés, twists of fate, coincidences, and confrontations, the novel is quite without literary merit, although its dramatic potential is unquestionable. The defects which mar the ending of the novel are circumvented in the film, a near miracle attributable to the discipline and subtlety of both Henry King and Belle Bennett.
35. The film had earned a reported $1,500,000 in profits by the early thirties. See Fox, p. 30.
36. *Ibid.*
37. Mordaunt Hall in the *New York Times*, December 28, 1925, p. 19.
38. Andrew Sarris, *The American Cinema: Directors and Directions, 1929–1968* (New York: Dutton, 1968), p. 67.
39. Herman G. Weinberg, *The Lubitsch Touch: A Critical Study* (New York: Dutton, 1968), p. 80.
40. *Ibid.*
41. No fewer than three Lubitsch pictures made the list that year, an unparalleled achievement. The others were *Forbidden Paradise*, with Pola Negri and Adolphe Menjou, and *Kiss Me Again*, with Marie Prevost and Monte Blue.
42. Colman, p. 59.
43. *Ibid.*
44. *Ibid.*, pp. 59–60.
45. *Kiki* was remade as an early talkie in 1931, with Mary Pickford in the title role and Reginald Denny in the Colman part.
46. Colman was on loan-out from Goldwyn to First National.
47. Mordaunt Hall in the *New York Times*, April 6, 1926, p. 26.
48. Of Miss Talmadge's comedic abilities, Clarence Brown later remembered: "Norma was the greatest pantomimist that ever drew breath. She was a natural-born comic; you could turn on a scene with her and she'd go on for five minutes without stopping or repeating herself." Cited in Brownlow, pp. 145–146.
49. Apparently, Lasky had also read the book and did not need much persuading. He too recognized its cinematic potential. See Colman, p. 63.
50. For the sake of comparison, *The Phantom of the Opera* (1925) cost $1,000,000, *Wings* (1927) $2,000,000, *The King of Kings* (1927) $2,500,000, and *Ben-Hur* (1926) $4,500,000. See Benjamin B. Hampton, *History of the American Film Industry: From Its Beginnings to 1931* (New York: Dover, 1970), p. 342.

51. Erich von Stroheim's celebrated remark regarding the Death Valley sequence in *Greed* (1924) is equally apt here: "140 degrees in the shade—and no shade."

52. Colman, pp. 66–67.

53. Paraphrased from Percival Christopher Wren, *Beau Geste* (New York: Grosset & Dunlap, 1926), p. 80.

54. Jeffrey Richards, "Ronald Colman and the Cinema of Empire," *Focus on Film* (Vol. 1, No. 4, September–October, 1970), p. 47.

55. *Ibid.*, p. 49.

56. Ironically, Colman was working for Paramount on a two-picture deal in 1939, but, alas, was not given the opportunity to reprise his greatest silent success.

57. Kevin Brownlow, *The War, The West, and The Wilderness* (New York: Knopf, 1979), p. 245.

58. *Ibid.*

59. Mordaunt Hall in the *New York Times*, November 29, 1926, p. 16.

60. Cited in Fox, p. 30.

61. Brownlow, *The War, The West, and The Wilderness*, p. 245.

62. "While there is nothing startlingly novel, as far as screen stories are concerned, in having a romance between a handsome gypsy chieftain and a lovely, flaxen-haired Princess, the idea is embellished when these characters are impersonated by Ronald Colman and Vilma Banky." Mordaunt Hall in the *New York Times*, January 25, 1927, p. 18.

63. Joe Franklin, *Classics of the Silent Screen* (New York: Citadel, 1959), p. 148.

64. Further similarities with *The Prisoner of Zenda* include the following: Princess Marie's steadfast decision to leave Montero and return to the duke prefigures Princess Flavia's resolve to remain with King Rudolph V rather than flee with Rudolf Rassendyll, whom she loves; in both films, an insider is designated to assist Colman—in *The Night of Love*, the court jester (John George) leaves the outer door open, permitting Montero to rescue the princess, while in *The Prisoner of Zenda*, Johann (Byron Foulger) attempts to lower the drawbridge to allow Rassendyll and his cohorts to rescue the real king; and finally, in both instances, Colman steals into the castle under cover of darkness to effect a daring rescue operation.

65. Cited in Colman, pp. 70–71.

66. Cited in James Robert Parish, *Hollywood's Great Love Teams* (New Rochelle, N.Y.: Arlington House, 1974), p. 33.

67. Cited in Quirk, p. 109.

68. Cited in Parish, p. 34.

69. *Ibid.*, p. 35.

70. Cited in Colman, p. 71.

71. *New York Times*, September 19, 1927, p. 30.

72. Cited in Helen Carlisle, "Too Temperamental," *Motion Picture* (Vol. 35, No. 3, April, 1928), pp. 84–85.

73. While in production, the picture was tentatively titled *The Passionate Adventurer*.

74. It is interesting to note that both Niblo pictures display similar plot structures: in *The Mark of Zorro*, Fairbanks portrays the foppish Don Diego by day and the tireless defender of threatened virtue by night; in *Two Lovers*, Colman plays Mark Van Rycke by day and the mysterious hooded avenger by night.

75. Cited in Quirk, p. 116.

76. *New York Times*, March 23, 1928, p. 24.

77. *Ibid.*

78. *Ibid.*
79. Parish, p. 38.
80. *New York Times*, January 14, 1929, p. 20.
81. Cited in Colman, p. 81.
82. *New York Times*, January 14, 1929, p. 20. The novel describes Lingard as "about thirty-five, erect and supple. The light chestnut hair curled close about his well-shaped head, and the clipped beard glinted vividly.... His mouth was lost in the heavy moustache; his nose was straight, short, slightly blunted at the end...." See Joseph Conrad, *The Rescue: A Romance of the Shallows* (New York: Grosset & Dunlap, 1929), p. 9.
83. A partial print of *The Rescue* surfaced in Kansas City, Kansas, in 1978, but before steps could be taken to preserve what was left, the film decomposed.

IV. Colman Crosses the Sound Barrier— The Goldwyn Talkies

1. Wild, p. 105.
2. Joe Adamson, *Groucho, Harpo, Chico and Sometimes Zeppo* (New York: Simon and Schuster, 1973), p. 70.
3. Fox, p. 31.
4. Kerr, pp. 47–48.
5. Fox, p. 32.
6. Cited in Colman, p. 90.
7. In 1916, Colman had appeared on the London stage in a bit part with du Maurier, whose restrained, naturalistic style greatly influenced his own.
8. Cited in Colman, p. 107.
9. *Ibid.*, pp. 107–108.
10. Wild, p. 123.
11. Julian Fox, "Colman," *Films and Filming* (Vol. 18, No. 7, April, 1972), p. 34.
12. William K. Everson, *The Detective in Film* (Secaucus, N.J.: Citadel, 1972), p. 62.
13. *Ibid.*
14. William Cameron Menzies was also nominated for Best Art Direction.
15. Cited in Colman, p. 87.
16. *Ibid.*, p. 86.
17. Everson, p. 62.
18. Colman, pp. 88–89.
19. "Colman" (March, 1972), p. 32.
20. Cited in Colman, pp. 104–106.
21. *Ibid.*, p. 103.
22. William K. Everson, unpublished film notes, Walker Art Center, Minneapolis, March 31, 1979.
23. See Colman, p. 108.
24. Mordaunt Hall in the *New York Times*, October 29, 1931, p. 27.
25. Father of one of Colman's leading ladies, Joan Bennett.
26. One of the many actors who later auditioned for the part of the High Lama in *Lost Horizon.*
27. Cited in Colman, p. 112.
28. *Ibid.*

29. See Fox, "Colman" (March, 1972), p. 32.

30. See *ibid.*

31. It might also be noted that A.E. Anson's portrayal of Gottlieb is marred by a German accent that is only passable, while Richard Bennett's attempt at a Swedish accent as the great Sondelius is simply appalling.

32. See Catherine Hunter, "Adventuring with Ronald Colman," *Screen Play* (Vol. 12, No. 83, February, 1932), pp. 64–65.

33. Cited in Arthur Marx, *Goldwyn: A Biography of the Man Behind the Myth* (New York: Norton, 1976), pp. 179–180.

34. Cited in Colman, pp. 112–113.

35. Hunter, p. 96.

36. The picture they see is Charlie Chaplin's 1918 First National comedy, *A Dog's Life.*

37. It is worth noting that, in the book, Jim Warlock's mistress compares him with Douglas Fairbanks, and later his wife mentions Ronald Colman! See Robert Gore Browne, *Cynara* (New York: Grosset & Dunlap, 1932), pp. 147, 182.

38. As always, Colman's ingratiating humor is much in evidence. For its sheer tongue-in-cheek approach, his impromptu speech before the assembled gathering at the swimming contest deserves notice: "Ladies and gentlemen, I count myself fortunate — I may say most fortunate — in having been asked here today. For it is indeed a great privilege to be here with you today in these godly surroundings; I use the word godly advisedly because, after all, cleanliness is next to godliness, isn't it. These — these water sports — uh — water brings cleanliness; clean bodies, clean minds, and pure hearts. Uh — they say that water seeks its own level. That is true, but water also levels all ranks. We have no class distinction here today. Our little prize — our little prize will be given to the girl with the loveliest figure, the quickest eye, and the best stroke. Accomplishment, skill, earnest endeavor; these are the things that count in the long run. And so I say, our motto should be today, as always — uh, well — one for all, and all for one!"

39. Colman, p. 117.

40. *Ibid.*, pp. 119–120.

41. Cited in Colman, p. 119.

42. Oddly enough, Colman was always somewhat reluctant to play dual roles, as he explained to an interviewer in 1933: "A dual performance really adds little or nothing to an actor's reputation and stature, but it doubly damages him if he is bad." Cited in Quirk, p. 154.

43. Cited in Jane Leslie, "Are Actors People?" *Motion Picture* (Vol. 33, No. 3, April, 1927), p. 114.

44. Cited in Colman, p. 121.

45. *Ibid.*, pp. 122.

V. The Image of a Star

1. Cited in Colman, p. 124.

2. Fox, "Colman" (April, 1972), p. 35.

3. *Ibid.*, pp. 36–37.

4. *Ibid.*, p. 37.

5. See Rudy Behlmer, ed., *Memo from David O. Selznick* (New York: Viking, 1972), p. 139.

6. Cited in Colman, p. 164.

7. *Ibid.*, p. 166.
8. See Everson, pp. 65–66.
9. See François Truffaut, *Hitchcock* (New York: Simon and Schuster, 1967), p. 86.
10. Everson, pp. 64–65.
11. R.J. Minney, *Hollywood by Starlight* (London: Chapman & Hall, 1935), p. 117–118.
12. Richards, p. 46.
13. *New York Times*, January 18, 1935, p. 29.
14. Cited in Colman, p. 135.
15. *New York Times*, January 18, 1935, p. 29.
16. So charmingly improbable that reviewer André Sennwald quipped: "Sometimes it seems as if anybody can write scenarios." *New York Times*, November 15, 1935, p. 20.
17. *Ibid.* Despite the cumbersome title, it was—at 66 minutes—the shortest talkie Colman ever made.
18. But even here, the enjoyment of the scene is diluted by the all-too-recognizably painted backdrop against which the exchange unfolds.
19. *New York Times*, November 15, 1935, p. 20.
20. *Ibid.*
21. *Ibid.*
22. Fox, "Colman" (April, 1972), p. 35.
23. Interview, Juliet Benita Colman with author, June 17, 1975.
24. Elizabeth Allan, Edna May Oliver, and Basil Rathbone were featured in both pictures.
25. See Brian Aherne, *A Dreadful Man* (New York: Simon and Schuster, 1979), pp. 34–35.
26. Cited in Colman, p. 179.
27. Although critics have observed that the picture every so often slumps into reliance on the printed page, it should be noted that, unlike *Clive of India*, the intertitles in *A Tale of Two Cities* always appear over action shots. Never obtrusive, they do not replace action, but merely underscore and intensify it.
28. Letter of June 3, 1935, cited in Behlmer, p. 84.
29. Cited in Fox, "Colman" (April, 1972), p. 39.
30. John Baxter, *Hollywood in the Thirties* (London and New York: Zwemmer and Barnes, 1968), p. 27.
31. Cited in Colman, p. 184.
32. "Colman" (April, 1972), p. 35.
33. Best Actor nominations went to Gary Cooper for *Mr. Deeds Goes to Town*, Walter Huston for *Dodsworth*, William Powell for *My Man Godfrey*, Spencer Tracy for *San Francisco*, and Paul Muni for *The Story of Louis Pasteur*. Muni won.
34. Leslie C. Staples, "The New Film Version of *A Tale of Two Cities*," The *Dickensian* (Vol. 54, No. 325, May, 1958), p. 120.
35. Ouida was the nom de plume of Louise de la Ramée, whose novel was first staged in 1870.
36. Colman, pp. 153–154.
37. Rosalind Russell and Chris Chase, *Life Is a Banquet* (New York: Random House, 1977), pp. 61–62.
38. Frank Capra, *The Name Above the Title: An Autobiography* (New York: Macmillan, 1971), p. 193. Long before he learned that Colman was available, Capra apparently had Brian Aherne in mind for the part.

39. Colman, p. 175.

40. Capra, p. 200.

41. *Ibid.*, p. 201.

42. *Ibid.*, p. 196.

43. *Ibid.*

44. Jaffe was not altogether a newcomer to Hollywood, however, for he had starred opposite Marlene Dietrich in Josef von Sternberg's *The Scarlet Empress* (1934).

45. Gene Milford and Gene Havlick also won an Oscar for Best Editing.

46. The observations in this paragraph issued from conversations with Thomas R. Tietze, to whom the author is gratefully indebted.

47. See Capra, p. 190.

48. Colman, p. 168.

49. *Ibid.*, p. 177.

50. Exploiting President Franklin D. Roosevelt's remark that the Doolittle bombers which raided Tokyo, Yokohama, and Osaka had come from "Shangri-La, for all I know."

51. Included among the scenes never used was the appearance of Chopin's former pupil, Montaigne, portrayed by a real former monk, John Tettemer, whose memoirs were published posthumously in 1952 under the title *I Was a Monk*. He can still be seen briefly, however, at the piano with Jane Wyatt.

52. This thumbnail history of an "incredibly shrinking film" issued from conversations with, and the research of, Robert Milton Miller, to whom the author is gratefully indebted.

53. See Marjorie Walker, "'Lost Horizon' Returns—SRO," *Hollywood Studio Magazine* (Vol. 13, No. 9, March, 1980), pp. 6, 7, 21.

54. Colman, pp. 177–178.

55. Thus begins *The Prisoner of Zenda*.

56. David Niven, *Bring on the Empty Horses* (New York: Putnam, 1975), p. 181.

57. Action expert W.S. Van Dyke was brought in to direct the fencing sequences.

58. Douglas Fairbanks, Jr., followed his father's advice ("Rin-Tin-Tin couldn't miss in that part"), made a shrewd suggestion of his own (that Rupert of Hentzau always appear in black), and, as the witty, charming villain, all but stole the show from Ronald Colman. See Douglas Fairbanks, Jr., and Richard Schickel, *The Fairbanks Album* (Boston: New York Graphic Society, 1975), p. 216.

59. The observations in this paragraph issued from conversations with Thomas R. Tietze, to whom the author is gratefully indebted.

60. Douglas Fairbanks, Jr., *The Salad Days* (New York: Doubleday, 1988), p. 274.

61. Cited in Behlmer, pp. 110–111.

62. See *ibid.*, p. 112.

63. Richards, p. 49.

64. My thanks are due Thomas R. Tietze for suggesting the "broken wing" metaphor.

65. It is generally believed that George Cukor was brought in to direct the renunciation scene with Colman and Madeleine Carroll.

66. Richards, p. 48.

67. By an odd coincidence, Farnum appears in a minor role in the Colman version.

68. Oreste Kirkop and Kathryn Grayson took the leads again when an unsuccessful musical adaptation was filmed in 1955.

69. Robert Milton Miller, "Preston Sturges: A Director's Life" (Master's thesis, University of Kansas, 1973), pp. 106–108.

70. *Newsweek* (Vol. 12, No. 15, October 10, 1938), p. 29.

71. Richards, p. 45.

72. *New York Times*, September 29, 1938, p. 31.

73. Frank S. Nugent in *ibid.*, December 25, 1939, p. 19.

74. Cited in Colman, pp. 187–191.

75. *New York Times*, December 25, 1939, p. 19.

76. Fox, "Colman" (April, 1972), p. 37.

77. *New York Times*, December 25, 1939, p. 19.

78. Fox, "Colman" (April, 1972), p. 37. It is interesting to note that Paramount originally intended *The Light that Failed* as a vehicle for Gary Cooper or Ray Milland, and announced that it would be shot in Technicolor.

79. *New York Times*, December 25, 1939, p. 19.

80. *Ibid.*, September 6, 1940, p. 25.

81. *Ibid.*

82. *Ibid.*, October 30, 1941, p. 27.

83. Richards, p. 46.

VI. Years of Diversification

1. Rosalind Russell recalled one of the British War Relief parties: "There were a lot of those parties for the English. I remember one where Highland pipes were playing, and all the English actors—Ronnie Colman, David Niven, Errol Flynn—performed as a chorus line; you never saw anything so good-looking as that line-up of men in your life." Russell and Chase, p. 93.

2. Cited in Colman, p. 215.

3. Colman later became godfather to McCoy's son Ronald.

4. Cited in Colman, pp. 232–233.

5. *Ibid.*, p. 233.

6. *Ibid.*, p. 246.

7. In attendance were George Sanders (whom Benita later married), Vincent Price, Jack Benny, Herbert Marshall, George Cukor, Gladys Cooper, Joseph Cotten, and Patricia Medina.

8. Bernard DeVoto, ed., *Mark Twain in Eruption: Hitherto Unpublished Pages about Men and Events* (New York and London: Harper & Brothers, 1940), p. 202.

9. While in production, the picture was tentatively titled *Three's a Crowd*.

10. *The Nation* (December 26, 1942). Reprinted in James Agee, *Agee on Film, Volume One* (New York: Grosset & Dunlap, 1969), p. 24.

11. *New York Times*, December 18, 1942, p. 36.

12. *Newsweek* (Vol. 20, No. 9, August 31, 1942), p. 2.

13. Fox, "Colman" (April, 1972), p. 38.

14. Thus begins *Kismet*.

15. Fox, "Colman" (April, 1972), p. 38.

16. It was also nominated for Best Musical Score and Best Sound Recording.

17. When M-G-M remade *Kismet* as a Technicolor musical in 1955, with

Howard Keel and Ann Blyth in the starring roles, the Colman-Dietrich version was reissued to television in black-and-white prints under the new title *Oriental Dream*, which made the film even less appealing.

18. Colman, p. 214.

19. Fox, "Colman" (April, 1972), p. 38. The *New York Times* quipped that the role "fit Mr. Colman as snugly as a well-wound turban." *New York Times*, August 23, 1944, p. 16.

20. Fox, "Colman" (April, 1972), p. 38.

21. *New York Times*, March 21, 1947, p. 29.

22. *Life* (Vol. 22, No. 16, April 21, 1947), p. 65.

23. *Newsweek* (Vol. 29, No. 13, March 31, 1947), p. 92.

24. Cited in Gavin Lambert, *On Cukor* (New York: Putnam, 1972), p. 199.

25. By a strange twist of fate, Guy Bates Post, who starred in the 1922 film *The Masquerader*, another dual-role melodrama which Colman later remade for Samuel Goldwyn, appears with Colman in the *Othello* sequences.

26. *New York Times*, February 20, 1948, p. 19.

27. *Time* (Vol. 51, No. 8, February 23, 1948), p. 99.

28. *Newsweek* (Vol. 31, No. 6, February 9, 1948), p. 74.

29. Cited in Quirk, p. 239.

30. Miklos Rozsa also won for Best Music Score. George Cukor, nominated for Best Director, lost to Elia Kazan (*Gentleman's Agreement*).

31. Perhaps the fact that the role *was* such an unusual one for Colman accounts for a theory which has gained some currency in recent years: that Colman's Oscar was primarily a belated, retrospective tribute to earlier—and greater— successes, somewhat the way many feel about John Wayne's award for *True Grit* (1969). While we have seen, for instance, that *Clive of India*, although often claimed to be one of Colman's finest efforts, falls short, the same cannot be said of *A Double Life*. His performance is an electrifying tour de force, and stands on its own merits.

32. Shot in New York's famous Empire Theatre, where Colman was playing with Henry Miller and Ruth Chatterton in *La Tendresse* when he was discovered by Henry King and Lillian Gish in 1923. The Empire was razed in 1953.

33. Cited in Colman, p. 225.

34. Cited in Lambert, pp. 197, 199.

35. Cited in Colman, p. 227.

36. Cited in Quirk, p. 239.

37. *New York Times*, February 20, 1948, p. 19.

38. Colman, p. 241.

39. Although similar to CinemaScope and Cinerama, the Todd-AO process was not merely wide screen but giant screen as well. Sixty-five mm in width rather than the standard 35 mm, it was vastly superior to Cinerama, since it was photographed with only one camera, rather than three, and projected with just one projector, not three. Its running speed was 30 fps rather than the standard 24 fps.

40. It was also his last, for Mike Todd died in a plane crash in 1958. The former Avrom Hirsch Goldbogen of Minneapolis, he once admitted, "I'm a showman. I'm not interested in social significance, symbolism or artistic triumphs that are financial losers. I worship artistic integrity, but in a public medium success is determined solely by public *acceptance*, and that is ascertained, unfortunately—or fortunately, according to the point of view—by the slight formality at the boxoffice." Cited in Art Cohn, ed., *Michael Todd's Around the World in 80 Days Almanac* (New York: Random House, 1956), p. 8.

41. Cited in Niven, *The Moon's a Balloon*, p. 306.
42. *Ibid.*, p. 307.
43. Cited in Colman, p. 270.
44. Fox, "Colman" (April, 1972), p. 39.
45. Cited in *ibid.*
46. Cited in Quirk, p. 246.
47. Cohn p. 42. Included in the regiments of extras were 6,400 Spaniards, 2,672 Japanese, 3,600 Moslems, 1,927 Arabs, 1,688 American Indians, 1,553 Englishmen, and 1,664 Frenchmen. *Ibid.*, p. 15.
48. Cited in Cohn, p. 15.
49. *New York Times*, October 18, 1956, p. 37.
50. Ezra Goodman, *The Fifty-Year Decline and Fall of Hollywood* (New York: Simon and Schuster, 1961), p. 196.
51. Director of such later "disaster" pictures as *The Towering Inferno*, Allen produced his greatest disaster with *The Story of Mankind*, about which he once boasted: "Me, if I can't blow up the world in the first ten seconds, then the show is a flop." Cited in Fox, "Colman" (April, 1972), p. 39.
52. Richards, p. 51.
53. *New York Times*, November 9, 1957, p. 31.
54. Cited in Colman, p. 272.
55. Fox, "Colman" (April, 1972), p. 39.

VII. Of Shadow and Substance— The Legacy of Ronald Colman

1. Cited in Fox, "Colman" (April, 1972), p. 39.
2. Fox, "Colman" (March, 1972), pp. 26–27.
3. Cited in Colman, p. 156.
4. *Ibid.*, p. 237.
5. Brian Aherne, *A Proper Job* (Boston: Houghton Mifflin, 1969), pp. 202–203.
6. Colman's identification with the theme of self-sacrifice, once fully established in *A Tale of Two Cities*, receives its most poignant expression here.

Bibliography

I. Books

Adamson, Joe. *Groucho, Harpo, Chico and Sometimes Zeppo.* New York: Simon and Schuster, 1973.

Agee, James. *Agee on Film, Volume One.* New York: Grosset & Dunlap, 1969.

Aherne, Brian. *A Dreadful Man.* New York: Simon and Schuster, 1979.

_____. *A Proper Job.* Boston: Houghton Mifflin, 1969.

Baxter, John. *Hollywood in the Thirties.* London and New York: Zwemmer and Barnes, 1968.

Behlmer, Rudy, ed. *Memo from David O. Selznick.* New York: Viking, 1972.

Bergman, Andrew. *We're in the Money: Depression America and Its Films.* New York: Harper & Row, 1972.

Brownlow, Kevin. *The Parade's Gone By.* New York: Knopf, 1968.

_____. *The War, The West, and The Wilderness.* New York: Knopf, 1979.

Capra, Frank. *The Name Above the Title: An Autobiography.* New York: Macmillan, 1971.

Cohn, Art, ed. *Michael Todd's Around the World in 80 Days Almanac.* New York: Random House, 1956.

Colman, Juliet Benita. *Ronald Colman: A Very Private Person.* New York: Morrow, 1975.

Connell, Brian. *Knight Errant: A Biography of Douglas Fairbanks, Jr.* Garden City, N.Y.: Doubleday, 1955.

DeVoto, Bernard, ed. *Mark Twain in Eruption: Hitherto Unpublished Pages about Men and Events.* New York and London: Harper & Brothers, 1940.

Dunning, John. *Tune in Yesterday: The Ultimate Encyclopedia of Old-Time Radio, 1925–1976.* Englewood Cliffs, N.J.: Prentice-Hall, 1976.

Easton, Carol. *The Search for Sam Goldwyn: A Biography.* New York: Morrow, 1976.

Everson, William K. *The Detective in Film.* Secaucus, N.J.: Citadel, 1972.

Fairbanks, Douglas, Jr. *The Salad Days.* New York: Doubleday, 1988.

_____, and Richard Schickel. *The Fairbanks Album.* Boston: New York Graphic Society, 1975.

Franklin, Joe. *Classics of the Silent Screen.* New York: Citadel, 1959.
Gish, Lillian. *Dorothy and Lillian Gish.* New York: Scribner's, 1973.
————, with Ann Pinchot. *The Movies, Mr. Griffith, and Me.* Englewood Cliffs, N.J.: Prentice-Hall, 1969.
Goodman, Ezra. *The Fifty-Year Decline and Fall of Hollywood.* New York: Simon and Schuster, 1961.
Hampton, Benjamin B. *History of the American Film Industry: From Its Beginnings to 1931.* New York: Dover, 1970.
Higham, Charles, and Joel Greenberg. *Hollywood in the Forties.* London and New York: Zwemmer and Barnes, 1968.
Kerr, Walter. *The Silent Clowns.* New York: Knopf, 1975.
Lambert, Gavin. *On Cukor.* New York: Putnam, 1972.
Macgowan, Kenneth. *Behind the Screen: The History and Techniques of the Motion Picture.* New York: Delacorte, 1965.
Marill, Alvin H. *Samuel Goldwyn Presents.* New York: Barnes, 1976.
Marx, Arthur. *Goldwyn: A Biography of the Man Behind the Myth.* New York: Norton, 1976.
Miller, Robert Milton. "Preston Sturges: A Director's Life." Master's thesis, University of Kansas, 1973.
Minney, R.J. *Hollywood by Starlight.* London: Chapman & Hall, 1935.
Morley, Sheridan. *Tales from the Hollywood Raj: The British, the Movies, and Tinseltown.* New York: Viking, 1983.
Niven, David. *Bring on the Empty Horses.* New York: Putnam, 1975.
————. *The Moon's a Balloon.* New York: Putnam, 1972.
Parish, James Robert. *Hollywood's Great Love Teams.* New Rochelle, N.Y.: Arlington House, 1974.
Perry, George. *The Great British Picture Show: From the 90s to the 70s.* New York: Hill and Wang, 1974.
Pratt, George C. *Spellbound in Darkness: A History of the Silent Film.* Greenwich, Conn.: New York Graphic Society, 1973.
Quirk, Lawrence J. *The Films of Ronald Colman.* Secaucus, N.J.: Citadel, 1977.
Robinson, David. *Hollywood in the Twenties.* London and New York: Zwemmer and Barnes, 1968.
Russell, Rosalind, and Chris Chase. *Life Is a Banquet.* New York: Random House, 1977.
Sarris, Andrew. *The American Cinema: Directors and Directions, 1929–1968.* New York: Dutton, 1968.
Schickel, Richard. *His Picture in the Papers: A Speculation on Celebrity in America Based on the Life of Douglas Fairbanks, Sr.* New York: Charterhouse, 1973.
Truffaut, François. *Hitchcock.* New York: Simon and Schuster, 1967.
Ursini, James. *The Fabulous Life and Times of Preston Sturges: An American Dreamer.* New York: Curtis, 1973.
Wagenknecht, Edward. *The Movies in the Age of Innocence.* New York: Ballantine, 1971.
Weinberg, Herman G. *The Lubitsch Touch: A Critical Study.* New York: Dutton, 1968.
Wild, Roland. *Ronald Colman.* London: Rich & Cowan, 1933.

II. Articles

Carlisle, Helen. "Too Temperamental." *Motion Picture*, Vol. 35, No. 3, April, 1928, pp. 31, 84–85.

Connor, Edward. "Revisiting *Lost Horizon*." *Screen Facts*, Vol. 1, No. 2, 1963, pp. 50–60.

Everson, William K. Unpublished film notes, Walker Art Center, Minneapolis, March 31, 1979.

Finlay, Ian F. "Dickens in the Cinema." *The Dickensian*, Vol. 54, No. 325, May, 1958, pp. 106–109.

Fox, Julian. "Colman." *Films and Filming*, Vol. 18, No. 6, March, 1972, pp. 26–32.

_____. "Colman." *Films and Filming*, Vol. 18, No. 7, April, 1972, pp. 34–39.

Frank, Sam. "*Lost Horizon*—A Timeless Journey." *American Cinematographer*, Vol. 67, No. 4, April, 1986, pp. 30–39.

Hall, Gladys. "Ronald Colman Reveals His Greatest Secret!" *Motion Picture*, Vol. 45, No. 2, March, 1933, pp. 49, 86.

_____. "The Star Diggers." *Motion Picture*, Vol. 36, No. 3, October, 1928, pp. 106–107.

Hunter, Catherine. "Adventuring with Ronald Colman." *Screen Play*, Vol. 12, No. 83, February, 1932, pp. 64–65, 96–97.

Jacobs, Jack. "Ronald Colman." *Films in Review*, Vol. 9, No. 4, April, 1958, pp. 175–189.

Leslie, Jane. "Are Actors People?" *Motion Picture*, Vol. 33, No. 3, April, 1927, pp. 60–61, 100, 114.

MacCulloch, Campbell. "The Vanishing Screen Stars." *Motion Picture*, Vol. 40, No. 1, August, 1930, pp. 28–29, 88.

Manners, Dorothy. "Are You the Type?" *Motion Picture*, Vol. 39, No. 4, May, 1930, pp. 48, 112.

_____. "Five Big Stars Are Retiring in 1933." *Motion Picture*, Vol. 45, No. 3, April, 1933, pp. 28–29, 81, 83, 85.

Maxwell, Vivian. "Colman Sees War in China." *Motion Picture*, Vol. 43, No. 5, June, 1932, pp. 52–53, 77, 79.

Moak, Bob. "Ronald Colman's Dream Girl." *Screen Secrets*, Vol. 8, No. 56, November, 1929, pp. 54–55, 109.

Monroe, Keith. "Top Man on the Totem Pole." *Motion Picture*, Vol. 73, No. 3, April, 1947, pp. 40–41, 108–109.

Mook, Samuel Richard. "Barriers Burned Away." *Picture Play*, Vol. 32, No. 3, May, 1930, pp. 44–45, 104.

Morley, Malcolm. "The Stage Story of *A Tale of Two Cities*." *The Dickensian*, Vol. 51, No. 313, December, 1954, pp. 34–40.

Pryor, Nancy. "They Deny It." *Motion Picture*, Vol. 40, No. 6, January, 1931, pp. 48–49, 93, 96.

Richards, Jeffrey. "Ronald Colman and the Cinema of Empire." *Focus on Film*, Vol. 1, No. 4, September–October, 1970, pp. 42–55.

St. Johns, Adela Rogers. "Ten Handsome Men of the Screen." *Photoplay*, Vol. 29, No. 2, January, 1926, pp. 32–33, 109.

Sammis, Edward R. "The Dark Angel of the Films." *Paris and Hollywood Screen Secrets*, Vol. 4, No. 35, February, 1928, pp. 48–50.

Shaffer, Rosalind. "Unwritten Chapters." *Motion Picture*, Vol. 41, No. 1, February, 1931, pp. 50, 92–93.

Spensley, Dorothy. "Desert Stuff." *Photoplay*, Vol. 30, No. 2, July, 1926, pp. 40–41, 136–137.

Staples, Leslie C. "The New Film Version of *A Tale of Two Cities.*" *The Dickensian*, Vol. 54, No. 325, May, 1958, pp. 119–120.

Walker, Marjorie. "'Lost Horizon' Returns — SRO." *Hollywood Studio Magazine*, Vol. 13, No. 9, March, 1980, pp. 6, 7, 21.

Washburn, Mary. "When Stars Come Down to Earth." *Motion Picture*, Vol. 35, No. 5, June, 1928, pp. 31, 120.

Waterbury, Ruth. "His Double Life." *Photoplay*, Vol. 33, No. 1, June, 1948, pp. 46–47, 113–115.

_____. "Ronald Talks at Last." *Photoplay*, Vol. 29, No. 2, January, 1926, pp. 29–30, 121.

III. Reviews

Life
New York Times
Newsweek
Time

Index

Page numbers in **boldface** *indicate photographs.*